our cosmic journey

Christian Anthropology
in the Light of Current Trends
in the Sciences,
Philosophy and Theology

our cosmic journey

Hans Schwarz

AUGSBURG PUBLISHING HOUSE
Minneapolis, Minnesota

OUR COSMIC JOURNEY

Copyright © 1977 Augsburg Publishing House

Library of Congress Catalog Card No. 77-72460

International Standard Book No. 0-8066-1592-3 (paper)
International Standard Book No. 0-8066-1551-6 (cloth)

Scripture quotations unless otherwise noted are from the Revised Standard Version of the Bible, copyright 1946, 1952, and 1971 by the Division of Christian Education of the National Council of Churches.

MANUFACTURED IN THE UNITED STATES OF AMERICA

Contents

PART I
STRUCTURES OF HUMAN EXISTENCE

PART II

OUR JOURNEY: BETWEEN CHAOS AND PROVIDENCE

*No other epoch has accumulated so great and
so varied a store of knowledge concerning man
as the present one: . . . But also, no epoch is
less sure of its knowledge of what man is than
the present one.*

MARTIN HEIDEGGER,
Kant and the Problem of Metaphysics

Preface

Information about the human species abounds. We already know so
much about ourselves and the world around us that we are awed
whenever we think of the volumes which are added daily to our existing knowledge. Astronauts have stepped into outer space; physicists
have surveyed the properties of minute atomic particles; psychiatrists
have described our psychic make-up; and behavioral scientists have
compared our behavior with that of other living species. Yet the farther we have gone and the more we have acquired the more uncertain
we have become about ourselves.

We are not just overfed with data and information, but we have
largely lost the frame of reference in which to place and to arrange
our findings. Instead of feeling at home on this earth we inhabit, we
are more like stranded astronauts drifting disoriented in outer space.
We do not know in which direction we are moving. We seem to
plunge in all directions without knowing which way is up or down.
We are straying as through infinite nothingness. As we read the front
pages of our newspaper the chills often creep up our spines. We feel
that this world has become a colder place. There is such immense
cruelty and hatred in this world. Yet it is not so much the poor and
dejected that cry out for vengeance. It seems the more educated and
affluent we become the more we demand from each other and the
more we want of the earth's resources. Humanity seems under a magic
spell of constantly exceeding the limits of what is presently available,
insatiably plundering and exploiting the earth and its own kind. Yet

9

there is no visible satisfaction connected with this activity. The faster our pace, the higher our living standards, the more we want and the more dissatisfied we get. Here the question that Jesus posed: "For what does it profit a man, to gain the whole world and forfeit his life?" (Mark 8:36), becomes very real to us. We are indeed about to lose our life while we frantically attempt to gain everything.

Clouds of despair and disaster are looming ever more threateningly on the horizon. We have largely harnessed the earth, but in doing so we are pursuing a dangerously self-destructive course. We have lost our measure for right and wrong and have sacrificed our sense of orientation. Our immense knowledge and our tremendous technological achievements seem to be turning against us. We are no longer frightened animals under a threatening sky. We are rather people who are afraid of each other and of our own potential for self-destruction.

In this situation it is imperative to rediscover the origin, direction, and goal of *Our Cosmic Journey*. We must learn anew who we are, what our true potential is, and how this potential might beneficially be realized in the future. The most appropriate way for self-assessment is to tap the immense resources that science has uncovered concerning the origin and history of the universe, of life within the universe, and of our own kind. We must also listen to the important things science has to say concerning our potential for self-improvement, the peculiarities of human behavior and its possible modification, and our psychic potential for good and for evil. Lest we be trapped by a schizophrenic compartmentalization we must then ask ourselves how these data should be related to the traditional Christian doctrines of creation, sin, and divine providence. Such theological reflection upon the findings of the life sciences is even more necessary, since the life sciences can only project a warranted future as an extrapolation of the past. Since the future of the stream of life is basically unpredictable, such extrapolations cannot suffice as a trustworthy foundation on which to build the future.

If the future of *Our Cosmic Journey* is to be more than a continuation of the past and more than a wishful dream, rays of hope for its future can only come from the Judeo-Christian tradition. Here the end of all history is proleptically anticipated in the life and destiny of Jesus Christ. Therefore this tradition may yield justified clues concerning the future. Since we must acknowledge that scientific insights are not static but have a history of refinement and clarification, it is only proper to acknowledge a similar progressive understanding of God's involvement with the world and of our status as part of God's creation. Thus we must investigate the scope of the biblical witnesses on these points and the appropriation of these insights at various crucial instances in the history of the Christian faith.

It may seem that such an understanding of humanity, evolving from the dialog between the Christian faith and the life sciences, exceeds the possibilities of one person and the limits of one book. Yet all the inevitable omissions and obvious shortcomings notwithstanding, such an analysis and synthesis of the various aspects of humanity must be ventured unless we really lose sight of who we are, where we stand, and which direction we are going and should be going. I do not intend to consider here most aspects of the Christian understanding of God, since I have dealt with this subject in an earlier book, *The Search for God*. I also do not want to reiterate what I have said earlier about our prospect for the future, especially as it deals with Christian eschatology, since I have written on this in my book *On the Way to the Future*. With these omissions granted, the discerning reader will still detect many places where more could have been said or more literature could have been cited. To some extent I have attempted to compensate for this in the selective bibliography in which many works are listed that are not explicitly mentioned in the text.

The material content of this book has attracted my attention during the past ten years of my theological journey. It has been presented many times in classes at our seminary, in adult education classes, in papers at regional and national meetings of the American Academy of Religion, and on many other occasions. Some readers will undoubtedly discover familiarity with this or that aspect of the book and perhaps also recognize some of their own input through questions, suggestions, and criticism. At this point I would like to thank the various publishers for their generous consent to allow reprint of the passages quoted. I also want to express my gratitude to my colleagues Wilbur France, Clarence Heinke, and Terrill Long of the Science Hall of Capital University, who carefully read parts of the manuscript dealing with the natural sciences, for their criticism and suggestions. I must thank too my colleague Leland Elhard for his helpful comments on the chapters dealing with the human predicament and sinfulness. My special thanks go to my colleague James Schaaf who undertook the thankless task of improving my style. His wife Phyllis who typed various drafts of the manuscript with unfailing speed and accuracy surely deserves thanks too. I must also thank Phyllis Dawson who typed most of the final draft with exceptional precision. Sharon Hilfiger deserves thanks too for the painstaking job of making the final checks on all English language references by comparing them with the original sources. She also helped considerably with proofreading and compiling the indexes. I must also thank again Ronald Grissom for final proofreading and for compiling the indexes. Of course, any inadequacy of the text, which the discerning reader will detect, is still solely my responsibility. The Aid Association for Lutherans awarded me the Fredrik A. Schiotz Fellowship and therewith enabled me to start with this project. My deep gratitude must be expressed for their most generous seminary and faculty support system. I would also like to say special thanks to the students and colleagues of the Augustana Hochschule in Neuendettelsau, Germany, whose deep Christian fellowship and cordial friendship I enjoyed so immensely on my sabbatical leave 1973-74 and in whose midst the first chapters of this manuscript were written. Finally I must thank my wife May and growing Hans and Krista for their continued patience and endurance while I was writing the manuscript.

Since this book is very much concerned with the history, present status, and future of humanity, it is only fitting that we remember that we only enjoy a clearer vision of the future, if we do not turn our backs on our ancestors, but accept their support, stand on their shoulders, and peek into the same future that they attempted to map out before us. Therefore, I want to dedicate this book to my grandfather Johann List from whose wisdom and faith I have learned much and continue to learn.

Hans Schwarz
Columbus, Ohio

Introduction

What does it mean to be a human being? What is our position in this universe? These age-old questions are asked with renewed strength and intensity today. The liberation movements of the southern hemisphere, the Marxist philosophers of the eastern hemisphere, and the angry voices of mistreated minority groups in our own country are pressing for a redefinition, nay, even a transformation of the human situation. Reading the daily newspapers and watching the news on TV we indeed gain the impression that there is something fundamentally out of balance with the world we live in. We seem to have lost our sense of orientation and direction on our cosmic journey. The firm foundation on which to build our lives has disappeared from our sight. Our world is in turmoil and our lives are threatened by the impact of technology that made our lives more changeable than ever and increased the pace in modern living to such an extent that truly "our years come to an end like a sigh" (Psalm 90:9). We have domesticated the world in an unprecedented way, but we have lost our souls and each other in the process. At no point in history have we had so much knowledge about the world that surrounds us and so little insight into our own place in this world and so little understanding for each other.

Humanity in turmoil: World War I, World War II, Jewish extermination camps, Korean War, Vietnam War, Congo, Palestine Liberation Organization, Rhodesia, Lebanon, Northern Ireland, etc., etc. Each of these names, and we could continue our list almost indefinitely, stands for the fact that we are able to commit cruelties beyond imagination. But it is not only our wars which contribute to a world in turmoil. Our technological progress too is a good ally to foster turmoil and destruction. It should make us blush with shame, for instance, that more Americans have been killed on their highways by peace-loving citizens than in all the wars we have ever fought.

Much more subtle infringements upon our accustomed ways of life are encountered daily in the technological civilization which we inaugurated. Through increased specialization we have imposed upon us a structure of life from which there is no escape. The so-called intimate sphere of life is a luxury of bygone days. Everything private, from sexual copulation to dietary habits, is subject to the scrutinous eyes of surveyors of "public opinion" and more and more personal data are being deposited in memory banks for governmental use and for the benefit of loan and finance companies.

Our technological civilization has also managed to put everybody into a splendid though rigorous isolation. The existence of countless specialists shows that more and more people are excluded from general fields of competency which are then divided and taken over by narrow specialists. Even within one family it is difficult to know what the other members are really doing. The work world of the father is not intelligible to the mother, and, because many mothers are now "gainfully" employed, the fathers find it more and more difficult to understand their wives' activities. Since school curricula are continuously being changed, the parents are often unable to provide help for the children for their school work and thus another partner within the family is being isolated.

Another segmentation is provided through developers and city planning. The problem of deteriorating inner cities and expanding suburbs is only one expression of the idea that each category of housing should be segregated and separated from all other categories. One lives first in an apartment, then moves on to another area, in which the so-called starter houses are located, then climbs up to the executive developments, and finally arrives at one of the retirement communities of the sunny South. Each phase of life is self-contained without much interaction from other brackets of age and income. We have no firsthand knowledge of how older or younger people actually live and what their problems are unless we watch their "stories" on TV. The segregation goes so far that in some retirement communities families with children are regarded as unwelcome intruders from another sphere. The naturalness of rich and poor, and old and young living together has been converted to the unnaturalness of a segmented and segregated society. That humanity is in deep turmoil becomes even more evident when we consider the phenomenon of transitoriness.

Transitoriness is something fundamental to life. Older forms of life are waning away and new ones are arising. But we have accelerated transitoriness to such a degree that it threatens our very existence. Let us illustrate this point with a few examples. Today in all fields of knowledge information is so quickly outdated that students often question whether they should still memorize facts. Even the most thorough preparation for certain professions no longer suffices because either new jobs with different requirements spring up overnight or old jobs become obsolete and with them the training received for them. Alvin Toffler's *Future Shock* is a vivid description of a society in transit in which nothing can be taken for granted and everything is in flux. Sacral structures are also affected by this trend. While the squarely built Roman churches expressed a confidence of man living on this earth and while the slender upward-reaching Gothic churches symbolized the yearning of medieval man for heaven, modern sacral structures at most resemble the tents of our present nomadic society.

Traditions that served as a guide for our attitude towards agriculture, family structure, religion, etc., more and more rapidly lose their binding character, and no longer are replaced by other traditions, but by steadily varying trends. It is not only that old foundations are shaking but that new ones are not built with the same strength and duration. We become more and more uncertain which way to move. Our own identity becomes increasingly uncertain, since the more possibilities there are to pursue the future, the more choices we must make and the more we realize that in making them there is nothing to rely on except our own self. This identity crisis shows itself in the crumbling of traditional professional images, in the uncertainty about what the roles of husband, wife, and children are within the family context, in the indecision concerning the liturgical and theological self-expression of the churches, and even in the questioning of one's biological role within the normal aging process.

Though having renounced the static existence of our forefathers, even today we seem unable to live a completely transitory existence. We could still justify the disintegrating structures of families, and neighborhoods by explaining them as part of the rapid social change we witness. But we are more at a loss to justify the psychosomatic reactions to our turbulent times. Increasing disturbances of the ner-

vous, digestive, and cardiac systems are signs of disease rather than
of progress.[1] We can only live in a state of permanent stress and insecurity, caused by our transitory life, if we sacrifice our mental and
physical health.

To arrive at an answer to these vexing issues, one is sometimes
inclined to resort to old standards and reinforce them with rigor. The
results are political, religious and cultural dogmatism which easily
finds open ears in an uncertain society. The other possibility would be
to ignore humanity's forward-reaching tendency by abandoning the
accelerating ship of continuous change. The results are what Theodore Roszak has vividly described as counterculture, a protest against
uncertainty and an attempt to find values outside the established
society.[2] Yet we wonder if either of these solutions, resorting to the
value of the good old days or simply bailing out entirely, is a helpful
remedy to overcome uncertainty. They ignore the intrinsically forward-reaching aspect of humanity and fail to see that, in the long run,
reactionary positions are self-defeating. They cannot overcome the
fact that life is transitory and forward-reaching.[3]

While we do not and cannot revert to a static existence, we are
unable to swim "constantly out upon the deep and with seventy thousand fathoms of water under us," as the Danish philosopher Søren
Kierkegaard once described our existence in faith.[4] We need something to cling to on our journey, a point of orientation and a point
of reference. This becomes especially necessary at a time when most
of the traditional points of reference have become unreliable and
obsolete. But how should we orient ourselves? One way of achieving
this is to relate us humans to the phenomena by which we are surrounded, or to the human matrix.

Redefining the human matrix: A matrix is "that which gives origin
or form to a thing, or which serves to enclose it." Confronted with
the immense turmoil in which humanity finds itself, essence, place,
and destiny of humanity must then be defined in relation to the items
which give origin and form to humanity and which enclose it.[5] This
means a human self-definition would be of no avail to solve our
existential anxieties, since we are neither our own boundaries nor our
own creators. Also a definition by one or several external referents
could at most result in a dogmatic position, since it would have to
absolutize a selection of the creative and formative causes of our
existence. If we want to address ourselves seriously to the question
"What does it mean to be a human being?," we must pursue the relational character of the question with utmost rigor and inclusiveness.

Since in our following treatise we attempt to rediscover the origin, present course, and possible destiny of *Our Cosmic Journey*, we want to refer to the essential reference points on this journey only in a kind of preview.

The first reference point for our journey is *matter*. It surrounds us, and we ourselves are at least in part composed of matter. Especially in the 19th century, in the wake of the first industrial revolution, humans were often compared with machines. Already in 1747 the French physician and philosopher Julien Offray de Lamettrie had written his provocative book *Le'homme machine* and a century later Ludwig Feuerbach claimed that man is what he eats.[6] This materialistic tradition is still maintained by the Marxist movement, since its founders, Karl Marx and Friedrich Engels, were in close contact with Feuerbach and the advocates of stringent evolutionism, both of whom reduced everything living to a variety of matter.

The next reference point is the *stream of life* as it evolves and unfolds itself in the universe. The origin and possible direction of life provides us with valuable information as to the unique character of life on earth and our special place within life on our planet. We are also confronted here with the amazing unity of life and our affinity to other forms of life.

Closely associated with this is another reference point, the *animal world*. Comparative anatomy, psychology, and embryology have discovered many analogies and similarities between humans and animals. We still have many instinct patterns that resemble those of animals and, of course, our skeleton is very much like that of other mammals. In the first exuberance following the publication of Darwin's theory of descent even serious scholars were inclined to regard humans just as higher mammals. The tendency to follow this line of thought is still strong. For instance, the insistence on naturalness in moral matters, such as sex life and marriage, is an indication that one does not perceive significant distinctions between humans and animals. However, the more carefully we compare ourselves with animals the more we notice the differences. We must mention here our unique openness toward the world and our lack of strong instinct patterns that control our inter-relational conduct.

In going beyond the animal world we come to the *human family* itself. Cultural anthropology and paleoanthropology are some of the disciplines that attempt to show the historical peculiarity of tribes, nations, and races. We notice that humanity's culture and appearance underwent considerable changes and that there is still an immense difference in the customs, languages and living standards of different nations. Yet at the same time we realize that the human family forms a basic unity which renders all distinctions as secondary. Though the Bible tells us that God created *all* humanity, and though the Stoic philosopher Cicero claimed that the basic difference between people is whether they are human or inhuman and not whether they are Romans or non-Romans, for some people today there still exist "Whiteys" and "Niggers." [7] We also remember that in World War II some people were called Japs and that even Cicero's contemporaries distinguished between Romans and barbarians. While in 1945 the United Nations declared inalienable human rights for all people, we know that this document was violated many times by the same member countries that signed and adopted it. Humans do not seem to be a good reference point to learn more about humanity, since they often treat their equals as unequals.

Yet there is another reference point that seems to shed some light on humanity, namely the *divine*. At the temple of Apollo in the city of Delphi in ancient Greece there was an inscription which read: *Gnothi seauton* (know thyself).[8] This was an encouragement not to reflect on the grandeur of humanity, but to recognize the fact that in entering the temple we approach a divine reality of which we are not a part. In other words, the inscription admonishes us: know that you are human and not divine. The psalmist put the same insight in the form of a question when he asked: "What is man that thou (O God) art mindful of him?" (Ps. 8:4). We are surely not divine, but God still cares about us. Yet this care does not seem to be a unilateral process. The church father Augustine wrote in the opening chapter of his *Confessions* the unforgettable words: "Thou hast made us for thyself and restless is our heart until it comes to rest in thee (O God)." [9] Evidently there is a restlessness and a yearning in us that remains unfulfilled unless it results in union between ourselves and our creator. To discover whether we really need God in order to find ourselves will be one of the major tasks of this investigation.

The union between the created and the creator, however, is neither a starting point nor something that has already been attained. Therefore, any redefinition of the human matrix and any mapping out of our journey would be grossly inadequate if we understood humanity just from the perspective of available reference points. To obtain a complete view of our journey, we must also consider our fundamental alienation from the intended goal. Then we realize that the human predicament is precariously extended between self-inflicted chaos and

God-wrought providence. By alienating ourselves from our creator we have estranged ourselves from each other and from our environment. Though our course borders dangerously close on self-destruction, there are two reasons for hope. First, we are under God's providential care, enjoying the trustworthiness of the natural, moral, and historical processes he has set in motion. Secondly, we have the promise of a new humanity and the privilege of its proleptic anticipation. This could provide sufficient incentive for reorienting ourselves so that something of the new humanity can be realized fulfilling the age-old dreams of the human family and persuading us to create a better world to live in.

PART I

STRUCTURES OF HUMAN EXISTENCE

When a human being is born and launched on its journey, it soon discovers that it is not alone. Humans are born into a *world*. Our existence is both defined and limited by the physical, biological, socio-philosophical, and metaphysical structures of this world. Though we can influence these structures in many ways with the aid of modern technology, or even through revolution and social change, we receive from them the limitations and the possibilities of our own existence. They are reference points for our life's journey, and only close scrutiny will tell us whether they are irrevocably binding, moderately flexible, or open to change. We shall soon notice, however, that many of them are not nearly as fixed as we first assumed. For instance, we will see that the components of our environment have an origin and a history. The big existential problem, however, is not solved, once we have discovered the origin and history of the structures. There are still the bewildering questions of what we can and shall do with them. In other words, we must then also address the issues of how we fit into this environment and whether our position is of accidental or providential nature.

1.

The Universe

In the 19th century the question whether the universe conforms to a specific plan or whether its structure is purely accidental was often solved in a relatively confident fashion. For instance, the collaborator with Karl Marx, Friedrich Engels, declared:

> It is an eternal cycle in which matter moves, . . . wherein nothing is eternal but eternally changing, eternally moving matter and the laws according to which it moves and changes. . . . But however often, and however relentlessly, this cycle is completed in time and space, . . . we have the certainty that matter remains eternally the same in all its transformations, that none of its attributes can ever be lost.[1]

This confidence in a causal mechanistic world view in which matter obeys the eternal laws of nature was nothing exceptional in the 19th century. Still today it is the creed of many materialistically inclined people. Yet over fifty years ago matter, or the existence of an absolute object, as one of the basic building blocks of the universe lost its absolute and unchangeable character.

1. The Search for Absolutes

a. Matter

It is fairly safe to take for granted the absolute character of the objects we encounter. Most things remain basically the same, regardless of how we look at them. For instance, if we examine a rock in a laboratory, the rock remains a rock whether we look at it during the day or at night, whether we look at it with our naked eyes or with the help of a magnifying glass. If we change the actual form of an object, e.g., grind our rock to fine sand, there still remains an object (sand) which is equivalent to the earlier object (rock) plus the energies involved in the transformation process. An object always remains an object. At the most it enters the scene of investigation in a different gown.

Yet, in his second antinomy of pure reason the German philosopher, Immanuel Kant, showed that our reasoning concerning an absolute object results in a basic conflict.[2] On the one hand, he argued, we can assume that we can divide every composite object into parts and these parts again into smaller parts and then continue infinitely with this dividing process, obtaining smaller and smaller parts. With equal right we could assume that this process ends at one time when we have reached the ultimately smallest and hence indivisible parts. Kant concluded that both assertions are logically possible and that we actually cannot decide through experience or perception which of these assertions is right. When scientists investigated the realm of the microcosmos they encountered the same antinomy in a very baffling way. While we in our visible world are able to divide the objects of investigation into smaller and smaller parts, this does not seem to work in the invisible world.

First, it was discovered that by a process of atomic fission a noticeable amount of matter could be directly converted into energy. This discovery was expressed by Albert Einstein with the well-known formula $E = mc^2$ (energy equals mass times the square of the speed of light), and describes the mass-to-energy conversion that is going on in an atomic explosion and, in a more tamed and useful way, in nuclear reactors. Since Einstein had expressed with this formula a universal relation, it applies as much to the combustion of coal or wood and oxygen into carbon dioxide and energy (heat and light), as it describes the nuclear reaction of radioactive substances. Yet in the latter case the release of energy is so enormous that the decrease of mass is measurable, while in the former it is too small to be detected. The inference could now no longer be avoided that the idea of an absolute and basically indestructible object had become untenable while the mass/energy relation emerged as a new and fundamental constituent of all things.

Another bewildering factor that contributed to the dissolution of the absolute object was Heisenberg's uncertainty principle.[3] Werner

Heisenberg discovered that in the subatomic realm the "product" of the uncertainty with which the velocity and the location of a particle can be measured never falls below a certain value and is likely to be higher. If we picture an atom in analogy to our solar system this phenomenon may become more comprehensible. Let us imagine that the core of the atom, the nucleus, is surrounded by many electrons like the sun is encircled by planets. Several of the planets can be observed with the naked eye and others with telescopes. With little difficulty we can determine their exact location and their speed. The reason why we are able to observe these planets is because they emit or reflect some light which then meets our eyes. The interaction that the light rays establish between us observers and the observed matter (planet) is so small, though certainly greater than zero, that we do not change the velocity or the location of the planet simply by looking at it.

But we cannot "look" at the electrons that encircle the nucleus of an atom with extremely high velocity, or at any other particles that serve as the elementary building blocks for atoms and molecules and finally for our visible world, and simply "see" them. Even sophisticated microscopes are of no help. We have to "touch" them with rays (such as light rays) or other particles that are somehow equivalent in "size" to these electrons if we want to observe them. Unfortunately we cannot use anything that is so much smaller than the object we want to observe that our observation would not disturb the observed object. There simply does not exist anything that small. When we observe an electron by means of rays we affect it so much that it considerably changes its course and its velocity. Depending on how we design the experiment, we can choose whether we want to observe either the location or the velocity of the particle more precisely. The more exactly we observe the one, however, the more inexactly we can determine the other. In other words, the observer can determine what he wants to observe, but he cannot get a total picture of the object at one and the same time.

Perhaps we can illustrate this situation with a snowball fight in the dark. If someone is hit with a snowball, we can approximately determine the location of the person who was hit by the surprise cry, but it is difficult to determine from the cry the velocity of the ball that hit the person. If we would throw another snowball into the same direction, we could not be sure that we hit the same person since the former hit does not give us any clues whether the one who was hit will stay in the same location or whether he or she will move. This is approximately the situation we encounter in the subatomic realm. We can determine certain features of an object under investigation by conducting experiments, but we are unable to know what happens from one experiment to the next. We can, for instance, locate a certain electron at one time here and another time there, but we do not know how it came from here to there.

Someone could object that someday rays might be found that are small enough not to affect the velocity or the location of the observed particles to such an extent. Though this seems unlikely, the remote possibility of such a discovery must be conceded. But would not then these newly discovered and more tiny rays be the actual building blocks of our universe? Again we would be confronted with the task of determining their basic features in order to explore the structure of the universe.

The last phenomenon we want to mention in this context is the duality of light. The question about the nature of light has aroused the curiosity of scientists for a long time. Isaac Newton had already suggested that light consisted of certain particles. This idea can best be substantiated through the so-called photoelectric effect. If the light emitted from a certain source consists of particles, they would hit a surface with a certain impact. Indeed it can be shown that this impact is strong enough to eject electrons from the matter that is hit by light "rays." [4] If a metallic plate, such as a zinc plate, is attached to a negatively charged electroscope and is exposed to light rays produced by an electric arc, the spread leaves of the electroscope will gradually collapse. This indicates that the electric charge has been lost through emission of (negatively charged) electrons on the metallic plate. When we decrease the amount of light or use a metal that is less chemically reactive, it takes longer for the charge to disappear. If we decrease the frequency but not the amount of light below a certain point, no electrons will be ejected from the metal plate. Finally, if we use a positively charged electroscope, little or no charge will be observed, since the electrons emitted from the plate are attracted back by the positive charge of the electroscope. From these observations Albert Einstein concluded in 1905 that light consists of massless particles, or photons, and that the energy of each photon is proportional to the frequency of light. Thus the assumption seemed to be right that light consists of small energy "particles" that can even eject electrons from matter.

However, other observations with the phenomenon of light lead to the conclusion that light consists of waves. For instance, when we send a light beam from a light source through a small slit behind which a screen is mounted, we observe that on the screen the pattern of light is not rectangular as we could have expected if the light only consisted of corpuscles or of particles. The picture on the screen resembles the "frozen" surface of a pond after we have thrown a stone into the water; it looks like a picture of concentric rings. When we have two slots parallel to each other and send light through them, we observe a phenomenon analogous to that caused on a pond if two stones are thrown simultaneously into it. The two ring patterns overlap and result in alternating dark and light bands, dark where the two "systems" cancel each other out and light where they reinforce each other. Thus we conclude that light consists of waves.

How can we reconcile these conflicting assumptions? After all, a particle cannot be a wave or vice versa. Scientists have tried hard to find a solution but with no lasting success. Finally, the Danish physicist Niels Bohr suggested that we assume that light is *neither* corpuscle nor wave, but that it has features of both, features that complement each other but which can never be produced at the same time with the same experiment.[5] It depends on the observer's choice of experiment whether he will observe the effects of light as corpuscle or as wave.

Yet this duality, or complementarity as we should say more precisely, is not only characteristic of light but also of electrons and other elementary particles. They produce both interference phenomena and photoelectric phenomena. Thus we cannot actually visualize the ultimate building blocks of our universe. Depending on our methods of investigation, they appear to us in certain ways but their actual "essence" is beyond our perception. Having recognized this, it is rather difficult to maintain the absolute character of matter as an empirical fact.

b. Space and time

While matter in its essence is beyond our conception, there still seem to remain two absolutes in our universe, space and time.

Yet Immanuel Kant in his *Critique of Pure Reason* already cautioned: "Those who maintain the absolute reality of space and time, whether as subsistent or only as inherent, must come into conflict with the principles of experience itself."[6] Kant himself assumed that space and time are forms of outer intuition, they are means with which we perceive object matter and they are not constituent of the object matter. With this definition he rejected the notion that space and time are simply "boxes" within which the objects of our perception are located.

Later scientific discoveries verified Kant's notion that space and time are not independent entities. By defining space and time as forms of outer intuition, Kant, however, turned them into part of the conceptual apparatus of the observer. This means that Kant proceeded the opposite way to Albert Einstein, who first postulated and then even proved that space and time must be related to the object matter and cannot be perceived apart from it. Already many centuries before Einstein the church father Augustine was not far from this insight when he claimed that to ask what happened before the creation of our world does not make sense, because we perceive time only in such a way that we observe a change of events. "Time does not exist without some movement and transition." [7] Because nothing existed before the creation of the world, there also was no time. Space and time presupposes matter, or at least a configuration of objects, while empty space would be similar to a hole with nothing around it.

Albert Einstein's theoretical foundations for our new understanding of space and time is laid down in his theory of relativity. In his *Special Theory of Relativity* Einstein postulated in 1905 that the velocity of light is always constant relative to an observer. This means that light emitted from a source does not change its velocity regardless of whether source or observer are moving. This seems contrary to all moving objects of which we know. For instance, if a rocket is moving away from an observer with a velocity v and a bullet is fired from the rocket with a velocity u in the direction the rocket is moving, the resulting speed of the bullet for the "stationary" observer is not $v + u$, as might be expected. Einstein made it clear that simply adding the velocities or subtracting them results in an approximate value, a procedure which can only be used with relatively small velocities. When the velocities approach the speed of light, we must be more careful in computing the resulting speed by resorting to an equation which prevents any two velocities ensuing in a speed higher than that of light: $V = \dfrac{v+u}{1+vu/c^2}.$ This equation pertains also to lower velocities, but there it can be simplified to a level of merely adding the velocities.

The principal that the velocity of light is always constant relative to an observer, together with a second principle of relativity, that all motion is relative, caused a radical reorientation in our concepts of space and time. Before this discovery it was commonly accepted that the whole universe was filled by some kind of world ether in relation to which everything else could be defined in the world, like the chairs in relation to the walls of a room. However, Einstein abandoned the idea of a world ether and came to the conclusion that there is no fixed world center. We can only define something moving by defining its motion in relation to the motion of something else. For instance, when we go by car on the turnpike, then we assume that the turnpike is at rest. But actually the turnpike is part of the earth and the earth is moving annually once around the sun and once each day the earth is revolving around its axis. The sun is rotating around its axis and also moving within the milky way. The milky way itself is moving, and so on. Thus everything is in motion, nothing is at rest, and the idea of a fixed world center is a wishful dream.

The correlative motion of bodies does not only determine their respective location, but also their extension, mass, and even their time. Flying in a jet plane perhaps we have noticed that we seem to get heavier when the jet accelerates and takes off. Yet what we feel is not an actual increase in mass, but the effects of acceleration on the inertia of our body. When we would travel at speeds very close to that of light, however, an *actual* increase in mass would take place which would be proportional to the velocity of the body. If a body would reach the speed of light, its mass would have increased infinitely. It has already been observed that protons having a velocity so close to the speed of light in particle accelerators, such as huge synchrotrons, became more massive than uranium atoms. It is impossible, however, to accelerate particles to the speed of light because, to reach this goal, an infinite amount of energy would be necessary. Hand in hand with the observed increase in mass goes an observed decrease of the length of the body. Again this decrease is relative. It can only be observed by someone who moves with a relatively lower velocity than the object in question. If we would dwell on the fast-moving body itself we would not notice a decrease in length. Yet the space between us and objects outside our moving system would contract immensely and if we would reach the speed of light distances would dwindle to zero.

Time is subjected to these changes too. For instance, if we would leave the earth in some imaginary jet with a speed close to that of light, all our body functions would slow down considerably. We would not notice this in our jet, however, since all other gadgets in our jet, including all time-keeping devices, would slow down accordingly. But a stationary observer on the earth could notice a retardation of

our aging, perhaps once we would have returned from a long interstellar trip, traveling all the time with extremely high speed. While
such retardation of the aging process due to the relativity of time
may sound like science fiction, it has actually been observed that time-
keeping devices, when highly accelerated, slowed down in that function relative to a stationary observer.

With time being relative too, the question arises whether simul-
taneous events are possible.[8] While we cannot deny that events occur
at the same time, it is impossible to observe their simultaneity because
light always takes time to reach an observer from the objects or events
he wants to observe. He always sees things of the past; for him they
may have happened at the same time, but they actually occur at
different "local" times.

If we sum up our findings concerning the nature of matter, space,
and time, we must conclude that scientific investigation has stripped
them of the absolute or infinite character they once were believed to
possess. Space and time are so closely connected with matter that they
cannot exist independently from it. But even the "essence" of matter
remains hidden from our eyes. Matter can be transformed into energy
and it can appear as either corpuscle or wave. It can even increase
or decrease depending on its relative speed. Of course, we can still
rejoice in the infinite space of the sky or the eternal roaring of the
sea when its waves crash against the shore. But in either case we
should remind ourselves that the terms infinite or eternal have only
metaphoric value. They denote a finite reality, an entity with boundaries. The elementary building blocks of our universe are only of
relative character.

c. Cause and effect sequence (determinism)

We have recognized that space and time do not exist independently
of matter, and that matter itself leads to the duality of corpuscle and
wave. But does this actually mean that all the structural elements of
our universe are of finite character? We cannot claim space and time
as absolutes since they are attributes of matter, and with regard to
matter we have discovered the duality of corpuscle and wave. Yet we
have only changed the names, while the assumption is still valid that
every effect is determined by knowable causes.

Corpuscles and waves emerge as the new coordinates through
which every event can be sufficiently defined. There can be nothing
new in our world, since every cause and effect is determined by these
coordinates which belong to our world and are constantly validated

by experimentation. Anything unforeseen seems to be excluded by the
mere fact that, at least in principle, every event can be predicted.
The French mathematician Pierre Laplace had claimed:

> Given for one instant an intelligence which could compre-
> hend all the forces by which nature is animated and the
> respective situation of the beings who compose it—an intelli-
> gence sufficiently vast to submit these data to analysis—it
> would embrace in the same foundation the movements of the
> greatest bodies of the universe and those of the lightest
> atom; for it, nothing would be uncertain and the future, as
> the past, would be present to its eyes.[9]

This was written before anyone knew of the possibilities of a computer. For us, this view would mean that once we feed a computer
all available data of our universe it could tell us the detailed future
of any part of the universe.

Despite the attractive character of this stringent causal nexus, according to which everything is predictable to the last atom, such a
mechanistic world view is only wishful thinking. The first argument
comes from the logical impossibility of a computerization of the
world. We can never program all the causes of the same time
level, since our world is not steady, but constantly changing. These
changes would require a continuous reconsideration of the already
programmed causes. Besides this, a total programming would also
necessitate a programming of the programming process, otherwise
some potential causes would be omitted. By its very nature such a
process would never be completed. The only relief could come from
a "supermind" that is not connected with our world and its cause
and effect system. Or to put it in a more old-fashioned way, only God
could know all causes and effects in our world.

Another argument against a stringent causal system comes from
the structure of matter itself. In viewing the duality of matter we
notice that we can determine whether matter should appear to us in
its corpuscle or in its wave character. Matter itself does not determine
its characteristics but we choose between the two possibilities.[10]
When we investigate the causal nexus in the subatomic structure of
matter, we discover an even more surprising indeterminism.

One of the best-known phenomena of radioactive materials is
their spontaneous decay. Radioactive substances disintegrate into
substances of less atomic mass whereby part of their former mass is
converted into energy. If the radioactive material is available in con-

siderable quantity, we can know exactly when half of it will be decayed. But if we had just one radioactive atom, we could never accurately tell when this individual atom would decay. In a similar way as we can know how old the average American will be when he/she dies, we can statistically determine when a sizeable quantity of atoms will be decayed, for instance 30 percent, 50 percent, or 80 percent. We know that the higher the intensity of the radioactivity of a specific substance, the shorter the lifespan of its atoms. Therefore we can even determine the mean life, or average life expectancy, of the atoms of a radioactive substance.[11] But we cannot know when a *specific* radioactive atom will decay just as we cannot know when a *specific* American will die. Of course, we could get the person's health checked and perhaps could arrive at a somewhat reliable prediction. But this method would not help with an individual radioactive atom, because an atom does not get sick or decrease in vigor. It is fully "alive" and then, from one moment to the next, it decays without predetermination and without any obvious cause. Of course, one could argue that this example does not provide a sufficient basis for rejecting a causal mechanistic world view, because some day we might find the cause for this seemingly spontaneous and undetermined decay. But even if we would, one could then ask, who would determine the determinator of the radioactive decay. In other words, we have pushed stringent determinism and causal mechanism one step further without arriving at an ultimate foundation.

Another objection against a deterministic world view comes from quantum mechanics. As early as 1900 Max Planck assumed to everyone's surprise that energy is not infinitely divisible. He claimed that it always appears in one or a multitude of energy bundles or quanta.[12] When an atom changes its energy level, it either absorbs or emits one or several of those quanta. Since the electrons thereby jump from one energy level to another, these changes are called quantum jumps. Again we are confronted with non-causal events; we do not know when a certain electron will jump and which energy level it will assume afterwards. Werner Heisenberg was the first to assert that quantum mechanics excludes a deterministic structure of reality.[13] He argued that after an event has occurred we can always list all factors that led to its occurrence, but we cannot predict in advance a certain event with absolute certainty.

Some people may claim that this theory does not at all affect our everyday life, because we are never personally confronted with quantum jumps or with the problem of the mean life of radioactive atoms.[14]

While we must admit that the subatomic realm is inaccessible to most of us, it nevertheless provides the "bricks" and the structure for our macrocosmos. Even more, quantum jumps are responsible for all polymerization, crystallization, and melting processes which then express themselves in the structural changes of the final product. Though, for instance, the crystalline structure of cast steel conforms to strictly determined patterns, the subatomic starting point of each of its crystallization processes is due to quantum jumps. When a piece of metal breaks or ruptures, the course of breaking or rupturing conforms mostly to the fixed crystalline structure, but in part also to quantum jumps that determine the exact micromolecular point from which the breaking starts. This means that a splinter of an exploding grenade barely missing a civilian walking down the road is difficult to explain as a strictly predetermined event.[15] The same indeterminancy must be recognized, for instance, in the blowout of a tire which did not seem to be worn out and which led to the deaths of the car's passengers. We could cite many other situations in which the effect of undetermined quantum jumps on our everyday life becomes evident. They play their role not only in fateful occasions, but in such common events as the boiling of water or in the use of household electric current. This leads us to a completely different understanding of the laws of nature.

In our everyday world we usually operate with large quantities of atoms. For large quantities, as we have seen from the discussion of the mean life of radioactive substances, static and deterministic laws are sufficient. But we have noticed that the substructure of reality is not founded on determinism. Determinism emerges only as the result of statistical laws when applied to large quantities of undetermined acts. Of course, a deterministic approach is necessary for our everyday life; we need to predict and manipulate the future to act with certainty and determination. For instance, how could an architect design a bridge that can withstand the forces of wind and weather if there were no macrocosmic determinism? Determinism serves as a pragmatic basis for our own actions although it rests on an undetermined substructure.[16]

The undetermined substructure of reality also becomes evident when we remember how laws of nature are postulated. They are projections from a series of *a* to a totality of *a*. A limited, observable basis serves as the starting point for non-observable postulations. This does not mean that laws of nature are wrong. Within their limits, they are necessary and reliable and all anticipated events, as soon as they belong to the past, can be checked whether they have fulfilled the predictions of these laws. But these laws are of an irrevocably hypothetical nature. They are not laws according to which events must occur, but laws patterned according to our experience of the way events generally happen. As nature shows its orderliness in following certain patterns, we should speak rather about *orders* of nature than about *laws* of nature viewed mechanistically.[17]

While at first glance everything seems to be structured in a causal mechanistic way, we soon realize that this is not so. The causal picture is the view we get when we look at the surface of our world. But penetrating its surface structure, we see that its very foundation is undetermined. The German physicist Pascual Jordan rightly called this change in our view of reality much more thrilling than all novels of world literature.[18] Regardless of the direction we turn, whether to the "infinity" of space and time, to the "eternal" duration of matter, or to the "determining" cause and effect sequence, we discover that the basic constituents of our universe are of irrevocably limited validity. Though we need them in our daily activities and have to regard them there as being of unchangeable or absolute character, we dare not forget that such pragmatic actions have no ultimate sanction. The basic structural elements of our universe are only tools to be used for specific and limited purposes, they do not suffice as an ultimate foundation for our lives. To make the outcome of our journey trustworthy, our lives must be grounded on something other than the elementary building blocks of our world or on the sequence of the building materials. Perhaps in looking at the universe as a whole we might gain a more confident answer about the trustworthiness of the future.

2. The World—Eternal or Episodic?

When Albert Einstein had convincingly postulated the inexorable connection between space, time, and matter, the question emerged for him, as well as for others, about the implications this theoretical observation would have for our understanding of the universe. Especially the question whether the existence of our universe was unlimited regarding age and extension of space, time, and matter had to be raised anew. In his *General Theory of Relativity* (1916) Einstein attempted a partial answer to these questions.[19]

He suggested that gravitational fields produced by masses distributed in space and moving in time are equivalent to the curvature of the four-dimensional space-time continuum they form. If applied to the forces of gravity this would mean that the light emitted from distant stars, just grazing the sun, is deflected somewhat towards the sun when it passes by the sun and its immense gravitational pull. This curvature is high enough that it can be verified by observation. For instance, if two stars have an angular distance slightly larger than the angular diameter of the sun, it can be observed that the angular distance between these two stars is slightly larger when the sun has "moved away" from this part of the sky than when it comes to stand directly between the two stars. Of course, one needs the help of a total solar eclipse to measure the angle between the two while the sun stands between them.

Einstein now attempted to generalize this gravitational pull by applying it to the structure of the whole universe. He suggested that the whole space-time continuum associated with the mass of matter contained in our universe is bent and curved. For a while the question remained unsolved, whether the curvature is positive which would mean that the universe is finite, or whether the curvature is negative which would prove the infinity of the universe. It was relatively easy to decide that the curvature is not unsteady like that of a banana, but uniform like that of a ball, because the galaxies seem to be very homogeneously dispersed throughout the observable part of the universe. But to decide between a negative and a positive curvature on the grounds of observable phenomena is very difficult. Einstein suggested that the curvature was positive and thus the universe finite. However, he held the curvature of space to be independent of time and consequently conceived of a space-time continuum similar to a cylinder with the time axis running parallel to the axis of the cylinder and the space axis perpendicular to it.

In 1917 Willem de Sitter, a Dutch mathematician, showed much more convincingly that both space and time must be curved (which seems more logical according to the presuppositions in Einstein's *Special Theory of Relativity*) and in turn suggested an expanding universe, similar to an expanding globe with a longitude serving as the space coordinate and the latitude as the time coordinate.[20] In this model of the universe, "history" would not repeat itself because, unlike the model proposed by Einstein, a light ray would not travel a complete circle. It would rather travel in a perpetually expanding spiral.

In 1922, the Russian mathematician Alexander Friedmann applied Einstein's theory to the universe as a whole and proved there were no static solutions to account for the structure of the universe. Einstein, however, was horrified about this solution and in turn introduced his cosmological constant according to which the universe would neither expand nor contract. Only much later, after the American astronomer Edwin Hubble discovered that the light coming from distant galaxies is subjected to a redshift in its special lines which increases with the respective distance of the galaxies from us, Einstein admitted that he had made "the biggest blunder of his life" and corrected the shortcoming of his own proposal.[21] This redshift is analogous to the "distorted" sound of a car that passes us on the road and moves away from us. The universe seems to be in a state of uniform expansion, whereby the mutual recession velocities between any two galaxies in space are proportional to the distance between them.

It is interesting here that Friedmann's proposal was nothing peculiar to Einstein's theory. Classical Newtonian mechanics had no static solutions either for interpreting the structure of the universe. According to Newtonian mechanics, if at any moment the galaxies were static, they would certainly have to start moving toward each other under their mutual gravitational attraction. This would lead to a contracting universe. The only alternative would be for the universe to be expanding so the galaxies have enough residual velocity to move away from each other against the contrary gravitational drag. We can exemplify this with a ball that we throw up in the air. This ball does not remain standing motionless in the air. It continues its upward move, away from the earth and its gravitational field, until it stops and then starts falling. Amazingly, the idea of an unchanging eternal universe exerted still such fascination for an innovative scientist as Einstein in the early decades of this century. Yet, together with Friedmann, he laid with his mathematical work the ground for the so-called big bang theory.

a. Cosmic egg or "big bang" theory

The Belgian astronomer Georges Lemaitre in 1925 proposed along the lines of de Sitter's version of Einstein's model of the universe a constantly expanding universe and then projected it back to its origin.[22] He assumed that if the universe is constantly expanding it must have had a beginning or a zero point at which it had almost no extension. This zero point of cosmic time must date further back than the age of the oldest surface rocks on our earth or the age of meteorites. It can be estimated by retracing the most distant galaxies to a state where they were all assembled at the same starting point. These different calculations converge upon approximately the same date. Various investigations have shown that the age of the oldest surface rocks is roughly 3.5 billion years, that of meteorites 4.7 billion, and the big bang model would yield little less than 10 billion years. This means that roughly 10 billion years ago mass must have been packed together so tightly that no individual atoms could exist, but only, as Lemaitre called it, a "cosmic egg" or "primeval atom" of extraordinarily high radiation. Lemaitre concluded that his primeval nucleus of immense proportions broke with a burst to form the atoms we know today. Very massive atoms would be formed, breaking down further to produce less massive atoms until we arrive at the permanently stable chemical elements, such as hydrogen, helium, carbon, iron, etc. Once we admit an initial big bang, this theory sounds very convincing. Yet it does not agree with the facts, since it would result in a universe chiefly composed of heavy elements. In reality, however, the universe is made up of 90% hydrogen, 9% helium, and only 1% heavier elements.

Together with Hans Bethe and Ralph Alpher the Russian-American astrophysicist George Gamow in 1948 presented a different approach to the big bang theory.[23] Gamow claimed that the cosmic egg was so highly compressed that it did not contain individual atoms, but only a "ylem" mass consisting of protons and electrons packed together so tightly that they formed a mass of electrically uncharged particles called neutrons. At the early state of the expansion, approximately "five minutes" after the big bang, the universe had already cooled down sufficiently to allow the aggregation of protons and neutrons into complex nuclei, namely deuterons (H^2), tritons (H^3), tralphas (He^3), alphas (He^4), and others. Yet within "thirty minutes" after the big bang the temperature would have been below that required to sustain thermonuclear reactions in light elements and the free neutrons, being abundant at the beginning but having a half-life of only thirteen minutes, must have virtually disappeared. They were used up in the formation of elements or decayed to protons to form the nuclei of hydrogen atoms.

The physicists Enrico Fermi and Anthony Turkevich studied the thermonuclear reactions that Alpher, Bethe, and Gamow had postulated and came to the conclusion that if their hypothesis had been correct, it would have resulted in an equal amount of hydrogen and helium and about one percent of deuterium from which the heavier elements could have been formed by capturing neutrons. However, Gamow himself noticed that his theory would account only for the formation of hydrogen and helium, but not for the existence of heavier elements except in very unlikely circumstances. The reason for this is that once the atomic mass of four (helium) is reached, a simple addition or a capturing of a neutron or a proton leads to extremely unstable elements. Since there is no stable nucleus with atomic mass five, the amount of heavier elements, calculated on the basis of this theory, would be much lower than the amount actually observed.

To the aid of this situation came the British astronomer Fred Hoyle, suggesting that hydrogen is the only original material while everything else is formed within stars and added to the interstellar material.[24] Together with the American nuclear physicist William Fowler he discovered that the observed decay period of supernova luminosity of fifty-five days coincides with the natural decay period of the spontaneous fission of californium-254. Thus they concluded that large amounts of californium are formed in the process of a supernova explosion. Furthermore, it had been observed that the spectrum of certain stars shows the presence of technetium. This element is radioactive and possesses no stable variety. The most stable form is technetium-99 with a half-life of about 220,000 years. If we allow 5 billion years for the average life of a star this would mean that only one billionth of the originally present amount of technetium-99 would remain. Yet there is still a sufficient amount of technetium in the stars to show in the spectral lines of their light. There are two possibilities to account for this phenomenon. Either technetium was present in rather huge amounts, which would be rather unlikely, or it was formed in the interior of the stars. The latter possibility would support Gamow's thesis of how the chemical elements were formed. If Hoyle's thesis is true that this process goes on in the stellar core, the density of matter would be so much higher there than in open space that the chance of a helium-4 nucleus being struck by two particles essentially simultaneously would be much more likely. Thus heavier atoms that lead to stable varieties could be more easily formed. By 1970, however, this idea of a nucleosynthesis in the stellar bodies through which the heavier elements were formed was gradually abandoned in favor of an explosive nucleosynthesis, such as in supernovae, through which a star explodes to end its career.[25]

At present one usually reckons in the big bang theory with a primordial fireball that exploded.[26] In a first step, the radiative era, nearly all energy that resulted from the explosion was in form of subatomic particles of high energy but without electric charge, the so-called photons. Most of the photons that compose the cosmic background radiation seem to stem from this original explosion. Within these first minutes hydrogen, helium, and a small amount of "heavy" hydrogen and lithium was formed. Within the next thousand years a gradual change from a radiation dominated universe to a matter dominated universe took place. The universe cools down considerably and galaxies are being formed from the "interstellar" matter. Once galaxies begin to condensate, they heat up and in turn heat up the intergalactic matter. Yet the decreasing density of intergalactic matter made conditions rather unfavorable for further condensation. We can assume that all galaxies were formed at approximately the same stage of the evolutionary process, between eight to ten billion years ago. The first stars in these galaxies consisted of hydrogen and helium. Since these first generation stars were often considerably larger in terms of their mass than our sun, they ended their development in the huge aforementioned explosions through which much of the production of the heavier elements occurred.

If the explosion of a cosmic egg marks the beginning of time, we should ask what was before that zero point. Of course we could conjecture that the once stable cosmic egg suddenly or gradually became unstable. Yet the question which then emerges is what made it change from its once stable state to an unstable one. If the big bang theory is assumed to be true, the dilemma is often solved in such a way to say that there was a state prior to the cosmic egg where matter/energy existed in a form similar to the intergalactic matter that we experience today.

Such exceedingly thin gas is subject to its own vastly diffused gravitational field. But such a universe was not static. Slowly the gas collected and the universe drew closer together. As the substance of the universe grew more compact, the gravitational field became more and more intense until, like a snowball rolling down the hill, the matter contracted at an ever increasing rate. Since the matter was compressed into a smaller and smaller volume, the universe heated up. This heat increase countered the gravitational pull and the contraction began to slow down. The inertia of matter, however, kept it contracting, passing the point where temperature and gravitation were balanced. The universe approached its minimum volume represented by the cosmic egg or the ylem state of matter. Finally the temperature was so high and the radiation so intense that the outward pressure due to the hot gases exceeded the inward pressure due to gravity. The substance of the universe was pushed out faster and faster and the big bang occurred. The universe had a definite beginning, the immensely thin gas, which went through a stage of condensation and, through the big bang, to a subsequent expansion.

When we ask about the future of our universe, it is very difficult to arrive at a definite answer. Following the theory of a constantly expanding universe, the decisive question is whether the velocities with which the galaxies recede from each other are large enough for mutual escape. The problem involved can be illustrated with a ball we throw up in the air. If we throw it with an initial velocity that is high enough the ball escapes into space and does not return in spite of the ever present force of gravity. If the velocity is not high enough, then the initial velocity with which the ball is thrown "upward" will decrease to zero and then increase again with reversed sign until the ball hits the earth. Many scientists indeed suggest that the first possibility bears closer resemblance to the future of our universe. The recessional velocity of the galaxies is believed to be high enough that the galaxies will continue to expand in spite of gravitational attraction between them. Thus astronomers speak of a hyperbolic structure of the universe or an ever expanding universe. Every galaxy outside our own will continue to recede with an increasing velocity, corresponding to the increasing distance between the galaxies and the diminishing gravitational attraction. The galaxies will grow dimmer and dimmer and finally they will approach the limit of the observational universe. Though this would not affect us directly, our own galaxy and our own planetary system is not exempted from this irreversible aging process. Our own sun will pass through the red giant stage, in which its heat and radiation will increase immensely and then sink back to the white dwarf stage and make our planetary system uninhabitable. Thus we are at a point of no return and "eternal" could easily mean doomed to death without any rejuvenation to follow.

b. Pulsating universe and steady state theory

Though this kind of future does not sound very promising, other scientists project a different one. They suggest that the expansion of the universe will slow down at some point and then, after becoming zero, it will reverse to contraction. The galaxies act in a way similar to the thinly dispersed gas before the cosmic egg and will contract to a cosmic egg that in turn will explode again. Since the first law of thermodynamics or the so-called law of the conservation of energy states that within an energetically closed system no energy can be lost, this fluctuation between an expanding and contracting phase could even last forever. Therefore this theory is often called the theory of a pulsating universe.

Matter-anti-matter universe: If one assumes that the existence of our universe is paired with the existence of an anti-universe, one can arrive at a similar theory. In 1929 the English physicist Paul Dirac postulated on a purely theoretical basis that for each type of particle there should exist an "anti-particle" with the exact opposite key characteristics.[27] In studying cosmic rays the American physicist Carl D. Anderson discovered in 1932 the anti-particle to the electron, the anti-electron or positron.[28] However, it was not until 1955 when scientists working with the Bevatron at the University of California at Berkeley, produced and observed the first antiproton. It took another ten years until physicists at the Brookhaven National Laboratory succeeded for the first time in building an artificial anti-nucleus by combining an antiproton and an antineutron to an antideuteron, the counterpart of the nucleus of ordinary heavy hydrogen.[29] Encouraged through these discoveries, some scientists, such as the American physicist Maurice Goldhaber, suggest now that besides a universe of matter there is also an anti-universe consisting of anti-matter.[30]

This hypothesis can provide a pulsating model of the universe, in which universe and anti-universe merge in the process of contraction, whereby matter and anti-matter annihilate each other and form a cosmic egg of gamma rays.[31] Perhaps the immense radiation pressure of these photons is sufficient to account for a subsequent big bang and an outward push through which equal amounts of particles and anti-particles are formed. The American science fiction writer and scientist Isaac Asimov introduced a slightly different model when he suggested that universe and anti-universe are similar to two connecting balloons.[32] While the one contracts it expands the other and vice versa. Thus the whole system would be static while each universe in relation to the other is in an unceasing process of expansion and contraction.

The obvious symmetry between matter and anti-matter is very suggestive of the hypothesis of a universe and an anti-universe. Yet matter and anti-matter in close proximity will annihilate each other. No star could contain a close mixture of matter and anti-matter. Otherwise it could explode more violently than a supernova. Observation of cosmic radiation did not lead to the detection of sufficient gamma radiation to suggest as much matter-anti-matter annihilation as would be produced if the interstellar or intergalactic gas were to contain large amounts of anti-matter. Even to suggest that matter and anti-matter must be attributed to respective galaxies leaves us with the question of how matter and anti-matter could be neatly separated in respective galaxies if they were created together. As far as we know the gravitational interaction between matter and anti-matter is identical to that between matter and matter, suggesting an indiscriminate mixture rather than a distant segregation. Even the assumption has been abandoned that all the vast energy releases observed in quasi-stellar-objects, commonly called quasars, could be explained in terms of annihilation of matter and anti-matter.[33] We may, however, concede that the presence of large amounts of anti-matter in the universe cannot be ruled out completely, nor can we reject the idea totally that some cosmic sources of intense radiation might indeed be due to the annihilation of matter and anti-matter.

Regardless of these concessions, it is unlikely that the total amount of anti-matter in the universe is anywhere close to the fifty-fifty percentage that a matter-anti-matter cosmology assumes. Perhaps we should follow here Hannes Alfvén who advocates the existence of matter and anti-matter galaxies, yet cautions that any statement about the existence of equal amounts of matter and anti-matter in the universe has to be founded on an artificial assumption that is not subject to observational tests.[34] If the hypothesis of a matter-anti-matter "creation" of the universe could be verified, it would, however, not necessarily overrule the depressing thought of an irreversible aging process of the world. Instead of starting with a primordial fireball of "ylem" as in the big bang theory, one would now start with ambiplasma, containing both particles and anti-particles. Through initial gravitational contraction and subsequent radiation pressure, due to proton-antiproton annihilation, we would then encounter an expanding universe, which we still observe with our telescopes.

Steady state theory: A very different approach towards cosmogony was taken by the proponents of the steady state theory or the theory of continuous creation. To some extent this theory seems to return to Einstein's earlier model of a stationary universe.[35] The founders of the steady state theory were sympathetic to Einstein's original model of an eternal and unchanging universe. Yet they rejected the idea that in a static model matter could have been created at some point when the universe began to exist. The three English astronomers, Hermann Bondi, Thomas Gold, and Fred Hoyle, therefore introduced the hypothesis that matter has no beginning but is continuously being created even today. To underline this idea they advanced in 1948 the so-called perfect cosmological principle.[36] According to this principle the universe appears the same at all times and in all places. Two main objections seemed to contradict this assertion. First, we remember that the galaxies are constantly receding from each other and thus our universe becomes more and more dispersed. Second, we have heard that in stars, such as our sun, hydrogen is steadily being transformed into helium, and therefore the hydrogen content of the universe is constantly decreasing.

Bondi, Gold, and Hoyle tried to overcome these observations that seem to contradict their hypothesis by reformulating the law of conservation of energy. They said that contrary to common opinion this law does not suggest that energy is never created out of nothingness, but it only states that energy has never been observed to be created out of nothingness. They now claimed that such a creation, a continuous creation, actually takes place and compensates for the loss that occurs through the receding galaxies and the production of helium. The continuous creation they suggested is so minute that only one hydrogen atom is created per year in one billion liters of space. Such a profoundly small amount suffices to balance the hydrogen loss, but is still much too small to be ever discovered.

Since the perfect cosmological principle does not allow room for a big bang or a cosmic egg, the recession of the galaxies must have a different origin. Hoyle, for instance, claimed that "the new material produces a pressure that leads to the steady expansion," while the British astronomer Raymond A. Lyttleton suggested that the positive charge of the proton is slightly stronger than the negative charge of the electron.[37] Though the difference of these charges is much too small to be detected through direct measurements, it would allow for the building up of a strong enough amount of positive charges in galaxies that they undergo a continuous mutual recession, similar to the repulsion of the same poles of two magnets.

The steady state theory certainly has attractive features. It suggests a self-rejuvenating universe that has no beginning and no end. Our universe always has been and always will be the same. Hoyle himself sees the essential difference between the steady state theory and the former theories like this: "Without continuous creation the Universe must evolve toward a dead state in which all the matter is condensed into a vast number of dead stars. . . . With continuous creation, on the other hand, the Universe has an infinite future in which all its present very large-scale features will be preserved." [38] Small wonder that confronted with this kind of "eternal vision," Hoyle has not much positive to say about the Christian understanding of life eternal.[39]

Yet the steady state theory itself is not as well founded as its proponents first believed. For once, one wonders by which principles certain physical laws are picked out for modification while others are left unaltered.[40] It almost seems that there are certain a priori principles at work that are subsequently applied to reality. However, it was exactly a better understanding of this reality that made the steady state theory falter. Since this theory was first proposed, several hundred quasi-stellar objects or quasars have been discovered and observed individually that emit microwaves and some of them even visible light. Another estimated one million quasars have become accessible through large radio telescopes. The emission lines of these quasars show a unique redshift that seems to indicate that these objects are receding from us with velocities several times higher than those of usual galaxies. In the mid-sixties the American astronomer Allan Sandage announced the discovery of what might be aged quasars.[41] Again they possess huge redshifts in their spectral lines. They also lack the microwave emission and look like ordinary bluish stars.

The increase in redshift, however, is usually interpreted as being in proportion to the distance from us. This means that blue stellar objects and quasars are all very far away from us and were therefore formed many eons ago. Since none can be detected in our more immediate neighborhood, the universe does not seem to be as uniform in its appearance as the steady state theory proposes. In fact the process through which quasars and blue stellar objects were formed does no longer seem to be operative now in our more immediate environment.[42] Thus the conclusion is unavoidable that the universe changes its appearance and is undergoing an aging process, while billions of years ago, when these objects were still closer to us, their formation may have still been ongoing.

Also the cosmic background radiation, accidentally discovered in 1965, seems to discredit the steady state theory and gives renewed evidence to the big bang theory.[43] According to the big bang theory the intense radiation from the primordial fireball will expand with the universe and be steadily degraded in density and energy. Calculated from the estimated age of the universe this radiation will now appear at a temperature of 3° Kelvin, arriving uniformly from all directions of space. Though this faint radiation is rather difficult to distinguish from other cosmic "noises," radio astronomy seems to confirm the existence and projected value of this radiation, allowing us to "hear" the initial big bang. If we can now even hear the birth pangs of our universe, does this imply that we live in an aging world and in a universe that is gradually running down?

c. A run-down universe?

The experience of natural and human history is often interpreted in such a way that the future becoming present and the present becoming past continue as a never ending process. When in 1842 the German mathematician J. Robert Mayer proposed in his essay *Remarks on the Forces of Inorganic Nature* the law of the conservation of energy, the eternal flow of time seemed to have been endowed with scientific sanctification. This law asserts that in an energetically closed system the quantity of energy remains constant, while just the form of energy is changeable. Energy can only disappear to re-enter the scene in a different gown. The energy of electricity, for instance, can be transformed into energy of light and of heat. Or the kinetic energy of flowing water is transformed into electric energy. Energy can also be produced by burning materials that disintegrate into burned substance giving off light and heat.

The decisive question is whether our universe is such a closed system that it neither loses energy nor gains it from outside. As far as scientific investigation has shown us, it is unlikely that our universe will be subjected to energetic forces from without. Of course, we could reckon with the interference of an almighty God, but then we abandon a strictly scientific line of argument. This would mean that our universe will always remain the same; it has no point of origin and the future will only bring a predictable modification of the past. Such an "eternal" universe is undoubtedly attractive; it provides steadiness within all changes. Nineteenth century materialists happily proclaimed the eternal course of nature that will always prevail. On the other hand, it is rather devastating to realize that regardless of how hard we try, our universe will basically remain the same. We cannot add one ounce of energy to it.

Soon, however, the law of conservation of energy was supplemented by the law of entropy. The German physicist Rudolf Julius Emanuel Clausius in 1850 and the British scientist William Thomson, the later Lord Kelvin, in 1851 discovered independently from each other that though the quantity of energy in a closed system remains always the same, this cannot lead to a *perpetuum mobile*.[44] The entropy or non-convertibility of energy of an isolated system never decreases, it either remains constant or increases. For instance, when we place a pot with boiling water in a cold room, the energy of the water disperses into the room and heats up the room a little, while the water cools. Though it is theoretically comprehensible that the room could cool down again and the water be heated by the energy released from the room, the law of entropy tells us that this is impossible. Although not lost, the energy is in a sense used up and is no longer convertible. Similarly, we can run a movie backwards and get the effect of water running back into the pipe or of a diver leaping back from the pool onto a platform, but the amusement of the onlookers already tells us that in reality these reversals do not occur. Thus, some scientists talk of the "time arrow" that bars events from being repeated.[45]

When we think of our universe and the obvious eternal recurrence of the same, it is difficult for us to realize that all the movements of the stellar bodies are singular and not repetitive. The interstellar gas dispersed throughout the universe is slowing them down, not noticeably, but enough eventually to use up their kinetic energy. Like an old clock gradually slows down before it comes to a complete stop once its spring is totally unwound, so our universe will become cold, dead, and homogeneous, with no changes of any sort occurring anywhere.

There is, however, the possibility that our universe will not go on expanding forever until a state of maximum entropy or of heat death sets in.[46] In a cyclic model the point of maximum expansion will immediately be followed by a contraction. It will start very slowly but increase in speed as it picks up momentum until, similar to the gravitational collapse of a star, all matter and energy will again be compressed to an immensely compact fireball.

In recent years this primordial fireball has increasingly been interpreted in analogy to the black holes that are supposed to form in the life of certain stars. If a star is considerably larger than our sun, its final collapse will not be halted on the stage of a white dwarf. It continues to collapse beyond this stage ad infinitum. All matter collapsing into this emerging black hole will be compressed to near infinite density so that it loses most of its properties. Even light within a certain radius from the center of this hole cannot escape the immense gravitational pull. Since such a black hole is unobservable, except for the influence on material which is close by, there has been no sufficient verification that black holes do indeed exist.

Transferred to the scale of the universe, the implosion or collapse of the universe into a black hole would eventually be followed by an explosion and a new stage of expansion would occur. One could assume that our universe therefore will oscillate between stages of expansion and contraction. Yet as an overall phenomenon, these pulsations would not be exempt from the law of entropy, they too would decrease in magnitude and finally come to a halt. However, one could also argue that for this model the law of entropy is not applicable, and that each new cycle of expansion and contraction is governed by an entirely new set of natural constants. Yet following this assumption we would have no possibility of projecting what such a new cycle would be like. At the most we would have the prospect of an uncertain and unknown future, though of infinite duration, that by continuing from one cycle to the next would wipe out all life as we know it.[47] But this would also mean that we have no reliable means of retracing the history of our universe beyond this "magic black box" out of which our present universe emerged. Thus, according to this theory, both beginning and end of our universe are shrouded in impenetrable mystery.

We could tell ourselves that our planetary future is still fairly secure, since the state of an ice death at which everything levels to the state of an energetic equilibrium, or the beginning of a new cycle of expansion and contraction is still billions of years away. Einstein has taught us, however, that time is only a relative measure, and depending on our perspective, it elapses more slowly or more quickly. Furthermore, scientists have discovered that another fate is threatening us in the more "immediate" future. Within the next two to five billion years the surface temperature of our sun will increase by one hundredfold.[48] Through nuclear reaction hydrogen is constantly transformed into helium in the interior of the sun. Helium, however, is less heat permeable and thus the more helium is produced the more the sun heats up until the heat pressure is high enough to counterbalance the helium pressure on the surface and to establish a new equilibrium of pressure. The resultant heat increase will cause all water on our earth to evaporate and to make the surface of our planet similar to that of the planet Venus. Needless to say, this kind of heat death, finally followed by the final heat or ice death when all energy levels will have attained an equilibrium, will make life impossible.

However, one could follow the French Jesuit paleontologist Pierre Teilhard de Chardin who claimed that entropy is perhaps a sufficient theory for inanimate nature, but it does not pertain to life.[49] Life shows at every moment that it is progressing towards a bigger complexity and diversity; by its very success it clearly counteracts all physical entropy. Thus, there cannot be a total death of the animate world, because in all adversity the stream of life is irreversible. This is certainly a persuasive argument against a final and total equilibrium at all energy levels. However, we must remember the source of the building bricks of life. Only through exploitation of the inanimate world is life sustained. What happens when the natural resources are exhausted and the sun stops giving its life-nourishing light? We cannot exempt life from its context with the rest of nature. It may be uncomfortable or even offensive for us to face, but there is no eternal force within our world. The world in which we now live is doomed to death.

Summary

Six items seem to stand out most prominently in this brief survey of the structure of the universe:

(1) The phenomenon of relativity has shown us that there are no independent and self-subsistent entities out of which our universe consists. Space, time, matter, and even causality, the basic "building blocks" of our world, are inextricably interrelated. They have no meaning apart from each other and consequently they are no fixed items. Their magnitude changes depending on the correlating system.

(2) This basic relativity notwithstanding, we have recognized that none of the cosmological theories starts with a void. There is always something given (matter/energy) the evolvement of which is then hypothetically extrapolated and to a larger or smaller degree empirically verified.

(3) There also seems to be a deep desire to conceive of nature either in strictly symmetrical models (matter-anti-matter, expanding-contracting) or to endow something in nature with constancy and eternal endurance (Einstein's static model of the universe, Hoyle's steady state theory). Both intents seem to express the fundamental conviction that there must be something which gives our existence permanence.

(4) The mere fact, however, that all cosmogonic theories start with a given does not imply a perpetual and self-rejuvenating universe. Apart from the purely hypothetical steady state theory, all cosmogonic theories indicate a gradual run-down of the universe, or, in the case of the hyperbolic universe, a total discontinuity between one cycle and the next.

(5) By their very nature, however, scientific cosmogonic theories cannot but start with something given (matter/energy) that is at least potentially empirically verifiable. If they would go beyond this and claim ultimacy or infinity as their starting point, they would leave their scientific grounding and venture into philosophy or theology. The transgression against these limits became evident with Fred Hoyle when he attempted to infer metaphysical claims from his "physical" postulates. With the postulate of a black hole at the beginning and end of our universe we could observe, however, an especially lucid case of science attempting to stay within its self-defined limits.

(6) This restraint in terms of ultimacy necessitates that scientific cosmogonic models, while helpful in illuminating pieces of our past and parts of our future, only contribute to a holistic picture of our existence, but cannot provide such a picture on their own. In a similar way this would be true too for philosophical or theological cosmogonic theories. While they provide a holistic approach, they need the assistance of science to endow their picture with particularity and specificity.

2.

The Phenomenon of Life

One of the most prominent scientists of classical antiquity, Archimedes of Syracuse, once boasted: "Give me but one firm spot on which to stand, and I will move the earth." [1] We have heard the French astronomer and mathematician Pierre Laplace claim with similar enthusiasm that if a supermind would know everything that has happened up to now, it could predict the course of the universe in detail for all eternity. Both eminent scientists evidently overestimated their own possibilities. The earth is not yet moved and the frequently revised weather forecasts demonstrate how unreliable the future can be. We know the general lines along which the cosmos will develop, but to determine every facet of it as Laplace thought once feasible is wishful thinking. The solid place to stand which Archimedes demanded has also long been recognized as a metaphysical postulate. Within our universe there is nothing solid. Everything is in motion and in constant change. Unless one reckons with the interference of someone or something that is exempt from the causal nexus and is above and beyond our world, we are unable to change the world's arbitrary course or to predict any individual future with certainty.

We noticed that Teilhard de Chardin's optimism about the eventual victory of the stream of life over the law of entropy is unfounded. While we recognize the ultimate limits that this law imposes upon the future of life within the cosmos, we are fascinated as is Teilhard that life developed from dead matter in such an amazing variety

49

and that it has attained ever higher degrees of complexity and diversity. Does this ongoing evolvement of life indicate that there might be some directive in the stream of life, perhaps urging on to self-fulfillment and self-transcendence? Were people mistaken when, in the wake of Charles Darwin's discovery of the theory of evolution, they claimed that human life might ascend to new and unprecedented heights?[2] The question that emerges here is whether we can discern any direction in the still ongoing development of life which in turn could illuminate the origin, present course, and ultimate destiny of our own journey. To investigate this issue we must first pursue the question of how life originated.

1. The Origin of Life

If we want to trace the origin of life we are at once faced with a whole set of questions: What is the difference between a living and a non-living being? What constitutes life? When did life originate? How did the origin of life come about? It is evident that we cannot attack all of these questions at the same time. Yet one of the first questions we have to deal with is the one of the distinctiveness of life. After all, how can we trace the origin of life if we have not sufficiently clarified what life is.

a. Narrowing the gap between the inorganic and the organic

A Latin proverb says: *Ex ovo ovum* (an egg comes always from an egg). This would mean that life always presupposes life. Consequently there must be a distinct difference between organic and inorganic matter. Yet throughout the Middle Ages it was commonly accepted that many lower animals, such as rats, worms, bees, fish, and even mice were spontaneously generated from decayed meat, slime, water, filth, and leaves.[3] Even Shakespeare in *Antony and Cleopatra* seems to suggest this, though with tongue in cheek, when he has the half-drunk Roman Lepidus say: "Your serpent of Egypt is bred now of your mud by the operation of your sun. So is your crocodile." [4] Of course, Shakespeare knew better. Yet it took until 1668 when the Italian physician and poet Francesco Redi showed by experiment that decayed meat does not produce flies, just attracts them.

When magnifying glasses were finally introduced, the tiny eggs of flies serving as the connecting link between one generation of flies and the next remained no longer undetected. The Latin proverb of an egg coming only from an egg seemed to regain strength. But only in 1860 did the French chemist Louis Pasteur show that even microscopic forms of life, often causing disease in man and animal, do not generate spontaneously. The surrounding air, or dust floating in the air, contains myriads of microscopic living beings, such as bacteria, and they spread as soon as they are exposed to a favorable environment, such as meat. As scientists learned more and more about procreation of life, even of bacterial life, not only the superstition about spontaneous generation was abandoned, there also seemed to open a wider and wider gap between the living and the non-living, the organic and the inorganic. By the mid-nineteenth century it was generally believed that life and products of living organisms could only be gained from living organisms.

The whole growing conviction of the fundamental difference between the organic and the inorganic was badly shattered in 1828 when the German chemist Friedrich Wöhler succeeded in producing urea from ammonium cyanate. Barely twenty years earlier, in 1807, the Swedish chemist Jöns Jacob Berzelius had distinguished between two classes of chemical substances, inorganic and organic ones. He claimed that inorganic substances occurred in nature independently of life, while organic substances were produced only by living beings. Of course, Wöhler's results refuted the idea that organic substances could be produced only from organic beings through the presence of a "vital force." Ammonium cyanate was considered an inorganic chemical, while urea was definitely an organic substance. Long before Wöhler's experiments the presence of urea had been discovered in urine. Yet the ardent defenders of vitalism, claiming a life force necessary to bring forth organic substances, were not convinced that an organic compound could have been produced from inorganic substances. They claimed yet in Wöhler's time that urea was only an excretory substance, the result of a breakdown and not of a synthesis sustaining life. Soon, however, "other chemists began to synthesize other organic substances out of inorganic ones" and today many known organic substances can be gained this way.[5] While it is still convenient to distinguish between inorganic substances and organic ones, defining the latter as compounds containing carbon atoms in their molecules, the vitalistic claim of a strict distinction between the two has been abandoned.

We still might assert that there is a fundamental difference between a dead organic substance and a living individuum. But again it is difficult to draw a strict line between the two. It is even difficult to arrive at definite characteristics which distinguish a living individuum from inanimate matter. For instance, reproduction, growth, irritability, and self-regulation are not exclusive features of life.[6] Scientists do not talk about only growing cattle, they also talk about growing crystals in a chemical solution. Once the crystallization process has started, a crystal grows according to a certain pattern determined by the chemical structure of the crystal. If we disturb a crystal in its growth, perhaps through the presence of a solvent or a corroding agent, it develops in an abnormal way, showing in this instance a depression on the face of the crystal.

Viruses may serve as another example to illustrate how difficult it is to distinguish the living from the dead.[7] Viruses, such as the tobacco mosaic virus, can be crystallized like most organic and inorganic substances. Once crystallized they show no observable traces of life. They consist essentially of nucleoprotein arranged for each type of virus in a characteristic form. While the usual protein molecules have an atomic weight of between 30,000-35,000 (this means that they are built of approximately 2,000 individual atoms), one of the tiniest viruses, the tobacco mosaic virus, has an atomic weight of approximately 17 million (this means that one virus is built of more than one million atoms). However, these huge virus "molecules" are living entities and not dead matter. If put on the right host material they reproduce, and within 30 minutes can "give birth" to another 200 newly formed viruses. It does not matter how long they were in their crystalline stage or in an environment in which they could not reproduce. Scientists have found viruses, caught thousands of years ago in glacial ice, which, when put into a favorable environment, were as reproductive as others. Viruses are adjustable to their environment and can also undergo mutations. This has been observed especially painfully, when a newly developed medicine suddenly is no longer effective against a certain virus. The virus has become immune or even has undergone a mutation and thus has escaped the deadly threat of the medicine. Especially the influenza viruses that were first isolated in 1933 seem to undergo continual changes, always calling for new vaccines to immunize against their attacks.[8]

Of course, there is still a big step from viruses to amoebas or to other one-cellular beings. Yet we have noticed that the distinction between the living and the non-living is in flux and it can even be bridged in laboratory experiments. Should this indicate that people of antiquity and of the Middle Ages were right after all when they assumed that organic forms could spontaneously develop from inanimate matter? To answer this question we have to deal more directly with the issue of the origin of life.

b. How did life originate?

One way of considering how life on earth may have originated is to recreate the conditions that existed when life presumedly started. While today our atmosphere consists mostly of oxygen and nitrogen, the atmosphere during the early stage of our earth was quite different. Since there was hardly any free oxygen in the atmosphere, no ozone was formed to protect our earth with an ozone layer and to absorb most of the ultraviolet radiation of the sun. The atmosphere must have consisted primarily of hydrogen and combinations of hydrogen, such as methane, ammonia, and steam.

The American physical chemists Harold C. Urey and Stanley L. Miller reproduced this primeval atmosphere in their laboratory in Chicago in 1954.[9] For one week they transmitted sparks through a capsule containing a mixture of these gases and subjected the capsule to intense ultraviolet radiation, thus duplicating events which could have been expected in the primeval atmosphere in which intense thunderstorms and a high sun radiation were probably common. To the surprise of all, they produced through these experiments organic compounds including some of the simpler amino acids. This result becomes even more remarkable when we consider that amino acids are the building blocks out of which proteins are composed, and proteins are common to all forms of contemporary life. Of course, it is a long way from simple amino acids to a living cell or even to man, but in principle a "natural" transition from inanimate matter to living beings might now be conceivable.

The argument for a natural generation of life gained new strength when the American biochemist Sidney W. Fox reported in 1960 that under presumably primeval conditions on earth spontaneous production of proteinoids was possible.[10] He claimed that these proteinoids differed only slightly from the natural proteins of low molecular weight. The molecular weight depended on the temperature at the time of origin, allowing for molecular weights up to 8,600 compared with a value of 6,000 for insulin. The proteinoids also had a tendency to assume cell-like shapes in aqueous solutions and their amino acid units showed some degree of order which is the same in repeated polymerizations.

Sidney Fox, however, is very cautious in his conclusions. He is not convinced that at present we can experimentally demonstrate how life began. Yet if it were possible to start life now by producing a cell which metabolizes and reproduces itself, he argues that we might be in a better position to determine whether the conditions under which this cell was generated are "conditions associated with the current earth, with what we believe to have been the prebiological earth, and with conditions prevailing on other planets." But he continues: "Although we can with certainty say only that life arose at least once, there is increasing reason to believe that life can, or even must, arise in many places at many times." [11] Of course, such a hypothesis of a polygenetic origin of life always presupposes a primeval atmosphere. It has been shown by the American astrophysicist Carl Sagan and by others that as soon as the (laboratory) conditions become oxydizing, i.e., a sizable amount of free oxygen is present, such as in our present earth atmosphere, no amino acids are formed.[12] This seems to suggest that reducing conditions are necessary for prebiotic synthesis of amino acids. Once amino acids are available, proteinoids are frequently produced in contemporary air in which oxygen is present.

So far we have discovered that all the essential building blocks of life may have been produced in sizable quantities on primitive earth. But the question remains how these prebiological compounds were formed into self-replicating, mutable molecular systems that interact with their environment. The main difficulty here is to explain the spontaneous origin and/or development of the genetic code.[13]

In its present form the genetic code is usually located in the genes which consist of huge molecules of deoxyribonucleic acid (DNA). These DNA molecules are responsible for replication and control of developmental processes. DNA contains groups of atoms, or nucleotide units, formed of one of four bases: cytosine (C), guanine (G), thymine (T), and adenine (A). In 1953 James D. Watson and Francis H. C. Crick discovered through X-ray diffraction the actual structure of the DNA molecule.[14] It consists of a twisted double strand of atoms. At regular intervals a projecting nucleotide in each strand is linked by a hydrogen bond to a nucleotide in the opposite strand. Thus the whole molecule looks like a twisted microladder in which an A unit on the one strand is always connected to a T unit on the other strand and a G to a C unit. Now it was possible to explain the replication of the genes: two strands separate by breaking their hydrogen bonds, each strand can attract partner nucleotides from the surrounding fluid and build a new partner-strand identical to the one from which they broke away.

We have now seen how the genes as the carriers of the genetic information can be duplicated. Yet we still have not touched the question of how they actually regulate the developmental processes. To understand the regulatory process, we must remember that the protein molecules of living organisms are built of 20 different bricks, the 20 amino acids. In the 1960s gradually the process was discovered through which the DNA of the genes controls the formation of amino acids into proteins.[15] In a simplified way we can say that the DNA remains in the cell nucleus and influences the rest of the cell through its almost identical pattern, the messenger-RNA (ribonucleic acid), which is built complementary to one of the two strands of the DNA. Short transfer-RNA segments have nucleotide projections on the one side that match those of the messenger-RNA, and they have bonds on the other side that attract specific amino acids and hold them in place until they link together into protein chains. This means that the nucleotide sequences in the DNA determine the precise order of the amino acids in the protein chains via the DNA duplicate of the messenger-RNA and via short transfer-RNA segments.

One might wonder how four different nucleotides (A, C, G, and T, or U [uracil] for T in the RNA) of the genes can determine the arrangements of 20 amino acids. Experiments have shown that triplets of these nucleotides correspond always to one particular amino acid. Thus it is very easy to specify each of the twenty common amino acids with four "letters" (nucleotides) grouped in three-letter "words" (triplets). The twenty basic "words" are then arranged in "sentences" of varying order and length to specify particular proteins. For instance, the protein phenylalanine is specified through UUU UUC and tryptophan through UGG. It seems that chains consisting of groups of these four nucleotides constitute the genes of all living beings from ant to man, and that the DNA, or in some cases the RNA, carries the genetic information for all possible and actual forms of life.

How did this amazingly simple yet precisely working mechanism of the genetic code originate and develop? The French Nobel Prize Winner in Medicine, Jacques Monod, sums up the issue of the origin of the DNA or of the genetic code very appropriately: [16] One possibility is that there is stereochemical affinity between a certain unit of the genetic code and a specific amino acid. If this were true, there would be a necessity for the structure of the genetic code as it is. Another possibility is that the structure of the code is chemically irrelevant. The code as we know it is the result of historical accidents that have then been frozen. Crick seems to opt for the latter possibility when he suggests that there were three steps in the formation of the genetic code: (1) The Primitive Code, in which a small number of amino acids were coded by a small number of triplets. (2) The Intermediate Code, in which these primitive amino acids took over most of the triplets of the code in order to reduce nonsense triplets to a minimum. (3) The Final Code, as we have it today.[17] This means that the number twenty and the actual amino acids specified through the code are at least in part due to historical accident.[18]

Yet Crick does not want to leave everything to chance. At first, he declares, the Primitive Code would code specifically for only a few amino acids.[19] However, as the process of development of the genetic code proceeded, "more and more proteins would be coded and their design would become more sophisticated until eventually one would reach a point where no new amino acid would be introduced without disrupting too many proteins." At this point the development of the genetic code stopped, since further progress would no longer give any advantage. This would mean that the genetic code evolved, at least from some stage onward, according to the interaction with the enduring proteins it specified. These conclusions are not really surprising, since the building blocks of the genetic code, namely amino acids, nucleotide bases, and sugars, are formed with surprising ease from a few single molecules such as formaldehyde, hydrogen-cyanide, and cyanoacetylene.[20] Perhaps biochemist Leslie Orgel is right when he concludes therefore that neither proteins without nucleic acids nor nucleic acids without proteins could have developed for long without their mutual assistance.

We must remember, however, that there is an immense difference between protein and proteinoid, the latter being a preprotein conceptually, and that by contact with water proteinoids form vast cell-like microstructures (proteinoid microspheres). Sidney Fox and others have shown that these microspheres produce bud-like appendages which when separated from the microspheres behave as physical nuclei around which polymers accrete to yield full-sized acidic proteinoid microspheres.[21] These newly emerged microspheres in turn frequently form junctions with one another. Tiny pockets of proteinoids, endoparticles, separate within the walls of the microspheres and pass through these communicative junctions from one microsphere to another. When released from their acidic microspheres to the outside through holes in the walls the endoparticles function as accretion nuclei which accumulate fresh acidic proteinoid of their own kind to form a "second" generation of microspheres. Since the microspheres are still prior to the actual protein and yet have cell-like features, it seems likely that between proteinoids and the later protein some kind of protocell emerged. This protocell was then able to make the kind of internucleotide bond (communicative and specifying channel) that characterizes nucleic acids. Once we arrive at the level of proteins, however, they necessitate corresponding nucleic acids to regulate their own structures.

The avenue along which the genetic code evolved seems now even more clarified through the observation of a mechanism by which a protein directly controls expression of its own structural gene.

> The essence of this regulatory mechanism is that a protein specified by a given structural gene is itself a regulatory element which modulates expression of that very gene. Thus, the protein regulates the rate at which additional copies of that same protein are synthesized as well as the rate of synthesis of any other protein encoded in the same operon.[22]

Though growth and development of protein chains seem to stem from these choices themselves, once growth and development have taken place, a correlated genetic code insures that the newly acquired features are preserved for further use.

The nucleic acids seem to function like super-administrative macromolecules that insure that that which is manifested is selected once it survives. How the nucleic acids and the "corresponding" proteins worked together to the actual breakthrough from the prebiotic stage to the biotic is still a matter of conjecture. Sidney W. Fox and Klaus Dose, for instance, claim:

> Two approaches have been evident in the modeling of the origin of nucleic acids. One is the search for models of prebiotic nucleic acid. The other is the conceptualization that many biologists have entertained—the concept that nucleic acids as superadministrative macromolecules came after protein and cell. This kind of thinking is Darwinian in the premise that what survives is selected after it is manifested, rather than that it is directed before it is expressed. Nor is this mode of thinking inconsistent with phenotypic expressions in succeeding generations. The range of possibilities can be determined by protein biosynthesis, and selected by the nucleic acids.[23]

Yet we wonder whether these two approaches are that far apart, especially if cell is understood as "primitive cellular constellations" and proteins as "proteinoids." Most likely many separate and rather diverse instances of the origin of life have occurred on primitive earth. Yet eventually only one line survived and developed and every organism on earth today would be a descendant of this line. This hypothesis can be backed up with a very interesting phenomenon.

In chemistry scientists distinguish between levo-rotatory (L) and dextro-rotatory (D) organic substances. These chemicals are absolutely identical except that they are built mirror-like, such as a left-hand glove is different from a right-hand glove. When these optically isomeric molecules are produced in the laboratory from combinations that do not show isomeric properties, half of the resulting molecules are levo-rotatory and half dextro-rotatory. However, in nature the levo-rotatory form dominates the dextro-rotatory. For instance, wine acid produced in the laboratory consists of 50 percent levo-rotatory and 50 percent dextro-rotatory wine acid molecules. In natural fruit juice, however, we find only levo-rotatory wine acid molecules. When we take the symmetric wine acid produced in the laboratory and put mold in it, it turns out unsymmetrical because only dextro-rotatory acid is left. The reason is that the fungi in the mold "distinguish" between levo-rotatory and dextro-rotatory acid and can utilize only the levo-rotatory derivation.

Similarly, all amino acids that occur in proteins have levo-rotatory configuration with the exception of a few small proteins (peptites) that occur in bacteria.[24] In bacteria D-alanine and some other D-amino acids have been found. Yet these peptites are toxic to other bacteria and are used in medicine as antibiotics. On the basis of laboratory experiments we might expect an equilibrium between D-rotatory and L-rotatory substances in living matter. Yet the discovery that the overwhelming majority of life on earth is made up of L-rotatory organic compounds may be an important argument in favor of the unity and uniqueness of life on earth.

But we must also take into account the discovery of organic matter in carbonaceous chondrites, i.e., stony meteorites consisting of clay-like hydrous silicate minerals, carbonate and sulfate minerals, iron oxides, and sulfur. Though there is always the chance that these meteorites were contaminated by earth products when they fell to the earth, "there is little doubt that the bulk of the organic matter in meteorites is indigenous." [25] Yet studies of meteorites show that the frequency of the L-configuration of amino acids found in them resembles that of recent sediments and soils on earth.[26] This would indicate that a possible evolution of L-rotatory compounds is not confined to the earth. It has been suggested that the organic compounds in meteorites have been formed by catalytic reactions of CO, H_2, and NH_3 in the solar nebula and that these reactions may be the source of prebiotic carbon compounds on the inner planets, and of prebiotic interstellar molecules.[27]

The Russian biochemist Aleksandr Oparin, one of the pioneers in the quest for the origin of life, even claims that that evolution of organic matter began

> before the formation of the Earth—on cosmic objects such as planetesimals and particles of gas and dust. After the Earth had formed, and its lithosphere, atmosphere, and hydrosphere had developed, monomeric and polymeric matter became more complex. Then the first forms of life evolved, and the elaboration of their structures and metabolism continued.[28]

Though such cosmic synthesis of prebiotic compounds is possible, it still does not enlighten the predominance of the L-configurations.

Yet we should also consider the discoveries connected with the Murchison meteorite, a large meteorite that fell in 1969 near Murchison, Victoria, Australia. Through careful and elaborate experiments, Keith Kvenvolden and others found that "the D and L enantiomers of amino-acids in the Murchison meteorite are almost equally abundant."[29] Furthermore, Kvenvolden suggests the indigenous nature of the amino acids and hydrocarbons in this meteorite.[30] This claim is underlined by the discovery of two amino acids in the meteorite which are generally not found in biological systems. These findings seem to reassure one observation made so far: Organic compounds are generated with surprising ease and in an amazing manifoldness. Yet the multitude of prebiotic substances and forms seems to narrow down remarkably once we turn to the kind of life that is traceable on earth.

Jacques Monod, for instance, who is convinced of a totally mechanistic evolution of life, concedes concerning the possibility of the appearance of life on earth: "The present structure of the biosphere far from excludes the possibility that the decisive event occurred *only once*. Which would mean that its *a priori* probably was virtually zero." [31] But then he asserts that "through the very universality of its structures, starting with the code, the biosphere looks like the product of a unique event. It is possible of course that its uniform character was arrived at by elimination through selection of many other attempts or variants. But nothing compels this interpretation." Monod prefers to leave open the issue by admitting that "at the present time we have no legitimate grounds for either asserting or denying that life got off to but a single start on earth, and that, as a consequence, before it appeared its chances of occurring were next to nil."

Other scientists are less hesitant to assume the unique character of a spontaneous generation of life on earth. The German physicist Pascual Jordan, for instance, argues from the predominance of the L-rotatory substances for a monogenetic origin of life.[32] Like others he assumes that sun-radiation and thunderstorms caused the formation of amino acids in the primeval atmosphere of our earth. They grouped together, but still these bricks of life did not have the faculty to reproduce. Then, however, he claims that through a quantum jump that caused a mutation there originated one single levo-rotatory molecule able to reproduce. Thus life began, and all organic substances are descendants of this one, levo-rotatory, reproductive molecule. Had this mutation from the unreproductive to the reproductive molecule happened at many places or in a large number of molecules, it would be much more likely that dextro-rotatory and levo-rotatory molecules would have originated at the same amount. A mutation from which life ensues must be so unlikely that it could only happen once on our earth. Thus we have almost exclusively levo-rotatory organic substances in nature.

Whether we follow Monod who leaves the issue of polygenetic origin of life on earth undecided, or whether we side with Jordan who opts for a monogenetic origin of life on earth, both options are very much alike in their assessment of life beyond this earth. The existence of organic or even intelligent life in other parts of the universe cannot be denied a priori. As we have seen in the case of meteorites, there are prebiotic organic compounds to be found outside our earth. Exobiology, the biology that concerns itself with extraterrestrial life, is a serious scientific enterprise and not a part of science fiction.[33] What we have found so far, however, are building blocks leading toward life and not remains of (once) alive beings. Even the bonanza of organic molecules on the surface of the moon, expected by many scientists, ended in disappointment. Scientists examining the lunar findings of the Apollo program discovered only a few amino acids, perhaps deposited on the moon by the solar wind.

Organic life originates and develops through mutations. The more mutative steps that are required to yield higher forms of life, the more unlikely parallel developments between life on earth and possible life on other planets become. Thus the possibility for a similar development of life on different planets even with identical environmental conditions is more likely to be negated than affirmed. The myriads of other humanities of which Giordano Bruno dreamed centuries ago and which Immanuel Kant accepted as a reality, seem to be unsustained speculations.[34] Though in our position as *living* beings we might be "rivalled" by other living beings beyond our earth, in all likelihood our situation as *human* beings is unique with regard to extraterrestrial life as it is with regard to life on earth. Perhaps the American anthropologist Loren Eiseley is right when he says about us earthlings:

> Nowhere in all space or on a thousand worlds will there be men to share our loneliness. There may be wisdom; there may be power; somewhere across space great instruments, handled by strange, manipulative organs, may stare vainly at our floating cloud wrack, their owners yearning as we yearn. Nevertheless, in the nature of life and in the principles of evolution we have had our answer. Of men elsewhere, and beyond, there will be none forever.[35]

2. The Great Chain of Being

The realization that we are lonely beings beneath a starry, ice cold sky is a relatively recent experience. Through the centuries humankind had brought more and more regions of this earth under its dominion and its members seemed truly destined to rule the world. But then the thought gradually emerged in the Middle Ages and gained strength in the Baroque Era that there might be other worlds with many other humankinds on board.[36] This idea of extraterrestrial competitors undoubtedly challenged our unique position. Yet there was still the age-old concept of a Great Chain of Being that gave humanity a definite position in this infinite world with its plurality of globes. This Great Chain of Being was thought to extend from the highest and purest being to the most simple inanimate forms, with humans having a definite place on the scale.

Plato expressed the concept of the Great Chain of Being first in his *Timaeus* when he advocated an emanatistic understanding of the world, descending gradually from highest forms of being to lower and lower ones.[37] With regard to nature Aristotle refined this idea when he declared:

> Nature proceeds little by little from things lifeless to animal life in such a way that it is impossible to determine the exact line of demarcation, nor on which side thereof an intermediate form should lie. Thus, next after lifeless things in the upward scale comes the plant, and of plants one will differ from another as to its amount of apparent vitality; and, in a word, the whole genus of plants, whilst it is devoid of life as compared with an animal, is endowed with life as compared with other corporeal entities. Indeed, as we just remarked, there is observed in plants a continuous scale of ascent towards the animal.[38]

There is a continuous Chain of Being and the anterior link somewhat overlaps the posterior.

While scholastic theologians did not show much appreciation of the Great Chain of Being since they felt it might impair God's freedom, it was a cherished idea in the Renaissance period and especially in the 17th and 18th centuries. Arthur Lovejoy rightly comments that in the 18th century "the conception of the universe as a Chain of Being, and the principles which underlay this conception—plenitude, continuity, gradation—attained their widest diffusion and acceptance."[39] Contrary to what one might expect of an idea stemming from Greek antiquity, the 18th century discussion was not restricted to learned circles. "There has been no [other] period in which writers of all sorts—men of science and philosophers, poets and popular essayists, deists and orthodox divines—talked so much about the Chain of Being." It is especially remarkable how this idea invaded poetic literature. Already John Milton has Adam reply to his angelic schoolmaster in *Paradise Lost* (1667):

> The scale of Nature set
> From center to circumference, whereon
> In contemplation of created things
> By steps we may ascend to God.[40]

Here the Chain of Being is understood as a stairway which we may use to reach God.

Alexander Pope in his *Essay on Man* (1732) was somewhat more restrained than Milton when he admitted that the end of the scale cannot be reached by humans:

Vast chain of being, which from God began,
Natures aethereal, human, angel, man,
Beast, bird, fish, insect! what no eye can see,
No glass can reach! from Infinite to thee,
From thee to Nothing!—On superior pow'rs
Were we to press, inferior might on ours;
Or in the full creation leave a void,
Where, one step broken, the great scale's destroyed:
From Nature's chain whatever link you strike,
Tenth or ten thousandth, breaks the chain alike.[41]

Every link in the chain has a necessary and essential place. If one is destroyed, the whole chain collapses. The importance of the Great Chain of Being is emphasized again by James Thomson who writes in his poem, *The Seasons* (1727):

Has any seen
The mighty chain of beings, lessening down
From infinite perfection to the brink
Of dreary nothing, desolate abyss!
From which astonished thought recoiling turns? [42]

What influence these poets had can be seen in Immanuel Kant's *General History of Nature* (Allgemeine Naturgeschichte) in which he quotes Pope several times (especially Preface to Part I in which Pope's statement on the Great Chain is mentioned). Kant himself assumed in this pre-critical work (1755) that "human nature occupies as it were the middle rung of the Scale of Being" . . . "equally removed from the two extremes." [43] Yet humanity was not understood as occupying the central point within the Chain of Being. While some people, such as Edward Young, thought that our position would permit us to think rather highly of ourselves, many others thought this to be reason for humility.[44] For instance, John Locke assumed that

we have reason then to be persuaded that there are far more species of creatures above us than there are beneath; we being, in degrees of perfection, much more remote from the infinite being of God than we are from the lowest state of being, and that which approaches nearest to nothing.[45]

Even with this emphasis on humanity's relatively low position within the Chain of Being it still enjoyed a secure place. Humans had a fixed place in which to live and a sense of direction of what was above and below them.

The Great Chain of Being, of course, can become a rather static and rigid scheme to interpret the world. This tendency is expressed especially clearly in Gottfried Wilhelm Leibniz' *Monadology* (1714). According to Leibniz the supreme author of all things has created each entity or monad in such a way that it represents the universe according to its point of view and that it has all its perceptions and desires as thoroughly and well-ordered as is compatible with the rest.[46] The monads are distinguished only through the degree of clarity of perception and range from the consciousless, naked monads to the soul monads (plants and animals), spirit monads (men and genius), and to the highest monad of total perception, namely God. Leibniz asserts that "the perfect agreement of so many substances which have no communication whatever with each other can come only from a common source." [47] God has ordered the whole universe as a pre-established harmony. One might easily get the impression that such a world order has rather stifling effects on humanity. But Leibniz assures us that we are not confined to a static existence. He says: "Our happiness will never consist, and ought never to consist, in complete joy, which leaves nothing to be desired and which would stupefy our spirit, but in a perpetual progress to new pleasures and new perfections." [48]

It was not only humanity's enterprising spirit that objected to the concept of the Great Chain of Being. The new findings in science especially seemed to conflict with this idea so blatantly that people such as Voltaire or Samuel Johnson felt that they had to abandon this idea completely. Paleontology, for instance, found more and more species that no longer existed. Since the Great Chain of Being was usually understood as immutable, all species should be coexistent at all times. Other species were observed to be on the brink of extinction. Furthermore, there were still gaps between the existing species and only a few of the so-called "missing links" had been found. Finally Voltaire objected to the existence of the vast hierarchy of immaterial beings above humanity that the Great Chain presupposed as something that modern reason would no longer accept.[49]

Not everybody was willing, however, to abandon the idea of a Great Chain of Being. Already Leibniz talked about a perpetual progression of humanity and Kant went a similar route. In his *Système de la Nature* (1770) the French Count Paul Heinrich Dietrich d'Holbach reinforced the tendency toward a more dynamic conception of the Great Chain of Being:

> Of those who ask, why does not nature produce new beings, we ask in turn how they know that she does not so. What authorizes them to believe this sterility in nature? Do they not know whether, in the combinations she is at every instant forming, nature is not occupied in producing new beings without the cognizance of these observers? Who told them whether nature be not now assembling in her immense laboratory the elements fitted to give rise to wholly new generations, that will have nothing in common with the species at present existing. What absurdity, then, would there be in supposing that man, the horse, the fish, the bird, will be no more? Are these animals such an indispensable necessity to nature that without them she cannot continue her eternal course? Does not all change around us? Do we not ourselves change? . . . Nature contains no constant forms.[50]

Yet before Holbach, the French philosopher Jean Baptiste Robinet had published his five-volume work *De la Nature* (1761-68). In the first two volumes he still advocated that God has already created all the species, all possible matter, all possible intelligence, and all possible beings and it is only up to us to discover the beings that are still hidden to our eyes. Yet he did not advocate a strictly static Chain of Being, since he allowed for the expansion and perfection of each species though within limits that were preordained.[51] In volume V of his monumental work, however, Robinet has adopted an evolutionistic interpretation of the Great Chain of Being. He now declares:

> The existence of nature is necessarily successive. . . . A state of permanence does not befit it. Germs created all together do not all develop together. The law of their generations, or manifestations, brings about these developments one after another. . . . It is true that Nature never has been, and will never again be, precisely what she is at the moment at which I am speaking. . . . At least it appears certain that Nature has never been, is not, and never will be stationary, or in a state of permanence; its form is necessarily transitory. . . . Nature is always at work, always in travail, in the

sense that she is always fashioning new developments, new generations.[52]

Robinet did not slide into the path of materialism. Nature itself is the creative force that in ever new variations brings forth the plenitude and diversity of species. When Robinet talks about the travail of nature one is almost reminded of Teilhard's evolutionary understanding of the creative process in nature. With Robinet, however, the time was ripe for an evolutionistic understanding of nature.

a. Evolution of life

The term evolution is connected with Charles Darwin. Yet Darwin neither used the term nor was he the first to propound evolutionary ideas. Even his most cherished ideas, such as struggle for survival, sexual selection, and survival of the fittest, were not first introduced by him. Already his grandfather, Erasmus Darwin, a renowned poet and physician, wrote in his *Zoonomia* (1794): "The final cause of this contest among the males seems to be, that the strongest and most active animal should propagate the species, which should thence become improved." [53] Erasmus Darwin suggested here that through a process of natural selection weak or unfit individuals are eliminated, a process which leads to constant improvement of future generations.

In 1809 then appeared the *Zoological Philosophy* written by the French zoologist Jean Baptiste de Lamarck. Again he provided a clearly evolutionistic view. However, he attempted to explain evolution by pointing to the cumulative inheritance of modifications induced by environmental influence. These modifications can become constant and lasting and even lead to the modification of old organs or to the need for new ones. The prime and most well-known example for Lamarck's point is the giraffe. Lamarck claimed that since the giraffe lives in places where the soil is nearly always arid and barren:

> it is obliged to browse on the leaves of trees and to make constant efforts to reach them. From this habit long maintained in all its race, it has resulted that the animal's forelegs have become longer than its hind legs, and that its neck is lengthened to such a degree that the giraffe, without standing up on its hind legs, attains of height of six metres.[54]

This idea that environmental influences significantly affect the evolutionary process was later picked up by Karl Marx and Friedrich Engels who believed that this type of inheritance could be used to facilitate future improvements of the human race. Still today the improvement of humanity through environmental or rather societal change is an important part of popular Marxist thinking.[55]

Before we turn to Charles Darwin and his own teachings, we must mention one more person who contributed to Darwin's evolutionary theory, namely the British economist Thomas Robert Malthus. In his famous *Essay on Population*, the first edition of which appeared in 1798, he suggested that the human race always tends to outrun its means of subsistence and thus can only be kept in bounds by famine, pestilence, or war, or through prudential checks, such as the postponement of marriage.[56] Charles Darwin confesses the strong impact Malthus had on his thinking when he writes:

> In October 1838 . . . I happened to read for amusement Malthus on *Population*, and being well prepared to appreciate the struggle for existence which everywhere goes on from long-continued observation of the habits of animals and plants, it at once struck me that under these circumstances favourable variations would tend to be preserved, and unfavourable ones to be destroyed. The result of this would be the formation of new species. Here then I had at last got a theory by which to work.[57]

Yet Darwin was not a plagiarist. He wanted to make sure that the ideas he received from Malthus could be substantiated by observable data. He conducted experiments, read, and traveled. Finally by 1844 "Darwin had convinced himself that species are not immutable and that the main cause of their origin was natural selection, but he continued to work on year after year to gain yet surer evidence."[58] Perhaps his famous book *On the Origin of Species by Means of Natural Selection, or the Preservation of Favored Races in the Struggle for Life* would have never been published it there had not been outside pressure.

The English botanist Alfred Russell Wallace had also come across Malthus' *Essay on Population* and this book triggered in him the idea of the "survival of the fittest." Inspired by Malthus, Wallace sent a paper to Darwin which he recognized had striking similarity with Darwin's own ideas. Yet Darwin was fair enough not to claim priority over the ideas of the then to him completely unknown Wallace. Advised by his friends, he sent Wallace's paper to the Linnean Society together with an explanatory letter to the secretary and an abstract of his own theory written in 1844. Both papers were read in 1858 at the Linnean Society and published in its Journal.

Now Darwin saw the time ripe for his own ideas and as the result of more than twenty years of work he published in 1859 *The Origin of Species*. The main tenets expressed in his book are: [59]

1) There are random variations among species.
2) Living beings increase at a geometrical rate and, as a result, there is a severe struggle for life at one time or another.
3) Since there are variations useful to organic beings, individuals with useful variations "will have the best chance of being preserved in the struggle for life."
4) Individuals with useful variations will pass on the beneficial traits to the next generation and "will tend to produce offspring similarly characterized."

Thus Darwin arrived at the idea of the survival of the fittest by means of natural selection. Though he claimed that this leads to an improvement of each creature in relation to its organic and inorganic condition of life and also in most cases to an advance in organization, he was well aware that this evolution does not wipe out lower and simpler forms of life, since they will endure as long as they are well fitted for their simple conditions of life. Darwin's conclusions in terms of the future of species were quite optimistic. Since he thought that "natural selection works solely by and for the good of each being," he could claim that "all corporeal and mental endowments will tend to progress towards perfection." [60] But in terms of the means of modification he was still modest, stating that "natural selection has been the main but not the exclusive means of modification." [61]

While demonstrating a basic unity of life and of its gradual evolution, he was still hesitant to make definite assertions about the actual course evolution took. While he believed that animals developed from at most four or five progenitors, and plants from an equal or lesser number, he held it immaterial whether one can really assert that "all the organic beings which have ever lived on this earth may be descended from some one primordial form." [62] Darwin's emphasis in *The Origin of Species* was not so much on an all-embracing evolutionary picture of life. He rather attempted to show that plants and animals are not fixed but tend to develop and show a basic cohesion among themselves.

Considering all his predecessors, people should have been prepared

for Darwin's *Origin of Species* when it appeared in 1859. Nevertheless, it was met with eagerness and with outrage. The first edition of
1,250 copies sold out on the day of publication and a second edition
of 3,000 copies soon afterwards.[63] Even his friend, the British geolo-
gist Charles Lyell, pleaded pathetically with Darwin to introduce just
a little divine direction into his system of natural selection.[64] The
American botanist Asa Gray too, a warm and sincere Darwinian, suggested that variations might be divinely guided.[65] While at least from
the second edition of *The Origin of Species* onward Darwin claimed
that "there is grandeur in this view of life, with its several powers,
having been originally breathed by the Creator into a few forms or
into one; and that . . . from so simple a beginning endless forms most
beautiful and most wonderful have been and are being evolved," [66]
he felt that the more divine guidance in variations he admitted, the
less reality would pertain to natural selection.[67]

Charles Darwin was far from finished with his work on natural
selection. As soon as he was convinced that species are mutable pro-
ductions, he "could not avoid the belief that man must come under
the same law." [68] In 1871 then appeared *The Descent of Man and
Selection in Relation to Sex* in which he tried to show how all human
characteristics might be accounted for in terms of gradual modification of man-like ancestors by the process of natural selection. Again
this book was prompted by outside pressure. The German zoologist
Ernst Haeckel had just published his *History of Creation* (1868), in
which Darwin found most of the points he was ready to make.[69]

Darwin now claimed that "man is variable in body and mind; and
that the variations are induced, either directly or indirectly, by the
same general causes, and obey the same general laws, as with the
lower animals." [70] He indicated how upright posture, larger brain
size, and other distinctive changes might have been produced, and
insisted that human moral and mental faculties differ in degree rather
than in kind from the capacities of animals, among which there are
rudiments of feeling and communication.[71]

Even religion is drawn into the evolutionary picture, when Darwin
claims that "there is no evidence that man was aboriginally endowed
with the ennobling belief in the existence of an Omnipotent God." [72]
Darwin assures us that such absence of a belief in a "universal and
beneficent Creator" does not say anything about his existence. Yet
he feels it unwarranted and even dangerous to conclude from the
universal knowledge of the existence of God that he indeed does
exist. Darwin also assures us that "there can be no doubt that the

difference between the mind of the lowest man and that of the highest animal is immense." Yet with the same breath he asserts that this difference, great as it is, "certainly is one of degree and not of kind." Human existence is now brought within the sphere of the laws of nature and analyzed in the same categories applied to the rest of the animated world. This becomes especially clear in the second part of *The Descent of Man* when Darwin tries to show that in analogy to the arthropodes, such as insects and spiders, and vertebrates, such as rats and monkeys, humanity transmitted the beneficent character traits gained through the process of sexual selection.[73]

The reception of *The Descent of Man* was quite different from that of *The Origin of Species*. Some people still protested against a view that seemed to relegate God to total inactivity with regard to the evolutionary process. But by now most people did no longer oppose Darwin's ideas; they had come to accept evolutionary thinking. The British educator Sir Alexander Grant summed up this sentiment well when he stated: "There is very little that is absolutely new." [74] An evolutionary "fever" now seemed to have set in. Before the publication of Darwin's *Origin of Species* the English philosopher Herbert Spencer had begun to turn evolution into an all-embracing concept. He defined evolution as "an integration of matter and concomitant dissipation of motion; during which the matter passes from an indefinite, incoherent homogeneity to a definite, coherent heterogeneity; and during which the retained motion undergoes a parallel transformation." [75] According to Spencer, evolution assures continuous progress. Spencer's evolutionary philosophy was eagerly embraced in the then expanding United States and contributed to the emphasis on "rugged individualism" and *laissez faire,* undergirding the exuberant optimism of the 19th century.[76] At the same time the German philosopher Friedrich Nietzsche proclaimed his idea of the emergence of a superman with radically different ethical standards.

When Karl Marx, at the suggestion of Friedrich Engels, finally read *The Origin of Species* in 1860, he commented that "this is the book which contains the basis in natural history for our view." [77] From then on Darwin's doctrine of natural selection was usurped as the ideological basis of dialectic materialism. Humanity was considered a product of heredity and environment and, upon change of the environment in terms of Marxist revolution, humanity will naturally ascend to a higher socialist future. Here Darwin's own caution had been forgotten that "our ignorance of the laws of variation is profound. Not in one case out of a hundred can we pretend to assign any reason why this or that part has varied." [78] Though Darwin himself was basically optimistic concerning the evolutionary progress, Darwin's theory is haunted by the mystery of spontaneous variations.[79] Why do variations occur and how do they actually effect the hereditary picture? Darwin could only give vague answers at this point. Here the work of the Augustinian monk Gregor Mendel proved to be decisive and sobering.

In his monastery garden in Bohemia, Gregor Mendel had been working for eight years crossing certain kinds of peas, beans, and hyacinths. He published the results of his experiments in two booklets with the title: [80] *Experiment on Plant Hybrids* (1866) and *On Hieracium-Hybrids Obtained by Artificial Fertilisation* (1869). Working with more than 60,000 plants, he discovered that they cross according to certain rules, the so-called hereditary laws.[81] If, for instance, he took a parent generation (P_1) of garden peas that had either smooth (AA) or wrinkled (aa) seeds, then in the next generation (F_1) the crossing of two parents resulted in smooth (hybrid) peas (Aa). When through self-fertilization these smooth peas brought forth another generation (F_2), three-fourths of the offsprings has smooth seeds (⅔ Aa as hybrids, and ⅓ AA as pure) and one-fourth has wrinkled seeds (aa as pure). The next generation (F_3) obtained again through self-fertilization resulted only in wrinkled seeds from the wrinkled ones, now showing that the wrinkled ones in F_2 had indeed been pure, and only in smooth ones from the purely smooth ones. The smooth hybrids, however, again yielded three-fourths in smooth seeds and one-fourth in wrinkled ones.

Mendel had shown through these experiments that all "new" characteristics that we obtain by crossing members of the same species are only new combinations of the characteristics already evident or hidden in the ancestors. This means that crossing or breeding does not change the biological potential of the parents, it only combines it to form new variations of already present potentialities.

It is one of the ironies of history that in the wake of late 19th century evolutionary thinking Mendel's discovery was completely ignored. When European botanists in 1900 discovered these laws for a second time and checked the literature, they found that Gregor Mendel had obtained both experimental data and general theory explaining the data 34 years earlier.[82] Today, however, Gregor Mendel is recognized as the founder of genetic research. Mendel's discovery made it plain that selective breeding could not account for the evolutionary progress Darwin had claimed.

Environmental pressure too, as Lamarck had once proposed, could not account for the biological evolution of life. For instance, when we transfer a butterfly in its chrysalis stage from a moderate environment into a cooler environment, the resulting butterfly will develop a hairy film. The same happens when we transplant a flower-plant that grew in good soil and in warm temperature to poor soil and a cold environment. It will grow leaves which are smaller and covered with a hairy film. However, none of these paravariations is an actual mutation which results in a change of inherited characteristics. When we return the specimens to their traditional environment, the "new" characteristics disappear.

Even human biological constitution remains unaffected by changes in the environment. As we know from the Old Testament, circumcision is a very old custom among Jewish people. However, thousands of years after the first Jew was circumcized, this operation must still be performed, because the biological make-up has been unaffected by this custom. Or consider the oriental custom of crippling the feet of women in their early childhood so that they walk with graciously small steps in tiny sandals. When the Communists banned this cruel custom in China, the next generation had feet as normal as women of all other nations. If none of these changes of the environment resulted in a change in the biological constitution, a clue to the evolutionary progress of life could perhaps be gained from a further investigation of the causes for "random variations." We remember that according to Darwin these variations are in part responsible for biological evolution. Indeed a major breakthrough occurred when the genetic basis responsible for such "variations" was discovered.

At the *Fifth International Congress of Genetics* in Berlin in 1927 the American geneticist Hermann J. Muller read a paper on "The Problem of Genic Modification" in which he reported about experiments with the fruit fly *Drosophila melanogaster* with which he had worked since his graduate studies under Thomas H. Morgan at Columbia University. Subjecting the fruit fly *Drosophila* to X rays, Muller gained an abnormal percentage of gene mutations, both in sperm and in eggs, and in the ovarian cells of the fly.[83] Some of the mutations were lethal; others led to sterilization. It was discovered that in some flies the linear order of some genes was rearranged, a characteristic which was inherited, and that often the X rays had a fractional effect on the genes. Muller also observed that the intensity of these effects varied with the x ray dosage to which the objects were exposed.

Now it seemed clear that the variations Darwin had postulated at the basis of the evolutionary change are actually mutations of the genetic structure of living species which in turn are handed on to subsequent generations. Darwin was right, too, when he claimed that such "variations" occurred at random since it had been shown with *Drosophila* and other objects of investigation that mutations are generally non-directed, with detrimental constellations far outnumbering favorable ones. The theory of evolution became essentially a synthesis of Darwinian thought and of genetics with the principle source of hereditary variations found in genetic mutation and the random shuffling involved in sexual reproduction.[84]

Once Muller discovered that mutations could be artificially induced by exposing *Drosophila* to radiation, he wondered "whether the mutations that occur in untreated material are caused by radiation of a similar type from radioactive substances naturally occurring." [85] He concluded that because of the low concentration of natural radiation most of the mutations in untreated flies cannot be caused by this source.[86] Of course, this result was somewhat disappointing, especially since the artificially induced mutations were of the same kind as the spontaneous ones. Muller, however, concluded, that:

> natural radioactivity, while of no consequence in flies, may appreciably influence human mutation frequency. For the long duration of the human generation sometimes allows the reception of ten or more *r* [roentgen]. Thus, under special conditions, the amount might conceivably be enough to be significant in evolution.[87]

Today we know of many more mutation causing factors, in addition to x-rays and natural radioactivity. For instance, all ionized radiation, such as ultraviolet light, cosmic radiation, and, under certain circumstances, even visible light can lead to mutations. Increase in temperature and certain chemicals, such as formaldehydes and alkaloids, can also increase the rate of mutations. Due to the large number of genes in humans it is estimated that every fifth child is born with a newly mutated gene.[88] Fortunately most of these mutations are either recessive so that they are not noticed in the human phenotype, or they have such slight effects that they are taken as normal variations in human development. With the discovery that new inheritable characteristics are due to a change in the genetic structure of a living being, the origin of evolutionary change was withdrawn from our eyes and relocated in the atomic realm. To understand what is taking place there we must take another look at the structure of the genetic code.

We have noticed that the genetic code works according to rather simple and uniform principles in order to regulate the developmental and hereditary processes. Yet looking at nature we observe that this does not result in a uniformity or monotony of life. For instance, each human being has in its cells 46 chromosomes and each single human chromosome forms a string of thousands of genes, containing altogether more than one billion nucleotides. Just in one cell the length of the DNA is approximately one yard, normally wound up in a small cell of far less than .001 inch. This shows how complicated a duplication of one cell is and how many possibilities there are in the hereditary process, knowing that in each successive generation we have available the whole genetic input of two parents. Each set of genes of a single cell contains the whole genetic code of an individuum and the order of this code controls the embryonic development, the instinctive behavior, and the physiological structure of each forthcoming individuum.

Mutations are then caused when parts of the DNA molecules are damaged or changed or when the code is defectively or incompletely duplicated, as in the case of a translocation of a single chromosome resulting in the inheritance of mongoloid characteristics.[89] Considering the complexity of the genetic information we should not be surprised that mutations do occur. We should rather be amazed at the immense precision with which the tradition of genetic information occurs and how infrequently "mistakes" are actually made. Let us, for instance, assume in all modesty that a human parent has a set of 1000 genes, each of which is able to assume 10 different forms. Thus the offspring is the result of a choice of 10^{1000} different combinations which means more possibilities for variations than there are atoms in our universe. Little wonder that each human being has its own gene pattern (genotype), its own individual face, and its unique fingerprint. Each new individuum is a strictly novel occurrence.

It is still undecided what kind of mutations promoted the whole evolutionary process. Representatives of the neo-Darwinian school, for instance, Julian Huxley and George G. Simpson, claim that evolution consists of an accumulation of small changes.[90] Others, such as Theodosius Dobzhansky and Ronald A. Fisher, suggest that the small mutations observable in laboratory experiments are not the cause of evolution. Dobzhansky, for instance, asserts that "evolution is a gradual and continuous process, but it results from the summation of many discontinuous changes, mutations, a great majority of which are small." [91] Scholars, such as Richard B. Goldschmidt and Otto H. Schindewolf, go one step further. They rightly remind us that laboratory experiments have only resulted in changes within the species, but not in formations of new species.[92] Besides that, paleontologists have found only a few fossils indicating a transition between species, and much less between major types. (An exception is the *Archaeopteryx lithographica*, a petrified bird resembling a transition between reptiles and birds with teeth in the beak, claws on the wings and a long tail spine.) Therefore, they assume that in exceedingly rare cases new species or even new classes are produced through gross mutations that drastically alter the whole structure of a being in its early embryonic stage and still are viable as creatures. However, it is difficult to adduce much evidence for such radical mutations.

Already Darwin has cautioned us that there are still many "missing links," since the uncovering of past generations in the evolutionary chain is largely haphazard. We might add that some details will perhaps always remain in the stage of hypotheses because the genetic processes of past aeons are forever withdrawn from our eyes. But it would be unfair to claim that evolutionary theories are only the result of wishful thinking. Of course, they can become that too, as is shown by the example of Piltdown man. Bones of this allegedly primitive form of humanity were "discovered" on Piltdown Commons near Lewes, England, in 1912. After roughly forty years of discussion, however, the fossil remains were exposed as forgery.[93] Apart from such unfortunate incidences, there are, however, good evidences that show a basic and amazing unity of living species and also indicate a historical evolvement of these species.

b. Unity and evolvement of living species

The first set of evidences for a unity of living species can be derived from comparative anatomy. With the exception of a few parasitic forms the roughly one quarter million different species of flowering plants have the same basic root structure, stem-bearing branches, leaves containing chlorophyll, and flowers made of modified leaves. They also live in the same way, absorbing dissolved chemicals through their roots and converting it with the help of sunshine and chlorophyll and carbon dioxide into more of their own substance. The amazing variety of flowers we view seems to go back to one basic structure or to one basic ancestor.

When we survey the more than one quarter million species of

insects, we again detect a basic unity in their structural design. Their body plans all show the same division into head, trunk, and abdomen, they have three pairs of legs and two pairs of wings, and their mouth parts are again built alike, although some of them use their mouths for sucking and others for biting. Coming to the vertebrates, again we notice a surprising similarity. Though the bones have been modified in accordance with their different uses, the fundamental structural plan is the same. Whether lizard, mole, eagle, wolf, ox, or gorilla, they all have similar skeletons, forming one big family. Whether with four feet, two feet and two arms, or stunted feet, they all look somehow similar and the conclusion can hardly be avoided that there is a basic unity in this individual diversity.

Often the same parts, however, are only present in either further developed or reduced parts. In some fish, for instance, the electrical potential in specialized muscles has been increased to such an extent that through electric discharge other animals can be killed or paralyzed. Quite often, the parts have receded to so-called rudimentary parts. When we look at a whale, for instance, its hind legs are hardly noticeable. Similarly, the wings of an ostrich are no longer fit for flying. Humans themselves have more than thirty of these rudimentary parts, the most bothersome being the appendix. For us it no longer serves a useful function, but in plant-eating mammals it is a sack in which bacteria digest the cellulose cell walls of vegetable food. Again the assumption could be made that these rudimentary parts point to a common ancestor from which different species developed into different directions.

At this point Ernst Haeckel introduced the so-called fundamental biogenetic law in which he claimed that embryos recapitulate in their development the development of their species in an immensely fast review.[94] Though this law can no longer be maintained, since often later developments are already anticipated at a younger (embryonic) stage,[95] we are still amazed at the similarity, for instance, between the vertebrates at their embryonic stage. Again we are inclined to think of a common ancestry.

A second set of evidence for a basic unity of living species can be derived with the help of biochemistry. The most striking evidence here can be obtained from serology.[96] Blood transfusions show that the blood from one human being can be received by another without complications for the latter, if both belong to the same blood group. However, if a person were to receive the blood of a dog, he would immediately show signs of being poisoned. His body would fight the foreign blood by producing antiparticles or antitoxins which react against it and the morbific agents that it contains. The antiparticles immunize a body against foreign blood and are constantly present in the blood after such an immunization. In a separator we can sort the red blood corpuscles from the pale yellow liquid of the blood serum that contains the antiparticles. If we take the blood serum which contains the antiparticles and treat it further with blood from a dog, the animal species against which the blood was immunized, the serum thickens and the foreign blood plasma falls out as an insoluble product.

Obviously the antiparticles react against the type of blood by which they were caused. Similarly, a vaccination against one disease does not help against a different one. Yet it was discovered that human serum or any other serum which was treated with dog blood, will also react, though more weakly, with wolf blood, and, still more weakly, with blood of foxes or hyenas. This means that the blood serum reacts with blood that is closely related to the blood with which it was treated. The stronger the reaction the closer is the chemical affinity. When we label the strongest reaction with 100 and the weakest with 0, we get the following scale: humans, 100; gorilla, 64; orangutan, 42; baboon, 42-29; and spider monkeys, 29. We notice that there is a closer chemical affinity between human blood and blood of the anthropoid apes than between human blood and the blood of other species. Of course, the scale does not prove that there exists an actual blood-relationship, but such a conclusion may not be unfounded.

There are two other striking phenomena we should at least mention here connected with the enzyme cytochrome c and the pancreatic enzyme insulin.[97] Both phenomena again seem to imply that some species are more closely related to each other than others. Cytochrome c, which carries out part of the respiratory process in the cells of most animals and plants, is somewhat differently arranged in each place of occurrence. The degree of variation enables us to determine to some extent the respective relationship between the species in which this enzyme occurs. It is not a farfetched conclusion to assume a common ancestor of cytochrome c from which the different varieties of the enzyme evolved. A similar phenomenon occurs with the enzyme insulin which is made up of 51 amino acids. Again the arrangement of the amino acids varies with the species we investigate. A closer similarity of the order in which the amino acids are arranged could be interpreted as a closer affinity of two species and a not-so-close similarity as a more distant relationship between the two.

We remember that in the idea of a Great Chain of Being one already reckoned with a basic unity of all living (and non-living) beings. However, now one assumes that this unity is not only horizontal, embracing all being, but also vertical, stemming from a common ancestor(s). From a common relationship that exists now, we have indeed inferred a common origin or ancestry that may have existed in the distant past. More and more evidence for an evolutionary process is also adduced by working with different time levels, as is done, for instance, in paleontology.

Apart from the Rockies, we rarely encounter original formations of the earth's crust. Usually we are confronted with secondary formations or sediments that owe their existence to the destructive forces of wind, water, and temperature changes. Through measurements of radioactive decay, especially carbon 14, uranium 234, and beryllium 10, we can approximately determine the age of these sediments and thus the age of the geological periods involved. Most of these layers contain fossils, petrified plants or animals, that are long extinct. The younger the sediments, the more fossils we obtain and the closer they resemble species that are still alive. The oldest fossil-containing layers are in the pre-Cambrian and date back about 2-3 billion years. These objects seem to resemble fossilized bacteria and blue-green algae.[98] One billion years ago we find true green algae and fungi and the first trace of an animal, a worm, is found 800 million years ago in the Pre-Cambrian. In the Cambrian period, 570 million years ago, the non-vertebrates are already well differentiated. In the next layers, Ordovician and Silurian, fishes are the highest animals. Amphibias appear in the Devonian and reptiles in the carboniferous strata that also contain our coal. Finally the mammals are presented in the Cretaceous barely 130 million years ago. Humans themselves are latecomers and we must confine ourselves to the last 20 million years to find traces of them.

How should we interpret these fossils? We can no longer follow the arguments of the British naturalist Philip H. Gosse who, two years before Darwin's publication of the *Origin of Species,* advocated in his book *Omphalos* a pre-chronic development of the life history of this world to reconcile the geological evidence for evolution with a literal six-day creation. The findings of geology proved for him only that God had created the world "with fossil skeletons in its crust—skeletons of animals that never really existed." [99] Bone analysis and arrangement and structure of teeth allow us today to tell even something about the climate in which these animals lived that are now fossilized and which diets they enjoyed. Both conclusions usually coincide with the environment we can reconstruct from the sediments in which they were found.

We can also no longer argue in the line of catastrophism. While paving the way for paleontology the French naturalist Georges Cuvier, with whom the term catastrophism is often associated, was wrong when he assumed in his book *Essay on the Theory of the Earth* (1818) that sudden floods, of which Noah's flood was the most recent, had destroyed entire species of organisms. The reason for introducing catastrophes into the evolutionary process was his conviction that each species was so well coordinated that it could not undergo developmental change. Therefore once a catastrophe had wiped out an entire population of all the countries at present inhabited, the devastated land would be populated by a small number of animals, if not by humans "that escaped from the effects of that great revolution." [100] Though disallowing a succession of different species on a global scale, Cuvier's theory at least attempted to account for the succession of different species in limited areas.

Cuvier, however, was not completely wrong when he assumed a rigid fixity of species. While today fossils of extinct species are usually explained by means of evolutionary changes, it is also assumed that they were no longer strong enough to survive and consequently they were displaced by more advanced and better equipped offsprings of the same species. Sometimes even whole species died out and were supplanted by other, presumably better equipped species, as we see in the case of the disappearance of the dinosaurs. Only places which were early cut off geographically from the main evolutionary struggle for existence, such as the Galapagos Islands or Australia, could retain some archaic relics and could go their own ways within the overall evolutionary process. Thus the marsupialia, such as the kangaroo and the koala bear, could evolve in abundance in Australia, and the Galapagos Islands are still inhabited by huge turtles that are long extinct in other less secluded areas.

The conclusion is almost inescapable that there is an evolutionary movement within the living species that proceeds from simple to more and more complex species. This upward movement is traceable by evidence of fossils both within the individual species and from one species to another. There also seems to be an evolution from mammals to human beings, the youngest traceable animated species. The findings of archeology and paleoanthropology even seem to indicate that there is an upward development within the ancestry of humanity, from the hominoids *(Pliopithecus* and *Proconsul)* over 20 million years ago, to the prehominids *(Ramapithecus)* more than ten million years ago, and finally to the *homo sapiens* (Neanderthal Man) a few 500,000 years ago.[101]

The most important question in the context of human evolution is when and where humanity first emerged. Contrary to occasional claims of an African genesis or of the origin of humanity in China, these questions are difficult to answer. Perhaps we should follow here the German anthropologist Gerhard Heberer who assumed an "animal-man transition field." [102] This phase of hominization, lasting roughly 600,000 generations, would mark the transition from man-like beings *(Ramapithecus)* to humans themselves *(Australopithecus)*. Since this was also the time when the anthropoid apes emerged, this would mean that neither *Pliopithecus* nor *Proconsul* can be understood simply as the ancestor of human beings. *Pliopithecus* and *Proconsul* are equally closely related to the *Pongidae* or the anthropoids, including gorilla, chimpanzee, and orangutan, as part of their ancestral family.[103]

In the search for the beginnings of humanity we must introduce here L. S. B. Leakey as one of the most astounding paleoanthropologists of our time. In 1948 his wife discovered the remains of the first *Proconsul* on an island in Lake Victoria, Kenya, following his earlier excavations there.[104] Excavating again together with his wife Mary in the late 1950s in the Olduvai Gorge in East Africa he now found that some *Australopithecines* may have used simple tools. Since these primitive pebble tools "were made of a kind of stone which is not found in the rock shelters where the bones were found, they must have been deliberately collected and altered." [105] This means that the *Australopithecus* was the first tool maker. Another important human characteristic was discovered by Teilhard de Chardin in a cave in Choukoutien near Peking when he noticed that the *homo erectus* (upright man) found there must have made use of fire.[106] Fossils of the *homo erectus* were also found in the Olduvai Gorge, but there fire was missing. This shows that it is difficult to pinpoint the exact date when the pre-human ceases and the human starts. It is equally difficult to locate the origin of humans geographically. While it is perhaps correct to assume that the change from *Australopithecus* to *homo erectus* took place in East Africa (Olduvai Gorge),

Australopithecus was very likely known in Asia too.[107] *Homo erectus,* however, is found in northern China, Java, East Africa, Northern Africa, and Europe.

In our more immediate past we are confronted with the Neanderthal Man. Again he appears in many different locations. But he is not our immediate ancestor. About 35,000 to 40,000 years ago the Neanderthal race was apparently rather suddenly replaced in Europe by people whose bone structure was like ours. These Cro-Magnon people evidently came from outside Europe. Toward the end of the Pleistocene period (10,000 years ago), they are already in Eastern Asia, Australia, Africa, and America. From what race they arose, we do not know. It is most likely that there were not several distinct geographic fields in which the transition from man-like beings to human beings like us took place. The human family is therefore a species that evolved toward a basic unity. There were occasional dead ends though in the human development that, as far as we know, led to nowhere. We can see this in the case of *Paranthropus,* a cousin of the *Australopithecus,* who did not evolve any further and became extinct. But the emergence of the human family did not come to a halt.

When we arrive at the *Australopithecines,* even more at the Neanderthal race, we notice an amazing variety among them.[108] They represent different stages of our more and more immediate ancestors, and can no longer be classified as different species, such as the species of human beings and the species of anthropoid apes, but are "evolutionary processes within a single species." [109] If one nation prevails over another, usually the gene pool of the losing nation is not eliminated but merges with the winning nation. Similarly, we may understand the successions between *Australopithecus,* Neanderthal Man, Cro-Magnon, and *homo sapiens.* After many battles and amalgamations finally one nation emerged, called modern humankind.

Summary

Confronted with the phenomenon of life, we are truly astounded about the wealth and accuracy of information that science has been able to amass. Six items stand out most prominently for us:

(1) Life demonstrates a fundamental unity and coherence. The basic building blocks of life are widely uniform, suggesting an intimate interrelation between all living beings.

(2) It has been difficult to point out a clear demarcation line between the living and the non-living. Life is not a separate entity superadded to this world. As the early emergence of organic substances indicates, life is an integral factor in the history of our world.

(3) Being aware of the unity between living and non-living and between the living beings themselves, we should not underestimate the peculiarity of each living species. Considering humanity especially, we have realized that the old slogan that "man descended from the apes" is too simple to be true. Though we are more closely related to one living species than to another, each species pursues its own individuality. This is even true for each human being. Though all humans are equal members of the human family, each has its own unique characteristics that endow its existence with singularity.

(4) In a similar way, however, as we were unable to explain why the universe evolved as it did, are we unable to answer the question why life evolved in all its diversity. It would not even suffice to resort to the idea of a self-expression of life, since the very fact of the uniqueness of all forms of life attests to their haphazard occurrence. This means that the issues of origin, goal, and destiny of life have not been sufficiently clarified if we refer only to life's material basis. Life could be as easily interpreted as a gift as it could be understood as a blind fate, and we have no reliable means to know its ultimate course or its final meaning.

(5) While often the question of ultimacy is left undecided with regard to non-human forms of life, we are usually dissatisfied with such ambiguity when our own lives are concerned. The idea that we come into existence without reason, that our lives drag on without meaning, and that we are snuffed out by chance, does not find many followers. The very fact that humans continuously extend themselves toward the future with hope and expectation might well indicate that they are not content with understanding themselves merely as a haphazard extension of life's material basis. Their yearning for new experiences and new insights expresses the conviction that there is more to human life than purely biological existence.

(6) Research into our biological level of existence has given us many valuable insights into our being by tracing the possible emergence of humanity and by relating us to other living species. But these endeavors still failed to illuminate adequately enough the origin, present possibilities, and ultimate destiny of our life's journey

to face it with confidence and assurance. Perhaps if we now move beyond the biosphere and pursue the question whether or to what extent there is something unique about humanity, we might come closer to receiving direction for our journey through space and time.

3.

Humanity—A Unique Species

We have traced the ascent of life and have also attempted to trace our own ancestors. Many details are still in the state of controversy and some of them will perhaps always be debatable. Yet two items should have become evident:

(1) There never has been a necessity for life to evolve the way it did evolve. The uniformity of life that we encounter today within all its diversity, cannot be accounted for by attributing it to innate laws or to necessary cause and effect sequences. The evolution of the tree of life, an image often used to depict the interrelatedness of different species, is a totally unique phenomenon. It is either the result of pure chance or the outcome of a guiding power from without, perhaps even a mixture of both.

(2) It is totally unfounded scientifically to claim in a traditional popularized Darwinian fashion that humanity descended from the monkeys as we have them today or from some kind of primordial apes. Undoubtedly chimpanzees and gorillas are closely related to us. Yet all the other living beings are related to us too, whether oxen or crocodiles, peach trees or violets. If we look closely at the evolutionary process, we might say that the present day primates branched off from the tree of life that ascended to modern day humanity.[1] This would mean that there is something unique about humanity, even with regard to its biological nature, that, its interrelatedness with all living beings notwithstanding, tells us something about its very nature. In this chapter we want to find out what is

unique about humanity, both by comparing it with other living beings and by reflecting upon its own potential.

1. Humans and Animals

Charles Darwin postulated that most of humanity's behavioral and ethical patterns can be explained as having gradually evolved from the animal stage. In comparing different animals with each other and finally with humans, we gain the impression that innate reactions that are due to rigidly fixed instinct patterns are becoming gradually less determined. On higher stages of life psychic faculties, intelligent thinking, and consequent actions seem to replace more and more the fixed and predictable reactions of less advanced forms of life. However, we remember that in comparing living beings with dead matter we observed that we could not draw a strict line of demarcation between the two. Yet at the same time we noticed that something fundamentally new had emerged with the phenomenon of life. Similarly, we must ask here, whether we can only talk about transitions from one form of life to another or whether with humans something truly unique emerged.

a. Distinction between humans and animals

It is often claimed that humans have a unique possibility to enlarge and transform their environment according to their needs and desires.[2] Yet a progressive world-openness and the liberation from the restrictive dependence on the environment is a characteristic of all vertebrates. Due to the physical development they can breathe through lungs, their extremities carry the body, some of them can even fly, their eggs have a protective cover or they bear young ones alive, and their blood temperature is no longer dependent on environmental temperature. Active transformation of the environment, however, as we detect in the often complicated structure of bird nests, is not a new acquisition on the vertebrate stage. When we look at the artistic structure of termite hills, we must admit that this faculty is already present in non-vertebrates. Yet there we may be safe in talking about the predominance or exclusiveness of instinctive behavior which regulates the transformation of the environment. When we reach the level of the anthropoid apes, we notice goal-directed experiments, planned shaping of tools, and the beginning of reasoning and a deliberating intelligence. Even a language of gestures can be observed, which may be classified as a lower form of human language and which enables the handing on of tradition.

We have seen that the earliest traces of humanity are often associated with bone and stone fragments that leave open the question whether they were planfully formed by human hand or whether they were accidental human products or just products of nature. It is difficult to determine whether primeval humanity used tools or intentionally produced tools which could be reused several times. Thus the exact location of the demarcation line between human and prehuman beings is imperceptible. Yet there is an immense difference between the first ambiguous human artifacts and the precisely hewn stone axes of the neopaleolithicum. And there is also a huge difference between the domination of the environment expressed in the occasional use of fire and the human self-expression demonstrated in the beautiful cave paintings of Altamira, Spain, barely 20,000 years ago. Yet what a difference again between these simple paintings and development and use of tools demonstrated in modern cancer research and in lunar landings.

We may agree with the German zoologist Bernhard Rensch that the peculiarities through which humanity was fundamentally elevated above the animal level developed barely 70,000 to 100,000 years ago.[3] But it was only in the last 10,000 to 20,000 years that humans became autonomous beings who learned to dominate the earth and to transform it through agriculture, animal husbandry, building of houses, roads, villages, and cities. When we talk about a transitional phase between man-like beings and humanity itself, we do not want to convey the impression that there is a clear-cut line when modern humanity commences to exist. We only want to indicate that somewhere within this phase human beings as we now know them were born.

It is noteworthy that the physical structure of humans has by far not changed as drastically as their achievements. But why is it that their achievements have accelerated to such an amazing pace? We could point here to the development of tradition which is often regarded as something distinctly human.[4] Tradition enables a rapid evolution of ways of conduct and of achievements. But again, it is not something specifically human. The German zoologist Adolf Remane, for instance, tells of titmice that started to open milk bottles in England that the milkmen had left at the doorsteps. This custom of opening milk bottles and stealing some of their content spread through tradition from a certain center where it was first initiated. In one part of the country only bottles with silver tops were opened, in other areas only ones with golden tops. This shows that tradition works very exactly. In weeks tradition can spread new customs over a territory for which strictly mutational change would need many generations. Tradition can "remember" items for many generations and it can enable intellectually less gifted members to participate in the discoveries of more intelligent ones.

There is no doubt that mammals especially can act truly intelligently. They can solve a problem through direct use of properties as a means to achieve a goal, not just on a trial and error basis. Intelligent thinking has become the foundation for technological accomplishments. Again, however, humans distinguish themselves only gradually and not qualitatively from the same faculties that animals enjoy. Even recognition is not something through which we distinguish ourselves from other living beings. The Greek poet Homer, for instance, mentioned in his *Odyssey* that the dog recognized his lord Odysseus when he returned to his home after many years of absence.[5] We also know that even after years mammals and birds can recognize their friends and enemies and their former homes. Again in the faculty to recognize items and beings of the past humans and animals differ only slightly.

The story is sometimes different when we investigate the power to remember. One of the classical examples is the one in which we put lettuce in a case and close it in front of a monkey. Through a hidden mechanism we remove the lettuce and put a banana in its place. When we open the box again the monkey will act surprised, a sign that he remembered that the box should have contained something else. But the span of remembrance for monkeys and apes is relatively short, approximately one to two days at the most. Similarly to small children, animals live almost exclusively in the present.

Human remembrance, however, spans almost a whole lifetime, from about the third year of life onward to the present. This immense difference between humans and animals allows for the development of an abstract conceptual language which is peculiar only to humans. Of course, we know of the elaborate language of bees or of the language of animals through which they warn their peers or beg for food. But this language is directed exclusively to the present or to the most immediate past. Even the interesting experiments of Allen and Beatrice Gardner with a young chimpanzee named Washoe did not change these results.[6] They were able to teach her in sign language such words as "please" or "door" or even sentences such as "please open quickly," but again all communication remained in the present. It is exactly this amazing power to remember that opens for humans the realm of thought and which provides the basis for culture.

One further characteristic of existence that needs illumination is behavior. We notice, for instance, that the social behavior of ants, termites, or bees is highly structured. There is a clear division of labor and each community leaves the impression of harmonious social coexistence. When we look at monkeys we discover many social traits that remind us of human behavior. While there is a definite social structure according to rank, the rank is not automatically conferred but gained through demonstrations of physical strength and intelligence, or, as in baboons, through age and wisdom. The groupings are loose and can be joined to larger groups or split into smaller ones. Often the family is not even a social unit but there can be promiscuity and the females stay together except for copulation. This is, for instance, different from the social behavior of storks for whom instinctive reactions insure durable pair relationships.[7]

Anthropoid apes who, except for humans, enjoy the longest childhood and youth among primates also exhibit the highest degree of individualization.[8] They often live in small groups of a changing membership. Adult members often leave their own group to join another. The more highly evolved the living beings are, the more freedom there is for them to choose their own group. When we reach the human level this tendency is furthered. However, we notice one additional phenomenon. While conspecifics among higher primates are usually spared from persecution, it is different with humanity. The broken bones and opened skulls of the *Sinanthropus* (Peking Man) and of some branches of the Neanderthal Man seem to indicate cannibalistic behavior.[9] Early humanity did not only kill and eat animals, it did the same with members of its own kind. Humans are the first, and so far only living beings that developed war to persecute and kill members of their own species. This phenomenon is missing in the animal realm and seems to be a by-product of our increased individualization.[10]

b. Inborn forms of human behavior

So far we have been able to show only the difficulty of differentiating between humans and animals. Yet there are some significant differences that show themselves first in the physical constitution and then in the human behavior.[11] The first characteristic difference is visible at birth and during infancy and adolescent stage. Though the form of the human growth curve is apparently a distinctive characteristic, at birth a human baby is much more helpless than the babies of its anthropoid relatives, the gorillas or the chimpanzees. Unlike a newborn anthropoid ape, the body proportions of a human baby are very different from that of an adult. This is mainly due to the larger brain size at birth. While the brain of most anthropoid apes weighs 180-200 grams, for human babies the weight is around 370 grams. Human babies also have larger body weight than the babies of anthropoid apes. While during the first year a human baby grows much more rapidly than that of anthropoid apes, its body development slows down considerably towards the end of the first year. This retardation of the body development continues for humans throughout their youth. For instance, an elephant is grown up at age fifteen and a chimpanzee at age ten or eleven. But for humans it takes nineteen to twenty-one years, or even twenty-four years as recent measurements suggest, until he/she is fully grown. The initial helplessness of a human baby requires close attention of at least one parent, while the slow development necessitates longer dependence on adults than in all other cases of living beings.

Within the last 100 years, however, there occurred a dramatic acceleration in the development of human beings. The age of sexual maturity has been lowered by two years and is now close to that of chimpanzees (10 to 11 years for chimpanzees against 13 years for humans). The medium adult body length too has increased by three inches in the United States and in European countries, and the human babies gain three to four pounds more body weight during their first year. The exact reason for this amazing acceleration is still unknown. Perhaps better food, more exposure to light through recreational activities, and more sensory stimulation in our technological world may be some of the factors that led to some of the problems caused by an accelerated body growth coupled with the usual pace in mental maturation.

When we compare the human development of the brain capacity with animals, we notice that in the development of a human baby its brain increases tremendously. While a newborn human has only 23% of its final weight of the brain, it has 83% when it is six and 96% in late youth.[12] With anthropoid apes, however, we observe only a doubling of the brain capacity, from 49.7% at birth to 100% at the end of their growth period. The human brain of adults is two to three times heavier in relation to their body weight than in comparison to anthropoid apes, while at birth the difference is only about 20%. It would be wrong, however, to assume that parts of our brain find no equivalent in the anthropoid apes. Again the difference is more quantitative than qualitative. The increase in volume of the human brain shows a progressive exponential evolution of the brain capacity.

With the appearance of Cro-Magnon man, however, the adult human brain has reached its maximum in size and form. Yet up to then the evolutionary increase in brain size has not been uniform. It was mostly the neocortex that grew, while the paleocortex regressed. The optical system in particular evolved and so did the associative parts of the brain, while the smell areas regressed. When we look at the sensory and motory parts of the brain we notice relatively large representation of the facial areas, especially lips, tongue, jaws, and of the arms and particularly of the hands, including each finger, and also of the feet and toes. This emphasis of the brain is physically represented in the development of language and in the upright posture.

Though anthropoid apes can walk a few steps without using their hands, only humans have achieved truly upright composure.[13] A newborn human has almost a straight spine and its pelvis is still fairly slanted. But soon the spine gains its typical S-like form and the pelvis is lowered. Through upright posture and by walking and standing on two legs, we gain the free use of our hands and arms. We can use tools or weapons with them while we walk, and our vision is now much more able to comprehend our environment. We need no longer sit up like a rabbit to survey our environment, or like a deer that stops eating to pay attention to dangerous sounds or smells. When we consider the many slipped or crushed discs, the prolapsed bowels, the varicose veins, and the circulatory diseases, we realize that we did not receive our upright posture as a mere boon. It has to be guarded carefully against its many misuses.

We should now consider human language as our last point of comparison between humans and animals.[14] The peculiarity of human language expresses itself rather obviously in the wide range of the human voice. When we talk we can span two octaves and in singing we can cover even three and a half octaves. This is a much larger range than that of anthropoid apes, where it extends, for instance, only one octave in gibbons. Usually animal language, especially among anthropoid apes, is not detached from gestures so that we could call it a mixture of voice and gesture language. Human language, however, has its peculiarity in its wide range of communication.

We can convey feelings, situations, objects, and most abstract and remote concepts, such as the cultures of extinct peoples.

A further advance in communication is the phenomenon of writing.[15] The first evidences for writing are the symbolic code-signs scratched on bones at paleolithic sites, the picture script in the cave paintings of the neolithicum, and the pictographs of prehistoric Eskimos and American Indians. The visual images induce associations with pictures of everyday life. At a more formalized stage we arrive at the syllabic scripts of China or of Egypt. There one needs as many images as one has syllables in a given language. Finally one comes to a total auditive stage when a word is characterized by a certain sequence of consonants and then also of vowels. This allows for strongest differentiation and for a continued creation of new words without burdening the memory with a huge amount of syllabic characteristics.

The development of language goes hand in hand with the development of a conceptual and symbolic world and allows for the development for the spiritual life of humanity. We could list many other characteristics of humans, such as the special form of the uterus, a life expectancy larger than that of other mammals, the non-specialization of hands, eyes, teeth, and ears, etc. But we only wanted to survey the most important characteristics that, at the same time, are the main contributors to the human element.

When we now concern ourselves more with the distinctive social behavior of humans, we must first ask whether there is anything normative about their behavior which they have "by nature." The search for the "natural" is complicated by the fact that it is very difficult to exclude all of our traditions and cultural conditioning. However, the experiments of Irenäus Eibl-Eibesfeldt, a student of the German behaviorist Konrad Lorenz, and of others yielded very surprising results.[16] He experimented with babies born deaf and blind who have, due to their impairments, no means for imitation and whose education is very difficult. Yet he noticed that such babies cry when they hurt themselves, they laugh when they are tickled, and they smile when they are patted. Of course, they never saw or heard these expressions from other people. When they are angry they frown like normal children, stamp with their feet, and sometimes even bite. This is true also for heavily brain-damaged children who could never learn this by touching other persons. As are other children, the deaf and blind are afraid of strangers whom they recognize through smelling, and they show signs of guilt and remorse when they have done wrong and then expect signs of forgiveness.

We can also observe that small children search for personal contact with a person to whom they can relate. If this desire is refused, there occur developmental disturbances.[17] Usually this contact is established naturally, since there is an instinctive bond between the mother and the newborn during the first half year after birth. Afterwards this bond is continued in a kind of voluntary partnership.

Since humans are social beings, the question has often been raised whether many of the specifically human characteristics are not inborn but the result of social conditions. Especially lately the issue has gained prominence whether the distinctive male and female modes of human behavior are the result of social conditioning. Observing primitive societies, Margaret Mead, for instance, suggested long ago: "If those temperamental attitudes which we have traditionally regarded as feminine—such as passivity, responsiveness, and a willingness to cherish children—can so easily be set up as the masculine pattern in one tribe, and in another be outlawed for the majority of women as well as for the majority of men, we no longer have any basis for regarding such aspects of behavior as sex-linked." [18] Ashley Montagu finally declared: "The notable thing about *human* behavior is that it is learned. It is nonsense to talk about the genetic determinance of human behavior." Of course, one should be aware that such a categorical statement can easily be refuted. We might think here, for instance, of the impact of certain hormones on the male/female behavior in humans, which enhances or diminishes sex specific behavior.

In human beings there are some gender-dimorphic behavior differences that are based on prenatal hormonal history.[19] But these differences do not automatically dictate or totally preordain the course of postnatal dimorphism of behavioral differentiation. Thus it is as wrong to say that males and females develop different patterns of preferred behavior *only* because they are treated differently, as it is wrong to claim that they are treated differently *only* because they demonstrate different behavior patterns right from the beginning. On the contrary, sex specific behavior patterns are partly given as a biologically conditioned potential and partly developed through cultural conditioning. There are biologically determined characteristics which contribute to subtle differences of potential between the sexes. In most societies these differences are implicitly recognized in the process of sex socialization. Thus the sex differentiated behavior indicates that certain models of behavior are more easily learned by one sex or the other.

The majority of ethnographic reports indicates that "males are more interactable, egoistic, spatially more explorative, rougher, less prosocial, and more peer-oriented, whereas females are typically more compliant, prosocial, less spatially explorative, less rough, and more involved in interaction with adults than are boys." One might still want to argue that these typically gender-oriented differentiations are expected by society and therefore are the result of cultural conditioning. Yet in observing Kalahari bushmen, Patricia Draper has noticed that these sex differences in the cultural behavior of children are not necessarily expected or intensified under certain cultural conditions. Other observations have also shown that when new items were introduced into the traditional bushmen culture, such as pictures of airplanes and automobiles, there resulted among the children specifically sex-related preferences of interests which had no precedence in their own culture. Under conditions of culture change to sedentary economy, however, certain elements of male and female differentiated behavior are indeed explicitly enhanced by society in the process of increasing sex differentiation.

Some of these sex-related modes of behavior, however, are not exclusively human characteristics. Irenäus Eibl-Eibesfeldt, for instance, reminds us that male characteristics, such as "a desire for higher rank and increased aggressiveness, are characteristics we share with other primates." [20] Since humans are also culturally conditioned beings, one must ask whether this common biologically engendered heritage should be culturally reinforced. For example, it would be an oversimplification to discard certain Pauline assertions on male (church) leadership (cf. 1 Cor. 7:4; 14:34) with the argument that they are culturally outdated. Yet the recognition that we encounter in these statements of Paul inborn norms does not automatically sanction them either. Perhaps Eibl-Eibesfeldt gives us a clue how to evaluate Paul's assertions when he says: "That women are inherently less curious than men must be doubted. More likely they are interested in different things than men." Naturally these interests are open to change through societal pressures as are any other "instincts." The question that must be left open at this point is whether and in which direction such change should be sought. Reference to nature alone will not suffice to solve this question.

There are also many biologically engendered human characteristics that are basic to both sexes. For instance, there is a distinctive inclination among adults to establish durable peer relationships. This does not necessitate monogamy, however, since polygamous arrangements can also be durable. Since the sexual activity is no longer restricted to special mating seasons, as in most animals, it can be used in peer relationships for mutual gratification and consequent deepening of these relationships. Also a rank relationship with the rule of some and the submissive and obedient behavior of others is biologically given as already Sigmund Freud asserted.[21] It has been shown in experiments that this behavior of natural obedience to authority can be exploited among humans and can lead to disasterous results, including the ruthless killing of fellow human beings. Fidelity of husbands, faithfulness of friends, courage in situations of extreme exigency, and even compassion and helpfulness are founded in our biological constitution and did not originate through cultural input.

Of course, biologically given norms of conduct need not be just a blessing or something that can be easily adapted to today's situations.[22] Our appendix shows us very drastically how painful biologically inherited relics can become. Today's anonymous mass civilization is very destructive of lasting relationships, and it impairs our "natural" feelings of compassion and helpfulness. More and more people find it easy to cheat the anonymous Internal Revenue Service or to steal in a supermarket, from an unknown and often unknowable business conglomerate. But the same persons who find cheating or stealing so easy, would have never dared to commit these crimes against the head of a tribe or in a local country store. Yet it is not just society that is to blame if "natural" norms cease to work. We are the ones who reduce the innate norms more through the dominance of our intellect over our instinctive behavior. For instance, we tell ourselves and others that our opponents are not human, but sub-human beings. Thus in World War II we depicted the friendly Japanese people as ape-like ugly Japs and the Germans as marauding Huns to eradicate any natural affection with our enemies.[23]

Beyond the strictly biological level there are other important formative sources of human behavior. The first one to be mentioned is the phenomenon of imprinting.[24] We mentioned that, once the instinctive bond between a newborn and its mother is waning, the newborn establishes a relationship with a caring person, usually the mother. This relationship with a caring person is established between the third and the 18th month and is constitutive for the infant's normal development. If all caring persons change several times after its second month, developmental disturbances, called hospitalism, will occur.

The impressions received during a child's fourth to the seventh year will predetermine which general features will be attractive for it in its future love relationship on the adult level. Any erotic attraction at this early stage, which especially Sigmund Freud emphasized with his concept of an Oedipus complex, is the exception rather than the rule. From the second year on discovery, curiosity, play, and imitation are characteristic for infants. These very different actions enable a young child to discover its environment, to develop all abilities which it has to learn, and to assume the conduct of the adults. In other words curiosity, discovery, play, and imitation prepare a child to become an operative member of the human community. In this context learning can be enhanced through spatial and temporal contiguity, through rewards and punishment, and through the readiness to discover, play, and imitate. Learning usually modifies instinctive, i.e., inborn action, but it does not result in a reduction of inborn reflexes.[25]

While willpower plays an important role in modifying human behavior, there are two important items that influence the willpower:[26] (1) the respective condition of life and (2) the milieu to which a human being was subjected during its childhood. For instance, if the food resources are scarce, people will attempt to satisfy their biological needs contrary to their intentions not to steal. Consequently burglaries will increase. If someone was frequently subjected to hunger as an infant, the person will show a tendency in its adult life to satisfy its oral needs excessively through eating, drinking, or smoking.

Yet none of these influences or tendencies are slavishly binding. If we arrive at a conclusion after having played through several options, we can attempt to enforce our will in opposition to the biologically or behaviorally conditioned patterns of conduct. However, the stronger these patterns are, the less chances our will has to enforce its choice. This means that we are not always free to do exactly what we want or will. Our actions are not as free as our reflections. Occasionally they are swayed by biological determination. Only human beings whose biological needs are satisfied and who understand the impact their environment has on them can act in true freedom. In order to further this kind of humanness, we do not want to advocate a return to the animal stage. But we must recognize and fulfill humanity's basic biological need for food and shelter and must understand the pressure its environment places on it. Once this has been accomplished, true freedom and not biological and environmental necessities will become the driving forces in the history of humanity.

2. The Human Potential

Ever since Charles Darwin explained the phenomenon of humanity within an evolutionary framework, it has been claimed that if humans have evolved so far, they could also evolve to new and unprecedented heights. That a change in humanity is taking place cannot be denied, for instance, when we consider that during the last 150 years each new generation has become taller than the preceding generation. We could also cite many other examples of change, such as increasing baldness and increasing recession of the so-called wisdom teeth. Yet these phenomena do not necessarily point in the direction of human betterment. If we want to assess the human potential for creative evolution three areas should receive prime attention, the neurological and genetic basis, the behavioral basis, and the socio-philosophical basis.

a. Neurological and genetic aspects

When we look at the human brain size we notice that since the Neanderthalians the adult brain has not been significantly enlarged.[27] We could conclude from this observation that the human brain is no longer evolving. Yet this would overstate the case. As the German neurologist Hugo Spatz points out, a child attains a nearly full-grown brain size between the age of seven and ten.[28] But this is the time when in the terms of learning and achievement most processes do actually start. This means there is a difference between the development of the cerebral potential and that of the cerebral efficiency. We might be safe to assume that it took hundreds of thousands of years until the human brain evolved to its present cerebral potential. This period may have concluded with the emergence of the Neanderthalians. Then started a period of evolution of cerebral efficiency which takes us from prehistoric time to our present history and even beyond. This period led to our cultural and technological evolution.

Hugo Spatz now turns to the question whether the evolution of the cerebral potential of the brain has already ended or whether there are certain parts of the brain that are still in a stage of development.[29] Mainly through comparison with closely related animals Spatz arrives at the conclusion that the outer parts of the human brain seem to be the youngest. Brain parts which are still impressible in the human skull are in a process of expansion and have not yet completed their evolutionary development. Spatz finds this true especially for the basal neocortex of the human brain. Its progressive development could lead to a future evolution of the human brain both in terms of cerebral efficiency and potential.

Of course, Hugo Spatz cannot avoid the burning question whether an increase in cerebral efficiency alone or in both efficiency and potential would lead to rather dangerous aspects.[30] He knows that some people fear that a further development of the human brain may lead to the extinction of humanity. Yet are such anxieties justified? Could a further development not also reinforce Darwin's claim that "of all the differences between man and the lower animals, the moral sense or conscience is by far the most important?"[31] When we look at the evident cannibalism of earlier human forms, or the pride with which Babylonian kings boasted of cutting off so many prisoners' hands and tongues, or when we remember the frequent human sacrifices in the religious cults of the Aztecs, we can hardly justify the longing for the good old days. We also realize, however, that technological evolution has given us tools for good and for bad that were undreamed of barely one hundred years ago. In many instances the results of technological evolution are used to torture political prisoners scientifically and to "pacify" enemies chemically. Yet the atrocities of modern wars and the tortures applied to prisoners are no longer a matter of national pride. These deeds are systematically concealed, since we know that we ought not commit them.

While Spatz mentions that our ethical differentiation has not kept pace with the technological evolution and that we can potentially destroy ourselves, he believes in a reconstruction of culture.[32] He points out that a damage of both hemispheres of the basal neocortex leads to psychic disturbances which go hand in hand with a dissolution of ethical behavior, while formal intelligence remains intact. Hence he assumes that there exist relations between a specific level of the development of the basal neocortex and a specific level of humanity. Confronted with the present demand for our responsible execution of history, Spatz claims it is important that the basal neocortex has not yet attained its ultimate development.

Instead of waiting for a possible evolution of humanity, others suggest that we should take evolution in our own hands. Especially the discovery and basic understanding of the function of the genetic code seems to have opened new vistas. Pierre Teilhard de Chardin, for instance, claims: "With the discovery of the genes it appears that we shall soon be able to control the mechanism of organic heredity

. . . we may well one day be capable of producing . . . a new wave of organisms, an artificially provoked neo-life." [33] Indeed, genetic research has established a definite relationship between a given genetic constitution and a certain disease so that more than a thousand diseases can be attributed to genetic causes.[34] With at least one hundred of these diseases pre-marital genetic screening can determine in advance whether one of the partners is afflicted by a deleterious dominant trait or whether both partners are carriers of a recessive deleterious genetic constitution. By taking genetic counseling seriously it is feasible that genetically caused diseases, such as Tay-Sachs disease or cystic fibrosis will be as much eliminated in medically advanced countries as typhoid and smallpox.

Some geneticists, however, do not want to confine themselves to detecting defective constitutions; they seek to change the very constitutions. One possibility would be to change the reproductive cells through a kind of genetic surgery. Due to the immense number of male sperm cells this seems impossible with man, but women ovulate only from 500 to 1,000 eggs during their reproductive period. It seems feasible that one could repair at least some genetic abnormalities in this relatively small number of cells and afterward replant the cells into the ovaries and let them develop naturally.[35] Apart from the technical difficulties with which these experiments are confronted, two big problems emerge. First, the human genetic system is so immensely complicated that we can neither identify nor locate all genes. Accurate localization, however, is mandatory for genetic corrections. Second, although accurate localization could be regarded as one of the technological difficulties which can be overcome, we would still have to clarify the exact way in which usually several phenomena are interrelated and cooperatively regulated by more than one gene. It seems as if from a technological point of view, specific genetic transformations are yet far away.

Notwithstanding these problems, even more radical types of genetic surgery have been advanced and it has been proposed to change the whole phenomenal appearance of humanity. The American geneticist and biologist Joshua Lederberg coined the term *euphenics* for this endeavor.[36] Through prenatal or early postnatal intervention, for instance, the size of the human brain could be regulated. Another possibility that has been highly publicized is the so-called cloning process or the non-sexual reproduction of body cells. The resulting genetic material is identical with one's own and thus one would no longer need to rely on organ donors, and the problem of rejecting transplanted organs through the immunization process would be eliminated. While it is possible to grow human tissue in cell cultures, the main difficulty seems to be that after a few divisions the cells are unable to regain their ability to differentiate the specific positions which they are going to hold within the developing organism, and thus they degenerate.[37] While this type of virtually unlimited organ replacement seems to point in a very promising direction, we are still far away from providing even the most simple spare parts through clonic reproduction.

Another possibility of genetic euphenics lies in the interference with human reproduction.[38] Already in the fifties cell nuclei of frog eggs were replaced by other nuclei upon which the eggs were parthenogenetically fertilized, i.e., without the aid of a male sperm. If one would apply this method to humans (which does not seem to be difficult), the resulting children would be as similar to their genetic parent and to each other as identical twins. Neglecting the influence of the environment, their pattern of conduct would be predictable to a higher degree than is possible with normally procreated children because they would now be subject to the genetic influence of only one parent. Due to their similar genetic constitution the children could learn from the mistakes of their parent. However, Joshua Lederberg rightly cautions that to produce such a human being artificially, *"we simply do not know enough about the question at either a technical or ethical level (and these are intertwined) to dogmatize about whether or not it should ever be done."* [39]

A far more promising possibility for the future was discovered in working with bacteria. When DNA (deoxyribonucleic acid, the determinator of the genetic code) was extracted from one kind of bacteria and purified and infused into another kind, this second strain adopted certain characteristics of the former. Although the experiments have been successful with different strains of bacteria, thus far they have failed with higher living beings.[40] Again this kind of euphenics seems to lie in the distant future. Similarly, breeding of humans with three or four sets of chromosomes seems to be a very remote possibility. Where such triploid or quadruploid sets of single chromosomes have occurred, they always had deleterious effects. Muller's prediction that "for a long time yet to come (in terms of the temporal scale of human history thus far), man at his present best is unlikely to be excelled, according to any of man's own accepted value systems, by pure artifacts" seems to be justified.[41]

But Hermann J. Muller, 1946 Nobel prize winner for physiology and medicine and professor of zoology at Indiana University, also wanted to influence the genetic constitution of humanity.[42] For over fifty years he advocated artificial insemination as a first step toward controlling our own future development. Artificial insemination has the economic advantage of being relatively inexpensive and the technical advantage of being easy to administer. Of course, such a prospect of artificial insemination does not actually enlarge the human potential. As we learned from Gregor Mendel we would be thrown back to the potential of our own genetic pool and even the most careful mating process would only result in new combinations of already latent possibilities.

b. Behavioral aspects

When we look at the behavioral basis for the human potential, we want to consider first the amazing behavior modification possible through the use of biopharmaca. It is, for instance, commonly known that the male hormones influence masculinity and aggressiveness while administration of female hormones increases the motherly instinct.[43] Within the near future psychotropic drugs will be available to deepen and vary one's feelings at will.

Already now we know four different groups of psychopharmacological agents which primarily influence human feelings.[44] There are first of all stimulant drugs, such as ephedrine, which decrease fatigue under certain conditions. However, they have some undesirable side effects on the central nervous system. Then there are antidepressant drugs, such as iproniazid, which may produce euphoria, increase verbal productivity, speed reaction times, and otherwise act as a stimulant. They are mainly used in combatting severe depressions of mental patients. Third, there are tranquilizers such as chlorpromazine, which are employed in the treatment of disturbed mental patients including schizophrenics. Finally, there are weak tranquilizers and sedatives, such as meprobamate, which relieve neurotic anxiety without producing the sedative effects of barbiturates and bromides. There is also a group of psychoactive drugs which causes transient psychotic states. These include psilocybin, mescaline, and LSD-25 (lysergic acid diethylamide) to name a few more. There are also medications in the experimental stage which increase the ability to learn and the inclination to be influenced. Though some of these mind drugs were used in ancient time for religious rites (Sybilic oracle, Peyote cult),[45] it has been only recently that we learned to what an amazing extent human behavior is not fixed and static, but open to modification.

The plasticity of human behavior is also emphasized by behavioral psychologists such as B.F. SKINNER. Fascinated by the work of the Russian physiologist Ivan Pavlov on conditioned reflexes and by the ideas of the first explicit behaviorist John B. Watson, Skinner concluded that "stimulation arising inside the body plays an important part in behavior." [46] Skinner attempts to understand human behavior largely in terms of physiological responses to the environment. Of course, he is well aware that environment cannot explain everything. Behavior is not endlessly malleable, primarily because of the restrictions set by one's innate endowment or one's genetic constitution. Yet Skinner encourages us "to examine the reasons for one's own behavior as carefully as possible because they are essential to good self-management." [47] Skinner even goes on to say that

> This is no time, then, to abandon notions of progress, improvement, or, indeed, human perfectibility. The simple fact is that man is able, and now as never before, to lift himself by his own bootstraps. In achieving control of the world of which he is part, he may learn at last to control himself. [48]

If we are to interpret this statement as an appeal for a new heroism, we are far away from what Skinner intends.

In his book *Beyond Freedom and Dignity* (1971), he made it clear that the abolition of autonomous humanity "has long been overdue." [49] Scientific analysis of behavior tells us that autonomous humanity does not exist. We are controlled by the world around us and in large part by other people. Yet we are not only victims, because our environment is almost wholly of our own making. Skinner considers the evolution of culture as a "gigantic exercise in self-control" . . . through which "the individual controls himself by manipulating the world in which he lives." Thus "the controlling *self* must be distinguished from the controlled self, even when they are both inside the same skin." [50] Such distinction, however, limits the role of self-expression, since we are always also reactors to circumstances. [51] This outside stimulus can be expressed by brutal force or by simply trying to get others to change their mind.

Since Skinner maintains that some kind of external control of human behavior is inevitable, the question is whether this control in effective cultural design should be left to accidents, to tyrants, or to ourselves. [52] Skinner is realistic enough to know that the danger of a misuse of power looms greater than ever. Yet Skinner sees an effective defense against tyranny in two steps: (1) The fullest exposure of controlling techniques and (2) restriction of the use of physical force. In understanding the techniques we realize when guidance becomes brainwashing and by eliminating physical forces we prevent the stronger from pushing around the weaker. As he has outlined in his utopian novel *Walden Two* Skinner is convinced that humans should be deliberately conditioned to certain behavior instead of leaving the behavioral results to mere chance.[53] "Automatic goodness" is for him a desirable state of affairs.[54] Skinner is aware that such egalitarianism of the good does away with heroic deeds. But in the long run, Skinner is convinced these will no longer be necessary. Gradually we will no longer need to submit to punishing environments or engage in exhausting labor. We will move more and more towards making food, shelter, clothing and labor-saving devices readily available. Skinner concludes that "we may mourn the passing of heroes but not the conditions which make for heroism." [55]

We could ask Skinner why he wants to reinforce a particular kind of goodness in the conditioning process. But he would easily justify his position by pointing to some of the values that evolved in the history of humanity.[56] Yet the decisive question has to come at the distinction between the controller and the controlled. If we are always both victim and victor, how can we be so optimistic in our attempt to bring about paradisiac conditions? Contrary to Skinner's assumption we are discovering that the nonman-made environment (e.g. natural resources) seems in the long run to pose bigger problems for human progression towards "the better" than the man-made environment does. Therefore our situation of being controlled and of living in a finite environment poses more restrictions than Skinner could envisage. The human potential expressed in the polarity of controller and controlled is in reality too analogous to the Christian understanding of *simul justus et peccator* (justified and sinner at the same time) to allow for self-redemption.

The Austrian Nobel prize winner and director of the Max Planck Institute for Behavioral Psychology, KONRAD LORENZ, seems to provide a more realistic appraisal of the human potential. Since Lorenz experimented with animals almost his whole life we are not surprised that he attempts to assess the human potential in strict analogy to the animal world. He disagrees with the German anthropologist Arnold Gehlen that humans are defective beings.[57] While humans lack explicit specialization in one specific field, Lorenz finds that their nonspecialized approach to the environment serves as an adaptive advantage. Even in physical respect their versatility to be able to jump, climb, swim, and dive distinguishes them from most animals. Similar to many higher animals this non-specialization is coupled with curiosity and leads them to become cosmopolitan. But in animals the exploratory and creative discourse with the environment ceases once adulthood is reached.

With humans, however, the openness to the world is a characteristic feature that accompanies them until senility sets in. This fundamental and significant characteristic of humans—their continuous, creative, and active discourse with the environment—can therefore be classified as a phenomenon of neoteny, of being mature while still growing up.[58] Humans always retain some of their "immature characteristics" in adulthood; they are always becoming and never definitely set in their ways. This allows for the peculiarly human freedom of action, uninhibited by rigidly structured norms for action and reaction. Humans can dialogically interact with their environment and become reasonable beings.

Yet Lorenz notices such an immense dichotomy between our success in mastering our environment and the failure to control our own affairs. Lorenz, however, does not resign to this situation by saying that social problems are simply more difficult to master than environmental ones. He finds rather the clue for this evident dichotomy in the way conduct is shaped in animal populations.[59] For instance, even among the highest animals their conspecific ways of conduct, i.e. their behavior against members of their own species, are much more determined by inborn components than by rational achievements. Their interaction with the extraspecific environment, however, is more governed by reason and less by innate patterns.

However, we do no longer live in our natural ways so that inborn components could decisively inform our behavior. Both with regard to our kin and with regard to those creatures and things not of our kin we have created our own environment. Experimenting in a dialogical and questioning manner with our environment, we increasingly dominate our surroundings. We also developed a language through which transindividual knowledge could be handed on to future generations and a culture could be founded. These developmental steps introduced such rapid and profound changes in our living conditions that the adaptability of the inborn components of our behavior to these new situations was overextended. Lorenz arrives at the conclusion that "man is not so evil from his youth, he is just *not quite good enough* for the demands of life in modern society." [60] What would happen, Lorenz asks, if animals were given different tools, for instance, if a chimpanzee would be given a hammer or a pigeon would be given the beak of a hawk? The results would certainly be devastating because the natural equilibrium between the possibility to kill and the instinctive inhibition to kill would be disturbed. Lorenz claims that this is the situation in which we find ourselves.

Already the first wedge in his fist gave man the possibility to kill his brother so quickly and surprisingly that the victim had no chance to activate inhibitions in the aggressor through cries or submissive posture.[61] With modern weaponry we are so removed from the consequences of our actions and from the victims themselves that our natural inhibitions to endanger or kill conspecifics are well "protected" against activation. For instance, a person who would be too inhibited to become aggressive enough to give his child a good spanking, would find it easy to push the button to launch a ballistic missile. In recent wars many gentle and caring family fathers flying high above the clouds mercilessly killed innocent women and children in air raids. But it is not just the rapid development of modern weaponry that brought in a precarious situation.

We are also not good enough for the demands of our increasingly anonymous world community that demands that we relate to any unknown person as we would relate to a personal friend.[62] Lorenz claims that through natural inclination we would obey those of the Ten Commandments that refer to our conduct toward fellow human beings without developing responsible morals, provided that the fellow human beings are well-known friends or associates. Yet overfed with social obligations of all kinds, crowded in small city apartments, with the constant stress of modern life upon us, interhuman relationships are becoming more and more shallow, and aggressive behavior erupts.[63] The demands upon us are mounting; we ought to restrain our drives and instinctive feelings and check in responsible self-examination the implications of our behavior for the future.

Lorenz realizes that our task to attain responsible behavior is getting more and more difficult. But in his influential book *On Aggression*, he does not end on a negative note.[64] He calls first for increasing research into the causes of our own behavior. Then he suggests that we look for responsible substitute objects in order to redirect the original form of our aggressive drives that no longer are allowed an outlet in modern society. Third, he points out that with the help of psychoanalytic research ways could be found to sublimate these drives. But he is not optimistic enough to assume that aggression can be eliminated through moral legislation or by removing triggering causes. Lorenz also rejects the idea of genetic manipulation to eradicate aggression, because aggression is tied in with many positive features, such as love, enthusiasm, energetic drive, etc. Insight into the causes of one's own behavior, however, is for Lorenz the first step in mastering conflicts in cases in which a categorical imperative alone would not suffice.

The most promising aspect, however, for the future is seen in the redirection of our aggressive drives. As a good way of redirection Lorenz advocates sports, because in sports aggression and fairness are paired. Though he is quick to caution that sports are not always beneficial in fostering understanding between nations. The best way to overcome national aggression would be for individuals from different nations to meet and get to know each other. Lorenz also advocates enthusiasm as a way to release aggressive energy. Here the arts and sciences deserve a boost as collective properties of the whole human family. Even humor is suggested as a means of showing brotherly spirit. Trusting in human reason and in the power of selection, Lorenz concludes that this, "in the not too distant future, will endow our descendants with the faculty of fulfilling the greatest and most beautiful commandment of true humanity." [65]

One may wonder, however, whether Lorenz' optimism is justified. The German biologist Bernhard Hassenstein, for instance, first doubts that there is an aggressive drive that needs periodic satisfaction.[66] Aggression is not an isolated phenomenon, but has been detected with certainty only as a support for other biological functions, such as procuring of food or attainment and defense of one's rank. Therefore Hassenstein asserts that "man can act according to a free will," i.e., without the pressures of his drives or of other coercive forces. Having played through the different possibilities we can freely decide what to do, regardless of how causally determined our nervous system functions. Secondly, Hassenstein suggests that there is no law in nature which prevents physically strong species, such as lions or rats, from killing their own kind.[67] On the contrary, strong animals living in societal groupings usually do not use submissive postures and do not have inhibitions against killing conspecifics if they do not belong to their own societal grouping. Hassenstein suggests that killing of conspecifics seems to be a natural means to avoid overpopulation. While Hassenstein concedes that we may have a biological inhibition against killing members of our own social grouping if we individually know them, one must leave undecided whether this inhibition also applies to people we do not know. This means that killing of con-specifics could be humanity's own natural way of self-preservation and of avoiding overpopulation.

Of course, if this analysis proves to be correct it would make it even more difficult to channel peacefully the aggressive drives set free and/or engendered by the life style of our modern industrial society. Lorenz may have sensed some of this dilemma when in a later writing on *Civilized Man's Eight Deadly Sins* (1972) he con-cedes that "there is no lack of obstacles to be overcome if humanity is not to perish. . . . When we consider all that has happened and is happening in the world today, it is difficult to argue with those who believe that we are living in the days of anti-Christ." [68] Perhaps we assess Lorenz' present position correctly when we say that by comparing humans with the animal world he perceives humanity's Promethean potential but at the same time is afraid that it may be misused in a self-destructive way.

c. Socio-philosophical basis

When we finally consider the socio-philosophical aspect of the human potential, we notice a peculiar ambivalence if not uncertainty concerning the human prospect. Western capitalism, for instance, has portrayed for a long time a naively optimistic picture of perpetual progress. We must concede that occasional dark clouds have been looming for quite a while on the horizon of the Western Hemisphere. There also have been ethnic and class revolts in many countries and occasional shortages of energy and of material resources. The overall picture, however, has been one of basic optimism, characterized by the yearly increase in the respective Gross National Product and docu-mented by larger paychecks.

Even when Alvin Toffler warned us about a *Future Shock* caused by a more and more accelerated change, he was convinced that the threatening effects of the future could be harnessed. [69] In a more recent book, *The Eco-Spasm Report*, Toffler has completely aban-doned the idea of expansion. [70] Our industrial civilization will break down, he suggests, and a wholly new civilization with different priori-ties will emerge. Toffler has not cut off the future, but like many others he has realized that there are limits to technological expan-sion. Unless we opt for a bleak future of humanity, as the Club of Rome has pointed out, there must be immediate steps taken to insure certain limits of growth. Otherwise growth in terms of more, bigger, and better will be limited by the exhaustion of energy and natural resources, the steady increase in human population, and the subsequent pollution of our environment.[71] The frequently used paradigm of the spaceship earth indicates that we are confronted with limited and exhaustible resources which can only insure us a bearable future if we take drastic steps to achieve a basic reorientation of life styles.

Others are less convinced that there are even enough resources to be shared regardless of which measures we implement. Therefore they advocate the method of a triage, dividing the human family into three groups, a first that will survive without outside help, a second that will continue to live if immediate help is administered, and a third that is beyond hope regardless of what we do.[72] Here we are provided with at least some kind of hope, provided that we belong to the right group. A similar selective method is advocated by Garrett Hardin with his parable of a lifeboat ethic.[73] The lifeboat leading to human survival has a limited capacity. Though it is not yet filled to the brink, it cannot harbor all the people attempting to get into it. Allowing any more people to get on board will potentially endanger the future of all who occupy it. Thus one reaches the conclusion to stay with the present occupants and concentrate on their survival. When we look at the increasing interdependence of humanity, especially in terms of energy supply, natural resources, and technological products, we wonder whether one can so easily distinguish between those occupying the lifeboat and those drowning outside. We could easily awaken to the dreadful realization that though we thought we were inside the boat, we are actually the ones in the chilly waves fighting for survival.

A similar insight seems to be expressed by the American economist Robert L. Heilbroner in his sobering book, *An Inquiry into the Human Prospect.* He tells us that today the

> sense of assurance and control has vanished, or is vanishing rapidly. We have become aware that rationality has its limits with regard to the engineering of social change, and that these limits are much narrower than we had thought; that many economic and social problems lie outside the scope of our accustomed instrumentalities of social change; that growth does not bring about certain desired ends or arrest certain undesired trends.[74]

Heilbroner, however, does not want to proceed in the usual manner, first painting a dark picture and then, nevertheless, coming out on a

positive note. It is our startling awareness, he says, that the quality
of life is deteriorating. The future can be no other than "a continuation of the darkness, cruelty, and disorder of the past" and, "the
question of whether worse impends" must be answered in the affirmative.[75] With this prospect before us, Heilbroner does "not intend to
condone, much less to urge, an attitude of passive resignation." [76]
"The human prospect," we hear, "is not an irrevocable death sentence.
It is not an inevitable doomsday toward which we are headed,
although the risk of enormous catastrophes exists." [77] Yet Heilbroner
does not assure us a rosy future. There will be a future all right, but
only a future of survival. To insure this future Heilbroner invokes
from Greek mythology the figure of Atlas who with endless perseverance bore the weight of the heavens on his shoulders. Heilbroner
concludes: "If, within us, the spirit of Atlas falters, there perishes
the determination to preserve humanity at all cost and any cost, forever." [78] If Heilbroner is correct that human survival demands an
Atlas-like perseverance, we wonder whether the human potential
suffices to carry the celestial globe. After all, we have come to realize
that we are both a product of this globe and confined to it. Does it
not border on wishful thinking to assume that we ourselves, even
the possible solidarity of the human family notwithstanding, can
carry our own foundation?

When we turn to Marxist Communism, we discover a much more
naive and unbroken trust in the human potential than in the capitalistic West. The German neo-Marxist ERNST BLOCH, for instance,
asserts: *"True genesis does not occur in the beginning but in the end,*
and it is only commencing when society and existence *(Dasein)* are
radicalized, i.e., when they get to their roots. The root of history,
however, is the working and creating man who changes the way
things are and surpasses them." [79] The world in its present state and
in its evolving shape is not an accident. We are its main agents and
it is up to us to shape the future. Bloch is realistic enough to know
that we cannot give the world any shape we desire. We cannot
neglect and deny the concrete realities which we face. Yet unlike
Western capitalistic thought Bloch does not see humanity pitted over
against nature or matter. In a midwifely function we are part of
nature or of matter. Going one step beyond Karl Marx, Bloch does
not just recognize that there are certain potentials in nature. Matter
is not a mechanistic and monolithic block, but a real potentiality, a
potentiality to be. There is an openness toward the future in matter.
Bloch even uses the terms finality and entelechy to describe the basic

characteristics of matter. In an anticipatory way potentiality is hidden in nature. Nature is not just tending toward certain concretizations, it is also mere potentiality.

Two items are therefore merged in Bloch's concept of nature, the creator and the created. Matter is a " 'being-in-possibility,' a potentiality pregnant with though distant modes of life—leading to the 'naturalization of man' and the 'humanization of nature.' " [80] Matter has become the unmoved mover that moves itself. In Bloch's approach we are reminded of Spinoza's philosophy of identity, because in both God and the world are merged into one. Through this merger matter becomes creative, obeying its own laws. Humanity is not vis-a-vis matter, but part of it, contributing the subjective element to matter. "The willing of thought, the thought of willing toward a common better life is a strong magnet, directed toward our future, toward the future of the world, as it constantly looks to us and withholds to the weak choice alone both bad and good." [81] Humanity is part of matter, albeit prominently engaged in securing its future and coaching it toward the better, the final goal, which will be the new homeland.

If humanity plays such a decisive role in the evolutionary process of the world, we would assume that it is endowed with exceptional qualities. Bloch does not concede such exceptional status to humanity. For instance, he reminds us of the Marxist notion of human self-estrangement when he asserts that we are not free and equal by birth, that we have to fight for the privileges of freedom and equality and acquire them. We are not surprised either to hear Bloch say that we are not a fixed species with static properties, since "the whole history shows a continuous transformation of human nature." [82] According to our inclination and to our formation we are a product of societal conditions. Therefore, we are neither good nor bad by nature. Bloch claims that the idea of an original goodness is as wrong as the idea of original sin. The *humanum* is not an a priori principle of deduction, but the historical goal. "It is the utopically not-at-hand but sensed, yet not the meta-historically fundamental and certain."

Freedom, equality, and brotherhood point to the future, to the realm of hope; they do not describe a present state of the *humanum*. This becomes especially evident for Bloch in looking at the state. According to Engels, the state will fade away in a classless society, since the goal of a classless society is freedom from being subjected to other people. Yet Bloch admits that this prognosis does not yet apply to one single socialist country, since the surrounding countries are still ruled by capitalism. When socialism has gained its victory in most or all countries, however, then Bloch is sure that the goal of the abolition of the state can be accomplished.[83] One of the prime ways to attain the goal of socialism is the change of humanity's attitude toward the means of production. After private property and private interest have been done away with, morality will have gained a decisive victory. Bloch is even convinced that in such a society jurisprudence will have trouble finding an adequate area of activity. Fraud, theft, burglary, embezzlement, robbery, and kidnapping will be relics of the past. Even emotionally caused delinquencies will be considerably changed, since the abolition of private property will give different meaning to envy, greed, and jealousy. Jurisprudence will then mainly be concerned with sexual and affective offences.[84]

One cannot but be impressed with this fundamental conviction of the immense potential for human betterment. Most capitalist projections look somewhat poverty stricken by comparison. Yet one should not be surprised about such confidence. For Bloch all restrictive forces have evaporated. There is no longer a principle or power that impresses from outside its will upon matter. Almost in messianic fashion (cf. Jer. 31:33) Bloch proclaims that there does not exist a dichotomy or even a distinction between the will of God and the eternal drive of nature.[85] Both are merged into one and humanity becomes matter's highest fruit. While matter implies in its goal humanity, it in turn implies the realization of the *humanum*. Thus, the ultimate goal of nature and of humanity is the realization of the *humanum* in the world. Is it realistic, however, to join Ernst Bloch in highly idealistic and neo-Darwinian fashion and claim that we are approaching a concrete utopia? If there is really this innate urge within the world toward gradual realization of the *humanum,* as Ernst Bloch assumes, we should be able to delineate a gradual verification of the *humanum*. While it is difficult to adduce any evidence in most parts of our earth, claims have been repeatedly made that a new humanity is appearing in China. Does this *Sinanthropus redivivus* indicate a new phase of the hominization process and allow at least for a partial verification of Bloch's claim?

Chairman MAO TSE-TUNG asserts that history has put upon the proletariat and the (Communist) Party in the present epoch of societal development the responsibility for right understanding and transformation of the world.[86] According to him, this process has already reached a historical moment in the world and in China, a moment of great significance, as it has never been known in history: complete removal of the darkness in the world and in China and transformation into a new bright world. The reason for these optimistic claims can be attributed to two factors: (1) Like most Communists, Mao Tse-tung is influenced by the Darwinian idea that "mankind makes constant progress and nature undergoes constant change," and (2) Mao's evolutionary thinking is paired with a dialectic movement which convinces him that "the history of mankind is one of continuous development from the realm of necessity to the realm of freedom." [87]

Like most materialists Mao regards spirit as secondary and subject to matter.[88] Yet he does not go along with them in conceiving of the spirit as simply an extension of matter. Though Mao rejects idealism rather vehemently, we wonder whether Frederic Wakeman is not correct in assuming that German idealism "first convinced Mao Tse-tung that will was not just an irrational instinct, and egoism not just selfish. Instead the will was free, rational, and universal." [89] Mao affirms on the one hand that "in the general development of history the material determines the mental and social being determines social consciousness." But then in dialectic fashion he asserts on the other hand too that there is a "reaction of mental on material things, of social consciousness on social being and of the superstructure on the economic base." [90] Of course, it is not any kind of pressure to which the material basis reacts. Therefore Mao claims it is the most important task to utilize the insights into the objective laws of the world actively to transform this world.[91]

If we ask what the objectives of this transformation are, even the so-called red catechism, the small red book of *Mao Tse-tung's Quotations,* does not give us definite clues. One objective is "to insure a better life for the several hundred million people of China and to build our economically and culturally backward country into a prosperous and powerful one with a high level of culture." [92] To achieve this end we must "have faith in the masses" and "faith in the Party." We must also abolish "the ruthless economic exploitation and political oppression of the peasants by the landlord class." Though the enemy, consisting of the Chinese reactionaries and "the aggressive forces of U.S. imperialism," will not perish of himself, "the socialist system will eventually replace the capitalist system." Mao considers this to be "an objective law independent of man's will."

"A tremendous liberation of the productive forces" will be brought about through the change toward socialism.[93] Yet it is not only an economic change that Mao envisions. He feels a tremendous responsibility in educating the peasants and in allowing them to participate in the evolutionary process. When he enumerates the virtues of a Communist, we notice that Mao envisions more than making China prosperous. We hear that

> at no time and in no circumstances should a Communist place his personal interests first; he should subordinate them to the interests of the nation and of the masses. Hence, selfishness, slacking, corruption, seeking the limelight, and so on, are most contemptible, while selfishness, working with all one's energy, wholehearted devotion to public duty, and quiet hard work will command respect.

Toward any person who has made a mistake in his work, the attitude of a Communist "should be one of persuasion in order to help him to change and start afresh and not one of exclusion, unless he is incorrigible."

When we ask to what extent these visions have been realized, we hear conflicting reports. On the one hand we are told that the people of China are moulding themselves and being moulded by internal forces derived from that messianic vision of a new society and a new world.[94] Undoubtedly, the little red book is the new bible whose sayings are religiously followed and "Mao's picture has replaced both altar and portrait." [95] Mao's sayings that could become a new classic in wisdom literature are not just recited, they are followed by many. His principles of equality, frugality, diligence, and hard work have made China rich and strong within an amazingly short time. Since we live, however, on a finite earth, in the long run there will be limits to growth even in China, whether it decides to live within a global community or whether it prefers isolation. Confronted with our finite planet the creativity and prosperity of matter will encounter its most serious limitation. But we know that Mao wants more than prosperity; his goal is not just affluence but a reign of virtue.[96]

However, we also hear that even the great Proletarian Cultural Revolution of 1966 and years of political education before and afterwards could not do away with three subversive elements.[97] These are (1) the traditional family attitude in which the authority of the clan reigns supreme, (2) the narrow mentality of the country people who still find deep satisfaction in the tales, myths, and customs of the past, and who are always more interested in their own survival than in that of others; and (3) the bureaucracy that instead of showing a spirit of service and dedication still lapses back to the old

Mandarin habit of superiority and autonomy. A comment at a regional conference attended by several leaders of a city is highly revealing: "We have got through the production barrier. We are still rough old fellows whether we study or not." [98] Does this mean that Mao overestimated the human potential as far as humanity's evolution toward a new being is concerned? When we look at Mao's premise that the history of humanity is one of continuous development from the realm of necessity to the realm of freedom,[99] we might find an answer to our question.

Mao assumes that human progression means freedom toward the good in a communal sense. He forgets, however, that freedom on a human basis is never just a communal action, but also an individual action. It is exactly at this point that the conflicting and "subversive elements" become noticeable when their individual good conflicts with Mao's notion of the common good. The primal concern with human self-preservation just does not allow for the completely unselfish human beings that Mao envisions as the perfect Communists. The attempt to secure one's own self-preservation can only be abandoned if one knows that one's preservation is guaranteed. But how can such knowledge be engendered by a philosophy that rejects any absolutes and in turn absolutizes as the common good an individual notion of good, namely Mao's way. Perhaps the Party's total grip on human life and goals, though bringing about tremendous temporary economic prosperity, is not that all-inclusive as it essays to be, because it misses the real humanity and therefore its real potential.[100]

When we now turn to PIERRE TEILHARD DE CHARDIN, who neither represents Western capitalism nor Eastern Communism, we notice at the outset a very different frame of reference for the assessment of the human potential. As are Marxist thinkers, Teilhard is convinced that there is a dynamic drive in nature.[101] His extensive studies in paleontology have led him to accept evolution as one of the main principles of explaining the position of humanity. According to Teilhard there are two main phases in the evolutionary process, an expanding and a consolidating one. The latter one is termed complexification, because at this state the evolutionary process is becoming more differentiated. Since the increasing complexification contributes to a higher degree of freedom, Teilhard can be rather optimistic about the constantly increasing pressure that originates when the human family is forced to crowd more and more closely together.[102]

Teilhard discerns three distinct phases in the development of the universe, the cosmogenesis whereby the cosmos came into existence, the biogenesis through which the organic life evolved, and the anthropogenesis or noogenesis when humans emerged. For Teilhard evolution is no longer a hypothesis but a new and all-embracing dimension of the universe. Yet, we must ask Teilhard why he can be so optimistic about the future of the evolutionary process. First he points to the evolutionary process itself. While admitting that the human future contains a certain unpredictable element, he sees in the world of humanity certain tendencies in its development, "of which we may safely predict that they are definitive and will only become accentuated with time." [103] Teilhard sees first a continuous rise of social unification within one nation and on a global scale as human society "organizes itself." Second, there is "a growth of generalized technology and mechanization." Finally, there is "a heightening of vision." The increased power of instruments leads to a growth of our reflective concept of the universe and the great wave of modern technical progress is "automatically accompanied by an ever-spreading ripple of theoretical thought and speculation."

As we have done with both Marxists and Capitalists, we must also ask Teilhard whether he does not overestimate the resources of our finite spaceship earth. Yet we will soon discover that he is aware that our energy resources in terms of carbon fuels and hydroelectric power are not inexhaustible.[104] He even wants to take seriously all warnings about environmental pollution and threatening famines and shortages of conventional fuels. Yet at the same time he is convinced that "science can foresee and indeed already possesses inexhaustible substitutes for coal, petroleum and certain metals." The feeding of our increasing population by direct conversion of carbon, nitrogen, and other simple elements seems to indicate for him another possible means of overcoming an insurmountable threat to human progress. While he admits that we must be cautious, since "we still have feet of clay," the proviso "still" will be changed to a "no longer." Notwithstanding all difficulties, there is "an instinct of planetary preservation" and there is "a sense of the species" that conveys the feeling of a common destiny which will result in a truly democratic world society.[105]

One wonders whether this almost naive and blind trust in the future is not as unreliable as that of Communist utopia. Teilhard would not agree with this assumption, because he assures us that "worldly faith is not enough in itself to move the earth forward." [106] He sees a decisive difference between the Marxist anthropogenesis (the birth of the new humanity in Marxism) and his christocentric view of progress. Because Marxism rules out the existence of an irreversible center at its consummation, it can "neither justify nor sustain its momentum to the end." He claims that it is not enough to inspire and polarize the human molecules, such as in Marxism, so that the new humanity is supposed to be born through some kind of collective reflection and sympathy.[107] It is rather because there is at the summit and heart of a unified world an autonomous center of congregation which is "structurally and functionally capable of inspiring, preserving and fully releasing . . . the looked-for forces of unanimization" that we can have hope in humanity and in the future. Knowing about such a central source, he feels he can be optimistic that humanity and the universe can reach the natural goal of evolution without the aid of external violence.[108]

A Christian understands, Teilhard says, that the process of hominization is only a preparation for the final parousia. Yet christogenesis, when everything will be received and end in Christ, is not a natural phenomenon or a product of evolution. There is an ascending anthropogenesis and a descending permeation of christogenesis. The natural evolution up to humanity and the "supernatural" descent in the incarnation have merged to form a unity in salvation history.[109] The unifying movement of the human family (upward-slanting and forward moving) and the activity of Christ in salvation history (from above and permeating the whole reality of humanity) are fused in the christogenesis. Thus hominization serves as a preparation for and a way toward the parousia. We notice the incarnation receives prime emphasis in Teilhard's view, because in the incarnation God united himself with the world he created, unifying it, and in some way incorporating it in himself. It becomes clear that life is not an accidental phenomenon in the material universe, but the essence of the universe.[110] Similarly, Teilhard is convinced that humans are not accidental to the biological world, but a higher form of life. The social phenomenon in the human world too is not a superficial arrangement, but an advance of reflection. And finally, Christianity is not a coincidental phenomenon, but the direction of the socialization process.

While the genesis of humanity is constitutive for the genesis of Christ in the human family through his church, it is this descent of Christ that superanimates humanity.[111] Not the crowding upon each other of the human family warms the human heart, but the union through love and in love brings individuals together. In Christianity, Teilhard claims, we have witnessed the birth of love.[112] He sees it central to the Christian faith that the human individual cannot perfect himself or exist in fullness except through organic unification of all people in God.[113]

The universal movement forward to the future and upward in an evolutionary and metaphysical sense does not express a downgrading of the personal. The personal and universal at the summit of evolution rather endows our individual and corporal existence with meaning and direction.[114] Teilhard asserts that in Christianity alone the faith in a personal and personalizing center of the universe is alive and has a chance of surviving today.[115] In Christianity the hope is kept alive, growing, and set to work that one day

> the tension gradually accumulating between humanity and God will touch the limits prescribed by the possibilities of the world. And then will come the end. Then the presence of Christ, which has been silently accruing in things, will suddenly be revealed—like a flash of light from pole to pole. Breaking through all the barriers within which the veil of matter and the water-tightness of souls have seemingly kept it confined, it will invade the face of the earth. And, under the finally liberated action of the true affinities of being, the spiritual atoms of the world will be borne along by a force generated by the powers of cohesion proper to the universe itself and will occupy, whether within Christ or without Christ (but always under the influence of Christ), the place of happiness or pain designated for them by the living structure of the Pleroma.[116]

The whole evolutionary process is directed toward and finds its fulfillment in the parousia of Christ, in the creation of a new heaven and a new earth. Contrary to Marxist thought, Teilhard believes that the spirit will gain the victory over matter and, conditional upon this first victory, he is convinced of the victory of the risen Christ whose Pleroma (fulness) will be accomplished when he will be all in all.[117] The creative evolution that we see in Henri Bergson or in Charles Darwin as non-directional is supplemented in Teilhard through a christocentric view of a creative union.[118]

We could still question whether Teilhard does not view the evolutionary process too monolinear, when he judges, for instance, the notion of original sin to be primarily an intellectual and emotional straightjacket.[119] We might also wonder whether Teilhard does not see the evolution of humanity and the kingdom of God or salvation in and through Christ too much as two sides of the same homogeneous process.[120] Lastly, we might ask whether Teilhard does not grossly underestimate the strain our growing population and our technological civilization puts on the environment and its diminishing resources. Though we should not pass over these questions too lightly, we should not forget the immense difference between Teilhard's view of humanity and the secular assessment of the human potential so far reviewed.

Unlike Teilhard the secular valuations of humanity see our potential in para-Mendelian fashion as an extrapolation of that which we now enjoy within our human possibilities. In cases where they go beyond this, their utopian dreams face the grave limitation that occurs as soon as finite humanity is made the guarantee of an infinite future. Here Teilhard's view of humanity provides a notable exception and necessary correction. Though as scientist he does not belittle humanity, as theologian he need not rely solely on humanity in assessing our potential for the future. In an eschatological vision he asserts that our finitude is overcome by God's promise, partly and proleptically realized in Christ, to create a new humanity. Therewith God in Christ, the ultimate referent for humanity and its environment, is encountered, the one who according to the Christian tradition brought all things into being and who will bring them to their final conclusion.

Summary

Concluding this chapter on the uniqueness of humanity we are again confronted with the phenomenon of a basic unity of life.

(1) It has become impossible for us to assert a qualitative difference between human and animal characteristics. All forms of life are related to each other.

(2) Yet there is something distinctive about human beings. We must mention here our continual openness to the world, our ability to assimilate ever new experiences, our differentiated language, our immense span of remembrance, and the possibility to hand on vast amounts of information.

(3) Some features that are often claimed to be culturally conditioned, such as interests and roles exhibited predominantly by one sex, the inclination among adults to establish durable pair relationships, obedience to authority, and compassion and helpfulness are found to be part of our natural endowment. This does not mean that

these features are oblivious to cultural conditioning. They can either be considerably suppressed or enhanced.

(4) When we look to the future of the human race, we notice that neither biologically nor socio-politically this future is closed to us. We are still evolving.

(5) The frequent attempts to spell out in detail what the human goal and destiny will be are confined to extrapolations of present possibilities. Where they go beyond this natural limitation they result in wishful dreams. The future of our human journey will be enacted partly as an extrapolation of present possibilities and partly as the novel and unpredictable interplay between these possibilities. Therefore we can speak with certainty about the future only from a point at which the future is already past.

(6) In Teilhard, however, we have encountered the claim that in the Christ event the final goal of history has occurred in proleptic anticipation. As Christ stands for God, who is usually understood as co-equal to all time differentiations, his self-disclosure might be able to illuminate the direction in which the future can and should be enacted. Since the future is continuously approaching us, this would also throw light on our present state of affairs.

4.

God's Own Creation

In our attempt to understand the origin, present course, and possible destiny of our cosmic journey we have tried to define the basic structures of space, time, matter, and the causal sequence. We have also discussed various scientific theories concerning the origin and development of the world, of life, and even of the human family. Confronted with this massive scientific evidence for a "natural" history of the world we may wonder whether there is any need now to refer to God. To introduce God simply as an additional structural component of our existence would indeed be ill-advised. The rise of the scientific theories concerning the origin and history of the world is paralleled by an increasing uncertainty as to the proper place for God in a world which has become more and more of our own making. Especially the Darwinian revolution concerning the origin of humanity brought a profound uncertainty of how to relate the biblical witness to the evolutionary data.

We have noticed that science can provide us with many valuable insights into the structure, origin, present course, and possible destiny of our universe and our place within it. For science, however, the final reference point in explaining our cosmic journey is the cosmos itself. If scientific explanation would go beyond this built-in limitation, it would change its status to metaphysics. But any explanation shy of ultimacy cannot give us sufficient guidance in our understanding of personal and world history. We recognized that even socio-political theories, if they rely exclusively on science to illuminate the future, fall short of instilling our lives with lasting meaning.

We can receive reliable assurance about our present status and our future destiny only from a horizon which encloses all other horizons but itself is not enclosed. This horizon could not be an additional structural component of our existence, but one that illuminates all other components and endows them with ultimate reality. Such horizon comes to focus only in God, who, according to the Old Testament, is from eternity to eternity. This would mean that science, in its preoccupation with the particularity and specificity of the cosmos, and theology, in its endeavor to relate God to his ultimacy and universality to this same cosmos, are not opposed to each other but vitally interdependent. Science endows theology with particularity and specificity and theology gives to science ultimacy and universality.

Since both science and theology are concerned with us and the world in which we live, they are inextricably related to each other through their common object of inquiry (us and the world we live in), and they are distinguished from each other through their peculiar perspectives (particularity and specificity, and ultimacy and universality). To arrive at a total view of humanity, we cannot leave these two enterprises remain standing side by side. We must rather ask ourselves how they supplement and complement each other. This is even more necessary since often the impression is left that the perspective of science alone suffices to adequately illuminate our historic existence. After having elucidated briefly the structures of human existence from the perspective of science, we must now ask for their meaning from the vantage point of theology. In this pursuit we first want to fathom the relationship between God, the ultimate referent of theology, and the world, the ultimate referent of science, before we turn to the specific biblical assertions of our position within God's creation.

1. Defining the Relationship Between God and the World

In a world increasingly dominated by science, there are primarily two lines of thinking that have historically evolved as attempts to relate God to the universe, namely pantheism and deism or theism. We want to consider first pantheism as a way of bringing together God and the world. It is historically older than deism or theism and attained prominence in the 17th and 18th century.

a. The pantheistic approach

One might wonder why pantheism should be adduced here as a means to relate God to the world in a scientific age. There are already some pre-Socratic philosophers, such as Xenophanes, who show decidedly pantheistic notions in their understanding of God.[1] The Upanishad texts of ancient India tell us too that Brahman, through whom all beings come into existence, in whom they reside, and where they return in the end, bears distinctly pantheistic characteristics.[2] But in both instances the pantheistic overtones seem to arise from a critique of prevailing polytheism. Western pantheism, however, is predominantly influenced by Judeo-Christian monotheism. This is even true for seemingly Greek Renaissance movements, such as the Platonic Academy in Florence or the Cambridge Platonists.[3] In talking about Western pantheism, we must at least mention three figures who quite independently from each other stand at decisive points in the history of Western thought, namely Giordano Bruno, Baruch Spinoza, and Georg Wilhelm Friedrich Hegel.

The most celebrated of the Italian philosophers of nature, GIORDANO BRUNO, was deeply influenced by Copernicus' recent theory of a heliocentric world view.[4] Before coming in contact with Copernicus, he had learned from the German theologian, philosopher, and scientist Cardinal Nicholas of Cusa that all judgments about positions in the universe are relative so that the world has no given center. Yet it was Copernicus' theory of the earth moving around the sun that led him to reject entirely a geocentric and an anthropocentric conception of the universe. The space of the universe, we hear Giordano Bruno say, is infinite, and neither reason nor nature can assign to it a limit. This universe is filled with an infinity of worlds, "similar to our own, and of the same kind." [5]

Since all worlds are in motion one wonders whether Bruno arrives with Aristotle at the notion of a first unmoved mover. While quoting Aristotle extensively, he feels that there is no separate first mover and thence no gradation of motion. All mobile bodies are equally near to and equally distant from the prime and universal motive power. There is no longer a central point from which or toward which all bodies move and the Hellenistic concept of ethereal spheres is irrevocably gone. Yet Bruno maintains that "from a single infinite and universal motive force in a single infinite space there is but one infinite universal motion on which depend an infinity of mobile bodies and of motor forces, each of which is finite both as to size and to power." [6]

Bruno has not abandoned the idea that there is a power which holds the universe together and which infuses into each part its respective motion. But how is this "world soul" related to the universe? Hearing of innumerable grades of perfection which unfold the divine incorporeal perfection, we are reminded of Leibniz's monadology. But when Bruno, in contrast to Leibniz, continues that "our earth, the divine mother who hath given birth to us, doth nourish us and moreover will receive us back," we sense the pantheistic inclination in his thoughts.[7] Bruno no longer draws such a strict distinction between God and the world as did Nicholas of Cusa. Yet neither does he want to identify the infinite world with God. God is seen as

> completely infinite because he can be associated with no boundary and his every attribute is one and infinite. And I say that God is all-comprehensive infinity because the whole of him pervadeth the whole world and every part thereof comprehensively and to infinity. That is unlike the infinity of the universe, which is comprehensively in the whole but not comprehensively in those parts which we can distinguish within the whole.[8]

Bruno emphasizes the divine immanence without abandoning the distinction between God and the world. God still remains the integrative power that sustains and guides the universe.[9]

We are not surprised that the church objected very strongly to Bruno's speculative thoughts. Yet were they dangerous enough to label him as a heresiarch and finally to burn him at the stake in 1600? Evidently it was not just a religious trial that was conducted. Bruno's influence had spread far beyond Roman Catholic quarters and thus, in the face of his almost constant refusal to repent, the Roman authorities felt they had to resort to extreme measures.[10] While the man was consigned to the flames, his thoughts could not be that easily extinguished; they were echoed throughout the centuries.

The immediate influence of Giordano Bruno can be traced at such faraway places as England. People at the English Court and English poets and scientists, such as Edmund Spenser and Francis Bacon, picked up his idea of innumerable other humanities. But his continuous influence is most obvious in the work of the Dutch philosopher BARUCH SPINOZA. Though Spinoza nowhere directly cites Bruno, he seems to have been familiar with Bruno's central ideas.[11]

When one initially reads Spinoza, one may wonder whether he does not by far exceed Bruno in the radicality of his approach. We hear, for instance, that "in the infinite understanding of God no substance can be more perfect than that which already exists in Nature." [12] Spinoza then continues to say "that of Nature all in all is predicated, and that consequently Nature consists of infinite attributes, each of which is perfect in its kind. And this is just equivalent to the definition usually given of God." [13] In other words, God and nature seem to be equated. This becomes even clearer when Spinoza refers repeatedly to "God and Nature" indicating at least their intimate relatedness if not interchangeability.[14] We also hear that "Nature results from no causes . . . and must necessarily be a perfect being to which existence belongs." [15] This is exactly how theologians such as Thomas Aquinas and Anselm of Canterbury once talked about God.

We might conclude that such evident identification of God with nature might degrade God. But Spinoza would not agree with us. Since he understands God as a being of whom all attributes are predicated, all other things are intimately related to him. God is a cause of all things.[16] Through God's providence which we find in the striving of the whole of nature and in individual things, they maintain and preserve their own existence.[17] While we detect here an analogy to Bruno's understanding of the integrative power of God, the similarity between Bruno and Spinoza becomes even more explicit when Spinoza "divides the whole of Nature . . . into *Natura naturans* and *Natura naturata.*" *Natura naturans* (creating nature) he now defines as "a being that we conceive clearly and distinctly through itself, and without needing anything beside itself . . . that is, God." [18] That *Natura naturans* is nevertheless equated with God becomes clear when he says "that God is known only through himself, and not through something else." [19] But what is then *Natura naturata* (created nature)? For Spinoza it is the modes or creations which depend on or have been created by God immediately; it is specifically motion in matter and the understanding in the thinking thing. Spinoza concluded: "These, then, we say, have been from all eternity, and to all eternity will remain immutable. A work truly as great as becomes the greatness of the workmaster." [20] Yet unlike Bruno the distinction between the creator and the created is immediately immensely qualified when Spinoza allows for only two proper attributes of God, thought and extension.[21]

The difficulty for Spinoza in maintaining a proper distinction between creator and created seems to lie in his understanding of God

as substance. While he maintained with René Descartes the distinction between *res cogitans* (thinking being) and *res extensa* (extended
being), he differed from Descartes in changing the underlying inte-
grator *res* (being) into substance. When Spinoza states: "By God I
understand Being absolutely infinite, that is to say, substance consisting of infinite attributes, each one of which expresses eternal and
infinite essence," [22] the bind in which he finds himself becomes evident. Unlike Descartes he has conferred upon God such a determinative naturalistic characteristic that the equation of God with nature
is inevitable. In analogy to God and nature, God and substance too
have become interchangeable.[23]

It would be wrong to assume that Spinoza wanted to do away
with religion or with God.[24] Spinoza was convinced that true knowledge can only be attained by relating all our ideas to God, since he
is the source and reference point of all true knowledge.[25] With Martin
Luther, Spinoza rejected the idea that God is a long, broad, and
extended thing.[26] Yet contrary to Luther, he did not want to remove
the notion of extension from God altogether. Spinoza claimed that
extended substance is one of the infinite attributes of God, it is indivisible and its parts can never be really distinct. There is no vacuum
in nature and therefore nature or God form an infinite, indivisible
unity in which each "part" and incident attain their proper valuation.
Spinoza therefore concluded: "All things are in God, and everything
which takes place takes place by the laws alone of the infinite nature
of God, and follows . . . from the necessity of His essence." [27] This
pantheistic approach almost completely disallows for a distinction
between the creator and the created. Yet the question that must be
addressed to Spinoza is not primarily why one should still maintain
the God language if God and nature become interchangeable, but
whether his approach still provides a satisfying answer to the perennial question of philosophy: Why is there something and not just nothing? Do nature's own possibilities suffice to account for the difference
between nothing and something and between void and creation? In
his attempt to relate God closely enough to nature, Spinoza seems to
have failed to provide a satisfactory answer to this important question.

When we move closer to the contemporary scene we could cite
many philosophers and theologians who pursue a more or less pantheistic line of thinking. In England the most prominent pantheistic
thoughts seem to come from the Romantic movement, from poets
such as Percy Bysshe Shelley and William Wordsworth. In Germany
nearly all philosophers and many theologians were affected by pan-

theistic thought. We could name here Friedrich Schleiermacher, Gottfried Ephraim Lessing, Johann Wolfgang Goethe, Friedrich W. J. Schelling, and Johann Gottlieb Fichte, to mention just the most prominent ones. In many cases Spinoza's writings served as the main source of inspiration.

The most prominent representative of pantheistic thought, albeit of a very special kind, was GEORG WILHELM FRIEDRICH HEGEL.[28] His impact can be felt in English writers such as F. H. Bradley and Bernard Bosanquet, and in Italian philosophers, such as Benedetto Croce and Giovanni Gentile. In America Hegel's influence is noticeable in the Ohio Hegelians John B. Stallo, Peter Kaufmann, Moncure Conway, and August Willich, in the pragmatism of John Dewey, and in the speculative idealism of Josiah Royce. In Germany Hegel's philosophy dominated at the middle of the 19th century. Still in our century Karl Barth asked: "Why did Hegel not become for the Protestant world something similar to what Thomas Aquinas was for Roman Catholicism?" A partial answer to Barth's question may lie in the fact that immediately after Hegel's premature death in 1831 his influential left-wing followers usurped his system for their own purposes. Left-wing Hegelians, such as Bruno Bauer in his later years, David Friedrich Strauss, Ludwig Feuerbach, Karl Marx, Friedrich Engels, and Max Stirner identified Spirit and nature to such an extent that their philosophies turned largely materialistic and atheistic. But what did Hegel himself teach?

Contrary to Bruno or Spinoza, Hegel was not interested in revising the faith of his Judeo-Christian tradition; he wanted to interpret it. Especially the Gospel of John with its "dialectic" terminology and its emphasis on the logos attracted Hegel to the Bible. At the age of twenty-five he wrote a *Life of Jesus* (1795), the opening of which characterizes his thinking: "The pure reason, completely free of any limitations is itself the Godhead." [29] Later in his *Science of Logic* (1812) he explained this statement in his introductory remarks: "Logic therefore must be understood as the system of pure reason, as the realm of pure thought. *This realm is the truth as it is for itself without covering.* Therefore one can say that this content is *the description of God, as he is in his eternal being prior to the creation of Nature and a finite spirit.*" [30] Hegel wanted to witness to the living God in his philosophic system, because the whole universe, stemming from him, witnesses to the living God. This means that Hegel endeavored to draw religion and philosophy closely together. In his posthumously published *Lectures on the Philosophy of Religion*

(1832) Hegel even asserted: "The content of religion cannot be different from that of philosophy, since the absolute Spirit does not have two self-consciousnesses of itself which would have different and opposed contents." [31] The absolute Spirit is identified with God, since there can be no higher definition for God.[32] The absolute Spirit permeates art, religion, and philosophy and returns in these three forms to itself.[33] But what is absolute Spirit?

First we must distinguish the absolute Spirit from the subjective spirit that is in human beings and the objective spirit, the spirit of the human community.[34] The absolute Spirit is then the eternal, in itself same Spirit that becomes another and recognizes this other as itself.[35] This dialectic movement of the absolute Spirit leads to the higher definition of the absolute as absolutely disclosing, self-conscious, and infinitely creative Spirit. The absolute Spirit understands itself by positing being as its other self, by creating nature and the finite spirit, so that the other which it has created ceases to have any independence over against the absolute Spirit. The other is only a vehicle through which the Spirit attains its absolute being for itself, its absolute unity of being in itself and for itself, its concept and its reality.[36]

Through the dialectic movement of the Spirit Hegel saw no problems asserting that the world is created. The Spirit "becomes an other to itself: it enters existence. . . . It creates a World." [37] Hegel did not stop with these assertions, but also asked why God had to create the world.[38] The answer is already given in Hegel's definition of God as Spirit. Creation of the world is not something accidental or arbitrary that might or might not be. Creation pertains necessarily to the concept of God as ultimate Spirit.[39] It is part of God's true infinity that he posits a finite world. He does this in order to endow with reality the distinction to his infinity.[40] In this dialectic process the creation of the world is not analogous to the creation of the world from some primordial matter. God does not create from something material. Again the absolute Spirit demands that besides God there can be no eternal, self-subsisting matter, not even a chaos; God creates the world out of nothingness.[41] God creates absolutely out of nothingness, his creation is infinite activity, which is not directed against something at hand or present, it is creation of the world as something posited by him.[42] Only this unlimited priority has the character of creating. God posits the world over against himself as another, he wills a finite world. The world is at once opposition to

God and God's other, it has no independent existence and must be continually posited by God.

We notice at once the immense advantage of Hegel's system over against other attempts to relate God and the world. He neither digs an unbridgeable chasm between them, nor does he fall prey to the endeavors of Spinoza and of other pantheists who identify God with nature or with the world. As we will see later, Hegel's system is deeply informed and shaped by biblical insights. The sarcastic remark of his opponent Arthur Schopenhauer was certainly exaggerated when he claimed that by welding together philosophy and religion Hegel intended to back the official Prussian state religion. Therefore the official state religion served as the criterion for what could be thought in philosophy.[43] Yet we too wonder whether Hegel does not overestimate the possibilities of philosophy.[44] In his desire to perceive being as the manifestation of the infinite Spirit, he establishes a universal metaphysical system. The whole universe becomes the justification for God and vice versa. Contrary to Immanuel Kant's emphatic claim that for reason God is at the most a logical possibility and a moral necessity, God again becomes a logical necessity. Hegel attempted to demonstrate that to understand ourselves and the world we must understand God. Yet in order to "prove" these theological assertions Hegel had to pay the price of dissolving religion into philosophy. This meant that while he distinguished between God and world, he also had to equate them.

Hegel's followers, less ambitious to perpetuate a pure system, settled either for the equation of God with the world, such as the "atheists" Karl Marx and Ludwig Feuerbach,[45] or they resurrected a theistic approach of relating God and the world, such as the Roman Catholic theologian Johann Adam Möhler. The danger of Hegel's approach stems from the point at which we can also discern his highest accomplishment, the inextricable relationship between God and the world. This is true for a pantheistic approach in general. It is inclined to obliterate the distinction between God and world and therefore always bears in itself the danger that Schopenhauer once noticed saying: "Pantheism is only a euphemism for atheism." [46]

We should remember here, however, that Hegel rejected the notion that he or others had ever advanced a decidedly pantheistic approach to the relationship between God and the world.[47] He contended that God has never been conceived of as being everything or as being the sum total of all individual things. According to Hegel the divine has been conceived of at most as the Essence of things and that which lies at the foundation of all things. While we cannot follow Hegel in his sweeping attempt to erase pantheism from the history of thought, the matter is different with Hegel's own affiliation with pantheism. Iwan Iljin is certainly close to the truth when he says: "Apart from the divine reason-substance there is no self-sustained and self-determined 'being other' possible. For Hegel, therefore, 'theism' (belief in God) means 'pantheism,' and 'pantheism' means 'acosmism' ('there is no world') and 'panepistemism' ('the divine science is everything')."

Since Hegel, however, understands his system as an interpretation of the Christian faith, at the center of which is Christ as God incarnate, God is neither perceived as being in the world, as in pantheism, nor is the world in God, as in panentheism.[48] Yet the world has no existence and reality independent of God and, therefore, to know the true meaning of the universe, and of humanity, one must first know God. But can we really say that the reference to God solves all the problems? While we must affirm this in an ultimate sense, when God's kingdom will finally triumph, we would oversimplify matters if we attempted to ascertain this also in a penultimate sense. The progression of God's history is still too much contaminated by irrational and disparate elements that the reference to God alone suffices to make our world intelligible. The question we must pursue now is whether a theistic approach to relating God and world, which is also possible according to Hegel's principles, would bear more merit.

b. Deistic and theistic approaches

Theism is a historically evolved term which developed in gradual opposition to deism and pantheism.[49] Deism and theism were at first used almost synonymously, but drifted farther and farther apart, until theism was mostly attached to orthodox talk about God, while deism acquired a connotation of religious unorthodoxy. Theism usually stands for the belief in a personal God who is beyond and above the world, a God who has created the world out of nothing and preserves and governs it. The belief in a personal God who is seen in radical contrast to the world, but who is creatively and preservingly active in it, is often constituent for theism. With this kind of preliminary definition in mind we could name as theists many Western philosophers and theologians. Yet in our brief survey we want to mention only those who most significantly advanced a theistic understanding of the relationship between God and the world.

The term "theism" appears for the first time in European thought in Ralph Cudworth's introduction to his treatise *The True Intellectual System of the Universe* (1768). The lengthy work of the Cambridge Neo-Platonist RALPH CUDWORTH initially caused much suspicion in orthodox circles, but was then recognized as the standard text for the refutation of materialism and atheism. Cudworth claimed that he used the same tools as the atheists and showed that from the very starting point of the atheists, i.e., from atomism, atheism can be refuted and deprived of its own arguments.[50] While Cudworth affirmed the lawful orderliness with which science described the universe, he restricted any mechanistic explanation of the world to the explanation of individual events. All individualities, he asserted, form a harmonious cosmic entity which receives its life from its creator. Nature is not dead matter, but alive, and life is ultimately of spiritual nature. Cudworth claimed that the atheists cannot deny the existence of soul and mind in a human being, though these items do not fall under external sense experience. Consequently

> they have as little reason to deny the existence of a perfect mind, presiding over the universe, without which it cannot be conceived whence our imperfect ones should be derived. The existence of that God, whom no eye hath seen nor can see, is plainly proved by reason for his effects, in the visible phenomena of the universe, and from what we are conscious of within ourselves.[51]

Though leaning heavily on René Descartes, he rejected Descartes' "mechanistic theism" and his skepticism about our ability to discern God's purpose in nature. He also discarded Descartes' idea that animals are machines, and on the contrary affirmed that they are endowed with sensitive, though not immortal souls.

According to Cudworth there can be no dichotomy between the spiritual and the material worlds, because "there is a scale, or ladder of entities and perfections in the universe, one above another." This Great Chain of Being, tying the whole cosmos together, disallows for a separation between the spiritual and the material, and since "the production of things cannot possibly be in way of ascent from lower to higher, but must of necessity be in way of descent from higher to lower," the world and its phenomena cannot be interpreted in purely mechanistic terms.[52] Small wonder that the empiricism advanced by David Hume became the main target of Cudworth's vitalistic theism. Unlike Hume, Cudworth could never have admitted that the human mind was originally a mere blank or that the human soul is nothing but a higher modification of matter.[53] God as the eternal divine spirit endows all being in all its gradations with living harmony and order. Reality allows for discerning the presence of a spiritual basis within it. This spiritual basis comes from God and points towards God who manifests himself as the living and present one. This harmonious relationship between God and world that Cudworth assumed to be discernible in the world led him to believe in a harmony between reason, religion, and revelation.[54]

Turning now to ANTHONY EARL OF SHAFTESBURY, we notice that the harmony between reason, religion, and revelation is already reduced to a harmony between reason and religion. Shaftesbury first defended the apologetic method of Cudworth and praised him for depicting the position of the atheists with their own arguments before he refuted them. But then he went beyond Cudworth when he stated in his *Characteristics of Men, Manners, Opinion, Times, etc.* (1711):

> For as adverse as I am to the cause of theism, or name of Deist, when taken in a sense exclusive of revelation, I consider still that in strictness the root of all is theism, and that to be a settled Christian, it is necessary to be first of all a good theist; for theism can only be opposed to polytheism or atheism.[55]

While Shaftesbury was too much of a gentleman to attack the dogmas of the church, he confessed that human reason does not suffice to understand their secrets. He even warned against using Old Testament stories in poetry, because they did not reflect the true divine wisdom of goodness.[56] Revelation, though not discarded, is definitely reduced to secondary value in Shaftesbury's thoughts. Actually, to be a theist, he claimed, one needs no revelation. Since the universe is the result of majestic art and of infinite goodness and love, it convinces an impressible observer of the existence of an all-encompassing spirit who in his wisdom and goodness has linked all the parts to a harmonious unity.[57] While Shaftesbury conceded that there is distortion in nature, he is convinced that it does not diminish the discernment of God as the creative genius in nature. God is the "source and principle of all beauty and perfection" and when beings participate in this beauty and perfection, they are happy and flourish, but when "they are lost to this, they are deformed, perished, and lost." [58]

Again the Great Chain of Being necessitates a coherence of the created with the creator. Contrary to the deists, Shaftesbury did not want to relegate God to the position of a prime mover, but he conceived him to be in constant and living interaction with the creation.[59] As did Cudworth, he attacked both Hobbes and Descartes for making God an idle spectator of the universe. Though God is not an arbitrary God, his power is unlimited. The only "limitation" that Shaftesbury allows for is the control of God's activity through the laws of his own moral nature, because it is impossible "that Heaven should have acted otherwise than for the best." [60] "Everything is governed, ordered, or regulated for the best, by a designing principle or mind, necessarily good and permanent." [61] While Shaftesbury does not always clearly distinguish between God and nature, it is evident for him that God is the creative and ordering principle for nature. "God has created Nature and has endowed her with creative powers so that she might carry on the work of providence." [62]

When we come to François Marie Arouet, commonly called VOL-TAIRE, we obtain a different picture of God's involvement in nature. Voltaire is one of the greatest French authors who fought for tolerance, reason, and human rights all his life. During his three years of exile in England (1726-1729) he was strongly influenced by English deism and Newtonian mechanics.[63] He was convinced that Newton's whole philosophy necessarily leads to the knowledge of a supreme being who has created everything and arranged everything freely, while Descartes, though affirming a creator and cause of all things, is inconsistent in his philosophical conclusion.[64] But Voltaire's theism or deism no longer resulted from a harmony of reason and religion as was still the case with Shaftesbury. For instance, Voltaire discards the notion of an animating soul as a word covering up for our ignorance.[65]

In following John Locke he abandoned even the notion of innate moral principles. Voltaire recognizes in his *Treatise on Metaphysics* (1734) that that which is called a virtue in one place is rejected as a vice somewhere else. Nevertheless he asserts: "It seems to me for certain that there are natural laws with respect to which human beings in the whole universe must agree." [66] Voltaire does not seem to advocate a complete relativism of morals as we might at first have surmised, yet for him the fundamental moral laws are fairly restricted. They consist mainly in the admonition not to injure others and to seek one's own pleasure as long as it does not impair the happiness of one's neighbor.

God is not so much a God of humanity; he is a God of nature who is the wise author of a nature useful to us.[67] Voltaire comes close to comparing the universe with a clock which God as the divine watch-maker designed in his omnipotence when he observes about the orbits of the sun and the planets: "This Rotation from West to East is an Effect of the Free-will of the Creator, and this Free-will is the only sufficient reason that can be assigned to it." [68] The world therefore attains a rigid status and God is relegated to inactivity. While Voltaire still admits that nature tells us that God exists, God has been divorced from the world, he has been relegated to "the primordial and final cause of all." [69] Yet with the same breath Voltaire admits: "You can no more demonstrate its [God's] impossibility than I can demonstrate mathematically that it is so. In metaphysics we scarcely reason on anything but probabilities. We are all swimming in a sea of which we have never seen the shore." But moral reason demands God's existence for Voltaire. God sustains the moral order, he prevents crimes and maintains justice. Voltaire, however, does no longer perceive a harmony between reason, religion, and revelation. The notion of God and of his relationship toward the world is based mostly on reason, or, as Kant said three generations later, on pure practical reason.

Kant then finally introduced a clear distinction between deism and theism (Voltaire, for instance, though clearly deistic preferred to call himself a theist). According to Kant "the *deist* believes in a *God,* the *theist* in a *living God.*" [70] Theism proposed a natural theology and attempts to conclude from the arrangement, order and unity of the world the characteristics and existence of an originator of the world. A deist, however, believes in a primordial mover or a prime cause of all things. Kant, however, demonstrated that pure reason is unable to prove the objective reality of such a supreme being. The relationship between God and nature is not a principle to be deduced from nature. It is rather an interpretative means by which we understand nature. Once this insight was obtained the whole (rational) deistic or theistic attempt to arrive at a harmonious unity between reason, religion, and revelation had to collapse.

While the endeavor must be lauded for convincingly demonstrating that the findings of science and the assertions of the biblical witness are not opposed to each other, the possibilities of reason were over-estimated. The relationship between God and the world is as inaccessible to proof by scientific means, as the findings of science concerning the structure of the universe can be verified through reference to the biblical witnesses. Yet both enterprises, science (reason) and theology (revelation and faith), must be correlated to obtain a complete and coherent view of the world. But neither deism nor theism distinguished clearly between the impossible task to prove the validity of one perspective by reference to the other, and the necessary correlation between the two perspectives. Consequently they could not achieve the unity they sought to obtain between reason, religion, and revelation. In attributing to reason alone the task to delineate such unity they unintentionally contributed to reason's unduly elevated position and thereby downgraded religion and revelation.

In more recent years a second type of theism has been advanced.[71] This new type is also to be contrasted to the traditional theism in which God is understood as being in all respects absolutely perfect or unsurpassable and in no way and in no respect surpassable or perfectible. According to this second type of theism God is continu-ously interacting with the world and vice versa. This view, commonly called process philosophy, was first forcefully put forth by the English mathematician and philosopher, ALFRED NORTH WHITEHEAD in his book *Process and Reality* (1929).

Whitehead is dissatisfied with both the Aristotelian notion that God is the first unmoved mover, and the "Christian" notion that God is "eminently real." According to Whitehead, in the Western tradition both notions were fused into the idea that God is the "aboriginal, eminently real, transcendent creator, at whose fiat the world came into being, and whose imposed will it obeys." [72] Whitehead is concerned that the presentation of God under the aspect of power awakens "every modern instinct of critical reaction." [73] "If the modern world is to find God," Whitehead claimed, "it must find him through love and not through fear." [74]

To attain the notion of a loving God and not of a tyrant God, Whitehead suggested that we must limit the possibilities of God. He attempted this limitation by attributing to God a primordial and a subsequent nature. In his primordial nature God is "the unlimited conceptual realization of the absolute wealth of potentiality." [75] This does not mean for Whitehead that God is prior to all creation, but that he is with all creation. Apart from God there would be no actual world, since nothing could be actualized, and apart from the actual world with its creativity, there would be no rational explanation of the ideal vision which constitutes God.[76] Thus God needs the world as its arena of actualization and the world needs God as the granter of these actualizations. This interdependence becomes even more evident in God's consequent nature. Since all things are interrelated, Whitehead assumed that the world reacts to God. Thus God "shares with every new creation its actual world." [77] While in God's primordial nature all groundwork for the possible world is given, God in his consequent nature provides through a kind of feedback the weaning of his physical feelings from his primordial concepts. Therefore Whitehead described the nature of God's subsequent involvement in the world as "the perpetual vision of the road which leads to the deeper realities." [78] Since the subsequent nature is always moving on and integrates the actualities of the world into the primordial whole which is unlimited conceptual reality, God provides the binding element in the world. He confronts what is actual in the world with what is possible for it, and at the same time provides the means of merging the actual with the possible.

Both God and the world are the instrument of novelty for each other. But God and world move conversely to each other in respect to their processes. God, as primordially one, acquires in the interchange with the world through his consequent nature the multiplicity of the actual occasions and absorbs them into his own primordial integrative unity. The world, however, as primordially many, acquires in the interchange with God through his subsequent nature as integrative unity, which as a novel occurrence is absorbed into the multiplicity of its primordial nature. God and world are coaxing each other along, God being completed by the finite and the finite being completed through confrontation with the eternal. Whitehead summed up his thoughts by saying:

> What is done in the world is transformed into a reality in heaven, and the reality in heaven passes back into the world. By reason of this reciprocal relation, the love in the world passes into the love in heaven, and floods back again into the world. In this sense, God is the great companion—the fellow-sufferer who understands.[79]

CHARLES HARTSHORNE, one-time assistant to Whitehead, went along similar lines as his former teacher, advancing, as he calls it, this "theism of the second type." [80] Hartshorne was aware that such a notion of God as he introduced with his second type of theism could by no means be "the entire actual God whom we confront in worship," since it would still be an impersonal it and not a personal thou.[81] He was also aware that God cannot be defined, i.e., limited by human concept. But he wanted to push the possibilities of reason as far as possible and he is even convinced that we no longer have to choose between Spinoza and Jesus, because nature should not only be conceived of as God, as did Spinoza, but as God of love.[82] Hartshorne then concludes:

> The ultimate ideal of knowledge and of action remains this: to deal with the world as the body of a God of love, whose generosity of interest is equal to all contrasts, however gigantic, between mind and mind, and to whom all individuals are numbered, each with its own life history and each with its own qualitative—enjoying and suffering, more or less elaborately remembering and anticipating, sensing and spontaneously reacting—natures.[83]

We could mention works of many other prominent and promising theologians and philosophers that have learned from process theology, such as Daniel D. Williams, John B. Cobb, or Schubert Ogden. But the circle seems to close here. We have seen how some attempted to identify God with nature, such as in the pantheistic tradition, we have noticed how some tried to posit God over against nature, such as in traditional theistic and deistic fashion, and finally we have discovered that in the process view God is supposed to be one with the world and beyond it, both finite and infinite, eternal and temporal, necessary and contingent.[84] While the attempt of process thought to mediate between theistic and pantheistic modes of thought seems to hold much promise, we cannot but notice one serious shortcoming in all theories so far reviewed.

All these theories have as their point of departure the primacy of reason. Though we do not want to downgrade reason, we have observed that a harmony between reason, religion, and revelation cannot be established by relying on reason alone. It would be wrong to fault reason for its obvious limitations, nor could we blame religion or revelation for this "failure." It is only proper to refer here to Immanuel Kant and his antinomies of pure reason.[85] He stated there that if we want to prove anything beyond the limits of empirical knowledge with the help of pure reason, we at best arrive at an either-or: either there is something or there is not something, either it is so or it is not so. The primacy of pure reason only leads to possibilities, possibilities that can be too easily disclaimed. When we engage practical reason, however, as Kant himself did, we are not much better off, because God then becomes a practical necessity, or as Dietrich Bonhoeffer once said, a "working hypothesis." [86] While the material basis of the universe and of humanity can be adequately dealt with through reason alone by referring to the findings of science, we are at the most confronted with possibilities once we address to reason issues of ultimacy and universality. Here the question of how to relate God and the world gains renewed importance as the point at which the world of particularity and specificity intersects with the dimension of ultimacy and universality. Since we are aware of the limits of reason, we would then not want to make reason our prime resource in dealing with this question.

It would be dangerous, however, if we would now simply take refuge in divine revelation to come to terms with the dimension of ultimacy and universality. Such a move could easily be interpreted as repristinating authoritative thought structures of bygone days or even as an escape into credulity. Wrestling with the trustworthiness of the Christian faith, young Hegel discovered that it would be tedious and futile to attempt to prove that the Christian faith still contains a few reasonable insights which could be used to illuminate the issues of ultimacy and universality.[87] Such an approach would at best be a piecemeal defense of the Christian faith, and inquisitive minds would interpret it as an open invitation to refute with the help of "reason" one of our reasonable arguments after another. By resorting to "reasonable" arguments in the defense of the Christian faith we would still bow to the primacy of human reason. However, Hegel also showed that there is another approach possible which may disclose to us the dimension of ultimacy and universality. If we give any credence to God eternal as the source of all wisdom, as Hegel claimed, "we must link the eternal with the accidental in our thinking" and we must consider the needs of human nature and show in this situation that the Christian faith is both natural and inevitable. This means that the Christian faith as a whole illuminates our nature and therefore is inevitable if we want to be true to ourselves as religious and God-dependent beings.

Giving prime attention to revelation as reflected in the Judeo-Christian tradition, we might receive trustworthy guidance of how to assess the human potential toward the good or how to evaluate the origin and direction of the evolutionary process. We might discover, too, that from this perspective, which envisions God as its ultimate horizon, the insights of science lose some of their particularistic limitations and come to stand in a more comprehensive context. We would also avoid the danger that Martin Luther pointed out, namely that we have no criterion for distinguishing God from the created and for understanding the created.[88] Luther even goes so far as to say that "nobody knows what a man or a woman is, unless he faithfully recognizes them as a work of God."[89] "But it is our duty," he continues, "to read and to instruct others, in order that from Holy Scripture we may gain knowledge of the creatures, and from the creatures of the Creator." Revelation therefore does not replace reason, but it illuminates the findings of reason by referring to their true reality discernible in them. Thus we must take seriously the claim of the Judeo-Christian tradition that God is not a God out there, beyond the world, nor one who is in the world and identical with it. The world and its movements are rather God's works in which he is present. The whole world can now be understood as pointing to God as its ultimate reason for existence and purpose. This God has revealed and continues to reveal himself to human reason. Therefore revelation is not constitutive for human reason but contingent upon it, since only reasonable beings can "know" about revelation.

2. The World as God's Creation

If we want to understand the world as God's work, we are immediately tempted to look at the creation accounts in Genesis. Statistical evidence will tell us, however, that there are many places apart from the first chapters of Genesis in which assertions are made about the world as God's creation. Actually, to appropriately understand the world as God's work, it would be best initially to pass by the creation accounts in Genesis. The reason for so doing is not a contempt of these accounts, but the realization that in talking about the world in its totality we must first of all talk about God, the ultimate referent for the world. Both in the Old and in the New Testament, however, God is first introduced to us as redeemer and then as creator. How this redeemer or savior God is to be understood can be seen from Hosea 13:4 when we hear him say: "I am the Lord your God from the land of Egypt; you know no God but me, and besides me there is no savior."[90] Yahweh is not one of the many gods; he is the God who does not tolerate any other gods. As this one God, however, he should not be confused with some kind of primordial principle. He can tell the Israelites that he is their God, because he is associated with certain events that constitute their history. The realization that

God is the maker of history is one of the most fundamental insights in the Old and New Testament.

a. God as the maker of history

When we read the Decalog in Exodus 20:1ff. we are again confronted with the prominence of history. Yahweh does not simply decree the commandments for Israel. Before commanding them to do anything, he reminds the Israelites that he is the Lord of their history by saying: "I am the Lord your God, who brought you out of the land of Egypt, out of the house of bondage." The Israelites in turn recall over and over again God's mighty deeds, especially as they occurred in connection with their Exodus from Egypt. These deeds are referred to when the farmer brings his gifts to the sanctuary (Deut. 26:5-10), they are mentioned when the father initiates the son into the meaning of the commandments (Deut. 6:20ff.), and even the prophet Ezekiel reminds the Israelites that they came from Egypt and that there they became God's people (Ezek. 20:5). In spite of the prominence of the Exodus events, it would be misleading to speak with Ernst Bloch about a principle of Exodus which results in a principle of hope.[91] The Exodus events themselves are not the ground of Israel's hope, because God's "mighty arm" and not the events he caused are the focus of these references. The intention of these references is not to stimulate hope that one can expect further events in analogy to the Exodus, but that one can expect the continued presence of the mighty God who made the Exodus possible. The emphasis therefore is not on history but on God who makes history possible.

The emphasis on God as the maker of history becomes especially evident in the creed of Deuteronomy 26:5-9. Here the main events in the salvation history are recapitulated beginning with the time of the patriarchs and concluding with the conquest of the promised land: [92]

> A wandering Aramean was my father; and he went down into Egypt and sojourned there, few in number; and there he became a nation, great, mighty, and populous. And the Egyptians treated us harshly, and afflicted us, and laid upon us hard bondage. Then we cried to the Lord the God of our fathers, and the Lord heard our voice, and saw our affliction, our toil, and our oppression; and the Lord brought us out of Egypt with a mighty hand and an outstretched arm,

with great terror, with signs and wonders; and he brought
us into this place and gave us this land, a land flowing with
milk and honey.

Though the passage cited does not just contain objective facts, we
nevertheless notice a close concentration on objective facts. The
general outline of Israel's history is seen in the light of God's actions.
In other words, the biblical events in this creed and in most other
parts of the Old Testament are a concentration and sometimes even
distillation of historical events, events that are at the same time
interpreted as God's action.[93]

Thus the Old Testament presents the course of history as a kind
of salvation history which was shaped and led to fulfillment by a
word of judgment and salvation continually injected into it. The
continual and progressive reinterpretation of the traditions of Israel
are necessitated through the factual course of history and make this
course part of the tradition. This means that the older promises are
never abandoned or superseded by the actual progression of history
but are incorporated into it in a fulfilled, modified, and expanded
way. The tension between promise and fulfillment was not replaced
by the simple advance of Israel's history, but was strongly creative
of Israel's historic progress.[94]

Israel's understanding of salvation history was not only expanded
toward the future, it was also expanded into trans-national and trans-
human terms. We have seen that the prophets already understood
that other nations were included in God's plan for Israel and vice
versa (cf. Isa. 2:2-4; Amos 1:6-8, etc.). But it was especially in the
period of apocalyptic that not just the world of individuals and
nations but the whole cosmos was understood to be involved in God's
salvation history. This historicizing of the whole cosmos in terms of
a universal salvation history is of tremendous importance for theology.
Without apocalyptic the Israelite salvation history would have been
"bogged down in the ethnic history of men or the existential history
of the individual." [95] Having started with the patriarchs, God's salvation history eventually included all Israel, all nations, and all the
world. This means that at the beginning of the New Testament,
history was understood as the working out of God's purposes or
simply as salvation history.[96]

The question whether this perspective of a universal salvation
history is continued in the New Testament, is difficult to decide.

Apart from a few passages in Luke-Acts and some brief references in Letters of the New Testament, that imply a cosmic dimension of salvation, we are confronted with the history of just one person, Jesus of Nazareth, and not with the history of a people or of a community. However, there is no doubt for the early Christian community that the history of Jesus cannot be divorced from the history of God with his people. The Letter to the Hebrews therefore opens with the well-known words: "In many and various ways God spoke of old to our fathers by the prophets; but in these last days he has spoken to us by a Son" (Heb. 1:1f.).

But the history of Jesus is not simply a continuation of the history of God with his people, because the history of Jesus is the history of the "last days," or, as Paul says: God sent his Son "when the time had fully come (Gal. 4:4). Rudolf Bultmann captured this new situation very appropriately when he observed that the emerging church

> understood Jesus as the one whom God by the resurrection has made Messiah, and that they awaited him as the coming Son of Man. For it is apparent that in that very fact they understood his sending as God's decisive act. In expecting him as the Coming One they understood themselves as the Congregation of the end of days called by him. For them factually—no matter to what degree it may have been clearly conscious—the old had passed away and the world had become new.[97]

History and salvation history have reached their goal and thereby "history is swallowed up in eschatology." [98]

Does this mean that we are reverting again to an earlier Israelite understanding of God's history, which comprises only God's particular history with his people while leaving history outside the particular salvation history untouched? Bultmann seems to make a strict distinction, if not separation, between history and salvation history. He asserts that contrary to New Testament expectations "history did not come to an end, and, as every schoolboy knows, it will continue to run its course." [99] Yet Bultmann suggests that Paul and the Gospel of John did not expect the eschatological event as a dramatic cosmic catastrophe but as happening within history, "beginning with the appearance of Jesus Christ and in continuity with this occurring again and again in history, but not as the kind of historical development which can be confirmed by any historian." [100] Consequently, the meaning and future development of history becomes secondary for a

Christian. Decisive is only the confrontation with the eschatological event, with Jesus Christ, in the proclamation of the church. This proclamation demands a decision from us and enables us to understand us to be free from the world and its historical process, yet still a part of this process. While we remain historical beings, we receive God's forgiving grace. Therefore, we are not just the resultant of our past but are allowed to have a genuinely new beginning.

Many of Bultmann's students share his strictly dialectic view of history.[101] Other theologians, however, are more reluctant in divorcing God's saving event from history. Karl Barth, for instance, claims in his *Church Dogmatics* that "the history of salvation is *the* history" which encloses all other history and to which in some way all other history belongs as its illustration and reflection.[102] But he warns us not to confuse salvation history with the history of religion or the history of the religious spirit, because in so doing we would downgrade it to be only one history among many. Barth understands salvation history as "the nexus of the particular speech and action of God for the reconciliation of the world with Himself which at its center and climax is the history of Jesus Christ." [103]

Especially Oscar Cullmann, largely in dialog with Bultmann and his followers, emphasized the importance of salvation history for our understanding of history in general. According to Cullmann the coming of Jesus signifies the midpoint of history. Thus the whole New Testament holds the view that the midpoint of time lies no longer in the future but in the past.[104] The reason for this notion is not just that the New Testament was written from the perspective of Christ's resurrection. Jesus himself emphasized that the kingdom of God is already in the midst of the people when they saw him expelling demons by the finger of God, healing the sick, checking the power of death, and forgiving sins. Yet at the same time Jesus maintains the future character of the kingdom. In the light of the Christ event as the midpoint of history the whole Old Testament history is seen as a preparatory history moving toward this midpoint.[105] This view is especially dominant in the Gospel according to Matthew in which Jesus is depicted fulfilling a multitude of Old Testament promises and carrying a large number of Old Testament messianic titles. However, the history of salvation after this midpoint is described in the New Testament as an unfolding of the Christ event. The first Christian community regarded the Christ event together with its New Testament interpretation as the revelation of the divine plan according to which salvation history will continue to develop up to the end.[106] Of course, the question that interests us at this point is how one can distinguish between salvation history and history in general.

Cullmann is aware that a secular historian would not describe the history of Israel, including the emergence of Christianity, as salvation history but as connected with the histories of other peoples.[107] However, Cullmann claims that salvation history rests on "the *divine selection* of events within the whole of history." It forms a very narrow line which continues on "for the salvation of all mankind, leading ultimately to a funnelling of all history into this line, in other words, a merging of secular history with salvation history." [108] Since all history finally merges into salvation history, Cullmann would find it exciting to show the hidden ways in which, in the light of the biblical revelation, the preparation for salvation was made in the history of the Gentiles and their religions.[109] But Cullmann refrains from attempting a historical proof of the factuality of salvation history, knowing that the events of salvation history are experienced as divine revelation in such a way that God's actions as well as the meaning of his actions can only be grasped through faith.[110] With this concession, Cullmann admits that salvation history does not consist of pure historical facts but of an understanding of these facts which together with their occurrence is attributed to God's self-disclosure.

Wolfhart Pannenberg seems dissatisfied with a view that, in connection with God's saving activity, emphasizes the historical occurrences, while ultimately leaving it up to God's faith-empowering action to make us aware of God's self-disclosure contained in them. Pannenberg does not want to distinguish between a special salvation history and the rest of history because "God's redemptive deed took place within the universal correlative connections of human history and not in a ghetto of redemptive history." [111] Consequently Pannenberg postulates: "In contradistinction to special appearances of the Godhead, revelation in history is open to everyone. It has universal character." [112] The Holy Spirit or faith are not necessary to recognize God's self-disclosure in the events attested to in the Bible.[113] These events have convincing power if they are perceived in their historical context, because then they speak the language of facts and God has disclosed himself in that language.

Yet Pannenberg is aware that the mere acknowledgement of history is not enough.[114] History, and this means especially the history of Jesus, must be grasped as an event that has bearing on one's existence. "*Mere* historical faith, which is satisfied with the establishment that the event happened and does not allow itself to be grasped by this event, thus has precisely not understood aright the inherent meaning of this history, but has diminished it." Pannenberg realizes too that not everyone accepts the Christ event as something that touches one's own existence. Thus he cannot but admit that an illumination is necessary for someone to apprehend psychologically the significance of the Christ event. Nevertheless Pannenberg wants to reserve the term faith for the trust that that which has occurred in proleptic anticipation in the life, destiny, and resurrection of Jesus Christ, namely the end of history and the fulfillment of revelation, will be brought to its final completion. In other words, for Pannenberg faith lies in the trustworthiness of that for which Christ stands, namely God and his future.

Pannenberg has convincingly elaborated the dynamic thrust of the Christ event. He has also pointed out that to recover the meaning of the Christ event one has to perceive it in its historical context, i.e., of Jewish apocalyptic. Yet to recognize that this part of history which started with ancient Israel and culminated in the Christ event is not just a piece of Near Eastern history but the history from which all other history receives its illumination, direction, and judgment, we need more than a rational proof. Notwithstanding his immense effort to show the intelligibility of this history, Pannenberg has to concede that we need illumination to accept this history's decisiveness for our own future. Ultimately it is God's own doing that opens our eyes to perceive the significance of this little piece of history, called salvation history, for the understanding of all other history, including our own.

In mentioning that salvation history, culminating in the Christ event, illuminates, directs, and judges all other history, we do not want to convey the impression that only salvation history is wrought by God. All history is God's history, while salvation history is like a red thread which guides us on our way through history. For instance, when God is introduced as the one for whom nothing is impossible and who determines the course of history, this is not done to impress upon us the notion that the whole of world history runs according to God's preconceived plan, but to express the conviction that God will bring his plan of salvation to completion (Gen. 18:14 and Luke 1:37). The mighty acts of God performed throughout the history of salvation serve as a constant reminder that God is at work in the whole world for the penultimate and ultimate benefit of humanity. They show us that God's plan of salvation will eventually prevail even over the most adverse obstructions.

b. God as the creator of the world

In this context, however, it becomes important that the God who ordains the present course of history is also understood as the one who brought the world and its history into being. Yet "strange as it may seem to us, Israel came to believe that Yahweh was creator of all things only as a kind of corollary to her faith in the God of exodus." [115] Unlike our creeds that start with the belief in God the creator, the first great affirmation of Israel's faith always has been: "Yahweh has freed us from the land of Egypt, from the house of bondage" (cf. Exod. 20:2; Deut. 5:6; 6:21; Ps. 81:10; etc.). Since Israel's faith was founded on God's mighty acts in history, it is only understandable that the belief in God the creator was relegated to second place.

In sharp contrast to the deities who were venerated in the neighboring nations, Yahweh was not a God of nature. The Israelites did not find it necessary to treasure sacred myths for the explanation of the material world. Thus in the Old Testament the doctrine of the creation of the world does not stand on its own, forming the main theme of a passage in its own right. Gerhard von Rad has pointed out very precisely that the doctrine of creation "has always been related to something else, and subordinated to the interests and content of the doctrine of redemption." [116] It is only in the wisdom literature of Israel that we encounter unequivocal, self-justified statements of the belief in creation. Yet when we consider Psalms 33, 74, 136, or 148, we notice that the psalmist does not just dwell on the creation accounts. After rejoicing in the God who spoke and it came to be, who commanded and it stood forth, he immediately connects this with the affirmation: "The Lord brings the counsel of the nations to nought; he frustrates the plans of the peoples. The counsel of the Lord stands for ever, the thoughts of his heart to all generations. Blessed is the nation whose God is the Lord" (Ps. 33:10ff.).

When we come to Deutero-Isaiah, we are confronted with the same phenomenon of the intimate connection between the belief in God the creator and the trust in his power. "At no point in the whole of *Second Isaiah* does the doctrine of creation appear in its own right." [117] In Isaiah 44:24ff., for instance, we hear: "Thus says the Lord, your Redeemer, who formed you from the womb." After further references to the creation the assurance is given that Jerusalem will be inhabited and the cities of Judah will be rebuilt from their ruins. Here the reference to God the creator is used to strengthen the faith of the prophet's audience. If God has created the whole world, it should be easy for him to fulfill his promises concerning the outcome of history.

Yet the belief in God the creator is not simply a cosmic backdrop against which soteriological pronouncements gain in persuasiveness. The creation of the world and the order of nature themselves are in their deepest sense of soteriological significance.[118] This can be seen in the creation Psalms 8, 19, and 104. Here the whole cosmos is understood as a witness to the wisdom and power of God. Of course, one might argue that these Psalms are not originally intended as a witness to Yahweh as the creator (Psalm 19, for instance, in its first part only talks about El) and that they even show influences of Egyptian thinking.[119] But then one might also argue that they seem to be closely related to the Israelite wisdom literature, a category in which we ought to find self-justified statements about God the creator. Wisdom literature especially emphasizes the primal ordering of God in his creative activity. But again we notice that this "cosmic" orderliness witnesses to God's continued activity and reemphasizes the trustworthiness of God's promises.[120] There just is no separation possible between the God of creation and the God of redemption and no actual distinction between God's creative and redemptive activity. Both are seen in continuity with each other. The notion that something went wrong in God's original creation and therefore he had to devise a redemptive plan, is totally foreign to the biblical understanding of God's activity. God's activity can never go wrong so that there is no need to replace his creative activity by his redemptive involvement.

When we now turn to the prime witness to God the creator, the first chapters in Genesis, we must concede at the outset that the Old Testament belief in the creation is only stressed at a later period and only developed into a more prominent element during the period of the later kings.[121] Since all nations in Israel's neighborhood regarded their principal God as creator, it is highly unlikely that the Israelites did not at all refer to Yahweh as the creator prior to the seventh or eighth century B.C. Unfortunately, we cannot prove this with literary documents. But we know that there was a considerable cultural and religious exchange between Israel and its neighbors, and therefore we may assume that the Israelites knew Yahweh also as a creator God. It is also safe to assume that the creation accounts in Genesis, as they now stand, must have been preceded by earlier forms, again dating back beyond the seventh or eighth century B.C.

Yet why did no one arise before the Yahwist, or the even later priestly writer, who went beyond the statements of the creed in Deuteronomy 26:5-9 to add in Genesis 1 and 2 the creation of the world as a prelude to God's salvific activity with his people? We might want to answer by saying that very likely it took Israel such a long time to bring the older traditions about the creation into an appropriate relationship with traditions about God's salvific activity. Then we would have to ask why Israel did not speed up this process? A solution to the whole problem might be found if we remember that no religion prior to 800 to 500 B.C. was more than a tribal religion, including the Israelite religion. Only from that time-span on, which Karl Jaspers called the pivotal age of history, can we trace the emergence of universal religions beyond their original tribal confinements.[122] It was during this time that modern humanity which we now encounter emerged. The growing awareness of the universality of God's activity led to an expansion of history in two ways: history was pushed back to the earliest beginning of history in the creation of the world (Gen. 1f.) and it was expanded to include all nations in God's salvific activity (Isa. 2:2f. or Isa. 49:6). The insight that God created the world is therefore not to be misunderstood as a hypothesis about the prime cause or the prime mover of the world. It is rather the corporate existential confession that the God who is presently at work in the world is no other than the one who brought it into existence and who will bring it to completion.

Looking at the Genesis accounts, especially the priestly account of God's creation of the world, we notice that God's creational activity is divided into the work of specific days. Often people have pondered how long the duration of each of these days was and whether the seven days of creation foreshadow a six-day work week with the seventh day as the sabbath. Attempts have also been made to discover from the genealogies following the creation accounts just how many years have passed since the creation of the world.[123] But these endeavors to derive a scientific chronology of world history from the Genesis accounts and related materials miss the main point of these references. By introducing specific days into the creation accounts and by connecting these events "chronologically" with our history, these accounts were irrevocably exempted from the timeless mythological context from which much of the imagery was borrowed. The creation accounts are no longer stories about gods, such as the Babylonian creation myth *Enuma elish*. These myths left only faint echoes in the priestly creation account.[124] God's creational activity in the beginning, these accounts tell us, did not take place in some kind of pre-history or supra-history. It made history possible and at the same time it is part of the historical process.[125]

The priestly creation account (Gen. 1:1-2:4a) starts with the simple statement: "In the beginning God created the heavens and the earth." Yet this statement is the most difficult one to interpret in the whole account. For instance, we could assume that this verse is a summary of that which in the following verses is unfolded in detail.[126] But would this imply not that God's creative activity was mainly one of subjecting the primordial chaos to orderliness? The priestly account then would be only a variation of the Babylonian creation myth. The creator God Marduk would have been exchanged for the Israelite God (Elohim), but the story would remain the same: [127] Tiamat, the threatening chaos-dragon of the sea and the personification of evil, is slain by the young god Marduk. Out of her slain body he forms the world; one part suffices for the heaven, another for the earth, the waters, and the clouds. He created stations in the sky for the great gods, i.e., the stars, organized the calendar, and caused the moon to shine forth.

Perhaps then the German Assyriologist Friedrich Delitzsch and other representatives of the Pan-Babylonian movement were right when they declared at the beginning of this century that the Israelite antiquity from beginning to end is inextricably connected with Babylonia and Assyria.[128] Therefore it might be better to study the original documents, the mythologies of Babylonia and Assyria than the inferior and later ones of the Old Testament. When Friedrich Delitzsch in his famous lecture in Berlin of January 13, 1902, on "Bible and Babel" advocated such thinking, he caught many by surprise. Even the German Emperor Wilhelm II cautioned that theologians should not disturb the believers by announcing premature results of their research. Though the claims of the Pan-Babylonists were certainly mistaken, especially when they labeled the Old Testament ethics as pre- and sub-Christian, it is now commonly accepted that the priestly creation account bears some resemblance to the Babylonian creation myth.

But a careful comparison between the priestly account and the Babylonian creation myth shows significant differences between the two. We have already noticed one important difference: the priestly account is part of history and no longer a timeless myth. The Hebrew verb for "created" in the opening verse of the priestly account is *bara*, a word used exclusively to denote a divine creative activity. We find it again in Genesis 1:21; 1:27 (twice); 2:3 and 2:4, in the priestly account. It is also used seventeen times by Deutero-Isaiah, who speaks of creation in the context of God's salvific activity, and at several other places in the Old Testament. Instructive are the uses in Exodus 34:10 and Numbers 16:30, because in both instances *bara* is used to indicate God's miraculous and mighty activity in history.[129] *Bara* is therefore a divine creative activity that has no analogy in the works of humanity. It is only God himself who can create, and he creates with extreme ease. For instance, the "deep" *(tehom)* over which the Spirit of God hovered bears only remote resemblance to the mythological chaos-dragon Tiamat. There is no struggle between two cosmic principles, God and the deep. Tehom has no power of its own, it is only mentioned because the creative will of God is above it.[130]

When we come to the actual creative process, we notice that a brief assertion of Yahweh's will suffices to bring the world into being. Contrary to the creation myths outside Israel, God is so high above everything else that he has no need to struggle to carry through his creative will. God says and so it is, is the thoroughgoing conviction of the priestly writer. Only in poetic language do we hear about Leviathan or Rahab, that God overcomes (Job 26:12; 41:1).[131] Yet even there a struggle is not implied; it is God's mighty word that makes a difference.[132]

If God created the world through his word, any understanding of the world as an emanation of the godhead, or a self-manifestation of the divine being or its powers, is excluded. The only continuity between God and his creation is his word. But it would be wrong to assume that God and the world are separated. God created the world; it is his own property and he is its Lord. The image of potter and clay (Jer. 18:1-6) serves as a constant reminder that the one who rules over history is also the one who rules over nature. He brings forth both and destines their courses.

In an almost ironic way we hear that "God called the light Day and the darkness he called Night" (Gen. 1:5). After separating light from the threatening darkness he gives each its proper name. Therewith he declares them to be under his authority. The same course is followed with the heavens, the earth, and the sea. When we come to the sun, the moon, and the stars the procedure is somewhat different. God simply made them and told sun and moon to rule over day and night respectively. Remembering the elevated status that the heavens, earth, sea, light, darkness, and the sidereal elements enjoyed in neighboring religions, we understand how revolutionary these

statements were. The elements of nature were robbed of the divine
power they possessed in these religions, because the Israelites understood that God had created the heavens and the earth and all that
is within it. God's creational acts are accompanied with the statement
"and God saw that it was good" (Gen. 1:4, 10, 12, 18, 21, 25) and
at the end the assertion is given again that everything he had made
was very good (Gen. 1:31). It is also mentioned that God finished
the work he had done. There was no unfinished business, not something that by accident just did not get done. Everything was very
good. This means that the created world is endowed with God's
approval. It is God's good world.

When we now take a brief look at the Yahwistic creation account
(Gen. 2:4b-25) we notice at once a much more modest scope than
the one provided by the priestly writer.[133] Not the threatening waters
of the sea but the waterless desert is presupposed here. It will become
the cultured land which we are supposed to till and to keep (Gen.
2:15). Only our immediate environment is described here. But again
it is God who made the earth and the heavens and who gives the
life-giving water. Unlike in the priestly account, in which everything
is leading up to the creation of the human race, here everything is
created around humanity so that it may feel at home in God's creation. We would not be wrong in talking about the Yahwistic account
as an anthropocentric view, in the appreciative sense of the word, of
God's creation. Unlike the deductive priestly account that almost
provides a bird's-eye view of God's creational activity, the Yahwist
represents the view of people who can say: "Look around you. God
has made all this just for you."

The important question that we have so far avoided is posed to
us by the opening verse of the priestly account and again by the
beginning of the Yahwistic account, namely: Does the assertion that
God created heaven and earth imply that God created the world out
of nothingness? Evidently the Genesis accounts do not explicitly state
that God started with nothing when he began to create the world.
They simply say that he started to create heaven and earth. Of course,
then they would leave open a possibility for the gnostic notion that
"there was once a 'Nothing' out of which God created the world, a
negative primal beginning, a Platonic *mê on*, a formlessness, a chaos,
a primal Darkness." [134] While Genesis 1:1 seems to contradict the
idea that a formless, watery, nocturnal, and abysmal chaos was present when God started to create heaven and earth, it is also difficult
to assume that he would have first created such a chaos out of which

he created everything. Perhaps the mentioning of this chaos, *tehom*, should be seen in line with the mentioning of the other entities, such as light, darkness, heaven, earth, sea, etc., that were customarily divinized in the neighboring religions. Chaos must serve God's purpose, namely that order arises, the ordered creation of the world.

The biblical writers no longer understand chaos as something to be afraid of, because the world is the Lord's and all that is therein. Of course, this does not answer our question of a creation out of nothingness and it cannot answer it. Here we encounter the limits of the biblical creation accounts. They were written in the language of their time, using the cosmological knowledge of that time. Though it has often been attempted, one cannot abstract from this cosmological knowledge and arrive at pure theological insights.[135] None of the statements in the Genesis accounts are just theological, and therefore still relevant, or just scientific, according to the knowledge of that time, and therefore outdated. They are statements of faith expressed in the then available conceptual tools. Understandably but unfortunately these tools do not convey our modern scientific insight that matter can either exist in an ordered or in a disordered state. Matter in disorder (chaos) and in a state in which one thing was not clearly distinct from any other thing was regarded by ancient people as not yet created.[136] When the world (for us: ordered matter) was created this meant for the priestly writer and the Israelite at his time that it was logically, but not chronologically (!) created out of chaos (for us: disordered matter). A similar understanding is portrayed by the Yahwist, with the difference that in his account the dry barren ground is substituted for the chaos of Genesis 1.

For us today it is only proper to regard creation out of nothingness as "the classical formula which expresses the relation between God and the world." [137] Contrary to process thought there is no "given" for God that influences him in his creative power or that resists his creative intentions. The affirmation of a creation out of nothingness also guards us against the temptation to identify God and the world as in pantheism. Creation was not a necessity for God, as Hegel thought, and it was also not an accident as one might assume from the findings of paleontology. The first event in history, as the Genesis accounts assert, was the movement from nonbeing to being.[138] Once being is assumed the scientific theories concerning the development of the universe have their proper testing ground.

If we want to rephrase the beginnings of the creation accounts into presently available and tenable scientific conceptuality, we should follow the persuasive suggestion of William Pollard and say: "When God began to create a universe, there was nothing; no space, no time, no matter; nothing at all. Then there was a black hole, shrouded in impenetrable mystery. Out of this black hole came an expanding space-time universe, initially a vast fireball filled with light, neutrons, protons, electrons, and anti-neutrinos, all governed by defined physical laws" (personal communication). Of course, as scientific insights progress, details of such a rephrased beginning of the creation accounts will be subject to constant revisions. Yet the basic theological intention of such statements will remain unchanged, whether they were formulated by the Yahwist, the priestly writer, or by us. They want to express the conviction that God is the author of all that is and that without him nothing would be. One might wonder, however, whether such theological intentions might not at times run counter to scientific evidence. Though clashes between theology and the sciences have often occurred, they are unnecessary if each discipline remembers its own limits. By their very definition the sciences confine themselves to assertions about variations within the space-time and matter/energy continuum, while theology goes one step further by reflecting also on how this continuum was brought into existence and to whom it owes its structure.

None of the scientific theories we have reviewed, moves beyond the confines of being; they simply try to delineate the development of being within the world itself. But theology cannot remain completely disinterested in these scientific discoveries. The reason for this is that the creation accounts do not just tell us that God brought the world into being, but also make statements concerning the arrangement of that which was brought into being. Admittedly, they do not want to rival a scientific study of the developmental process. But they want to be taken seriously when they point out the existence of an ontological and historical development within the world, the appearance of different levels of being, and the continuous struggle in the history of humanity. Since creation is understood here in the context of salvation, the evolutionary process which is described by science would be understood as part of the overarching historical-ontological process through which God is working out his salvific purpose.

This is also the proper place at which we can appreciate Teilhard's cosmo-historical view of the world by which he attempts to conceive as a basic unity the natural history of the world and God's salvation history. Similarly, we must be sympathetic to the Marxist notion of a unity between matter and Spirit. While agreeing with the Marxists that matter and Spirit move in the same direction, we cannot side with them in their attempt to merge both into a unitary system. The biblical witnesses caution us that it is exactly the prevalence of the Spirit which gives matter its momentum and significance. We are also able to historicize the concept of the Great Chain of Being as denoting the unity of all created being (but not of God and the created world, as originally understood) and the unity of all history.

In talking about God as the creator of the world, we cannot confine ourselves to the Old Testament. If it is true that creation is part of God's salvific activity, we should find ample evidence for this in the New Testament. Indeed mention of God's creation is made in the New Testament in two significant ways. First we hear that God created the world. Similar to *bara* in the Old Testament, the New Testament reserves *ktizein* (to create) as the special word through which God's creative activity is expressed.[139] Secondly, the mentioning of God as the creator of heaven and earth in the New Testament usually affirms a point only loosely connected with this doctrine, but is not intended to provide cosmological theories about origin and structure of the world. For instance, in the statement that "in those days there will be such tribulation as has not been from the beginning of the creation which God created until now, and never will be" (Mark 13:19), the reference to creation underscores the seriousness of the impending apocalyptic woes.

While the New Testament writers generally affirm the Old Testament tradition concerning the creation,[140] they become more precise at two points. First, it is now explicitly stated that God created "all things" (Eph. 3:9). In Colossians 1:16 too we hear that "all things were created, in heaven and on earth, visible and invisible, whether thrones or dominions or principalities or authorities." God is the one who "calls into existence the things that do not exist" (Rom. 4:17). These assertions leave no doubt that creation is not an emanation of the godhead or a creation out of some kind of primordial (chaotic) matter. Any metaphysical dualism is excluded here, a dualism perhaps between a creator god and a redeemer god, such as in Gnosticism, or between a primordial darkness and the god of light. Creation is strictly creation out of nothingness. Second, the New Testament authors become more explicit about the word through which God created everything. While Paul, for instance, reaffirms the Old Testament understanding that God created through his word (2 Cor. 4:6), he also mentions that the world is created and sustained through Christ (1 Cor. 8:6).[141] It is through his son, we hear in the opening sentence of the Letter to the Hebrews, that God created the world (Heb. 1:2).

When we come to the Gospel of John we have a very significant identification of the creative word *(logos)* with Christ. Already the first words take us by surprise, because the "in the beginning" of the Gospel of John is an exact translation of the opening words of the priestly creation account.[142] This *logos*, the Gospel of John tells us, was in the beginning; it was with God and it was God. It is the mediator of creation, the giver of life, and this word is Christ. Does this mean that the New Testament finally succumbed to the temptation of rabbinic writers to advocate a world reason or a semi-divine *logos* through whom the world was created? If that were true, we would witness a Hellenization of the biblical creation accounts, and Plato's idea of a world soul would no longer be completely foreign to biblical thinking. Though terminological affinities to speculative writings cannot be denied, the New Testament is not interested in such speculations.[143] Not even the idea of a primordial emanation of the *logos* or of a primal begetting could be justified.

While in Proverbs 8:22 wisdom says of itself: "The Lord created me at the beginning of his work, the first of his acts of old," the Gospel of John confesses: "In the beginning *was* the Word." [144] The word is already pre-existent, it needed not be created in a first act of creation. The word is identified with God though, but it is not identical with him. Both assertions, the word was with God and the word was God, must be equally emphasized. It is now understood that the creative word of God is not just his word, it is Jesus Christ, his son. The one God acts through himself as the father or through himself as the son, and it is through the son that he was created and does sustain everything. Christ therefore is God's life-giving word. This leads us to the other important point in the New Testament understanding of creation.

God did not just create the world, he is also creating the world anew. We hear Paul say that "if any one is in Christ, he is a new creation; the old has passed away, behold, the new has come" (2 Cor. 5:17). Christ therefore is not only the mediator of the creation in the beginning, he is also the one who brings about the completion of creation, or the new creation. This new creation is already present in those who claim Christ on their side, because through his resurrection Christ himself was the first born of the new creation. The whole creation therefore is longing and waiting for the eschatological fulfillment, when the creation "will be set free from its bondage to decay and obtain the glorious liberty of the children of God" (Rom. 8:21).

We have completed the course from the creation in the beginning to its eschatological fulfillment in the new creation. We have discovered that the history of nature and the history of God's salvific activity form an inseparable unity. The history of nature provides the object matter for God's salvific activity. Once we have experienced God and his activity we can perceive that nature is telling the glory of God and the universe proclaims his handiwork (cf. Ps. 19:1). On the other hand God's salvific activity provides nature with continuity, coherence, and purpose. Coming from the Christian understanding of creation both the evolutionary process and world history are not the result of blind chance. They are the result of God's creative and redemptive will. Yet how can we talk in a full sense about creation, unless we also consider humanity whom the priestly writer introduces as the apex of creation, and for whom, as the Yahwistic writer says, all creation was provided?

3. Humanity in the Light of God's Creation

In our attempt to understand humanity in the light of God's creation there are many facets on which we could dwell. We could mention our peculiar openness to the world, pointed out by Konrad Lorenz and others and theologically interpreted by Wolfhart Pannenberg as implying an openness for God. We could mention our dialogical structure, emphasized by Martin Buber, through which we become persons in being confronted with a thou. Again this has been interpreted as reflecting a relationship with God. Since we want to consider humanity in the light of God's creation, however, our relationship with God is already presupposed. Now it becomes important how we can best express this relationship. There seem to be two facets most prominent, simple though they may be. The one is the insight that humans are creatures and not the creator. The other is the acknowledgement that humans have a preferred place in God's creation as God's administrator.

a. Humans as creatures

The priestly writer devotes four verses in his creation account to the relationship between God and humans. Three times we hear in Genesis 1:27 that God *created* humanity, as if to emphasize that

humans are definitely creatures of God, not more and not less. However, it is almost frightening to watch how closely humans are associated with the animals.[145] No special day of creation is reserved for
humans. They are created on the same day as the land animals. Like
the fish and the birds, they are blessed and given the command to
be fruitful and multiply. They are even supposed to share with the
land animals the same food. The Hebrew word *adam* that is used to
denote a human being is a collective word, meaning actually humankind.[146] To insure that it is not misunderstood as depicting some
kind of archetypal primal androgynous being, the immediate qualifi-
cation is added that God created "them" male and female. The
sexual differentiation therefore is something given with creation.[147]
Humans are not created in solitary existence, but they are called to
be the thou of each other. The full meaning of being human cannot
be realized in an individualistic existence, it can only be realized in
the encounter between man and woman. This does not imply a glorification of the sexual nature of humanity, because sexuality is only
its nature and not its achievement. It is given from God and wants
to be used as a gift and not as a means of self-glorification.

When we turn to the Yahwistic creation account we notice again
our total dependence on God. While humans are cared for in many
ways, they have no life of their own. "The Lord God formed man of
the dust from the ground, and breathed into his nostrils the breath
of life; and man became a living being" is one of the classical insights
of Old Testament anthropology.[148] In reading this verse we might
first assume that a body-soul distinction is introduced here. We know,
however, that such a distinction is foreign to biblical thinking. A
human being is conceived of as a unity. What makes this verse so
peculiar is the intimate connection between *adam* (man) and *adamah*
(earth). Humans are made of dust. "You are dust, and to dust you
shall return" (Gen. 3:19), we hear again toward the end of the
temptation story. Humans and nature form a unity. Humans are taken
from nature and go back to nature. In analogy to the priestly writer,
the Yahwist does not say that God simply commanded the earth to
bring forth humans, as he did with the other living creatures. God
breathes life into a human being and it becomes a living being.
Human life cannot be taken for granted; it is a gift of God. We
receive our human existence through participation in God's life-
giving spirit. Perhaps today when we are wondering whether the
human family will survive the threatening signs of environmental
pollution, overpopulation, and scarcity of natural resources, this

insight into the character of human life as a gift assumes renewed importance. But it is not just the life of the human family in general that is understood as a gift from God.

The creator of the human family is at the same time creator of each individual human being (cf. Isa. 17:7).[149] About God's creative activity the psalmist confesses: "Thou didst form my inward parts, thou didst knit me together in my mother's womb. I praise thee, for thou art fearful and wonderful. Wonderful are thy works" (Ps. 139:13f.). Similarly we read in the Book of Job:

> Thy hands fashioned and made me; and now thou dost turn about and destroy me. Remember that thou hast made me of clay; and wilt thou turn me to dust again? Didst thou not pour me out like milk and curdle me like cheese? Thou didst clothe me with skin and flesh, and knit me together with bones and sinews. Thou hast granted me life and steadfast love and thy care has preserved my spirit.   Job 10:8-12

Though the writer knows about the procreative process, that the semen is ejected into the female organism and the solid embryonic body is formed ("Didst thou not pour me out like milk and curdle me like cheese?"), this whole process is at the same time understood as a work solely wrought by God. It is beyond the imagination of the Old Testament writers that nature should do its part and then let God do the rest.[150]

Luther captured the biblical understanding of the dependence of human life on God very well when he said: God "could easily create children without man and woman. But he does not want to do it. He joins together man and wife that it seems as if man and wife would do it, but nevertheless he does it hidden under such masks." [151] Each human being is totally God's work regardless of his or her line of descent. The question whether life evolved "naturally" (unaided) from inanimate matter, though scientifically very significant, is theologically secondary. Both inanimate nature and the living creatures are God's creation. Whenever and wherever human life appears, it is a gift of God.

But let us return to the Yahwistic creation story. Humanity's creaturely position is not only indicated by the Yahwist when he mentions that humans are taken from dust and created through the life-giving spirit of God. The reddish brown skin of the Israelites reminds him of the reddish brown dust of the earth. It is also emphasized when he points out humanity's close relationship with the animals.

Like humans they are created from dust and we find it almost embarrassing that animals are created as "a helper fit for him" (Gen. 2:18). Yet the idea that humans and animals could be on equal level is rejected, since we hear that the animals are brought to Adam so that he could name them and exercise authority over them.

When we come to the creation of the woman, we notice that God's creative activity does not tolerate any spectators. Adam falls in a deep sleep when Eve, the mother of all living, is created. We are only allowed to view God's creation retrospectively.[152] Though Eve is created last, she is not an afterthought; she is the final touch in God's original creation. It may sound strange for us that Eve is taken from a rib of Adam. Originally this figurative speech may have arisen from the observation that most of the human body is enclosed with ribs except for part of the abdomen. But for the Yahwist this image has taken on different meaning. It affirms that Eve is not on the level of the animals; she is not taken from dust. She is from the same kind of "material" as Adam. Man *(ish)* notices this immediately and calls her woman *(isha,* similar to the Old English meaning of woman, female man). Again we cannot escape the notion that man and woman belong together, they are created for each other.[153]

Then comes the interesting statement in the Yahwistic account that "a man leaves his father and his mother and cleaves to his wife, and they become one flesh" (Gen. 2:24). Contrary to Israelite custom and perhaps reflecting an earlier matriarchal culture, it is the man who leaves his family, not the woman. But this statement no longer describes a custom, it now describes a natural drive. Woman is taken from man, they were once one flesh and therefore their natural drive is again to attain this unity.

In concluding our brief survey we must admit that many differences in detail nothwithstanding, both the priestly writer and the Yahwist are unanimous in emphasizing humans as creatures, creatures in immediate vicinity of the animals, but created distinctively different from the animal world and created in a basic twofoldness of man and woman. When we now consider the biblical understanding of humans as God's administrators we will again notice that the human position has to be guarded against two temptations, to reduce a human being to the highest developed animal, or to elevate it to the position of God.

b. *Humans as God's administrators*

We cannot talk about the biblical understanding of humanity without attempting to clarify the meaning of being created in the image of God. The human position as God's administrator seems to stem from the claim that humans were created in the image of God. "Let us make man in our image, after our likeness," commences the priestly account of the creation of humanity and then it concludes: "So God created man in his own image, in the image of God he created him" (Gen. 1:27). This plural form "let us make" suggests that perhaps even the priestly writer felt uncomfortable with the daring statement that God created humans in his own image.[154] Thus the plural form implies that humans are created in the image of both God and all the heavenly beings associated with God. This sentiment coincides with the observation in one of the creation psalms that God has made humanity "little less than God" (Ps. 8:5). Again with reference to God and his heavenly court, Elohim, the plural form for God, is used (the notion of a heavenly court is not uncommon in the Old Testament; cf. Job 1 and Isa. 6). But what does it mean that humans are created in the image of God?

Passages such as Genesis 3:22, 1 Samuel 29:9, and 2 Samuel 14:17-20 indicate that God and his heavenly court are considered blameless and with knowledge of the difference between good and evil.[155] But the assertion that humans are created in the image of God does not refer just to the ability of a human being for moral decision, or to the dignity of humanity, or to our personality. Yet it also does not mean that humans are a replica of God, though this thought might be inferred. Moreover, the priestly writer is not especially interested in defining what the image of God entails, but rather emphasizes the purpose for which it is given. As soon as God decides to create humans, he destines them to have a special relationship with the animals that were created before them. They are to have dominion over the animals. Similarly, the Yahwistic writer, who does not mention humans being created in the image of God, knows that God conferred upon humanity certain responsibilities (Gen. 2:15-17) and that God wants humanity to make certain decisions regarding the creation (Gen. 2:19f.; cf. the significance of naming somebody or something). Humans are therewith placed in a special position within God's creation. Being called to have dominion over the animals, to subdue the earth, to till the garden, and to name the animals, also implies that humans are confronted with the creator. It is God who has called them to do these things and created the animals and the world.

Perhaps we can even determine more clearly in which respect humans ought to function in God's image, when we consider the

Near Eastern custom of setting up images of earthly rulers.[156] In the ancient Near East the erection of a picture or a statue of a king always indicated that the area in which the replica of a king was erected was the domain of the king who ruled over it (Dan. 3:1-6). If humans are introduced into God's creation as being created in the image of God or as God's image, this could then mean in analogy to this ancient practice of erecting symbols of authority that humanity exercises and symbolizes God's dominion over the world. Humanity's dominion over the world reminds everyone that God is in control of creation and also reminds us that we exercise this dominion on God's behalf.

One might wonder what kind of people can fulfill the demand to have authority over God's creation. Do the creation accounts envision absolute rulers who have a special gift for exercising authority? The answer is surprising when we consider that the dominion aspect is always connected with the plural "let them have dominion" (Gen. 1:26, 28). The focus is not upon a charismatic leader, but upon the human community.[157] Each one of us is asked to act as God's administrator. That the administration of God's creation is not delegated to exceptional people is reaffirmed by the psalmist. For instance, in Psalm 8 he rejoices that God has given us dominion over the works of his hands. But then he continues by asking: "What is man that thou art mindful of him" (Ps. 8:4). It is not an inherent quality coming to expression in exceptional people that justifies the insight of humans being made in the image of God. It is simply God's will that wants us to be his administrators.

It is significant for our understanding of the human position that the statement: "So God created man in his own image, in the image of God he created him" is immediately followed in the creation accounts by the remark: "male and female he created them." Neither the strong physical power of a man nor the reproductive faculty of a woman better resembles the human position of being created in God's image. It is only man and woman together, representing the human community, who exercise the privilege and obligation which this position entails. Very appropriately Gerhard von Rad observes: "The idea of man, according to P [priestly writer], finds its full meaning not in the male alone but in man and woman." [158] This would mean that neither a man nor a woman can obtain his or her full personhood without the other partner. It would be wrong, however, to understand this as an emphasis on sexuality or the procreative power. God's blessing upon man and woman and his command to be fruitful and multiply is referred to in a separate word. It is not given simultaneously with humanity's creation in God's image and with its creation as male and female. The procreative faculty is not a consequence of being created in the image of God; it is a gift of God to be used responsibly. Emil Brunner is right when he observes that the statement: "So God created man in his own image, in the image of God created he him; male and female created he them," is such a simple assertion "that we hardly realize that with it a vast world of myth and Gnostic speculation, of cynicism and asceticism, of the deification of sexuality and fear of sex completely disappears." [159]

Most animals seek out their sexual partners only for copulation and the procreative process, and after the young ones mature the "marriage" is dissolved. Humans, however, live always in the context of sexual differentiation. Once they reach their adult stage, they are never oblivious of their sexual status. We have noticed that some behavioral psychologists emphasize that the peculiarity of this differentiation is not just a biological and physiological differentiation, but one that finds expression in the spiritual and attitudinal realm. Cultural imprinting can reinforce this differentiation by relegating most men and women to clearly defined occupational and behavioral patterns, or it can seek to obliterate the differentiation by attempting to overcome them. Attempts to reinforce this differentiation often segregate men and women and therefore make the realization of full personhood through mutual interdependence more difficult. Tendencies to obliterate the differentiation regard men and women not as equal but as identical and consequently bereave man and woman of the mutual enrichment through which they become fully human. While efforts to reinforce the sexual differentiation are often associated with a so-called male-dominated culture, tendencies to obliterate the differentiation are sometimes associated with the so-called women's liberation movement. This movement, however, is much too multi-faceted to arrive at such a simple equation; to some extent it is only a countermovement to a so-called male-dominated culture.[160]

We have seen that the insight that humans are created in God's image can only be realized in the mutuality of the man-woman encounter. When they jointly approach their own being and the world that surrounds them, they can best exercise the dominion to which they are called. Yet there are certain phenomena that can raise doubts whether humans are actually fit to be God's administrators. First of all, one must ask whether the understanding that humans were created in the image of God does not overestimate their potential.[161] It may be true that humans can discern between good and evil, yet knowledge and will, reflection and action seem to go separate ways. The Old Testament history is a history of human disobedience, a history that seems to belie the assumption that humans were created in God's image.

When we consider today's scene, the validity of humans created in God's image primarily to have dominion over the earth becomes even more questionable. We are confronted with threatening or actual overpopulation in many parts of the world, with the rapid depletion of our natural resources, with a tremendous ecological imbalance. Knowing these facts, how can we still take seriously that we should be "fruitful and multiply, and fill the earth and subdue it"? Many responsible people today claim emphatically that our number one problem is a comprehensive and total population control. However, the priestly writer seems to demand the exact opposite. Furthermore, discerning people point out that, because of the tendency in the Genesis accounts to elevate humans above the rest of creation, humans have understood themselves as pitted over against nature. Lynn White, for instance, observes:

> Especially in its Western form, Christianity is the most anthropocentric religion the world has seen . . . Man shares, in great measure, God's transcendence of nature. Christianity, in absolute contrast to ancient paganism and Asia's religions (except, perhaps, Zoroastrianism), not only established a dualism of man and nature but also insisted that it is God's will that man exploit nature for his proper ends.[162]

We could, of course, attempt to argue that Christianity or the Israelite religion are no longer very influential in today's "post-Christian" world. Lynn White, however, rightly counters that our daily habits of action

> are dominated by an implicit faith in perpetual progress which was unknown either to Greco-Roman antiquity or to the Orient. It is rooted in, and is indefensible apart from, Judeo-Christian teleology. The fact that Communists share it merely helps to show what can be demonstrated on many other grounds; that Marxism, like Islam, is a Judeo-Christian heresy.[163]

When we remember that the understanding of God the creator finds its larger context in God as the author of history, we realize that humanity's creation in the image of God implies that humans are both historical and history-making beings. The ethical optimism, derived from the biblical understanding that humans are created in the image of God, therefore today finds its continuity in an historical optimism that history will continuously evolve and will necessarily evolve toward the better. The basically optimistic assessment of the human potential that we have observed in both Eastern Communism and Western capitalism largely evolved within and emerged from the Judeo-Christian context. Can we therefore blame Arnold Toynbee when he claims:

> If I am right in my diagnosis of mankind's present-day distress, the remedy lies in reverting from the *Weltanschauung* of monotheism to the *Weltanschauung* of pantheism, which is older and was once universal. The plight in which post-Industrial-Revolution man has now landed himself is one more demonstration that man is not the master of his environment—not even when supposedly armed with a warrant, issued by a supposedly unique and omnipotent God with a human-like personality, delegating to man plenipotentiary powers. Nature is now demonstrating to us that she does not recognize the validity of this alleged warrant, and she is warning us that, if man insists on trying to execute it, he will commit this outrage on nature at his peril.[164]

Lynn White, Arnold Toynbee, and others demand that we abandon our preferred position and perceive ourselves as fully integrated into the context of nature. The Great Chain of Being flowing from the highest to the lowest members of the universe would then be whole again. While we agree fully with the diagnosis of the problem—our exploitative and self-glorifying attitude—we must disagree with the proposed solution which advances a pantheistic world view and therefore a divinization of nature, plus our integration into the context of nature.

We must conclude from the fundamental interrelatedness between animate and inanimate nature that solipsistic beings cannot sustain themselves. We are doomed if we would try to live as if we were gods created in our own image. Yet today's problems cannot be solved if we go to the other extreme and resign ourselves to the natural. Our existence is vitally related to nature and its structures, which allow for our existence. But behavioral psychologists rightly warn us that our instinctive drives are not strong enough to dominate our behavior and to guide us in our complex industrial society. Since we are humans, we are reasonable beings and we are no longer fundamentally natural (instinct driven) beings. Here we must remember Hegel's reminder to link the eternal with the accidental in our thinking. There is something eternal that comes to expression in us. The Old Testament refers to the same phenomenon when it tells us that we receive our existence as human beings through participation in God's life-giving spirit. It would be wrong to limit the Spirit only to its animating function. It is also the spirit of all wisdom and truth to whom both the Old and the New Testament attest.[165] Since we depend with our whole existence on the participation in the Spirit, the Old Testament rightly understood humanity as theomorphic, created in God's image.[166] This means that the cause for today's uncertainty and bewilderment lies in abandoning our position as being created in the image of God. Therefore we weakened our participation in God's spirit both in terms of right judgment and full participation in (divine) life.

At this point the biblical understanding of humans as persons becomes crucial.[167] Persons live in conformity to God and as his representatives. This notion evolved to the characteristic Judeo-Christian and therewith Western idea of freedom to govern the world and to regulate the affairs of society and interhuman relationships. Freedom, however, was not to mean "do as you please." It carries with it the obligation to exercise dominion in accordance with God's life-giving spirit to further that which is good, true, and beautiful, and help to alleviate and eliminate that which is distorted and self-centered.

Since we always obtain meaning of our existence through the object matter whom we serve,[168] there are basically two possibilities for us to acquire such meaning: (1) If we serve God as his administrators, our existence gains meaning from God and our actions are done to glorify God. Glorification of God through overpopulation (Gen. 1:28 says: "fill the earth," it does not say "overpopulate it." This is the point at which the command to multiply has its limits.), exploitation of natural resources, and universal pollution is self-contradictory. Our experience of God as a caring and loving God, however, becomes normative for the way in which we as his administrators should be experienced by others. Being created in God's image would then call for a life style of authority yet in humility, of determination yet with compassion, of faithfulness yet in dignity.

(2) If we, however, serve as our own administrators, our existence must gain meaning from ourselves, and our actions are done to glorify

ourselves. We must perform heroic deeds, continuously triumphant over nature and over our own kind. We are then pitted against nature or against other people for short-term gains. Solitary humanity, as it emerges more and more today, may serve as a warning of the consequences if we abandon our position as God's administrators. Neglecting our responsibility to foster and cultivate God's creation, we consider it our own dominion and destroy its natural context. Erosion, climatic changes, overpopulation with certain animals and epidemics for humans, animals, and plants are some of the consequences. Attempting to gain the world for our own, we are about to lose it.[169]

Summary

In this chapter we finally made explicit reference to God to further elucidate the meaning of the structures of human existence. Thereby we noticed five significant points:

(1) Scientific inquiry attempts to explain the development of the world, and our own status within it, by referring to processes within the world. More and more specificity and particularity is achieved through this endeavor. Since our world is finite, however, scientific description lacks ultimacy and universality. Theological reflection on the structures of human existence accepts the scientific discoveries and at the same time interprets them in the light of God's ultimate and universal activity. This procedure endows the structures of existence with wholeness and lasting meaning.

(2) To attain a significant relationship between God and the world in which we live, God must be intrinsically present in us and in our world. At the same time he must transcend us and our world and be prior to them. But he must also be mindful of the world and us without being dependent on them in his actions.

(3) The Judeo-Christian tradition witnesses to a God who is the maker of history and the creator of the world. Both activities are intimately related to each other. Creation points primarily to the initiation of the primordial beginning of the universe and the ushering in of its ultimate fulfillment, while the maker of history stands for the God who is actively involved in the ongoing process to assure its final conclusion.

(4) We humans are God's creatures and administrators. We are part of the creative process and at the same time responsible for its appropriate execution. Since the creative process itself has no ultimate

reality, we are free to shape the world according to its and our inner-most possibilities. The direction for our involvement can be gained from the acknowledgment of God's spirit who is behind and within the creative process to assure its continuity and coherence.

(5) Our inquiry into the structures of human existence should suffice to illuminate our journey through space and time according to its origin, its present course, and its future possibilities. However, their life-enabling character is continuously threatened by our violations. Therefore, we must inquire whether our predicament is so grave that chaos impends or whether God's providential care and his inauguration of a new creation will finally prevail.

While we gradually seem to realize that we are on a dangerously self-destructive course, the question must be asked to what degree we can still alter the course. In other words, we must find out what the cause and extent of our sinful actions are and whether anything can be corrected.

PART II

OUR JOURNEY: BETWEEN CHAOS AND PROVIDENCE

At the conclusion of the last chapter we realized how difficult it is to analyze the structures of human existence without immediately referring to human sinfulness. But we did not want too quickly to label humanity as sinful and in need of God's grace. The reference to humanity's sinful nature is too frequently used as an excuse for maintaining the *status quo*. Since God is the one from whom all good things proceed, humanity in its sinful nature is also often misunderstood as an entity that does no longer belong to God's domain.

We have traced the human origin in the context of the animate and inanimate world, we have investigated the uniqueness of humanity and its potential for further development, and have emphasized the necessity for understanding humans as being created in God's image. Now it is equally important to discover the possible destination of our cosmic journey. We must see what humanity is doing with and in its unique position and how God responds to its doings. Thus we want to investigate first the relationship between the human predicament and the cause of evil. Then we will turn to the manifold dimensions of human sinfulness and finally we will see how the human condition is still one under God's response and care.

5.

The Human Predicament
and the Cause of Evil

The frequent calls for law and order indicate that our secular society is certainly aware that humanity is in turmoil. Yet to label this state as sinful would not solve anything, as Karl Menninger rightly observed, because the term sin and the meaning connected with it have largely disappeared in our society.[1] Words such as bad, wicked, immoral, and sinful have almost been eliminated from everyday vocabulary. With the rise of psychoanalysis these terms have often been understood as symptoms pointing to underlying causes that are void of moral quality.[2] Even the terms Satan or the demonic that are again becoming increasingly popular, are hardly associated with the cause of evil. There are at most bewildering and threatening phenomena largely connected with obscure and esoteric enterprises. If we want to fathom the dimension of the human predicament, however, we cannot neglect the issue of the cause of evil.

While we may have difficulty convincing most people that they are sinners, they nevertheless readily admit that the world is an evil place. The French existentialist philosopher Jean-Paul Sartre once said: "Hell is—other people!" [3] The human predicament is that we are tortured by others, those with whom we are forced to live. The evil character of the world is also documented by the system of law and order that each human community has developed. Each of these systems is a tacit admission that we do not conduct our lives the way we should. Thus laws and orders become necessary to guide us in the right direction. If we disobey, we will be punished or re-educated.

Even religious cults, from the most primitive to the most advanced, imply that humans are acting differently from the way they should.[4] Religious exercises are usually conducted to compensate spirits or God(s) for human wrongdoings. Often humans understand that they cannot even attain compensation or that they cannot redeem themselves from their wrong conduct. Thus other forces, stronger than humanity, have to intervene and save the human beings from the evil in which they entangled themselves. The very notion of salvation implies the assumption that we ought to behave differently. Wherever we look, whether in the secular or in the sacred sphere, we are confronted with the notion that the human predicament is not what it ought to be. This sentiment is largely shared by psychoanalysis.

1. The Psychoanalytic View of the Human Predicament

SIGMUND FREUD, the founder of modern depth psychology, espoused a very interesting and influential view of the human predicament. In a nutshell his view is contained in a statement concerning the interpretation of dreams:

> The ethical narcissism of humanity should rest content with the knowledge that the fact of distortion in dreams, as well as the existence of anxiety dreams and punishment dreams, afford just as clear evidence of his moral nature as dream-interpretation gives of the existence and strength of his evil nature.[5]

Human behavior is determined by the sexual behavior which is ambivalently both good and evil. While at first Freud distinguished primarily between the conscious and the subconscious in humanity, he soon realized that this differentiation was too simple. So he further distinguished between the *ego* and the phenomenon of conscience.[6] Through his research into self-punishment and the impact of World War I, Freud also introduced a death drive into his system. According to Freud this drive resists the lifegiving power of the *eros*.[7] Thus the manifoldness of the psychic life was reduced to two energies, the drives of love and of death which are regulated and emerge from three different authorities, *ego, id,* and *superego* (while the dualistic theory of the death instinct and the eros instinct is developed in *Beyond the Pleasure Principle,* this theory is coupled with the theory of three agencies—ego, id, and superego—in *The Ego and the Id*).

The ground of all psychic life is the id which consists mainly of chaotic and subconscious drives. Prominent among them is the procreative drive or the libido. But in all assertions of life the libido is mixed with the desire for death which has as its goal regaining the inanimate stage. In its origin and development the libido is intimately connected with the body, advancing from the oral stage (suckling) to the anal stage (control of bladder and bowel movement, both together called the pre-genital phase), and the oedipal stage (death wish against the father and incest wish with the mother).[8] Connected with the libido is the ominous power of a death instinct. This death instinct is directed primarily against humanity itself.

If humans do not want to destroy themselves, they have to direct the death instinct to the outside in the form of aggression or destruction. Freud states: "It really seems as though it is necessary for us to destroy some other thing or person in order not to destroy ourselves, in order to guard against the impulsion to self-destruction." [9] Yet it would be wrong to label the desire for death as something completely negative. Together with the libido it serves life in aiding the eros to dominate the objects of its pleasure and therewith helps us to attain control over nature. But it can always erupt in its naked power as aggression and destruction and endanger the culture made possible through the libido. Freud confesses that "in consequence of this primary mutual hostility of human beings, civilized society is perpetually threatened with disintegration." [10]

Freud is aware that most people do not like the idea that there is an instinct of death or destruction in humans.

> For 'little children do not like it' when there is talk of the inborn human inclination to 'badness,' to aggressiveness, and destructiveness, and so to cruelty as well. God has made them in the image of His own perfection; nobody wants to be reminded how hard it is to reconcile the undeniable existence of evil . . . with His all-powerfulness or His all-goodness.[11]

Referring to Goethe's Mephistopheles, Freud comments: "The Devil himself names as his adversary, not what is holy and good, but Nature's power to create, to multiply life—that is, Eros." [12] According to Freud all life essentially consists of this struggle between the instinct of destruction and the instinct of life as it works itself out in the human species.

So far we have restricted our observations of these instincts for life and for death to the id. But we also have to reckon with the ego. The ego emerges from the id as that part of the id which is turned to the external world. It functions in such a way that it recognizes internal and external stimuli, arranges them in sequence, and initiates reactions to these stimuli. Thus the task of the ego can be described as that of a mediator. This does not exclude that it also pursues its own interests as Freud admits when he says: Even when the desire for death "emerges without any sexual purpose, in the blindest fury of destructiveness, we cannot fail to recognize that the satisfaction of the instinct is accompanied by an extraordinarily high degree of narcissistic enjoyment, owing to its presenting the ego with a fulfillment of the latter's old wishes for omnipotence." [13] But the ego must also represent the demands of the outside world to the id. The corrective function of the ego is aided by the superego.

The superego originates through internalizing external authority by identifying with it. It is of special importance for humans as social beings. According to Freud, ideals and laws of a society are nothing but a collective superego.[14] The superego of the individual is formed through education by the collective superego and becomes the "vehicle of tradition and of all the time-resisting judgments of value which have propagated themselves in this manner from generation to generation." [15] The superego ties families and societies together when one submits one's own interests to those of one's parents and of society. Again we discover that the superego also has its negative side. It can assume cruel and demonic features which drive one into neurosis, melancholy, and even death. The "conscience" of the superego can lead to guilt or to aggression, and even to suicide.

In whatever direction we look, we observe that humanity always struggles to find its way between life and death, between preserving and creating life, and destroying it. We cannot escape the conclusion that Freud presents a definitely dualistic view of humanity, torn "between the life and death instincts." [16] Yet it is not only individuals in whom these drives appear. Even culture is torn between life and death.[17] But Freud widens the scope of perception even more when he says:

> And now, I think, the meaning of the evolution of civilization is no longer obscure to us. It must present the struggle between Eros and Death, between the instinct of life and the instinct of destruction, as it works itself out in the human species. This struggle is what all life essentially consists of,

and the evolution of civilization may therefore be simply
described as the struggle for life of the human species.[18]

If this dichotomy is so all-pervading, we may conclude that it is
impossible for us "to transcend the limits of the human condition or
to change the psychological structural conditions that make humanity
possible." [19]

CARL GUSTAF JUNG, one-time collaborator with Freud, soon abandoned Freud's sex-dominated theory of the human predicament in
favor of a more comprehensive one. Jung distinguishes between the
conscious and unconscious parts of the human psyche. The conscious
is turned toward the outside world and has its center in the ego. The
unconscious is divided into two distinct realms, the personal and the
collective unconscious. The personal unconscious contains the forgotten, the suppressed, and the unconsciously noticed, thought, and
felt, provided such things are in close relationship to the experiences
of the individuum.[20] The collective unconscious consists of the collective memory of the human family, such as situations of common
human nature, namely situations of anxiety and danger, battles
against an overwhelming majority, relationships between the sexes,
attitudes toward father and mother figures, the experience of the
powers of light and darkness, etc.[21]

Jung discovered the collective unconscious in working with patients
whose dreams contained picture motifs that were unrelated to any
concrete life experience of the patients.[22] These motifs, however, were
related to religious symbols which were consciously unknown to the
patients. He found further manifestations of the collective unknown
in religious rites, dogmas, and symbols, and in myths and fairy tales.
Jung called the power-laden picture motifs of the collective unconscious archetypes. "The archetype is, so to speak, an 'eternal' presence, and it is only a question of whether it is perceived by consciousness or not." [23] Similar to Freud's id, the archetypes have a peculiar
twofold aspect. According to Jung this already shows in the picture
of the snake in Genesis 3 when the snake becomes either the symbol
of the tempter or the symbol of the savior. Similarly, the great mother
can be the threatening *tiamat* or Mary, the saving queen of heaven.
The father image again is split between the violent, castrating demon
and the benevolent sage leading the way to the realm of the spirit.

Unlike Freud, Jung does not dwell almost exclusively on the negative side of the collective subconscious but emphasizes its positive

powers giving new impulses to life.[24] While in the collective unconscious the oppositions are still undistinguished, the situation is different when the *ego* emerges and things become conscious. Then the
paradise of the original unity and wholeness is irrevocably lost. Therefore Jung finds that "there is deep doctrine in the legend of the fall:
it is the expression of a dim presentiment that the emancipation of
ego-consciousness was a Luciferian deed." [25] Seeking to obtain discerning knowledge, the ego encounters irreconcilable opposition and
is torn between opposing forces, such as spirit and matter, male and
female, good and evil, life and death. Though we cannot return to the
primordial oneness, we can overcome it through individuation. This
means we become "a single, homogeneous being, and, insofar as
'individuality' embraces our innermost, last, and incomparable uniqueness, it also implies becoming one's own self." [26] Individuation therefore is equated with "coming to selfhood" or "self-realization." This
process of individuation is guided by, what Jung calls, the archetype
of the "self." Man now comes both to himself and to the collective,
because in his wholeness he also reflects the cosmos. "The individu-
ated ego senses itself as the object of an unknown and superordinate
subject." [27] Does this mean that eventually we arrive at a point at
which the dichotomy is overcome so that ego consciousness ceases?

If we want to determine the extent to which we can achieve wholeness, we must follow Jung one step further in his analysis of the
person, because he distinguishes from the ego another aspect which
is directed to the external world and which he calls *persona*. The
persona functions analogously to a mask in Greek theater, because
we play our role in society through it and it filters out everything that
one does not do in a given role. Everything that the ego considers
irreconcilable with its persona is relegated into the unconscious as a
"shadow." [28] Thus the shadow contains the undeveloped, the inferior,
the suppressed and therefore wild drives, the amoral, the evil, and
the destructive. Jung now calls for an integration of the shadow as
part of the individuation process, because "mere suppression of the
shadow is as little of a remedy as beheading would be for headache." [29]
We should rather love our shadow in analogy to the way Jesus called
us to love our enemies.[30] Similarly the way God integrates his own
shadow, evil, into a quaternity, we are summoned to overcome moral
suffering through integration of our shadow.[31] Of course Jung makes
it clear that we cannot overcome evil by ourselves. "We are dependent
here on higher powers," since the attempt of self-redemption is of
no avail for humanity.[32]

It is evident that Jung goes beyond Freud's dualistic picture of humanity, in which Freud portrayed a persistent dichotomy between good and evil in human beings. Jung acknowledges that there are evil traits in us and beyond us, at times even beyond reconciliation. But Jung insists that ultimately they serve the good. This is most evident when Jung suggests that evil, as the shadow of God, is taken up into the trinity, making it a quaternity. As we will see later, the biblical witnesses usually neither suggest the strikingly dualistic view of Freud, nor are they so optimistic as to suggest that evil will ultimately be absorbed into the godhead.

When we now mention briefly ERICH FROMM, we notice in him a compassionate concern with the unfolding of life,[33] deeply informed by the psychoanalysis of Freud and Jung, and by evolutionary thought. Fromm claims that "the growing process of the emergence of the individual from his original ties, a process which we may call 'individuation,' seems to have reached its peak in modern history in the centuries between the Reformation and the present." [34] Of course, the beginning of modernity did not cause all the problems, it only magnified them, because humanity's very existence poses a problem.[35]

While animals are guided by instinctive behavior, living completely within nature, humans lack this instinctive mechanism. Though living in nature, at the same time they transcend it, and are aware of themselves. In posing themselves over against nature they have lost their unity and feel unbearably alone, lost, and powerless. The same process can be discerned in the development of an individual human being. At first it feels at one with its environment, but gradually it becomes more and more aware of its individuality. "On the one side of the growing process of individuation is the growth of self-strength," but the other aspect is "growing aloneness." [36] Human existence implies "freedom from instinctual determination of his actions" and therefore the condition of human culture. The bothersome fact, however, is that both sides of the development, growing strength and growing individuation have not been exactly balanced. Consequently the history of humanity is one of conflict and strife and "each step in the direction of growing individuation threatened people with new insecurities." Since man is aware of himself, Fromm states, he "realizes his powerlessness and the limitations of his existence. He visualizes his own end: death." [37] Yet we cannot go back to the prehuman state of harmony with nature.

Fromm claims that a human being "must proceed to develop his reason until he becomes the master of nature, and of himself." [38] But can a human being really accomplish this? Fromm seems to give a partial answer when he admits that the short span of life does not permit humans to realize fully all their potentialities "under even the most favorable conditions." [39] Furthermore, instead of responding to their freedom with dedication and work in solidarity with nature, humans often attempt to get rid of their freedom either in sadistic domination or in masochistic submission of the object to which they are supposed to relate, or they even attempt to remove it through destructiveness.[40] But then Fromm reminds us that "the intensity of destructive strivings by no means implies that they are invincible or even dominant." [41]

Evil is a specifically human phenomenon for Fromm. He sees it expressed in the "syndrome of decay," consisting of love of death, narcissism, and symbiotic incestuous fixation. It prompts people to destroy for the sake of destruction and hate for the sake of hate. This syndrome of decay, which always symbolizes regression, is countered by the syndrome of growth, symbolizing progression, and expresses itself in love of life, love of humanity, and independence.

While Fromm admits that a human heart can harden and that it can become inhuman, he insists that it never can become nonhuman. "It always remains man's heart." [42] Even people like Hitler's or Stalin's officials, he insists, began their lives with the chance of becoming good people. Human nature or essence is neither good nor evil, we hear, though there is a contradiction rooted in the very condition of human existence. This conflict requires a solution and basically there are only two solutions possible, to regress or to progress. Even if these solutions create new contradictions, a human being should be able to resolve its dilemma either regressively or progressively. In the struggle between love for life (biophilia) and love for death (necrophilia) neither of the two is ever present in its pure form (saintliness or insanity). In most cases there is a particular blend of both forms of love and our mind set depends on which of the two is dominant. Of course, for Fromm the issue of which form will eventually dominate is largely solved, because unlike Freud, he claims that there is an inherent quality to life in all living substance. Thus he labels the "death instinct" "a *malignant* phenomenon which grows and takes over to the extent to which the Eros does not unfold."

The dichotomy in humanity, which Freud sensed, is changed for Fromm to a potential for life. Does this mean that Fromm does not assume a radical evil in humans or even outside of them? Fromm does not give a direct answer but instead insists on a "rational faith in man's capacity to extricate himself from what seems the fatal web of circumstances that he has created." [43] Confronted with potential human self-destruction and denying any metaphysical reference point, Fromm's daring faith in the unthinkable, namely in a progressive affirmation of reason and love among all people, is perhaps the only alternative lest we end up in despair.[44] But is such an attitude still *rational* faith?

2. Biblical View of the Cause of Evil

We have noticed a deep awareness of evil in the psychoanalytic view of the human predicament. Evil pervades human existence as an omnipresent actuality (Freud) or at least an ever present potentiality (Fromm). The cause of evil, however, is not something that is superimposed upon humanity, making us mere victims of outside forces. The cause of evil is inherent in the structure of human existence. This sentiment is largely shared by the Bible, though with some significant modifications.

To discover the biblical view of the cause of evil, we want to turn first to the Old Testament. Then we will survey extra-biblical and intertestamental materials in order to determine the possible extent of outside influence on the biblical sources. Finally we will venture to assess the New Testament outlook on the cause of evil.

a. Old Testament sources

When we consider the Old Testament understanding of the cause of evil our attention is immediately focused on the account of the fall in Genesis 3, a passage conspicuously isolated from the rest of the Old Testament.[45] The story of the fall is not picked up by the psalmist, the prophets, or any other writer in the Old Testament.[46] But we dare not treat it as if it expresses an isolated incident. It forms part of humanity's history and therefore it is only natural to perceive it in its context as the first link of a whole sequence of sinful events. It is immediately followed by the story of Cain slaying his brother, by the vindictive attitude of Lamech (Gen. 4), the marriage between the sons of God and the daughters of humans (Gen. 6), the flood (Gen. 6-9), and finally the construction of the tower of Babel (Gen. 11).[47]

The event depicted in Genesis 3, however, is not just one among many. It is the first sinful event occurring to the first woman and to the first man, whose name, Adam, is understood as a proper name in the latter part of Genesis 3. By talking about Adam as a specific man, the Yahwist wants to show the exemplary character of this event. The sin committed in Genesis 3 is not simply a violation of God's command not to eat from the tree of the knowledge of good and evil. Rather the distrust of God is at the center of the fall account. While the condition depicted in the Yahwistic creation account is characterized by innocence, "a pure childlike relationship with God, a life also reflected in the relationship between man and woman," the harmony between God and human beings is now broken.[48] The intention of connecting creation and fall so intimately is not to show how the once good creation got so bad. Even after the fall the world, including humanity, is still God's good creation. But the Yahwist wants to demonstrate the reason for our present human predicament.

It has often been claimed that the disruption of the initial harmony is actually beneficial because it leads to the actualization of the human potential. Hegel, for instance, understands sin as the logical necessity to recognize the good, since if man "does not know about evil, he also does not know about good." [49] He characterized the fall "as the eternal myth of man through which he becomes man." The German philosopher Friedrich Schiller thought along similar lines and concluded that the alleged disobedience against God's command, was actually

> the fall of man from his instinct, which brought moral evil into creation, but only to enable the moral good within creation. Therefore without doubt it is the happiest and greatest event in human history. From this moment onward his freedom is inscribed, here the first and remote foundation was laid for his morality.[50]

This idealistic notion of human sinfulness is affirmed by many psychoanalysts. For instance, 175 years after Schiller, Erich Fromm claimed: "This first act of disobedience is man's first step toward freedom." Man was expelled from paradise and is now able "to make his own history, to develop his human powers, and to attain a new harmony with man and nature as a fully developed individual instead of the former harmony in which he was *not yet* an individual." [51] Carl Gustav Jung was a little more restrained when he wrote: "There is deep doctrine in the legend of the fall: it is the expression of a dim presentiment that the emancipation of the ego-consciousness was a Luciferian deed." [52] Pursuing a different perspective, Teilhard de Chardin also came close to this idealistic notion when he asserted that evil is a necessary byproduct of evolution through which in manifold errors and trials nature progresses on its evolutionary course.[53]

The idealistic interpretations of the fall argue on the basis of an evolutionary process, in which a later stage of the process is perceived as more highly developed and therefore better. There are two objections, however, that have to be voiced. First, it is difficult to assert on strictly biological grounds that an evolutionary development toward a higher stage is necessarily better. Biologically speaking, humans are not better than fish though humanity represents a higher evolutionary development of life. The same case can be made for the cultural development of humanity. A highly developed culture is not necessarily better than a primitive one, even if one judges "better" here by moral standards. Secondly, while the account of the fall is not incompatible with evolutionary theories, it is not amenable to any kind of evolutionary interpretation. This becomes evident in two ways.

First, the eruption of sinfulness in Genesis 3 cannot be deduced by causal inference from God's good creation.[54] When Adam is questioned by God about his behavior he tries such a causal inference, saying: "The woman whom thou gavest to be with me, she gave me fruit of the tree, and I ate" (Gen. 3:12). In other words, he wants to excuse himself by blaming the cause of evil on God. The woman tries a similar causal inference, though not as daring, when she replies to God: "The serpent beguiled me, and I ate" (Gen. 3:13). Again the excuse is made that the cause of evil comes from outside. Yet none of these attempts suffices before God to account for the gravity of the situation. Secondly, there is also no causal connection between this first sin and the emergence of subsequent sins. We concede that the Yahwist demonstrates in the chapters following the account of the fall that evil spread like a forest fire. But he does not mention anywhere that the emergence of new sin is connected with prior sin and thus can be used to excuse the significance of each case.

Evil came into the world with the first appearance of man and woman and it continued to erupt with every further appearance of man and woman. It is important to remember here what behavioral psychology has told us about the phenomenon of aggression. In many ways aggressive drives are present already on the animal level. Yet there they are usually displayed to help and further the species instead of destroying it. This is true for aggression activated against other species (defense, hunting, etc.) as well as within the own species (rank and order, mating, etc.). However, once humanity emerged and began to dominate its environment and members of its own kind through the introduction of more and more sophisticated tools (and weapons), the aggressive drives became increasingly ambivalent. At the same time they furthered the potential good and the potential evil. Thus extinction of some species and domestication of others, genocide of parts of humanity and unification of others through large-scale cultures went hand in hand. As psychoanalysis rightly tells us, the activities of humanity are highly ambivalent, pursuing life and spreading death at the same time.

But the emergence of evil cannot be compared with a fateful decree against which humanity has no choice. We should not overlook the fact that not a human being but the serpent is introduced as the tempter in the fall account. Yet it is an overinterpretation of the temptation story to conclude that the woman has more immediate access to the dark sides of life than man because she is seduced first and in turn seduces.[55] What is emphasized, however, is that the essence of human beings was not sinful from the beginning, but that temptation had to come from the outside. But the cause of evil is not an anti-Godly principle outside of God's creation, such as in Gnostic thought. We remember that the serpent is explicitly introduced as an animal and as part of God's creation, and not as part of the heavenly court.[56] Why this part of God's good creation becomes the tempter is beyond the interest of the Yahwist, since the solution of this question does not contribute anything to the description of human sinfulness. There are two items, however, that still need clarification: What was the object that tempted humans and what were the consequences for them once they succumbed to sin?

The first couple was tempted to be like God, knowing good and evil. It is difficult to assume that God had created a creature which is to become his potential challenger, since man "carries potential Godhead within himself." [57] While it is also absurd for the Yahwist to surmise that anybody could be like Yahweh, it is much easier for him to suggest that a human being wanted to become like the *elohim,* that it wanted to become divine.[58] When humanity was tempted to know good and evil, it was not just tempted to know the distinction between good and evil, but also to know everything, from good to evil.[59] Human temptation was then, and still is, to know everything and to know it better. This attitude challenged any kind of harmonious relationship and should not be confused with the emergence of humanity's inquisitive spirit. It is rather humanity's destructive desire to disallow for any "thous" who have their own sphere, and to treat them as "its" who have no secrets. This human hubris effectively destroyed humanity's relationship with God.

However, God did not respond to humanity's sinful pride like an insulted tyrant. Admittedly, the harmonious unity with God was gone, and the couple was sent forth from the garden. But the threat that the day they eat from the tree of knowledge of good and evil they would die (Gen. 2:17), was not actualized once they had sinned. They were only reassured that they would return to dust from which they were taken (Gen. 2:7; 3:19). Almost as if in defiance to the original threat Adam now dares to call his wife Eve, i.e., the mother of all living.[60] Not even the obligation to work can be understood as the actual curse of the fall (Gen. 2:15). However, once the harmonious relationship with God was broken, the harmonious relationship between humanity and nature, and between man and woman had disappeared too. Life now, confesses the Yahwist, is drudgery, filled with hatred and passion, and longing for harmony. Yet life does not come to an end, because "the Lord God made for Adam and for his wife garments of skins, and clothed them" (Gen. 3:21). Instead of lamenting evil, the Yahwist points to signs of grace that are given to the first couple on their wanderings through life, the coat of skins and God's help in clothing them.[61] This compassionate act of God could be much more likely understood as the first sign of the gospel, than the verdict that there will be constant animosity between the snake and humanity.[62]

When we leave the Genesis account of the fall in order to determine the cause of evil according to other Old Testament sources, our task becomes even more difficult.[63] In Amos, for instance, we hear Yahweh asking his people: "Does evil befall a city, unless the Lord has done it?" (Amos 3:6). After disaster has struck Job he responds to his wife in similar fashion saying: "Shall we receive good at the hand of God, and shall we not receive evil?" (Job 2:10). In Deutero-Isaiah the bewildering question if God might be the cause of evil seems to be resolved in the affirmative when we hear God speak: "I form light and create darkness, I make weal and create woe, I am the Lord, who does all these things" (Isa. 45:7). From other sources we even hear that God can stir up people against each other (1 Sam. 26:19).

God is the only God, he knows good and evil, and everything depends on him. But then we also hear that there is a spirit of evil, distinguished from the spirit of Yahweh, that torments people (1 Sam. 16:14f.). This does not impair the understanding that God is the only power in control, because it is he who sends the evil spirit.[64] Of course, if the Israelites would have attributed good and evil to Yahweh simply to insure a monotheistic notion of God, we might rightly talk about a demonic God from whose evil acts one could never be safe. We recognize, however, that God's actions always intend to make his kingdom triumph, or in other words, to advance his salvific plan. Thus the psalmist is right when he says: "For his anger is but for a moment, and his favor is for a lifetime" (Ps. 30:5). This becomes especially clear when we consider the function of the accuser (Satan) in its historic context.

The word Satan could be used in the Old Testament simply to denote someone as an adversary. For instance, the commanders of the Philistines were afraid that David might become an adversary (Satan) to them (1 Sam. 29:4).[65] Often the adversaries are the enemies of Israel and accuse Israel in the name of Yahweh, pointing to the evil that Israel has accumulated (1 Kings 11:14).[66] The ancient passage of Balaam and his ass shows us that Satan can also denote a heavenly being, someone part of God's court. Since Balaam unknowingly does something against the will of God, God becomes his adversary and obstructs his way, hindering Balaam from carrying out his own will (Num. 22:22ff.).[67]

In the Book of Job the function of Satan as the accuser rises to prominence. According to the first chapters, Satan, as a member of God's heavenly court, questions whether Job really is as blameless and upright as he appears to be. Since Satan is not understood as a demonic power, but one of the sons of God, he needs God's permission to test Job's goodness.[68] Thus the assumption still is valid that ultimately God is the one who tests Job. It would be difficult though to see Satan functioning here as an accuser in strict analogy to human court procedures. There are too many life-threatening forces applied against Job, such as disease, death, plundering, and the devastating forces of nature. The "causing of evil," however, is done in agreement with God, and not "behind God's back" as it happens with the tempting function of the serpent in the fall story. But we cannot escape the impression that here Satan appears as a heavenly foe of peaceful life and worldly comfort.[69] The result of his activity is not destruction, as one might expect. Job reaches a deeper piety and completely surrenders himself to God.

In the fourth vision of the prophet Zechariah the accusing function of Satan becomes most striking. He is no longer introduced as one of the sons of God, but simply as the accuser standing at the right side of Joshua, the accused high priest, while both appear before the angel of the Lord (Zech. 3:1ff.). Satan still attempts to uncover the evil side of humanity, the misdoings of the high priest during the exile. But it is no longer evident that his intentions result in furthering God's kingdom, because God intervenes through the angel to show mercy and forgiveness to the high priest (Zech. 3:4).[70]

When we finally come to 1 Chronicles 21, the independence of Satan has grown even further than in the passages so far reviewed.[71] This is the only instance in the Old Testament in which Satan is referred to as a proper name. For instance, we read in 2 Samuel 24:1: "Again the anger of the Lord was kindled against Israel, and he incited David against them, saying: 'Go, number Israel and Judah.' " The chronicler, however, reports the same incident by saying: "Satan stood up against Israel, and incited David to number Israel" (1 Chron. 21:1). When we turn from the Old Testament to the New, however, a similar change can be found in the image of the wrathful God as "a roaring lion" (cf. Hos. 11:10), which in the New Testament is applied to the image of the devil (cf. 1 Peter 5:8). Evidently in the days of the chronicler the idea appeared offensive that God should incite David to sin. In both versions, however, Chronicles and Samuel, we read that God ordered punishment for David's sin. Satan is nowhere elevated to the position of a dualistic counterpart to God, with God being then restricted to serve as the principle of good. Ultimately even this Satanic temptation serves the salvific plan of God. Because of God's punishment David's royal power is decimated and he is more open than ever for God's will.

From our brief survey we can detect that initially God was indiscriminately understood as the source of both good and evil. However, there was a growing tendency to restrict God's involvement with the cause of evil to the act of punishing humanity for its wrongdoings. This meant that the cause for humanity's evil doings had to be found outside God, first in the temptation through someone of God's good creation, then in the image of a heavenly accuser, and finally in the growingly independent status of a (the) pernicious Satan. We have difficulty agreeing with Kluger in his otherwise very instructive book when he says that "the figure of Satan represents the result of a process of development within the divine personality itself." [72] Not the divine personality underwent a developmental change, but the Israelite understanding of God was gradually clarified. This process is reflected in God's ongoing self-disclosure, culminating in God's full self-disclosure in Jesus Christ. While this process of clarification is reinforced in the New Testament, we must remember one decisive point: Regardless to whom the cause of evil is attributed in a particular incident, the Old Testament unanimously agrees that the existence of an evil tempter outside humanity does not diminish humanity's accountability for its own actions. Even when temptation appears to be irresistible, the human responsibility for its actions remains unchanged.[73] We can see this very plainly even in the chronicler's version of David's temptation when David confesses: "Was it not I who gave the command to number the people? It is I who have sinned and done very wickedly" (1 Chron. 21:17).

b. Extra-biblical and intertestamental materials

Before we pursue the New Testament understanding of the cause of evil we should at least mention briefly the relationship of the Old Testament understanding of Satan to extra-biblical and intertestamental materials. Since the prime references to Satan (Zech. 3:1; Job 1f.) do not appear until the early post-exilic era,[74] it might well be that Babylonian and Iranian influences shaped Israel's understanding of Satan. Indeed there is a close parallel between the biblical Book of Job and the so-called Babylonian Job or the "Poem of the Righteous Sufferer." [75] This poem tells about a pursuer who inflicts diseases upon a righteous man. While this Babylonian pursuer or demon of sickness bears resemblance to the disease-inflicting functions of Satan, we remember that this is just one feature of Satan in the Book of Job. Furthermore, the Babylonian demon of sickness is opposed and finally overcome by the good god, while we hear in the Book of Job that Satan acts with God's permission. Thus the Babylonian righteous man ascribes his suffering to the adversary, while Job ascribes his condition to God. While we recognize definite textual parallels between the Babylonian and the biblical narratives, we notice that their theological implications are diametrically opposed at decisive points.

There is another interesting way in which Babylonia becomes important for our understanding of Satan. When Satan's actions are described in the Old Testament, they often resemble the divine court procedures recorded in Babylonia. According to Babylonian mythology the relationship between God and the people runs like the ordinary court procedures. God is judge and the people are the seeker for justice. In these procedures between God and the people an accuser appears. He is a royal official, traveling around the country and representing "the Eyes of the King." [76] However, the concept of "Eyes of the King" is also known in Media, Persia, and Egypt. If this

imagery was so widely used, we need not be surprised that we find
its traces in the accuser function of Satan in Job 1f., and in Zechariah 3:1ff.

Of much greater significance than these Babylonian parallels is the
influence of Zoroaster's teachings on the Old Testament understanding of Satan.[77] In the center of Zoroaster's or Zarathustra's teachings
is Ahura Mazda, the one supreme god, who governs the whole development of the world (Yasna 31:8). Since Zarathustra excludes anything evil in his understanding of Ahura Mazda, he only refers to him
indirectly as the father of twin gods, Ahra Mainyu (evil spirit) and
Spenta Mainyu (holy spirit) (Yasna 30:3f.).[78] The original monotheism is thus paired with a strict dualism. Actually Ahra Mainyu is
not an equal opponent of Ahura Mazda, because he is only a spirit
of Ahura Mazda, and has Spenta Mainyu as his direct opponent. But
the strict dualism is weakened, since behind Spenta Mainyu is the
supreme God himself who is one with Spenta Mainyu (Yasna 47:1).
Yet the twin spirits created the world, Spenta Mainyu being responsible for life and Ahra Mainyu for non-life. Each of them has his own
following, with Ahra Mainyu being identified with the lie, betrayal,
death, sin, and evil. When we ask, however, where does evil come
from, we cannot avoid the conclusion that Ahura Mazda is also the
father of the evil spirit. Thus Ahura Mazda contains in himself the
inclination towards both good and evil.[79]

We cannot but be struck with the similarity between some of
Zoroaster's teachings and the gradual realization of the Israelites that
the cause of evil has to be excluded from their understanding of
God and therefore must be attributed to causes outside God. We
will also notice that some of the characteristics associated with Ahra
Mainyu gain prominence in the New Testament understanding of
Satan. Having discovered, however, the emphasis that the Old Testament places on God as both maker of history and creator of the
world, and the careful attention that it gives to Satan as part of God's
ultimate domain, we must recognize the fundamental difference between the thoroughgoing Old Testament monotheism and the basically
cosmic-ethical dualism of Zarathustra.[80] Unlike Zoroaster the Old
Testament writers never dared to imply that Yahweh was the father
of Satan. While it was essential for the Israelites to assert that Yahweh
was the Lord of history, they had no interest in seeking to establish
a causal connection between God and Satan. That does, however, not
diminish the strong possibility of the catalytic influence of Zoroastrian-

ism upon the Judeo-Christian tradition through which its understanding of Satan was furthered and clarified.

In the intertestamental period, which in many ways prepares the stage for the New Testament message, Satan is commonly understood as the one who wants to destroy the relationship between God and humanity, and especially between God and his people.[81] In some ways, however, Satan functions still very much in analogy to Satan in the Old Testament. The *Similitudes of Enoch,* for instance, tell us that a number of Satans are ruled by Satan (1 Enoch 53:3). They usually have access into heaven and are able to appear before the Lord of the Spirits (1 Enoch 40:7). Their function is threefold:

(1) they accuse people before God (40:7);

(2) they tempt people to do evil (69:6);

(3) they act as angels of punishment (53:3; 56:1).

Satans are also seen responsible for the fall of the sons of God and their intermarriage with the daughters of humans (1 Enoch 69:4f.). In 1 Enoch 6 we are told that 200 angels, one of their leaders being Azazel (8:1), intermarried with the daughters of humans. In the *Book of Jubilees* we read then that these evil spirits "do all manner of wrong and sin, and all manner of transgression, to corrupt and destroy, and to shed blood upon the earth" (Jub. 11:5). So Noah prays that God will imprison the malignant spirits and hold them fast in the place of condemnation (10:5). We notice that sin is traced here to the fall of angels and to their progeny.[82]

At other places, we hear that while humanity is responsible for its own sins, sin can be traced back to Adam's fall (Apocalypse of Abraham 23 and 26).[83] Yet the fall, whether of the angels or of Adam, is not the cause of sin, but is only its historical origin. This is clearly expressed in 2 Baruch 54:15, 19:

> For though Adam first sinned and brought untimely death upon all, yet of those who were born from him each one of them has prepared for his own soul torment to come, and again each one of them has chosen for himself glories to come. . . . Adam is therefore not the cause, save only of his own soul, but each of us has been the Adam of his own soul.

While it is mentioned here that through Adam's fall physical death came into the world, an understanding that is taken up by Paul in the New Testament, the fall is not yet seen as the cause of spiritual death (this latter idea is only occasionally expressed in the intertestamental period, cf. 2 Bar. 48:42f., 4 Ezra 3:21). At times Adam is understood as the cause of perdition of the whole human race. But there is never a clear connection between Adam's sin and the sin of his descendants.[84] We read, for instance, in 4 Ezra:

> For the first Adam, clothing himself with the evil heart, transgressed and was overcome; and likewise also all who were born of him. Thus the infirmity became inveterate; the Law indeed was in the heart of the people, but (in conjunction) with the evil germ; so what was good departed, and the evil remained.   4 Ezra 3:21f.

This means that the free will of humanity is significantly weakened after the fall.[85]

The main tenor of the intertestamental period, however, is expressed in the admonition: "Know, therefore, my children, that two spirits wait upon man—the spirit of truth and the spirit of deceit" (Test. Judah 20:1). Humanity then must choose between light and darkness, between the Law of the Lord and the works of Beliar (Test. Levi 19:1). In the Qumran writings the command for a personal decision takes on cosmic dimensions. World history is perceived as a battle between light and darkness.[86] There is no neutral ground between the sons of light and the sons of darkness who fight in this world for their ultimate victory. But humanity does not become a tool in the struggle between the two "spirits." It receives its destiny from the hands of God. In the intertestamental period Satan, Beliar, Mastema, or Azazel, as the evil one is called, is understood as raging against God and rivaling his dignity.[87] Being confronted with a time of immense political and spiritual crises, the perspective of the intertestamental writers was certainly appropriate. But they did not simply surrender the world to an indefinite dualistic struggle. They still held God to be in control. Through the catalytic influence of Zoroaster's Parsism they were able to understand an antagonistic world and its history without compromising their Israelite faith in God. They arrived at a dynamic ethical dualism, the basis for which had already been laid in the Old Testament. This "modified dualism," as W. F. Albright calls it, deeply influenced Christianity.[88]

c. The New Testament outlook

The New Testament understanding of Satan is characterized by the absolute and irreconcilable opposition between God and Satan and the presence of the kingdom of God in Jesus Christ.[89] Jesus' whole mission can be understood as a continuous confrontation with

Satan.[90] This does not mean that Satan is mentioned on every page of the New Testament. Yet Satan appears at the decisive points in the life and destiny of Jesus, at the beginning of his ministry in the story of the temptation (Mark 1:12f.), and at the end of his ministry through the betrayal of Judas Iscariot (Luke 22:3). The story of Beelzebul (Mark 3:22-27) indicates that the whole demonic realm is understood as being under the control and supervision of Satan. Whenever Jesus casts out demons it is a manifestation of the greater work of casting out Satan.[91] This leads us to the peculiarly ambiguous position of Satan.

On the one hand the synoptic writers tell us that Satan has as his goal the total destruction of humanity and especially the destruction of Jesus of Nazareth as the bringer of the salvific reign of God.[92] Satan is the author of all kinds of life-impairing diseases (Luke 13:16) so that Jesus' healing ministry in turn is described as "healing all that were oppressed by the devil" (Acts 10:38). Satan, the enemy, is also the one who plants his seeds in the midst of the "sons of the kingdom" (Matt. 13:38) and he attempts through Peter to invalidate Jesus' ministry (Matt. 16:23). While the significance of the destructive power of Satan cannot be underestimated, the New Testament writers refute the idea that every personal calamity is due to some corresponding personal sin (cf. Luke 13:1-3). Satan is certainly the one who causes evil in the world. But the New Testament writers are not interested in establishing a causal connection between one's sinfulness and subsequent "punishment" through diseases or other kinds of punishment, as was popularly believed among the people of their time. The New Testament writers are much more interested in pointing out the salvational purpose of these evil occurrences.[93]

The New Testament writers tell us not only of the destructive powers of Satan, but they tell us also of his defeat through Jesus Christ. In the story of Beelzebul (Mark 3:27) it is clearly expressed that Satan has found his victor and it is reaffirmed with each subsequent deed of Jesus, concluding in his sacrificial death (1 Cor. 15:57). Satan still wants to accuse people before God, but Jesus intercedes for them so that their faith "may not fail" (Luke 22:32). Satan has even lost his preferred position and access to heaven, because as Jesus affirms: "I saw Satan fall like lightning from heaven" (Luke 10:18).[94] This coincides with the observation in the book of Revelation that "the accuser of our brethren has been thrown down, who accuses them day and night before our God" (Rev. 12:10). Since Satan is overcome we are not surprised that the disciples are promised that they can "tread upon serpents," which means that they have authority over the seductive anti-Godly powers of evil (Luke 10:19).

As we can see from the New Testament epistles, once Jesus was no longer physically present Satan is still active, attempting to destroy the growing Christian community. Jesus himself taught his disciples in the Lord's Prayer to pray that they might not be overcome by the evil one.[95] Satan attempts to render void the labor of the apostles through his temptations (1 Thess. 3:5). He persecutes the Christians (1 Peter 5:8f.), he disguises himself as an angel of light to seduce people through wrong teachings (2 Cor. 11:14), and Paul can even say that some of the delays in his missionary journeys are due to the influence of Satan (1 Thess. 2:18). The anti-Godly activity of Satan climaxes in the advent of the anti-Christ who will proclaim himself to be God (2 Thess. 2:3-9). Then Satan's aspiration, told in the apocalyptic book *Life of Adam and Eve,* that he will set "his seat above the stars of heaven and will be like the Highest" would come true (15:3). Though the Christians should not take Satan lightly, they need not be afraid. They are promised that "the God of peace will soon crush Satan under your feet" (Rom. 16:20). Through "the shield of faith" they can "quench all the flaming darts of the evil one" (Eph. 6:16) or they can simply avoid a tempting situation (1 Cor. 7:5). The Christians are not like the pagans who do not even realize that they are under the dominion of Satan (Acts 26:18).

The tendency to divide the world into two spheres of influence, one in which Christ rules and one which Satan rules, is clearly advanced in the Johannine writings.[96] In the Gospel of John, for instance, we hear that the devil is "a murderer from the beginning, and has nothing to do with the truth, because there is no truth in him. When he lies, he speaks according to his own nature, for he is a liar and the father of lies" (John 8:44).[97] Unlike the divine *logos,* he is not in the beginning, but from the beginning, and therefore clearly secondary to the *logos.* However, he is a murderer, the father of lies, the ruler of this world (John 12:31), and the people are his children. He who commits sin is of the devil, but he who is born of God commits no sin (1 John 3:8f.). Satan is definitely understood as the cause of evil.

But we still do not find a cosmological dualism introduced in the Johannine writings. The world is not divided in Gnostic fashion into an evil cosmos, the domain of Satan, and a celestial heaven, the haven of all believers in which the father in heaven rules. According to John the world is still God's creation, created through the *logos*.[98] The world is not divided into those who are saved and those who cannot be saved. A new birth is still possible (John 3:3), because "God sent the Son into the world, not to condemn the world, but that the world might be saved through him" (John 3:17). Once we have "overcome the evil one" (1 John 2:13) through faith in Christ, we are not lifted up into another sphere. We still live in this world and therefore the caution is still necessary: "Do not love the world or the things in the world" (1 John 2:15). Thus Rudolf Bultmann is right when he observes: "Each man is, or once was, confronted with deciding for or against God; and he is confronted anew with this decision by the revelation of God in Jesus. The cosmological dualism of Gnosticism has become in John a *dualism of decision.*" [99] But this dualism will not continue forever. "The world passes away, and the lust of it; but he who does the will of God abides for ever" (1 John 2:17). This is the hope which undergirds the New Testament faith.

If we want to sum up our findings on the correlation between the cause of evil and Satan, we must note that there is a growing awareness in the biblical writings that the cause of evil cannot simply be attributed to God. Especially in the politically confusing post-exilic time the trust in God as the giver of all good things could not be reconciled with God as the source of good and evil. From the very beginning, however, the power of evil was understood to be of so great a magnitude that it could not just be conceived of as stemming from humanity itself, individually or corporately conceived. But the relegation of the cause of evil to an outside force never did diminish the individual or corporate accountability for evil doings. Since God has always been understood as the creator of everything that is, the cause of evil had to come from God's good creation.

How it happened that part of God's good creation denied its own originator may be interesting for speculative minds, but it is unimportant for the biblical writers. It is also beyond the interest of the biblical writers to clearly define what is meant by evil. Though evil is often understood as that which is impairing the life-furthering process, it is most frequently conceived of as something that obstructs the furthering of God's kingdom. Even biological impairments, such as diseases, or physical disturbances, such as earthquakes, can be included under the category of evil. The reason for not distinguishing the so-called "natural evils" and the "spiritual evil" seems to lie in the biblical conviction that the world cannot be dualistically divided into two primordial principles, God as the cause of all good, and Satan as the cause of all evil. The biblical witnesses are convinced that ultimately and occasionally even pen-ultimately, the cause of evil cannot but glorify God (John 9:3).

We must ask, however, if the distinction between God and the cause of evil is not totally incompatible with what we have said about the structures of human existence. Teilhard, for instance, suggested that within an evolutionary understanding of the universe evil always tends to be understood as a necessary though unfortunate by-product of the creative process. Thus it would be difficult to assume that God and the causes of evil are operative on an equal level behind and within all processes. Yet Freud talked about drives at work within humanity and within society. But he did not seem to equate humanity or society as such with these drives. Similarly, Konrad Lorenz mentioned aggressive drives operative in all living things which only in humanity entail the potential for disastrous results. But we cannot equate these drives with part or the total constitution of any species. A living species is not co-extensive with the space-time continuum it occupies. In its interactive participation with the environment it extends beyond its own being. This is also true for humanity as a whole. Therefore it would be wrong to assume that good and evil, whether as cause or as result of human action, are ultimately human phenomena.

The biblical tradition did not measure good and evil by certain human standards, but by the extent to which they corresponded to God's will. Since it is God's will to make his kingdom triumph and to bring about his new creation, good and evil are intrinsically future-oriented. They intend to influence the inauguration of God's will and are constructive or destructive of the creative process. It would be an obvious contradiction within the divine reality to assume that God contains in himself both enforcement and hindrance of his will. Since our universe is both enactor and victim of evil, the cause of evil cannot be located either in the totality or part of our material universe. Perhaps we could compare here the cause of evil to some of the characteristic structural properties of anti-matter (without identifying anti-matter with the cause of evil!). While anti-matter is part of a larger field, it destroys the matter it encounters and radiates the results of this annihilation into the environment. In other words, the cause of evil is not on equal level with God. Since it stands in opposition to God's creation, it destroys the part of God's creation with which it comes in contact.

3. Personification of the Cause of Evil

When we now consider the possibility and extent of a personification of the cause of evil, we must ask ourselves at the outset whether such investigation is not a waste of time. Has not Friedrich Schleiermacher clarified the issue when he stated: *"The idea of the Devil, as developed among us, is so unstable that we cannot expect anyone to be convinced of its truth"?* [100] We must also remember Bultmann's objection that we no longer live in a primitive world. We generally know how the forces of nature function and we have discovered most of their laws. Therefore the belief in demons and spirits is rendered obsolete.[101] While we agree that in early Christianity "there is no christology without demonology," [102] we remember that none of the creeds adopted by the Christian church asks us to believe in Satan and his power.[103]

a. Non-created origin

We certainly do not want to revert to a pagan polydemonism that made fateful inroads into medieval Christianity and resulted in witch hunts and mass neuroses.[104] Yet we find it impossible to locate the cause of evil strictly in the human sphere or to consider it just as part of the natural process. We should not forget that at the height of the Enlightenment even Immanuel Kant in a book with the significant title *Religion Within the Limits of Reason Alone* insisted on the existence of a radical evil. Kant almost seems to have anticipated Konrad Lorenz' behavioral findings when he said: That man is evil cannot mean anything but that "he is conscious of the moral law, but has nevertheless adopted into his maxim the (occasional) deviation therefrom." [105] It is not humanity's natural make-up that makes it bad, but something that humanity is accountable for. It is a radical evil, however, working in every human being.

There are two ways, according to Kant, in which we could account for this radical evil in humanity.[106] It could first stem from human sensuality. But to relegate the cause of evil to the sphere of their senses would degrade humans to mere animals, indicating that they are not actually accountable for the evil they do. If human depravity, however, as some kind of malignant reason, would stem from our intellect, a possibility that Kant also considers, we would be the incorporation of the diabolic itself and would no longer act in true freedom. Thus Kant concludes that to seek the origin of evil in human sensuality would be too restricting, while extending it to the intellect

would be too all-embracing to account for the radical evil in humanity. For Kant, however, evil is a natural inclination that we freely
follow.[107]

If we assume a cause of evil outside humanity, do we then not
just push the causal nexus one step further without sufficient grounds?
Yet we remember that even psychoanalysis did not explain the phenomenon of evil by simply referring to humanity. With reference to
the destructive forces Freud talked about the (ambivalent) *superego*
and Jung about the (ambivalent) archetypes and a person's shadow.
In their destructive tendencies these phenomena were then explained
as a kind of haunting memory of the individual or of humanity as a
whole. As psychoanalysis wants to stay within the objectively given
(humanity), it cannot provide any further explanation for the destructive forces, unless it assumes a constitutive depravity of humanity.
But this notion had already been rejected by Kant.

Another possibility to account for evil would be to assume "meta-"
physical forces outside humanity. However, such explanation would
necessarily exceed the possibilities of science and philosophy. To
assume such a possibility for the origin of evil, however, might not
be too farfetched, if we remember that we were not content with
scientific cosmogonies and their objectively given (matter or energy)
in explaining the emergence of the universe. We were not even content with paleontology and its objectively given (the prehuman biological realm) to account for the emergence of humanity. So it might
be legitimate that we are not content with psychoanalysis and its
objectively given (the human psyche) to probe the depth of evil.
Analogous to our assertion that the emergence of the universe and of
humanity is due to God the creator, we may now assume that the
emergence of evil is due to Satan.

When we say "Satan" we do not want to revert to a primitive
mythological figure, but express "that there is a principle or force of
evil antecedent to any evil human action." [108] We must caution, however, against the assumption that the reality of Satan would allow us
a phenomenological distinction between the works of Satan and the
works of God. Martin Luther's warning against a theology of glory
must be heeded here, as he said in the *Heidelberg Disputation*
(1518): "Although the works of God are always unattractive and
appear evil, they are nevertheless really eternal merits." [109] Three
concerns are involved in this assertion:

(1) Though God's creation is good, the ongoing process of God's
redemptive history reminds us that it is not yet redeemed and per-

fected. This allows for the occurrence of many "natural" phenomena, of whom we know that they will not be part of the new creation. One of these phenomena is the necessity of death of one form of life to sustain and further other forms of life. We could call them "natural evil" to indicate that they are not anti-Godly constellations, but part of God's continuing creative and redemptive process. Gordon Kaufmann calls "natural evil" rightly a "somewhat inaccurate way of referring to this fact that God's hand cannot always be seen—that men often are, indeed, engulfed in what appears to be the very denial of loving purpose." [110]

(2) This leads to a second point, that God works through the appearance of the opposite. Especially Luther emphasized this by saying that God works like someone who is using a rusty and rough hatchet. "Even though the worker is a good craftsman, the hatchet leaves bad, jagged, and ugly gashes. So it is when God works through us." [111]

(3) The most bothersome concern, however, expressed especially forcefully in Luther's *The Bondage of Will* (1525), is that God works in evil people toward evil purposes. Though this reaffirms the biblical conviction that God can use Satan ultimately to achieve his purpose, even Luther was bothered by this statement and asked himself: "But why does he [God] not at the same time change the evil wills that he moves?" Luther does not indulge in speculations at this point. He simply admits: "This belongs to the secrets of his majesty, where his judgments are incomprehensible. It is not our business to ask this question, but to adore these mysteries." [112]

If it is the great philosophical mystery why there is something and not just nothing, it is the great theological issue why there is not just good but also evil. Here Satan becomes our ultimate referent in the search for the cause of evil. Insisting that God works evil in evil people, Luther did not dare to say in *The Bondage of Will* that God is the cause of evil. On the contrary, Luther affirms in the same treatise that humanity is either ridden by God or by the devil.[113] This shows us the paradox involved in our search for the cause of evil. While we must affirm that ultimately everything comes from God, we are aware of a power of darkness which is both integral to and contrary to God's redemptive history.

b. Sub-Godly limitation

The powers of darkness, however, have their limit in God. They cannot be understood as being on equal ground with God. If we cannot affirm the infinite superiority of God to all demonic or satanic powers, our trust in the ultimate triumph of God's kingdom is impaired. We would have to doubt that nothing is impossible to God and we would constantly be afraid that we were associated with part of the creative process that either is not under God's dominion or that shows a basic inevitable depravity. To avoid this dilemma of faith we must affirm with Luther that God is also the God of Satan.[114]

In classifying Satan as nothingness Karl Barth has picked up this emphasis on the sub-Godly aspect of Satan.

Barth affirms:

> Nothingness is that from which God separates Himself and in face of which He asserts Himself and exerts His positive will. . . . As God is Lord on the left hand as well, He is the basis and Lord of nothingness too. Consequently it is not adventitious. It is not a second God, nor self-created. It has no power save that which it is allowed by God. . . . Even on His left hand the activity of God is not in vain.[115]

When Barth continues that God's not wanting and not willing also has consequences because he is always active, even in his not working and willing, he comes close to denying the equally important insight that must be maintained together with the sub-Godly aspect of Satan, namely the non-creational aspect. Why and how it is that the cause of evil is and to whom it "owes" its being we do not know. Karl Barth seems to go beyond these limitations indicating that at least indirectly the "Nothingness" owes its being to God's inactivity. Of course, explicitly he rejects the notion that nothingness is created by God, but in his line of argument he comes very close to making the existence of nothingness dependent on God.[116]

c. Anti-Godly tendency

Besides the sub-Godly limitation and the non-created origin we must also mention the anti-Godly tendency of Satan.[117] Without neglecting the other two features, this aspect gains most prominence in the biblical story of the life and destiny of Jesus. Here we see best that God and Satan encounter each other on the same plane.[118] Karl Barth therefore is right when he stresses that the battle with Satan is primarily and actually God's own affair.[119] Luther, too, in his hymn "A Mighty Fortress Is Our God" warned us that "our ancient foe doth seek to work us woe." If we recall such abysmal attacks of the demonic as occurred in Auschwitz, Hiroshima and Nagasaki, and in

My Lai, we cannot escape the threatening character of the utter destructiveness and perversity of these powers.

This destructiveness and perversity surfaces prominently in the New Testament, when Satan is called the father of lies and a murderer from the very beginning (John 8:44). There also our observation is reinforced that these powers do not operate on our limited human level. They are in constant rebellion against God, fighting him on an equal level. Humanity's subsequent rebellion, however, though not to be taken lightly, is not an act of innate perversity or predetermined necessity. Humanity is willingly drawn into this battle, following on the footsteps of these forces, like them challenging God's authority and attempting to set itself up as a new god in full autonomy.

Looking at the story of Jesus' temptation we see both the power and the intention of these forces (Matt. 4:1-11). They attempt to win human allegiance so that they are worshiped instead of God, and in turn they promise us unprecedented influence. Since the Christ event, however, we know, as Martin Luther in "A Mighty Fortress Is Our God" affirmed that "one little word [Christ] shall fell him." As these powers recognized, Christ had come to destroy them and their influence (Mark 5:7; 1 Cor. 15:57). Claiming Christ on our side, we can join his victory over these powers.

It has become clear that these destructive powers do not confront us like an impersonal it, but like a persuasive and overpowering thou. Therefore a personification of these powers clarifies our perception of them. Since, however, neither Old nor New Testament has a consistent name for them, often leaving the impression that there are a multitude of anti-Godly powers, it might be appropriate to refer to them by their common intentionality as anti-Godly powers. The term anti-Godly powers would also relieve us of the possible misunderstanding that we are talking here about a devil or a satan in analogy to myths or to fairy tales.

Summary

Summing up this chapter in which we attempted to define the human predicament by analyzing the cause of evil, we want to reinforce the following points:

(1) Psychoanalysis suggests that the human predicament is determined by two conflicting drives, one urging for self-destruction and the other for preservation of life. These drives are intrinsic to human existence, but they need not result in human self-destruction.

(2) The biblical witnesses first understood God as the source of both good and evil. Only gradually, under the impact of a growing historical consciousness, they realized that evil is fundamentally destructive of God's creative process.

(3) The biblical witnesses emphasize that the first sinful act occurred within God's good creation. However, the origin of the cause of evil is neither ascribed to God nor to his good creation. Yet the all-pervading presence of the cause of evil is felt throughout creation. Humanity willfully succumbs to this cause and thereby denies God, the source and destiny of its existence.

(4) The Judeo-Christian tradition does not attempt to explain the origin of the cause of evil, but accepts it as a force that was not created evil, but chose to become anti-Godly in its tendency. The evil powers have their limitation in God and are not identical with the totality or a part of God's creation. Their personification underscores that we do not encounter them as an impersonal fate or a biological deficiency, but that their encounter usually results in actions for which we are accountable.

(5) As behavioral psychology and psychoanalysis indicate, our predicament, while serious, need not lead to destruction of humanity and its environment. But to attain a positive resolution of our predicament, the issue of human freedom needs further clarification. This can be done primarily by investigating the full extent of our sinfulness.

6.

Human Sinfulness

After trying to determine the location and magnitude of the cause of evil, it is now necessary to delineate how evil manifests itself in our human nature and to what extent we are still free to follow our own deliberations. Knowing about the seriousness of the human predicament, we could simply classify humans as sinners and therefore acknowledge humanity's basic depravity. Though we certainly do not want to take Genesis 3 lightly and diminish the magnitude of humanity's fallen nature, we realize that the fall did not make God's creation undone. Even under the spell of the fall we humans are still created in the image of God and remain God's administrators. When we now describe and evaluate the biblical and the church's understanding of human sinfulness, we must do this with reference to items such as humanity's actual nature, human responsibility, and humans being created in the image of God. While we must distinguish between actual sin and the original sin in the beginning which is reaffirmed by every subsequent actual sin, we will soon see that for the biblical witnesses the intention and structure of both actual and original sin point into the same direction.[1] Both are understood as aversion from God and implying that sinfulness is humanity's unnatural nature.

1. Biblical View of Sin

Approaching sin with the eyes of the biblical witnesses, we are first of all confronted with a multitude of expressions that describe sin.[2]

197

We also notice that none of the words used to denote sin has exclusive profane or theological character. In other words, sin is not understood as something which either occurs between me and my God, or only between me and my fellow people. Something occurring in the profane realm can have consequences for the relationship between God and us, and something happening in that relationship can have implications for how we relate to other people. In either case sin is foremost aversion from God.

a. Sin as aversion from God

In the picturesque account of the first sin, Adam replied to God's inquiry about why he was hiding himself: "I heard the sound of thee in the garden, and I was afraid, because I was naked; and I hid myself" (Gen. 3:10). Humanity breaks away from its close relationship with God and then experiences a basic insecurity in its subsequent confrontation with God.

Whether humanity trespasses against required norms, whether it attempts to reject any norms, or whether it is simply in error, in any case its activity is considered a sin against God. For instance, David certainly transgressed against the Hittite Uriah in the most blatant way when he asked that Uriah be sent on a fatal military mission so that David could take his wife Bathsheba as his own. But it was only after David was confronted with God through the prophet Nathan that he recognized: "I have sinned against the Lord" (2 Sam. 12:13). This conviction is reaffirmed when the psalmist confesses: "Against thee, thee only, have I sinned, and done that which is evil in thy sight" (Ps. 51:4). The continuation of the verse: "so that thou art justified in thy sentence and blameless in thy judgment" implies that recognition of this sinful act does not invalidate the binding value of God's norms but reaffirms them. God demands conformity with his will, but humanity becomes sinful and by avoiding God in its sins it implicitly attests to the unwavering will of God.[3]

Sin is everything that does not proceed from a trusting relationship with God. Paul puts this understanding of sin very precisely when he says: "For whatever does not proceed from faith is sin" (Rom. 14:23). Since sin is always defined by relating an action or its result to our ultimate destiny as promised by God, sin as such is not accessible to phenomenological investigation. The people in Sodom and Gomorrah, for instance, did not perceive their perversity as sinfulness. Only in the sight of Yahweh was their conduct understood as greatly sinful (Gen. 18:20). Similarly, we do not get the impression that

Isaiah was of wicked character. Being confronted with God, however, he discovered his sinfulness confessing: "Woe is me! For I am lost; for I am a man of unclean lips, and I dwell in the midst of a people of unclean lips; for my eyes have seen the King, the Lord of hosts!" (Isa. 6:5). If sin is aversion from God, we are not surprised to hear that a person who sins shall die (Ezek. 18:4). Once one turns away from the giver of life, the turnaround has implications for this life and beyond.

Sin is primarily a theological term, indicating the disruption of the life-giving and life-sustaining relationship between God and humanity. By contrast evil usually denotes in a phenomenological and evaluative description that which is bad or harmful. Unless grace intervenes, sin will always have ultimate consequences. Life cannot be indefinitely sustained or newly created without continuing relationship with God, the source of all life. But not all sinful acts manifest themselves in evil behavior. The reason for this is that finite beings are unable to assess accurately the long-range effects of each individual act. Quite often something is not termed evil, though it may have evil results in a relatively short time-span (cf. the proliferation of nuclear energy to aid underprivileged countries). Frequently also good and bad components are intermixed in a human action so that one is at a loss how to assess its propriety (cf. the dynamic leader that ruthlessly uses his elbows to achieve the good of the community). This dilemma shows the urgency for humanity to act in conformity to God's life-giving spirit to avoid ultimately and often pen-ultimately disastrous results. Reference to God, however, means to view an action in the light of ultimacy and universality. It means to discern whether an action contributes or distracts from the promised goal of a new creation. It also implies to check whether one's chosen methods for action are analogous to that of God's own action embodied in Jesus of Nazareth.

In Judaism there occurred a differentiation between mortal sins, such as idolatry, licentiousness, and bloodshed, and venial sins that were committed unknowingly.[4] For the former one attained satisfaction only through death, while for the latter one could atone through rites of purification, good works, and sufferings. Sin was then mainly understood as transgressing the divine law, behind which, God was still discernible. This sentiment of distinguishing degrees of sinfulness and of relating sinfulness directly to our attitude toward God was changed again in the New Testament times.

The Sermon on the Mount, for example, shows us Jesus' deep

awareness of the extent to which each person was hopelessly entangled in sinfulness. But Jesus did not just acknowledge humanity's
sinfulness, he tackled sin in an unprecedented way. First we remember that his whole ministry must be understood as a continuous battle
against the anti-Godly powers. His victories over the anti-Godly powers are not sporadic impacts on the domain of evil. They were manifestations that the time of salvation had commenced and that the
destruction of these powers had started.[5] This means that Jesus emphasized humanity's thoroughgoing sinfulness and, through his ministry,
even eliminated the very cause of sin, checking the anti-Godly powers
that tempt to sin. But Jesus did not stop there.

As the bringer of the kingdom of God, Jesus also established table
fellowship with sinners and pronounced forgiveness of sin (Mark
2:5-16). He did not separate himself from sinners, but as the one
who stands in the place of God, he established a new communion
with them.[6] These acts signal the beginning and foreshadowing of
the eschatological communion of God with his people when he will
no longer hold their sins against them. In Jesus therefore becomes
true what the servant of Yahweh had promised: "I, I am He who
blots out your transgressions for my own sake, and I will not remember your sins" (Isa. 43:25). The forgiving of sins constitutes an
eschatological moment; the new creation is proleptically anticipated
in which nobody will any longer turn away from God. However, the
proclamation of the kingdom of God and the forgiving of sins cannot
be taken lightly. They demand a response and ask for acceptance.
Those who reject God's Holy Spirit being present in Jesus' life and
destiny have forfeited their chance to return to God, they have
brought judgment upon themselves and committed an unforgivable
sin (Matt. 12:31f.).[7]

The life and destiny of Jesus is the great crisis for sin, as especially
the Gospel of John indicates. Jesus confronts the people with his
words and deeds and they realize in their confrontation that they are
sinners. They also know that in him they are offered the chance to
return to God. "If I had not come and spoken to them," we hear,
"they would not have sin; but now they have no excuse for their sin"
(John 15:22). In the confrontation with Jesus occurs the separation
between those accepting him and thereby accepting God and those
who reject him. By rejecting God in Christ the latter are judged and
their sins stand against them. Therefore we encounter the threatening
and at the same time comforting pronouncement: "He who believes in

the Son has eternal life; he who does not obey the Son shall not see life, but the wrath of God rests upon him" (John 3:36).[8]

When we come to Paul we notice a distinct difference between his understanding of sin and that of both the Old Testament and the Gospels. Though he builds on many of the Old Testament insights, his understanding of sin is determined by his own experience which in turn is shaped through his confrontation with God's self-disclosure in Jesus Christ.[9] Because of this confrontation, sin has become such a dominant theme for Paul that we get the impression that sin is humanity's second nature.

b. Sinfulness as humanity's unnatural nature

In the context of the Noachitic blessing we read the devastating words: "The imagination of man's heart is evil from his youth" (Gen. 8:21). This same statement that once brought judgment upon humanity (Gen. 6:5) now constitutes the premise for the pronouncement of God's grace.[10] Human beings are sinful from birth to death. The psalmist goes one step further when he exclaims: "Behold, I was brought forth in iniquity, and in sin did my mother conceive me" (Ps. 51:5). The psalmist does not introduce a traducianistic understanding of sin, as is often assumed, but he speaks of the "mother" Israel in analogy to Isaiah 54:1-5, alluding to the historic origin of Israel from her patriarchal ancestors (cf. Isa. 43:27).[11] This means that sinfulness does not just accompany the history of individuals, but the corporate history of Israel.

In following Jewish thinking Paul extends our perception of sin by saying that "sin came into the world through one man and death through sin, and so death spread to all men because all men sinned" (Rom. 5:12). Adam is the "gate" through which sin came into the world and sin is the "gate" through which death reached all people.[12] Paul does not want to put the blame on Adam for the emergence of sin and death. Sin for Paul *(he hamartia)* assumes almost anthropomorphic features, personifying the anti-Godly destructive powers that found their way into our human world through this first human being. However, Paul talks about the emergence of the age of death not just in a biological way. Symbolically this age had its head in Adam, who is the anti-type to Christ, the head of the age of life and the bearer of the new aeon.[13]

Many Western theologians, however, concluded from Paul's remarks that humanity had once been in an integer or original state, in which it had the possibility of not sinning and consequently of not dying.[14]

Death, sorrow, and pain were thought then to have come into the world through human sinfulness.[15] Only those outside the confines of orthodox faith dared to assert that already the first human being would have died, whether he/she had sinned or not.[16] Today most theologians rightly refrain from speculations about a pre-mortal, original state of humanity. Yet they too acknowledge that there is something peculiar about human death. Human death is not only a biological phenomenon, similar to the death of an animal.

We remember that a human being is the only living species that has an acute self-awareness, while humanity's predecessors had only rudiments of self-awareness or lacked it altogether. Theodosius Dobzhansky now made the important observation that

> self-awareness has, however, brought in its train somber companions—fear, anxiety, and death-awareness. . . . Death-awareness is a bitter fruit of man's having risen to the level of consciousness and of functioning ego. Self-awareness has developed as an important adaptation; death-awareness is not obviously adaptive, and it may be biologically detrimental.[17]

Humanity can never completely control this death-awareness. Contrary to animals in whom it often arises at the end of life, in humans it can emerge at any moment, even in the prime of life. It reminds human beings that they are mortal, that their efforts are ultimately in vain. While we can say that very likely death-awareness is an outgrowth and a necessary concomitant of self-awareness, and that it may be genetically conditioned, Dobzhansky warns us not to assume that there is a single genetic unit responsible for death-awareness.[18] There is not a special gene for death-awareness, but it is a basic human capacity derived from the whole of the human genetic endowment. Why is it then that human beings make death one of their primary concerns, as Ernest Becker pointed out? Why is it that from the earliest times of philosophical speculation, one of the primal concerns was the issue of death? Does this not indicate that Paul was correct when he asserted that the first human being was the gate through which sin and death-awareness entered the human world? Once humanity had alienated itself from the primordial conformity with its creator, death as God's condemnation of this sinful life-style threatened humanity and reminded human beings of their ultimate dependency which they rejected.

Like us Paul is not so much interested in the condition of the first human being. He wants to convey that we are born into the sinful context which the first human being ever to move on this earth initiated.[19] Nobody starts from the beginning, for we are all influenced in our self-assessment by the sins of the human family. This is what Paul means when he says: "By one man's disobedience many were made sinners." And "one man's trespass led to condemnation for all men" (Rom. 5:18f.). We rightly must talk here about sin as a hereditary affliction. At the same time, however, Paul appeals to personal accountability, because everyone knows about God and his word. Even the pagans, who do not have the (Old Testament) Law, have the law written in their hearts and they have a conscience that bothers them (Rom. 2:14f.). We are reminded here of Luther's insight that there is not a special law for the Christians, but the same "natural" law applies to both Christians and non-Christians.[20] We will see later that this understanding of common basic norms for human behavior is reaffirmed by the findings of behavioral research.

It is significant to find out how humanity expresses its sinful existence. Paul asserts that sinful humanity exchanges the truth about God for a lie and worships and serves the creature rather than the Creator (Rom. 1:25). This means that at the center of human sinfulness lies the abandoning of humanity's administrative position. The human family abandoned its position as God's administrators of the world and wanted to rule the world in autonomy. Since humanity is aware of itself, it recognizes its finitude and attempts to overcome it. There are two main ways in which humanity tries to accomplish this. Either it wants to expand its dominion to ever further horizons, an attitude which leads to self-glorification, or it is willing to surrender to that which surrounds it, a mind-set leading to religious idolatry. In either case, humanity prides itself of being in control of the situation.[21]

But humanity is deceiving itself, for it is not actually in control of its own situation. Instead of trusting the infinite God as humanity ought, an attitude which would enable it to have dominion over the world as God's administrator, it wants to have dominion over life as a whole and consequently trusts the finite world.[22] Thus humanity wants to dominate what it should trust, and trusts what it should dominate. Can we, however, agree that this perverse attitude results from humanity's own choice; that it lives by its own intentions contrary to the way it ought to live?

When we come to chapter 7 of Paul's Letter to the Romans we get the impression that sin has demonic character.[23] In confrontation with God's law, the nascent desires are awakened (Rom. 7:5). These desires or passions are not primarily sensual desires, but the whole gamut of sinfulness, from the basic pride to actual individual sins. Even the good and holy will of God is used to increase the power of sin (Rom. 7:13). In its natural (fallen) state human freedom is reduced to that of a slave (Rom. 7:14). Before its physical death humanity is already sold to sin and therewith to eternal death. Remembering his own situation prior to his conversion, Paul can identify with human sinfulness and exclaim:

> I do not understand my own actions. For I do not do what I want, but I do the very thing I hate. . . . So then it is no longer I that do it, but sin which dwells within me. For I know that nothing good dwells within me, that is, in my flesh. Rom. 7:15-18

Significantly, Paul does not identify flesh and sin, but only insists that human existence in the flesh is also an existence in sin. The human sphere of the flesh is a sphere of sin and dominated by sin. We can even draw the conclusion that humanity living according to the human sphere and in the human sphere, is enslaved by sin. Though humanity knows what to do and even intends to do it, it just cannot accomplish it. Actually this should not come as a surprise, since we have just seen that as long as humanity lives in and from itself it lives in pride and sin, turned away from God. That it still wants and wills the good, attests to the unnatural status of this behavior. Thus human nature has not changed, but humanity lives, however, in a totally unnatural way, so to speak with its back toward God.

It is evident that humanity's unnatural attitude need not effect the pen-ultimate quality of its doings. Very often we find high moral standards among pagans and among deliberate atheists. But already Augustine observed that the virtues "are rather vices than virtues so long as there is no reference to God in the matter." [24] The relationship to God is the deciding factor which determines theologically, but not phenomenologically, between a virtue and a vice. As soon as this relationship is broken, human action is sin against God, regardless of how "good" it is. Sin is aversion from God and must always be measured against this background.

Paul knows, however, that we are not condemned to live according to the flesh; we can also live according to the spirit. Right after the admission: "Wretched man that I am! Who will deliver me from this

body of death?" Paul exclaims: "Thanks be to God through Jesus
Christ our Lord!" (Rom. 7:24f.). The Christ event is the occasion
that liberates us from the bondage of sin (Rom. 5:21). Living according to the spirit means that we no longer live on our own and for our
own. Paul can therefore say that we are no longer on our own (1 Cor.
6:19). We are Christ's and belong to Christ. In the trusting relationship with Christ, enabled through the spirit, the basic alienation is
overcome. Similar to the basic sinfulness of natural humanity, however, this new status is not brought about through a biological or
genetic change. It is achieved through God's grace. Therefore it is
open to mistreatment and Paul constantly summons us to realize that
which we already are.[25] Since Christ has gained the victory over the
anti-Godly powers for those who claim Christ on their side, sin is no
longer dominant. Yet it still has to be fought in daily battles, battles
that still draw defeats, but that can and ought to foreshadow Christ's
victory over sin.

2. Understanding of Sin in the Tradition of the Church

When we now throw a few glimpses at how the church wrestled
with the understanding of sin, we can by no means be exhaustive,
but simply illuminate the main issues. The church's interpretation of
human sinfulness is very instructive, because it may easily and justi-
fiably be understood as a tradition of sin. The basic issue in the understanding of sin was whether there is still some goodness in humanity
or whether it is a totally corrupt entity. We would like to deal with
the question under the three headings under which it gained most
prominence in the church, namely the issues of freedom and responsibility, of humanity being both sinner and an image of God, and
humanity and the kingdom of evil.

a. Freedom and responsibility

The issue of freedom and responsibility twice gained unprecedented prominence in the history of the church, once in the formative
years of Western theology, climaxing in the struggle between Augustine and Pelagius, and then in the emergence of the Protestant Reformation. Shortly before A.D. 400, the ascetic monk PELAGIUS had
moved from Great Britain to metropolitan Rome. Worried about the
laxity of morals in Rome, he admonished the people to lead a good
life and appealed to their natural possibilities. Soon he found an
eloquent follower in Coelestius and even Bishop Julian of Eclanum

stood at his side. If God has commanded us to do the good, we must be able to do it, Pelagius argued.[26] Indeed humanity is free, he concluded, to decide to do the good or the bad, since it has freedom to do either of them.[27] As a reasonable creature a human being had this possibility since the beginning of creation, because God endowed it with a free will and gave it the ability of free judgment. So humanity was by nature capable of doing something good and something bad.[28] Though human freedom is from God, it is up to humanity whether it wants to do good or bad.[29]

Pelagius understands by freedom primarily psychological freedom, through which humanity freely decides what it wants to do. While this assessment of human freedom would not present any theological problems, Pelagius now equates this freedom of choice with moral freedom. In so doing, he ignores that moral life is not the resultant of individual acts but of a whole life attitude—whether one lives in conformity with God or not. However, he argues that there can be no sinful attitude or a sinful "nature," because if there were, what we call sin would then not be sin. It would rather be a fateful constellation for which God could not hold us personally accountable or even punish us.[30] Pelagius does not concede that humanity is without sin, but he insists that it could still be sinless.[31] Since sin consists only of separate acts of the will, the idea of its propagation by the act of generation is absurd according to Pelagius.[32] Adam was the first sinner, but there is no demonstrable connection between his sins and ours.[33] Newborn infants are therefore declared sinless and do not need baptism for the forgiveness of their sins.[34] According to Pelagius, humanity is born as biologically mortal. Through the example of Adam it then encounters the death of the soul.[35]

It would be easy to classify the position of Pelagius and his followers as self-redemptive moralism. They believed in the inherent goodness of humanity and actually did not need Christ's salvific deed to be able to return to God. When we consider Pelagius' assertions, however, in the context of classical antiquity, his position becomes more understandable.[36] In Greek mythology destiny *(moira)* was conceived as the overriding principle of life which even the Olympian gods could not master. The more the gods of mount Olympus lost in status the more people tended to resign themselves to fate or to luck. Even Plato agrees with traditional thinking when he says that even God could not oppose necessity.[37] Of course, he knows "that God is all." But God is not really in control of the affairs of the world. "Chance *(tyche)* and circumstance *(kairos)*, under God, set the whole course of life for us, and yet we must allow for a third and more amenable partner, skill *(techne)*." In the Roman empire the goddess of fortune (Fortuna) played a prominent role. Yet in Ovid's *Metamorphoses* we hear even Jupiter ask: "Does anyone suppose that he can so far prevail as to alter Fate's decrees?"[38] And Stoics, such as Cicero, resign themselves to the fact that "all things take place by fate," namely the order and series of causes.[39] The Emperor Tiberius is reported to have "lacked any deep regard for the gods or other religious feelings" because he believed "that the world was wholly ruled by fate."[40]

It is not surprising that in this environment of fatalism and determinism most theologians emphasized personal responsibility rather than the inevitability of sin. For instance, Theodore of Mopsuestia could assert very much like Pelagius "that it is only *nature* which can be inherited, not sin, which is the disobedience of the free and unconstrained will."[41] But then came Augustine and evidently left no room at all for human freedom.

AUGUSTINE emphasized that humanity has a free will and that sin is a voluntary movement.[42] If it were otherwise, God's precepts would be of no use to us. The first human being who was created was good and his will was directed toward the good.[43] With divine assistance the first human being could have stayed good and could have changed his possibility of not sinning and not dying to the impossibility of sinning and dying.[44] But Adam did not stay this way, he sinned and since in him are all people joined together, all people sinned through him (Rom. 5:12).[45] Therefore in Adam the whole human family became a corrupt entity.

Unlike Pelagius, for Augustine sin is not handed on through contact or imitation, but through procreation.[46] Sexual concupiscence expressed in the procreative act, though not sin for the reborn, makes the newborn child a victim of sin.[47] This emphasis on the concupiscence of the flesh is very likely a result of Augustine's monastic and ascetic attitude.[48] Nevertheless Augustine maintains that even as sinners we are "capable alike of good actions and of evil ones."[49] The inherited concupiscence is not determinative, it becomes sin through "willing consent."[50] Humanity can even at times avoid concupiscence and grave sins and instead select virtues of wisdom and fortitude.

Augustine would fully agree with Pelagius that a human being has the possibility to choose between virtues and vices. But he differs from Pelagius when he insists: "But this will, which is free in evil things because it takes pleasure in evil, is not free in good things, for the reason that it has not been made free. . . . Nobody has a free will to do the good without the assistance of God." [51] In other words, the good that the good do and the good that the bad do are not the same. Goodness before God does not just consist of individual morally good acts, it is the result of a life attitude which is in conformity with God. Therefore, the "virtues of the pagans are splendid vices." Once humanity revolts against God, the creator and sustainer, it is destroying the natural order of its existence, and it cannot undo this inclination through "good" activity. For Augustine sin is not just morally right or wrong, as Pelagius insisted, but he recognizes that it has much larger dimensions as the presumptuous attitude of being in control of one's own life. Sin is revolt against God; it is aversion from God and therewith pride and self-love.[52]

Of course, we might wonder whether Augustine does not eliminate personal responsibility for sin when he emphasizes God's predetermining will. But we must recognize that Augustine talks primarily about God's predetermining will toward salvation.[53] This would mean that humanity has even more of a choice toward the good, in individual acts as well as in its whole life attitude. Augustine makes it clear that for each individual act people still need God's grace so that they do not succumb to their sinful inclinations.[54] However, Augustine also talks about predestination toward damnation. But he remains rather silent concerning the reason for double predestination. He refers to God's will and to the mystery of grace, because "he who is delivered has good ground for thankfulness, he who is condemned has no ground for finding fault." [55]

Perhaps the church was wise when at the Synod of Orange (529) it reaffirmed Augustine's insight in humanity's total dependence upon God while at the same time passed over Augustine's ideas of double predestination with silence. Humans are free to choose between good and bad. We have heard this from Augustine and Pelagius as well as from representatives of the life sciences. However, their opinions differ, once they assess this occasional but persistent deviation from the good. In our time Konrad Lorenz concluded that "man is not so evil from his youth, he is just *not quite good enough* for the demands of life in modern society." In Augustine's time Pelagius made a similar remark with regards to the demands of life in urban Rome. Yet what might be excusable for a scientist is not excusable for a theologian, the failure to recognize that wrongdoing, once committed, cannot be made undone. Even if one forgives the evildoer and he attempts restitution, the sinful act cannot be taken back.

Today we notice this especially painfully when we admit our exploitative attitude toward nature. Once we have wasted the natural resources, we cannot put them back into the ground, and if we could the ground would not be the same as it was before we interfered. Only a truly creative power can accomplish the naturally impossible. This is exactly what Augustine envisioned when he insisted on the necessity of God's relationship with us to live a genuinely good life. Therefore the real freedom is not enjoyed in our inherent possibility to choose between good and bad. It rather lies in the freedom to become again children of God and to be touched by the power that promised to make all things new. This freedom is enabled through God's unconditional grace.

It is perhaps indicative of human nature that a thousand years after the Pelagian controversy the same issues were discussed again, even with similar arguments. In 1524 ERASMUS OF ROTTERDAM wrote his diatribe *On the Freedom of the Will* in which he attacked Luther's restrictions of humanity's free choice. He observed that "after his battle with Pelagius, Augustine became less just toward free choice than he had been before. Luther, on the other hand, who had previously allowed something to free choice, is now carried so far in the heat of his defense as to destroy it entirely." [56] Erasmus asked what the point of the many biblical admonitions and precepts is, if of ourselves we can do nothing, but God does everything? [57] Similarly he noticed too that we often read in Scripture of godly people, full of good works, who walked in the presence of the Lord. Again their good deeds cannot be simply sin. Of course, he conceded all good works are due to God without whom we can do nothing, but, he emphasized, even if the contribution of free choice itself is part of the divine gift, "we can turn our souls to those things pertaining to salvation, or work together with grace." [58]

We need not be surprised that LUTHER was shocked by Erasmus' failure to distinguish in Scripture between law and gospel and by his trust in the human potential of working together with God toward one's salvation. Luther answered in 1525 with his treatise *On the Bondage of the Will* in which he flatly renounced that a human being had a free will. He asserted that, like the Pelagians, Erasmus wanted to replace Christ as redeemer with our free will, since according to

Erasmus the free will can fulfill God's commandments.[59] For Luther sins are not just the big sins, but the sublime and at the same time profound sins of the heart.[60] Luther also disclaims that there is a distinction between venial sins and deadly sins. All sins are deadly sins,[61] because they are an attack on God. As Augustine had done he emphasizes that humanity does not just commit individual sins, but that its whole attitude is determined by sin. The source for this sinful desire is original sin which everybody inherits.[62]

Again Luther understands sin as concupiscence, a drive, however, that is not primarily sexual.[63] Humanity's procreative faculty is a divine gift, though polluted through human lust.[64] While Luther is more appreciative of human sexuality than Augustine, he agrees with Augustine that original sin is handed on through the procreative process.[65] Thus the inclination toward sin is handed on from generation to generation. Of course, we could ask whether it is not simply destiny that humanity is sinful. Luther, however, responds that humanity is never forced to sin, but does evil voluntarily.[66] God is not a demon who causes good or evil according to his wishes. "God cannot act evilly although he does evil through evil men, because one who is himself good cannot act evilly." [67]

It is significant here to notice the difference between Luther and Augustine in their understanding of predestination. Luther would agree with Augustine that we do not know why God acts in a certain way.[68] But he would reject the Augustinian notion that we cannot be sure of our predestination, if we are not sure of the continuance of our faith until death. All who look at Christ and hear him, Luther argues, can be sure of their predestination.[69] It comes close to suicide to speculate about the hidden God.[70] We should instead cling to the real God, to Jesus Christ. Thus predestination, even as double predestination, cannot become a source of temptation for the believers, but is rather their assurance of salvation.

According to Luther the free will of the sinner is an empty phrase. True freedom existed only in paradise and will again exist through grace.[71] Without grace, Luther says with Augustine, the human family is a corrupt entity, turned away from God.[72] Again sinfulness does not diminish humanity's moral choice. "The Ten Commandments" Luther asserts, "are inscribed in the hearts of all men." [73] There is wisdom in humanity and a drive toward the good.[74] We can build houses, found families, educate children, and establish good and just order in economy, commerce, and government.[75] But none of these activities make us more pleasant toward God, they only enable us to be more pleasant toward each other.

While emphasizing the total depravity of humanity, insofar as it might claim a natural ability to live in conformity with God, both Augustine and Luther agree with their opponents that there is still a possibility for moral goodness in humanity. Would this mean that sinfulness does not make us genetically inferior as Augustine and Luther seem to imply when they attempted to show how the inherent sinfulness is handed on from one generation to the next? Perhaps an investigation into the understanding of the relationship between sin and our creation in the image of God could clarify whether humanity is still to some extent in a state of original goodness.

b. Humanity's shattered image

We mentioned that humanity was created in the image of God. The question must now be raised whether this can still be said of sinful humanity. We have heard that the human family is a corrupt entity whose members can hardly be conceived of as living up to an image of God. Especially Irenaeus' distinction between image and similitude of God intends to assert both the sinfulness of humanity and its status as God's special creature. The distinction goes back to Genesis 1:26 in which two different Hebrew words (*zelem* and *demut*) are used to express that humanity is created in the image of God.[76] These Hebrew words are not identical. The second one tries to qualify the idea that an image could mean a replica. Some of the dogmatic conclusions, however, drawn from the different use of words go beyond their scriptural basis. Irenaeus claimed that through Adam's fall the God-intended development of humanity, through which it was to become immortal, was interrupted. Humanity lost its similitude, i.e., its relationship with God, while it retained the image, being a reasonable, and morally free creature. This distinction enabled Irenaeus to affirm that humanity did not change physically but only relationally once it had become a sinner.

The distinction between similitude and image, however, could easily be interpreted to mean that sinfulness only affected part of humanity, while the rest remained in a state of original integrity. This hazard is especially noticeable when Augustine uses neo-Platonic terminology and talks about evil as a deficiency of the good that results from a deficient cause or from a defect.[77] Such a train of thought could lead to the notion that humanity only needs to improve in order to be no longer sinful.

In late medieval theology the deficiency aspect of sin was even further developed. Thomas Aquinas, for instance, stated that "original sin in its material sense is indeed concupiscence, while in its formal sense it is certainly a defect of the original justice." [78] Original justice which Adam once enjoyed is now missing and therefore humanity was plagued with sin. This "corrupt disposition" namely the privation of original justice, is now called original sin.[79] But it can be corrected through a supernatural gift which achieves a sublimation of the rational creature beyond the human nature.[80] Human nature no longer needs a conversion but an addition or a sublimation. Grace was then understood as something supernatural in humanity or a supernatural quality.[81]

To perceive grace as a supernatural addition to humanity's natural state is as dangerous as the idea that a human being is not a totally corrupt and sinful entity, but only lacks the supernatural gifts of the similitude, i.e., original justice and integrity.[82] But the church thought differently. Therefore the Council of Trent decided in the "Decree on Justification" that through God's grace humanity can assent, cooperate, and dispose itself to God's salvific activity.[83] This meant that the church did not hold that humanity's sinful nature was really changed. Its properties as an image of God were still thought to be integral so that the lost similitude could be achieved through a supernatural addition.[84]

When we come to the Reformers, we notice that the distinction between image and similitude has been abandoned. "Man must be an image," we hear Luther say, "either of God or of the devil, because according to whom he directs his life, him he resembles." [85] Humanity is perceived as an entity and if it is sinful, the whole humanity is sinful. This reminds us of Luther's statement in *The Bondage of the Will* that a human being resembles an animal that is either driven by God or by the devil.[86]

John Calvin, though asserting that there is nothing left in humanity of which it could boast, claimed that there are "some remaining traces of the image of God which distinguish the entire human race from the other creatures." [87] Perhaps a little more cautious, this was the line of thinking that Lutheran Orthodoxy took. John Gerhard, for instance, maintains that "with regard to these most minute particles . . . the image of God was not utterly lost." [88] These "most minute particles," however, are inborn moral principles, humanity's dominion over other creatures, its intelligence, and its free will concerning the things which are under its control. We must agree here with Paul

Althaus that something important was emphasized here, but with inadequate conceptuality.[89] As aforementioned, humanity did not suddenly become stupid, lazy, and unreliable once it was drawn into universal sinfulness.

Karl Barth was right when he emphasized that the fact that humanity was created in the image of God did not get lost through sin. Even as sinner a human being is still God's creature and related to God.[90] The psalmist captured this insight very precisely when he exclaimed: "Whither shall I go from thy Spirit? Or whither shall I flee from thy presence?" (Ps. 139:7). As we have noticed, Genesis 1:26 does not talk about an ideal state of the distant past.[91] Still today humans are called to be God's administrators. To fulfill this task they are still endowed with the same gifts they always possessed. This does not mean that Luther was wrong when he stated that humanity has totally lost its status as being created in the image of God. We must remember that Luther was attacking the idea that some features in humanity were still integral while others were contaminated by sinfulness. Thus he insisted that the total human being was a corrupt entity. Emil Brunner seems to make the same point when he says: "The breaking of man's relation to God means that the image of God in man has also been broken. This does not mean that it no longer exists, but that it has been defaced." [92] The same stand is taken by G. C. Berkouwer when, in attacking any cooperative view of humanity, he emphasizes the total corruption of humanity.[93]

Today most Roman Catholic theologians have abandoned an ontological understanding of humanity being created in the image of God which so easily leads to the misunderstanding that part of a human being is still intact while the other part is corrupt. Michael Schmaus, for instance, mentions that according to the Genesis accounts the statement that humanity is created in the image of God should be understood in a functional way.[94] Humans are called to exercise dominion over the world. Only with regard to the new creation in the eschaton can we talk about an ontological understanding of the image of God when we will fully participate in Christ's being, made in the image of God (cf. Rom. 8:29; 2 Cor. 3:18). Very interestingly, Schmaus also mentions that according to the Fathers the statement that humanity is created in the image of God means that God reflects himself in humanity.[95] This implies that people can only realize themselves if they realize themselves as being created in the image of God. But we have seen that instead of reflecting God, people want to be like God.[96] We misuse the creation instead of exercising dominion over it and managing it in thankfulness to God. We are searching for ourselves in the creation instead of looking in it for the "footprints" of our creator. Therefore, in trying to discover the cosmos, we lose ourselves to the cosmos. Our world begins to resemble more and more a kingdom of sin rather than the kingdom of God.

c. The kingdom of evil

In the Gospel of John we hear the conviction expressed that the cosmos is ruled by the prince of this world. It was up to AUGUSTINE, however, to systematize and historicize in his classic *The City of God* the dynamic drives exhibited by the kingdom of God and the kingdom of sin. Augustine speaks of two cities, the city of God and the city of the world. One city "consists of those who wish to live after the flesh, the other of those who wish to live after the spirit, and when they severally achieve what they wish, they live in peace, each after their kind." [97] The two cities are not neatly separated, because the city of God lives like an alien in the city of the world.[98] The two cities or societies have been formed by two kinds of love: "the earthly by the love of self, even to the contempt of God, the heavenly by the love of God, even to the contempt of self. The former, in a word, glories in itself, the latter in the Lord." [99]

The decisive difference between the two cities does not lie so much in the material content of their actions, though Augustine observes that in the city of the world the rulers, and the people they control, are swayed by lust for domination, whereas in the city of God all citizens serve one another in charity. Augustine sees the decisive difference rather in the intentionality of their actions, whether one "lives according to himself" or according to God.[100] In both societies things essential to this life must be used, "but each has its own peculiar and widely different aim in using them. . . . The whole use of things temporal has a reference to this result of earthly peace in the earthly community, while in the city of God it is connected with eternal peace." [101] In the earthly city the possessions and comforts of this life tend to smear and block the way to God, whereas in the city of God they help to ease the burden of our life. Thus the believers are looking forward to judgment day when the city of this world will be dissolved and the kingdom of God emerge.[102]

Sin is here definitely understood as having a social dimension. It serves the self-glorification of humanity and is at least potentially self-destructive. Though Augustine knows that God can make a good use even of evil, we should not forget that he wrote *The City of God* under the impression of the devastation of Rome through the Gothic hordes of Alaric in 410.[103] Human history, as a history of the city of the world, is therefore interpreted as bringing upon itself its own judgment, which is at the same time part of God's judgment. The city of God is therefore a reminder and a corrective for the city of the world.

Nearly 1500 years after Augustine, ALBRECHT RITSCHL introduced the distinction between a kingdom of sin and the kingdom of God, to some extent very closely resembling Augustine's distinction and to some extent in deliberate opposition to it. This becomes evident when we hear him say that

> Sin, which alike as a mode of action and as a habitual propensity extends over the whole human race, is, in the Christian view of the world, estimated as the opposite of reverence and trust towards God, as also the opposite of the Kingdom of God—in the latter respect forming the kingdom of sin, which possesses no necessary ground either in the Divine world-order or in man's natural endowment of freedom, but unites all men with one another by means of the countless interrelations of sinful conduct.[104]

Ritschl rejected Pelagius' individualistic notion of sin, since he realized that the subject of sin is *"humanity as the sum of all individuals"* and that it leads to an association of individuals in common evil.[105] The kingdom of sin forms "a sinful federation with others" that "we become accustomed to standing forms of sin, at any rate in others, and acquiesce in them as the ordinary expression of human nature." [106] As a strict follower of Kant, Ritschl has abandoned the understanding of original sin as something inherited and instead emphasizes humanity's own choice.[107] The sinful desire and action of each individual "has its sufficient ground in the self-determination of the individual will." [108] We might wonder, however, to what extent the influence of others that Ritschl assumes, still leaves room for strict self-determination. The same question can be posed to Ritschl when he argues that there exists in each child "a general, though still indeterminate, impulse toward the good, which just falls short of being guided by complete insight into the good, and has not yet been tested in the particular relationships of life." [109] Yet does Ritschl really want to say that each child can be educated toward the good? Perhaps we get a clue to our question when we consider how Ritschl defines sin.

"Sin is the opposite of the good, so far as it is selfishness springing from indifference or mistrust of God, and directs itself to goods of subordinate rank without keeping in view their subordination to the highest good." [110] The Augustinian neo-Platonic notion of sin as a deficiency of the good is present here in Ritschl's definition of sin as well as the understanding of God as the highest good. Since sin, however, ultimately rests with humanity, individually and corporately conceived, Emil Brunner may be right when he said that Ritschl offers "a form of Pelagianism, intensified by social psychology." [111] But we should not forget that in his understanding of the kingdom of sin Ritschl rightly emphasized and reminded us of each human being's individual responsibility *and* sin's corporate dimension.

Due to Ritschl's influence, both aspects of sin, individual responsibility and corporate structure, were again emphasized by WALTER RAUSCHENBUSCH in his delineation of the kingdom of evil, and later also by Reinhold Niebuhr. [112] Walter Rauschenbusch claimed that "the doctrine of original sin has directed attention to the biological channels for the transmission of general sinfulness from generation to generation, but has neglected and diverted attention from the transmission and perpetuation of specific evils through the channels of social tradition." [113] Unlike Ritschl, however, he does not want to give up the hereditary unity of sin or the supernatural power of evil behind all sinful human action. [114] If we abandon one in favor of the other he is afraid that our sense of sin will become much more superficial and will be mainly concerned with the transient acts and vices of individuals.

Without indulging in medieval witch hunts, Rauschenbusch is convinced that the idea of the kingdom of evil gives to our modern minds an adequate sense of solidarity and a sufficient grasp of the historical and social realities of sin. [115] Since the life of humanity is infinitely interwoven, we cannot just talk about individual sins. "The evils of one generation are caused by the wrongs of the generations that preceded, and will in turn condition the sufferings and temptations of those who come after." [116] We are all bound together by the yoke of evil and suffering. "When the social group is evil, evil is over all." [117] But Rauschenbusch does not simply stop with the recognition of the corporate dimension of evil. He knows that often the leaders of human society have manipulated the fate of thousands of people for their own selfish ends. [118] But Rauschenbusch also knows of a kingdom of God. Yet a conversion from the kingdom of evil to the kingdom of God cannot be confined to our inner self and our personal interests. Conversion is both a break with our own sinful past and with the sinful past of our social group.[119]

With his notion of the kingdom of evil, Rauschenbusch very convincingly demonstrates that, similar to the fact that committing a sin is not just our own private decision, conversion from our sinful existence is not solely something that occurs between our own self and God. Conversion has interpersonal and—what Rauschenbusch did not recognize at his time—international consequences. Sin as aversion from God affects our attitude toward ourselves, other people, and nature; in short, it affects our whole person. We have noticed that humanity continually fails to realize that it ought to be God's administrator in this world. But we have also come to understand that even as sinful human beings we are not degenerated; we are still created in the image of God. God still gives us a framework in which to live. And we are as much accountable for the trespasses against this framework as for our basic attitude of aversion from God (cf. Rom. 2:15f.).

Summary

In this chapter we attempted to discover how evil manifests itself in our nature and to what extent we can still be regarded as truly free agents. In conclusion, we should remember several significant points:

(1) The biblical witnesses assert that humanity is free to choose between good and evil. But they vehemently emphasize that no human being has ever decided only for the good. Since in human actions the good considerably outweighs the bad, one might be inclined to view the human prospect rather optimistically. Yet such assessment could easily be misleading.

(2) No finite being can undo its evil actions, whether through restitution or by receiving forgiveness from other finite beings. Evil actions can only be undone by a power that is able to create history anew. Evil is not simply an action or method resulting in a bad constellation which could be changed. It is that which obstructs the furthering of the ultimate destiny of the universe.

(3) By themselves finite beings do not have an adequate comprehension of the ultimate destiny of the world. They calculate such destiny mainly by projecting past trends toward the future. Their finite horizon, however, limits them considerably in their ability to discern precisely between good and evil. Consequently, their sinful

action of turning away from God, the source of all good and the ultimate horizon of the universe, often results in evil actions of discernible magnitude. This is manifested then on an individual and corporate level and in humanity as well as in humanity's environment.

(4) Biological death is not the result of sin. Yet death takes on an entirely different meaning for humanity in alienation from God than for any other living being. Death confronts humanity in its quest for life's meaning and in its experience of the fundamental incompleteness of human life.

(5) Humanity is alienated from God, but it is not abandoned by him. Humanity is still God's creature and summoned to be God's administrator. Yet it only lives up to this position of reflecting God in its life-style when it opens itself for the ultimate destiny God has promised to humanity. As long as it seeks its own glory instead of God's it will continue to mistreat the world and itself in its pursuit of short-term gains coupled with infinite and often also finite losses. Yet God has promised in history and made manifest in the resurrection of Jesus Christ that his kingdom will finally triumph. Therefore we may hope that God's life-sustaining care will prevent humanity from destroying itself and its environment as it continues to exchange its infinite destiny for finite "values."

7.

Under God's Care

The narrative of our cosmic journey is nearly completed. We have outlined the basic structures of human existence and attempted to relate these structures in their specificity and particularity to the ultimacy and universality of God. And we noticed how humanity's fundamental alienation from God manifests itself in individual and corporate action. We realized, however, that humanity always remains God's creature. Humanity is not severed from God, even if it has abandoned its life of conformity to God and has gone its own way. In this respect Augustine's assertion that humanity deserted God and therefore was deserted by God is not true. Though we may live in agony and uncertainties, God's care is still present for us.

Our journey through space and time is not as haphazard as it may initially appear. God's promise to create a new world, a new heaven and a new earth, and to create us as new human beings continues to act as a mighty magnet in human history. To help our understanding of God's promise we must now investigate what is meant by God's care. Is it simply a preservation for the eschatological fulfillment or does God's preserving action already include features of newness? We will attempt to arrive at an answer by investigating the meaning of the terms general and special providence of God and how that which is envisioned in them relates to the world in which we live.

The idea of providence, troubling already to the ancient Greeks, is more and more questioned today. Facing an inhuman world, we are naturally inclined to exclaim in anguish: Doesn't anybody care? Confronted with the ever-larger prospect of global disasters, we are also more than ever prone to ask: Does the historical evolutionary process take any meaningful direction or is it simply governed by chance? While most of us long for the affirmation that our future will not approach us like an inescapable fate and that there is purpose and fulfillment in the cosmos, we cannot rid ourselves of the profound impact that the predominance of reason has had on us. Are the traditional religious sentiments concerning the course of the world still tenable if we subject every cause and effect sequence to rational scrutiny? Does it make sense then to speak of a divine governance or preservation of the world? We agree with William Pollard that "to speak of an event as an act of God, or to say that it happened because God willed that it should, seems a violation of the whole spirit of science." [1] It is not just secular rationalism, however, that makes it difficult to speak meaningfully about divine providence.

Modern technology has introduced heretofore unknown temptations to humanity. After Auschwitz and Hiroshima we can hardly agree with Gottfried Wilhelm Leibniz' confident optimism in which he declared that our world is the best possible one. Even Augustine's neo-Platonic idea that evil is merely a deficiency of the good seems untenable for us. We are rather tempted to agree with Richard Rubenstein when he ponders that if there were God he could not have permitted Auschwitz to happen, and if he had, we would have to strip him of his divine office.[2] Or we are inclined to agree with Arthur Schopenhauer when he rephrased Leibniz' assertion, saying that the world is "the worst of all possible worlds." [3] But it is not only God's special providence, or his miraculous activity, that is being challenged, it is also his general providence, or his benevolent being with his creation, that is being questioned. If we want to address ourselves to the question whether our present experience of the world and our notion of divine providence are two incongruous entities, we must deal with both God's general providence and God's special providence.

Since the biblical witnesses introduce us to the significance of God as the maker of history and the creator of the world, the understanding of God who is at work within the present order of nature should not pose any theological problems. Scientific objections too should virtually be eliminated, because we have seen that scientific investigations concern themselves with past events. For instance, only in retrospect can the historical and evolutionary process be viewed as a strictly immanent process. As soon as we can view an event, it is already past action. It is no longer an immediate occurrence. The now-point of an event is withdrawn from our immediate perception. Divine providence, however, concerns itself exactly with this now-point. It expresses the conviction that God is in control of the constellations of forces that decide at any given moment in which direction the future will be shaped. Moreover, divine providence also expresses the conviction that the future does not emerge in any conceivable way, but only in that form which God decides for it. Since providence does not primarily deal with the visible past, but rather with the invisible present and the amorphous dimension of the future, we need not be surprised that it is subject to many and differing interpretations.

1. Major Misunderstandings of God's Providence

There are especially three ways of interpreting divine providence which seem to clash most blatantly with the Christian understanding of God's providence. Nevertheless these three misunderstandings, namely the deistic or pantheistic notion, the fatalistic or Stoic notion, and the astrological or magic notion are more widespread than the Christian understanding of God's providence.

a. Deistic and pantheistic approaches

Originating in England and spilling over into France and Germany, the deistic notion of God's providence gained special prominence in the Enlightenment period of the late 17th and early 18th century. Yet it is not just a historical peculiarity. Its main tenets are still widespread today among common people as well as among scientists. God is conceived of as juxtaposed to nature. Often the whole universe is understood as resembling a huge clockwork. God functions primarily as the divine watchmaker who once constructed and wound up the magnificent clock of the universe and who now lets it run according to its own predesigned laws. God is held to be much too sublime and perfect to be actively involved in our daily lives or even guide them. Leibniz, perhaps, was the most prominent advocate of this kind of thinking.

According to Leibniz the whole universe forms a pre-established harmony consisting of many, self-enclosed, blind entities, which he called monads.[4] These monads, which can be atoms, inanimate bodies, living beings, or spirits, are coordinated like innumerable clocks. To ensure that there is perfect harmony in the universe, the monads do not interact with each other by their own volition. Each monad rather

acts like a minute soul which represents both its own bodily entity
and the whole universe with which it is coordinated. Depending upon
their function, the monads are not equal in their degree of perception; they range from almost imperceptive dead matter to the purest
perceptivity and activity which is God. In a detached manner God
reigns above the world and foreknows everything.

In their reverence of God and in their appreciation of his greatness,
deists are superior to many traditional Christians. The deistic emphasis on the non-interference of God reminds us how beautifully and
imaginatively God has arranged his creation. Every mechanistic process in nature may serve as another proof of the ingenuity of God.[5]
Yet a deistic God up there or out there is not a personal God who
cares about us or the world, but a God relegated to personal inactivity. Thus the magnificent order of the world becomes oppressive
for us, the laws of nature are experienced as ruling our destiny indiscriminately. Furthermore, the beauty and orderliness of nature can
be maintained only when we look for the most general and comprehensive lines which emerge in the history of nature. However, once
we consider individual events, the orderliness dissolves into random-
ness. We seem to encounter arbitrary constellations and a God who
plays dice. Suddenly the majestic grandeur of nature is replaced by
a picture of cruelty and disorder. Thus the evolutionary ascent of
life is reduced to the survival of the fittest, the blind alleys of the
evolutionary process, and the phenomenon of sickness and disease.
Since deists conceive of the history of nature as the immediate outcome of God's preordained plan, a deistic notion of providence could
as easily lead to the assertion that God cares as it could lead to the
idea that God does not care and never has cared.

The pantheistic notion of divine providence proceeds along the
pantheistic lines of relating God and world. Similar to deistic thought
God's providential plan and the history of nature are seen as one.
Contrary to deism, however, God is not perceived as a distant God,
but a God who is close at hand and present in every leaf of a tree.
God's providence encounters us in an unceasing way. In spring it
shows in the greening and blooming of nature, in summer in the
warm sunshine, in fall in the abundance of food, and in winter we
experience God who allows nature to rest and gain new strength for
the coming spring. The birds singing in the trees, the butterflies glid-
ing through the air, and the white clouds sailing across the sky remind
us of the beauty of God's creation and its wonderful arrangement.
We are thankful to pantheism for reminding us of this side of crea-

tion which we too often tend to overlook. God, however, is perceived there as hardly more personal and more caring than in traditional deism. This becomes evident, for instance, when we hear Friedrich Schleiermacher argue that divine providence is identical with natural causality.[6] Even sin, he says, is embraced under divine foreordination.

Yet if we identify God with nature as in pantheism, can we still call God a loving and caring God? Have not the life sciences shown us a different God when they tell us that one form of life can only be sustained by destroying other life? Furthermore, earthquakes that destroy flourishing cities, such as Lisbon in 1755, San Francisco in 1906, and Guatemala City in 1976, and floods that leave thousands of people without food and shelter, seem to tell us of a different kind of God than envisioned in pantheism. Nature in its grandeur, splendor, and profuseness is only one side of the coin. On the other side, however, nature with its basic laws of becoming and perishing remains impersonal, cool, and cruel. If we identify nature with God, as does pantheism, our world would also witness to a God who has planned everything with ice-cold, irrevocable determination. Our lives would no longer result from personal and responsible endeavors, but mirror the fatal and mechanistic routine that the laws of nature seem to reflect.

Even process thought or a theism of the second type is remarkably silent on these negative aspects of the historical and natural process. We remember that Whitehead and Hartshorne affirmed that we must conceive of God as a loving and caring God. But the intimate (pantheistic or panentheistic) relation they propose to exist between God and world, and their conviction of an upward and forward moving cosmo-historical process seem to stand in stark contrast to the almost frightening increase of the human potential for self-destruction. We might recall the projections of Erich Fromm, Robert Heilbroner, and Konrad Lorenz who point out the dangers of already existing partial realization of this potential. There is just too much negative feedback from the world that God would remain unaffected if he is as closely related to the world and even to some extent contingent upon it as process thought presupposes. David Griffin, for instance, admits this when he asserts that God "is also the universal recipient of the totality of good and evil that is actualized. . . . Stimulating the world toward greater intensity means the risk that God too will experience more intense suffering." [6a] Yet such an immensely involved god is no longer the freely guiding agent who can assure us that his redemptive promises will come true.

b. Fatalistic and Stoic approaches

The fatalistic notion of divine providence too seems to result from a radical identification of God's will with the natural processes. Unlike pantheism, however, God is usually not perceived as identical with nature. He is understood to be beyond nature with the latter serving as the extension of his will. In fatalism one is usually convinced that God governs and determines everything to such an extent that there is no possibility of escaping our predetermined fate. Since God has ordered the whole universe according to his will, it is useless and almost blasphemous to attempt to change the predominant natural or historical constellations. The appropriate attitude is not to take the initiative, but to resign ourselves to the divine fate so that God's will can prevail.

Especially in popular Islamic religion the belief is often held that one's fate or *Kismet* is settled beforehand by God, and that, whatever one may do, one can scarcely modify it. Muslim storytellers reinforce the idea that if something is Allah's will, all human endeavors are futile.[7] One might conclude that if the divine will is so overpowering the individual is relegated to total passivity. Though this conclusion is occasionally drawn, the bravery of Muslim soldiers points in a different direction. Since it is understood that Allah holds our destiny in his hands, all earthly powers can be defied. If it is indeed Allah's will that we should fall on the battlefield, we cannot escape his decree. However, if he has ruled differently, regardless how suicidal our courageous actions are, the enemy will not prevail over us.

Though Muslim theologians have repeatedly rejected a fatalistic interpretation of divine providence, their task is rather difficult.[8] While in the Qur'an the notion of both free will and strict determinism can be found, the name of Islam, meaning "surrender to God's will," seems to suggest in which direction the tension between free will and determinism ought to be resolved. The pre-eminence of divine foreordination does not allow on the human side for true freedom and responsible action. Humanity does no longer freely respond to God, it rather acts in spite of God in its daring endeavors lest it ends up in fatalistic resignation.

The Stoic notion of divine providence originated in ancient Greece. Greek religion never attained such a strict monotheism as did Islam. At best it developed the notion of a supreme god Zeus, ruling with a pantheon of other gods and goddesses. Consequently these gods and goddesses were not in control of human destiny. As the pre-Socratic philosopher Xenophanes observed, they looked and acted too much

like men and were subjected to the same destiny as humanity.[9] Unlike
the Muslims, the ancient Greeks did not conceive of an all-powerful
God standing behind the individual and corporate destiny. Therefore
destiny itself had to assume ultimate dimensions.

The Stoics captured this sentiment best when they advocated a
blind deterministic concept of fate. All foreknowledge leads at best
to the disclosure of a cycle of events from whom nobody is exempt.
At times the impersonal world reason or cosmic *logos* that lies behind
everything that happens in the world can assume features of a fatherly
providence that cares.[10] But most frequently God's care for individuals is not emphasized and providence is equated with destiny and
fate (*moira* and *haimarmene*). *Haimarmene* is even called the law
of the cosmos.[11] There is no escape for humans; what has been
decreed will be executed.

Though Greek life witnesses to a thoroughgoing pessimism, the
Stoics did not want to surrender to blind fate.[12] Realizing that the
impersonal destiny (*moira*) had the last word, they did not feel that
it was appropriate to resign to passivity. They steadfastly maintained
against the Greek Skeptics that the beauty and the interlocking purposes reveal that there is a benevolent will at work in the world.
They concluded that if one discerns the rules according to which this
world reason governs the course of the affairs and if one overcomes
one's own pettiness through virtue, one can lead a life of happiness
and fulfillment. Nature and history still run their course, but within
limits one can lead a life of self-determination, one is not a mere
victim. One of the early representatives of the Stoa, Cleanthes of
Assos, put this sentiment best when he confessed: "Fate leads the
willing, it drags on the unwilling." [13]

In times when people attempted to find direction in nature for the
foundation of their political and spiritual life, such as in imperial
Rome, in the Renaissance period, and during the Enlightenment,
Stoic ideas gained new popularity. People were convinced that at
least to some extent they could take their life in their own hands,
provided they pursue a prudent and heroic stand. Still today it is the
philosophy of the common people who want to enjoy at least the
small pleasures of life. They know too well that they are helpless in
changing the often unjust and oppressive structures of society.

But if we have no means to interfere and change our larger destiny,
if *moira* finally rules anyhow, then all self-control and self-determination has only modest value. At the most it provides temporary com-

fort, as for instance Boethius' *Consolation of Philosophy* indicates that
he wrote when he was unjustly thrown into prison by the Ostrogothic
King Theodoric and awaited his execution. Though there is no doubt
that Boethius remained a Christian in prison, the Stoic influence he
had imbibed in Rome led him to the classical Stoic assertion that
God is the foreknowing spectator of all events who will eventually
reward the good and punish the wicked.[14] Yet the indication of this
trust in God's benevolent providence stands in stark contrast to the
emphasis on divine foreordination. If God is really the ultimate source
of the historical process, it would be more logical to assume that he
distributes indiscriminately both good and evil.

c. Astrological and magic approaches

Touching upon the magic and astrological notions of divine providence we notice that its overpowering character has been diminished.
Unlike Stoicism, people are now convinced that they cannot only
know but to some extent even manipulate the future. In magic acts
the idea is expressed that through the use of certain objects and
rituals other objects and events can be affected. Cults are developed
to protect people and goods through manipulation with lucky numbers, amulets, and magic rites. Often these beliefs make use of Christian symbols, such as the cross, while they are actually remains of
primitive pre-Christian religions. They have made inroads in all higher
developed religions, reminding us that humanity's attempt to master
its own destiny is not a transitory phenomenon.

Some of the magic traits go back to the origin of humanity and its
religions. We must mention here first of all the belief in mana, a
supernatural invisible power that usually rests in a strong man, such
as a chief or a medicine man, and which can also be imparted to
animals, plants, and stones. In the magnificent wall paintings of
Altamira, Spain, hunters of the Paleolithic Age expressed the belief
that this magic power could be captured in symbols which would
then aid them in hunting. Still today many people wear an amulet
of some kind or have one in their cars to protect themselves from
unforeseen circumstances. Astrology supplements endeavors to master
one's destiny. It conveys the idea that cosmic constellations are
responsible for events here on earth and that by observing them it is
possible to predict the future and avoid undesirable consequences.

The belief in the providential power of stellar constellations is a
common feature in many religions. In the ancient empire of the

Aztecs, some years thousands of people were slaughtered to nourish the sun god and to dispose him favorably.[15] In other religions, e.g., the Egyptian, Greek, or Babylonian religions, customs were less cruel, but still the concern about the stars dominated the life of most people.[16] Even today the signs of the zodiac still play an important role, and a weekly magazine would be incomplete for many readers if it did not include the "prediction of the stars" for the coming week. Of course, many people will bluntly deny that they believe in such predictions. Nevertheless they read them eagerly every week and their decisions are more or less influenced by them.

We could simply reject the astrological understanding of divine providence as pure superstition and would be in good company. For instance, Martin Luther rejected astrology in no uncertain terms. Yet his time was full of the oddest superstitions and in many cases Luther was a son of his time.[17] Even Luther's close friend, Philip Melanchthon, thought much of astrology and attempted to establish a horoscope for Luther. He ridiculed Melanchthon's endeavor and whenever he had a chance he mocked at Melanchthon's love for astrology.[18] God would have to be pretty busy, Luther argued, if he would have to consult the stars before he could do anything. Luther was not interested in the exact date of his birth, a necessity for a good horoscope, and he was sure that heaven was not interested in it either.[19] It seemed strange for him that only a few stars should have such determining power over a human being, namely the stars of the sign of the zodiac under which one was born, but not all the stars in the sky.[20] It was especially ludicrous for him that the stars had to wait until someone was born to assume power over him, but they were not strong enough to penetrate the thin skin separating their rays from the unborn child. Rational arguments of this kind and the theological objection that God alone knows the future merged in Luther's scorn of astrology. Even today his criticism of astrology should not be taken lightly.

But what shall we say when the New Testament tells us that even God used a stellar constellation, possibly the conjunction of Jupiter and Saturn, to announce the birth of the savior? Should we simply reject this story as unbiblical and as an illegitimate influence of pagan religions? This would hardly be fair. But God is not the all-determining primordial tyrant at whose fiat everything comes into being. The Bible does not even deny that there are powers which are not immediately associated with God's reign. However, it constantly warns us against making use of them. For example, when King Saul tried to peek into the future by communicating through an occult medium with the spirits of the dead, this experience was devastating for him (1 Sam. 28:20).

Since all power is ultimately delegated from God, there is no actual reason to trust in the determining power of charms, amulets, or the movement of the stars. The endeavor to secure knowledge of the future through such secondary means is an attempt to bypass God and his power. This does not mean, however, that, without their dubious assistance we are left in the dark concerning the future. Knowing about God's redemptive activity, we have some foreknowledge of what God's ultimate future will bring. As God's representatives we are also encouraged to safeguard the future and administer it in accordance with God's will. But any cooperation with occult powers would contradict and obscure our position in relation to God. Instead of unconditionally obeying God's will, our actions would become contingent upon the assistance we believe these powers might give us.

Of course, God can use an unusual stellar constellation to indicate the beginning of one of his decisive acts with us. But signs are never self-evident. God himself has to interpret their meaning to us. When we carefully read the story about the star of Bethlehem (Matt. 2:1-12), we notice that the "wise men" did not expect God to be born in human form; they were looking for a mighty king. Only God, who is not subject to temporality, knows about the future and about the right interpretation of the signs that point toward it.

2. General Providence of God

When we now turn to God's providence by outlining the trustworthiness of the future, we must remind ourselves that though the future is hidden from our eyes, it is not dark for us. Neither the heroic stand of the Stoics nor the meddling attitude of magicians and astrologers is biblically warranted. In confrontation with God's redemptive history, we recognize that there is purpose and destiny involved in the creative processes. The discovery of purpose and destiny in our daily life is based on awareness that we have a future we can trust. The trustworthiness of the future has to be maintained in three areas, in the natural process of inanimate and animate nature, in the moral process of human behavior, and in the historical process of the human family's communal life.

a. *The trustworthiness of the natural process*

We have seen that the natural processes started once there was nature or matter. Yet there was no reason or cause that there should have been something in the first place. If there is no sufficient reason for the world's existence, the world is not absolute; it is contingent upon God's sustenance. The world being created out of nothingness is constantly threatened by nothingness. The divine providence consists then first of all in maintaining the creation. Luther, for instance, was much more impressed by the continuous sustenance of God's creation than by the creative act in the beginning, because Luther observed that many people start something, but most do not have the vigor to keep it going.[21] God, however, sustains his creation and is with it in every moment. Nothing is excluded from his sustaining guidance. He governs the orbits of the electrons as well as the encounter between two young persons that results in marriage.

The Old Testament understanding of *ruah* (spirit) serves well to illustrate God's sustaining and maintaining power.[22] When God gives his spirit something becomes alive and it lives as long as he leaves his spirit with it. But when he takes back his spirit, the people, or whatever it may be, is destined to perish. Thus the Old Testament people cry to Yahweh: "Cast me not away from thy presence, and take not thy holy Spirit from me" (Ps. 51:11). If God is the one without whom nothing can exist and without whom nothing can occur, he would be the sustainer of the earthquakes as well as of the spring rain, of devastating floods as well as the beautiful sunrise. Then we would come close to equating divine providence with the laws of nature or with all natural events. Yet would not such seemingly pantheistic identification of God with nature make it extremely difficult to resort to God in our understanding of nature? Would not nature itself be its highest principle of interpretation?

These fears would indeed be justified if we would forget that God makes the difference between nothing and something. As Hegel, for instance, emphasized nature is not equal with God, it is contingent upon him. Unless we perceive God as standing behind all the natural events, we are in danger of relegating God to the fewer and fewer instances in which we do not know the answer, or to a god of the gaps. Yet Dietrich Bonhoeffer warned us that with our increasing knowledge of the natural cause and effect sequences, God would be more and more edged out of the world.[23] If we want to avoid this danger, Bonhoeffer insisted that we rather affirm God in the midst of life, in the places in which we seem to know all the natural causes. Thus the affirmation of God's sustaining power in the face of the laws of nature and of all natural causes seems consequential and necessary.

But did we not now affirm a demonic god, a god who plays dice, and who builds up and destroys his creation with equal ease? At this point the issue of theodicy or the justification of God becomes important. To shed some light on this matter it is helpful to remember that the biblical writers do not divide all processes into two kinds, evil ones for which Satan is responsible and good ones which can be attributed to God. They are much more interested in showing that ultimately all processes will have to make God's kingdom triumph. This does not mean, however, that we are only enlightened about this ultimate and all-encompassing purpose of all processes while the individual events of history up to the eschaton remain dark and ambiguous. There are several degrees of dependability discernible even within the natural processes leading to that final goal: [24]

1. One kind of dependability is represented in the rising and setting of the sun and in the cycles of the seasons. It is a basic factor in the development of life on earth and, to our knowledge, it is completely reliable and dependable. Of course, we have noticed (cf. chapter 1) that not even the predictable movements of the celestial bodies can be taken for granted. Yet the probability for alternate modes of behavior than those we have observed is virtually zero. The dependability of the cycles of day and night and of the seasons is also reflected in the covenant with Noah when we hear Yahweh promise: "While the earth remains, seedtime and harvest, cold and heat, summer and winter, day and night, shall not cease" (Gen. 8:22).

2. A different form of dependability arises when several alternatives and large numbers of repeated instances are involved. We encounter this, for example, in the chemical reactions when wood and other fuels are burned, in the nuclear reactions in the core of the sun, and in the functions of our body cells. Without the dependability of these processes there would be no life on earth and no human history. Our very lives depend on the reliability of a huge number of these processes. Again the biblical witnesses remind us that God provides this kind of dependability. We hear that no sparrow falls to the ground without God's permission (Matt. 10:29), that all the hairs on our head are numbered (Matt. 10:30), and that God sends rain on the just and on the unjust (Matt. 5:45).

3. There is, however, a third kind of dependability which we en-

counter primarily in the evolutionary process of the universe and of life itself.

> So far as the laws of nature and the structure of things in space and time are concerned, the universe *could* have had many histories other than the one it has had. At the same time, however, it is equally true, under the stern requirements of the necessity of choice in temporal existence, that it *can* have only one of these histories.[25]

All other possibilities are gone and lost forever. The whole evolutionary process, especially of life on earth, is so accidental that the American vertebrate paleontologist George G. Simpson can rightly claim that "there is no automatism that will carry him [man] upward without choice or effort and there is no trend solely in the right direction. Evolution has no purpose." [26] We remember that even Charles Darwin wished that in all the accidental occurrences he could see a little more divine guidance in the evolutionary process. At the same time Darwin advanced rather strict principles according to which the advancement of life and the evolution of new species proceeds. Scientific research has refined Darwin's findings considerably, but it has not repudiated them. Jacques Monod also told us that there is chance and necessity in the evolutionary process. Therefore this third kind of dependability tells us on the one hand that the natural process is trustworthy, since it is ongoing, but it tells us on the other hand that it is open and undetermined.

Some conclude from the openness of the evolutionary process that humanity should take this process in its own hands.[27] Undoubtedly these calls have not remained unheard and humanity is effectively changing large parts of the evolutionary process. However, this interference has not altered the large scale picture of the process. As part of the natural process, our own doing is subject to chance and accident too. How many Nobel prizes in the sciences, for peace, or for literature, would not have been bestowed, for instance, if chance and accident had not been involved in the great contributions made to humanity? We, therefore, delude ourselves when we hope to master the natural process, not because we merely lack sufficient ingenuity and cleverness for the task, but because the natural process itself is fundamentally uncontrollable by humanity.[28]

It is exactly with regard to this third kind of dependability that we discern a peculiar train of thought in the biblical creation accounts. We hear that initially God said and it was so (Gen. 1:6f. et al.). This

is followed by the command for humanity to assume a certain responsibility (Gen. 1:28). And finally we are told that God takes protective care of humanity (Gen. 3:21: "And the Lord God made for
Adam and for his wife garments of skins, and clothed them."). This
means that the creative process itself and humanity's functioning
within this process do not suffice to make it dependable. Beyond
initiating and maintaining his creation God also has to abide with it.
We are reminded here of Luther's observation that we should not
think that God has retired and is sleeping on a pillow in heaven, instead he watches and guides everything. Luther was also much impressed with the fact that God did not abandon his creation after
he made it saying: "He [God] has not created the world like a carpenter builds a house and then leaves it and lets it be the way it is,
but he stays with it and sustains it the way he has made it, otherwise
it would not remain." [29]

God's care for humanity as expressed in the natural process is not
uniform. It proceeds on several layers of dependability involving
greater or lesser freedom. Within this freedom adverse constellations
have their place too, such as earthquakes and floods, or human man-
agement or mismanagement of the earth, and even to some extent
the seductive and devastating anti-Godly powers. Of course, we
could ask why God allows for a freedom that can also result in negative actions. Yet what other kinds of freedom could there be? If there
were only freedom towards the good there would only be coercion
but no actual freedom to choose between good and bad. God would
be the primordial tyrant at whose fiat everything occurs. Since the
overpowering providence expressed in Stoic or Islamic thought is foreign to the biblical experience, we arrive at a notion of providence
that sets forth but does not compel, that accomplishes and does not
dehumanize. The final goal and degree of dependability are known
and therefore the natural process is trustworthy though not foolproof.

In talking about the natural process we acknowledge that there is
a dynamic drive in nature. Scientific investigation has shown us that
nature moves consistently with and in space and time. Since, phenomenologically speaking, space and time are also nature's utmost
parameters, we have no reference point, however, to discern clearly
a teleological direction of this movement. Yet when this drive is
related to God, such a direction is provided. Now we recognize the
eschatological dimension of nature and hear that "the creation waits
with eager longing for the revealing of the sons of God" (Rom.
8:19). We also realize that nature is not an isolated phenomenon.

It is tied to and expressive of the phenomenon of life and therefore of humanity. Knowing about the God who cares for us through the natural process we can approach the future confidently.

b. The trustworthiness of the moral process

There is another major way in which God's general providence expresses itself. While in the natural process the aspect of God's continuous creation is dominant, in the moral process God's preserving action rules supreme. God maintains and guides his creation, and within creation especially humanity, to avoid their destruction and self-annihilation. God did not abandon the world once he had created it. Similarly, he does not let humanity go on its own, once humanity appears on the scene. God endows humanity with orders within which it can proceed and which may aid it in finding its proper place within creation.

The most obvious place to look for guidance is one's conscience. The name conscience is derived from the Latin *conscire* and means "being a witness to" or "knowing with" someone. In other words, the conscience is originally understood as a kind of moral self-reflection that scrutinizes one's activities. When we recall, however, how many crimes have been committed in nationalistic and fascist countries in the name of conscience, we wonder what kind of normative and autonomous voice this conscience is. We realize that our conscience itself is not a moral norm, but attests to such norms which it attempts to enforce.[30] Yet the extent to which these norms are perceived and enforced differs greatly. For some they seem to be hardly existent, while for others they are almost torture, for instance when we think of young Luther in his monastery cell. If we want to address ourselves to the trustworthiness of the moral process, we cannot just look at the conscience as the expression of moral norms. We must search for these very norms.

A promising way in our search for normative forces of human behavior is an investigation of the so-called natural law. The notion of a natural law goes back to the ancient idea that the gods gave their people a code of rules and regulations according to which they could and should conduct their lives. Aristotle cast this into a philosophical framework claiming that basic to all human law is a divine law, namely that which is justified by nature, and which serves as the critical norm and creative foundation of all human legislation and jurisdiction.[31]

At first, the Christian community was rather hesitant to adopt the idea of a natural law, prevalent especially among the Stoics. Yet primarily Origen paved the way for reception of the natural law in the Christian community when he identified Christ, the *logos*, with the world reason *(logos)*. At the same time, however, he pointed out that the existing positive law of the state could easily conflict with the natural law. For instance, he claimed that

> where the law of nature, that is of God, enjoins precepts contradictory to the written laws, consider whether reason does not compel a man to dismiss the written code and the intention of the lawgivers far from his mind, and to devote himself to the divine Lawgiver and to choose to live according to His word, even if in doing this he must endure dangers and countless troubles and deaths and shame.[32]

Soon Origen and other theologians, such as Lactantius, argued with reference to the world reason that to outlaw Christian congregations and to demand sacrifices to the gods was contrary to the natural divine law.[33] Thus for the first time an attempt was made to found and limit the state laws through the divine natural law.

When we come to Augustine we find a more explicit understanding of the natural law. He asserts now that we consider something as just because nature teaches us and not because we have arrived at it through human convention. With this statement he almost anticipated the heavy critique of the natural law a thousand years later by the English empiricists, such as Thomas Hobbes.[34] "The eternal law is the divine order or will of God, which requires the preservation of natural order, and forbids the breach of it." [35] The eternal law is not temporal, but it is concomitant with order, peace, and beauty.[36] At the same time this law is equal to the wisdom and will of God. The eternal law must be distinguished from the temporal law, which was given in Paradise, implanted in our hearts, and promulgated in writing.[37] The eternal law is eternally unchangeable and applies to the whole creation. Animals, however, are subjugated under this law in such a way that they have no part in it, while angels participate in it fully. Humanity is caught in the middle, in part subjugated to it like the animals and in part participating in it like the angels. The natural law belongs essentially to our humanity.[38] It is therefore made concrete and present in many ways, as the specific natural law, as the golden rule, as the Mosaic law, and as the law inscribed in our hearts. In these forms the temporal law is the reflection of the eternal law.[39]

Thomas Aquinas largely followed Augustine in his understanding of the natural law. For him "the eternal law is nothing other than the reason of divine wisdom according to which it serves as the directive of all actions and movements." [40] Contrary to Augustine, Thomas does not think that the term law *(lex)* is derived from reading *(legere)* or choosing *(eligere)*, but from that which is binding *(ligando)* on how we should act.[41] He therefore emphasizes the normative element in the law. "The law is an arrangement of reason for the good of the community which is to be furthered by those who are responsible for the community." [42]

Thomas distinguishes four different kinds of laws: Divinely revealed laws, directed towards supernatural purposes, positive human laws based on the natural law, the natural law itself, and the world law from which the natural law follows. The natural law then is "nothing but the participation of the eternal law in the rational creature." [43] This means that the natural law is connected with both the eternal law and the natural judgment of human reason. Through the human reason the eternal law gains binding power as a reasonable prescript. The natural law is therefore essentially reasonable.[44]

When Thomas based the natural law on the eternal law *and* reason, this was not just a boon which insured its binding character. Once reason went its own way, as happened from the Enlightenment onward, many things were introduced as reasonable which were clearly against any divine (eternal) law. We notice this to some extent in Thomas himself, when he argues for slavery on grounds that slaves are similar to material property. Slavery and private property exist for him "by human contrivance for the convenience of social life, and not by natural law." [45] Though he admits that slaves cannot be forced to convert to the Christian faith, he does not yet develop a natural law for individual freedom. Natural law, however, results primarily in reasonable action [46] according to body, soul, and mind. Therefore humanity establishes natural laws on the basis of the drive to self-preservation; it establishes natural laws on the basis of its animal nature for the purpose of procreation and nurture of its descendants; and it establishes natural laws on the basis of its reasonable nature, for instance, concerning the right and duty of education. Once it had been determined what the essence of humanity is, the law must be developed accordingly to further our humanity. Of course, besides the natural law of the individual Thomas does not neglect the natural law of the community as it applies to family, state, and church.

When we hear Luther say in his *Lectures on Romans* that there is much fantasizing about the natural law, we might conclude that he did not show much appreciation for this time honored concept.[47] When we also remember that he called reason a whore,[48] this might reinforce our picture of Luther's low esteem of humans as reasonable beings. But such a picture shows only one side of Luther's assessment.

Luther was convinced that God had ordered everything in the world, from the largest events to the smallest details. In his *Lectures on Galatians* of 1531 Luther stated with reference to Deuteronomy 22:5: "The male was not created for spinning; the woman was not created for warfare." [49] God has established a certain order in creation according to which each member has its specific place and function. Let the king rule, the bishop teach, and the people obey the magistrate. "In this way let every creature serve in its own order and place." [50] These orders extend over the whole of creation from nature to humanity itself. If nature is ordered by God according to certain structures, it is only consequential that inter-human relationships are ordered in a similar way. Indeed Luther is pointing out framework type of structures for family, government, and other inter-human relationships. For instance, God has instilled in the hearts of parents that they serve their children to the best of their ability, nourish them, care for them, and bring them up in diligence.[51]

Luther claims that these orders of relationships between people are best expressed in the natural law. For instance, everybody knows that we should obey our parents, since we are from the same blood and since they bring us up.[52] Likewise reason tells us that we should not kill anybody. From passages such as Matthew 7:12 and Romans 2:15 Luther concludes that the natural law contains all the precepts of the prophets and all other commandments.[53] To a large extent Luther finds the natural law identical with the Mosaic law. Since the Mosaic law, however, was given to the Jewish people, only that part of this law which is congruous with the natural law is obligatory for everyone. The matter is different with the commandment of love. Luther rightly recognizes that it is part of the natural law.

Since the natural law is inborn in us like the heat in fire or the fire in flint, it cannot be separated from the divine law.[54] It is a natural gift of God which was not lost through the fall. It enables and facilitates the communal life and serves as basis and corrective for all other forms of law. When Luther states, however, that "if natural law and reason were inherent in all heads," [55] all people would be equal in their conduct, he concedes that the natural law is no longer available in an absolutely normative form. While it is still inscribed into our hearts, because of our sinfulness its words do not have compelling power.[56]

In a similar way Luther assesses the power of reason. For instance, he admonishes a prince to "determine in his own mind when and where the law is to be applied strictly or with moderation, so that law may prevail at all times and in all cases, and reason may be the highest law and the master of all administration of law." [57] Yet reason does not function independently as the norm for the natural law, though Luther admits that the written law stems from reason as the wellspring of all law.[58] It can fulfill its normative function only insofar as it is imbedded in the ordering activity of God which surrounds and maintains it and which reason continuously presupposes.[59] Reason does not inaugurate the trustworthy moral process, but it discovers and forms the legal process according to God's ordering action. As long as reason and natural law are sustained by the ordering activity of God, they are the normative and formative forces of the moral process.

In the Enlightenment period, however, Luther's admonition concerning the relationship between God's ordering activity and the natural law was discarded. The notion developed that the natural law could be maintained on a strictly rational basis without reference to God. For instance, Jean Jacques Rousseau claimed that humanity is by nature good and that it could regain this natural state if it would turn away from the corrupting influences of society and civilization and be itself, instead of being simply a citizen whose value depends on the community in which one lives.[60] This idea is pursued further in his *Social Contract* (1762). While he realizes that human society is threatened by the tyranny of the people themselves, he is convinced that a true and just society cannot be based on mere force, it must rather be consistent with people as free and rational beings. Therefore he suggested that humanity be liberated from the tyranny of the human will. Rousseau insisted that no human being is isolated but part of a greater whole.[61] Freed from the narrow confines of its own being, a human being will find fulfillment in a truly social experience of fraternity and equality with citizens who share the same ideals.

The question must be posed to Rousseau whether one can count on such agreement by nature. For instance, in his *Essay Concerning Human Understanding* (1690) John Locke had already asserted that all our knowledge only stems from sense perception.[62] Following this empiricist trend David Hume finally discarded all metaphysics. Though he still allowed for an original moral sense in humanity, he distinguished between matters of fact, which rest on certain conventions of experience, and truths of reason which are based on certain conventions of reason. Thus there is no longer an eternal norm of justice, and law then becomes a matter of convention.[63] If there is no longer a directing moral influence, how can the sinfully inclined human beings, whom Rousseau portrays, become the citizens who strive for fraternity and equality? Humanity seems to be on a course leading to enslavement rather than to freedom.

When the ontologically grounded natural law was abandoned, however, not only its normative character, but also its outdated manifestations were discarded. For instance, the idea was increasingly challenged that there existed different classes of people with different rights and privileges. Undeniable progress could now be made by instituting inalienable human rights for all people and democratic procedures for dealing with each other. Yet in doing away with the metaphysically grounded natural law one was also prone to reject the notion that law is more than the expression of circumstances or mere convention. As Emil Brunner has shown, if there is nothing universally valid and no justice beyond ourselves that meets all of us as an undeniable demand, then there is no actual justice, only organized power play.[64] The alarming frequency with which totalitarian systems have emerged during the last one hundred years should make us wonder whether reason itself is a sufficient foundation for the moral process. Even during the reign of absolutism the kings and princes understood that they enjoyed their rule through the grace of God. But today's dictators exercise their rule in their own name. They do no longer feel themselves subjected to higher powers. The individual human being has become its ultimate measure for right and wrong.

But we should also remember Charles Darwin's assertion that human moral and mental faculties differ in degree rather in kind from the capacities of animals. If there is indeed a moral continuity between animals and humans, there should be even more ground to assume such continuity between one human being and another. Perhaps the reason why we tend to deny the basic unity of the human moral process lies in the fact of our sinful estrangement from each other. We are so far apart from each other that we tend to forget our common history and common destiny.

Wolfgang Wickler, a former student of Konrad Lorenz, points out our common moral history in his interesting book *The Biology of the*

Ten Commandments. He claims that the ten, specifically the fourth to the tenth commandments, are demands that have not just emerged on the human level. For instance, inhibition against killing of conspecifics, against theft and lying, and the summon to honor older members of the same social group are already present among animals.[65] This does not mean, however, that these commandments are immutable. As a foundation and summary of appropriate moral behavior they show a development even within the human family.

There are decalog-like collections of commandments known in Egypt, India, and even among the Masai in Kenya.[66] Especially the latter are instructive, since they portray a nomadic existence which necessitated significant changes in the decalog to adjust to the peculiarities of this form of life.[67] We are reminded here of Luther's insight: "What God has given from heaven to the Jews through Moses, he has also inscribed in the hearts of men." [68] Luther recognized the decalog as a basic norm which is known to everyone even without the Mosaic law. Ethological research has adduced more and more evidence that indeed there are some basic norms of human behavior. Arnold W. Ravin expressed this very appropriately when he said:

> Every culture has a concept of murder, that is a specification of conditions under which homicide is unjustifiable. Every culture has a taboo upon incest and usually other regulations upon sexual behavior. Similarly, all cultures hold untruth to be abhorrent, at least under most conditions. Finally, all have a notion of reciprocal obligation between parents and their children. These universal or near-universal ethics . . . do indicate some profound and fundamental needs in all men to behave within certain limits of ethical boundaries.[69]

This means that by nature the behavior of human beings is not as free and unspecified as we might initially assume. To be a human being means to act according to certain norms that enable us to live together and further our own species. The explicit forms which these norms assume, however, depends upon the environment in which the social behavior takes place.

The trustworthiness of the moral process enacted through the living out of these norms depends on our ability to develop these norms in such a way that they continue to be normative for interacting with the environment in which we live. If they are not developed in accordance with the changes we encounter and inaugurate we will become helpless victims of the environmental conditions under which we live.[70] For instance, unless we change our living habits, the crowded conditions in today's anonymous mass society may easily lead to the deterioration of individual partner relationships.[71] This means that contrary to our obligation of governing in this world and subduing it according to the moral norms within us, the world would subdue us and change our moral behavior accordingly.

These insights and conclusions have important implications for our understandings of the traditional theology of orders. Werner Elert is certainly right when he claims that the orders presupposed in the decalog with words of command and prohibition are orders of God's creation, an order to which we belong as its members. Appropriately they are called orders of creation.[72] We wonder, however, whether Elert is correct when he asserts that these orders are always orders that are and not orders that ought to be. Truly, the Sixth Commandment does not constitute marriage but presupposes it. Yet adultery was committed through acts that were considerably different in the ancient Israel of King David than in the medieval Germany of Martin Luther or in the Puritan England of the Pilgrim Fathers. Needless to say, in each epoch marriage was understood quite differently. This does not mean that the underlying norm "thou shalt not commit adultery" loses its binding value. But if we want to maintain the goal of a durable pair relationship which is envisioned in the commandment, the exact interpretation of its normative ought-character must be reevaluated with each changing situation.

Since we discovered that the moral norms are goal-oriented, intended to preserve the species rather than to constitute it, it might be good to follow the suggestion of Walter Künneth and talk about orders of preservation instead of orders of creation. Künneth does not intend to diminish the creational character of these orders, but he objects against a static interpretation of these orders and maintains that the creation must be perceived under the aspect of God's conserving activity.[73] This is even more necessary, since we know God's creation only in its fallen condition, under the aspect of preservation. According to Künneth the orders of preservation counteract the tendencies of the destructive anti-Godly powers. They are a sign that God does not want to destroy the world but conserves it for Christ's sake and towards Christ. The orders of preservation therefore have ultimately eschatological character, for they urge on towards the eschatological fulfillment in the new creation.

Since these orders are no longer evident in their original divine creational intention they assume the character of a law. But as law they enable and facilitate the living together of people. They express a mutual obligation and therefore have basically service character. Yet they are also susceptible to sinful distortion and can be misused to perpetuate injustice and inequality. Therefore, it is necessary never to divorce them from God as the originator and granter of these orders. This does not mean, however, that we should go as far as Karl Barth does when he claims that through its sinful existence humanity is in such a depravity that it has no possibility of knowing about these fundamental moral laws of nature. Barth therefore insists that these orders cannot be found anywhere, but they are disclosed to us through Jesus Christ in God's word.[74]

Dietrich Bonhoeffer attempts a similar christomonistic foundation of these orders as does Barth, when he claims that it is an empty abstraction to talk about the world without relating it to Christ.[75] The relationship "of the world to Christ assumes concrete form in certain mandates of God in the world. The Scriptures name four such mandates: labour, marriage, government, and the Church." The term mandates indicates very appropriately the obligatory aspect of these orders. Yet we are afraid that an exclusively christocentric approach to these orders—whether we accept their foundation in Christ or not—obscures the fact that the acknowledgement of certain moral norms is a necessary condition for human existence as such.[76] Since they are binding for both atheists and Christians, they are not a source of revelation.

Atheists can recognize these norms of moral behavior as partly inborn and partly handed on by tradition. In the light of God's self-disclosure in Jesus Christ, however, Christians perceive in these norms the preserving activity of God. They realize that through the evolving moral process God is preserving the human community against human self-destruction and against the destructive and seductive tendencies of the anti-Godly powers. Luther has expressed this once very picturesquely when he said: "If God would withdraw his protective hand you would become blind, or an adulterer and murderer like David, you would fall and break your leg and drown." [77] Through God's self-disclosure in Jesus Christ we are also reminded of the trustworthiness yet transitory character of the moral process. It will find its fulfillment and completion in the eschatological new creation, when the moral norms will be unimpaired and self-evident.

Then our moral behavior will be characterized through complete harmony with God.

c. The trustworthiness of the historical process

It has not been difficult for us to assert the trustworthiness of the natural process. We know that the universe has evolved in an amazing way over the aeons and there is little doubt that this process of unfolding will continue. Yet amid all the present-day uncertainties it has been more difficult for us to assert that there are basic moral norms which we can trust and which we must continuously develop. When we now consider the historical process, however, then its trustworthiness is even more difficult to maintain. Surely, we are informed by the Christian tradition that God is the Lord of history, but when talking about human history the question immediately emerges: On whose side is he?

In World War I the churches called upon God to bless the weapons on both sides of the trenches. After the Allies had dictated to Germany the terms of peace in the peace treaty of Versailles, the "German Christians" saw the special finger of God in Hitler's rise to power in 1933. Even in 1934 when many had discovered that Hitler was not just a blessing, a group of theologians in Württemberg contrived the following assertion:

> We are full of thanks to God that he, as Lord of history, has given our country Adolf Hitler, as leader and savior from our difficult lot. We acknowledge that we are bound and dedicated with body and soul to the German state and to its *Führer*. This bondage and duty contains for us, as evangelical Christians, its deepest and most holy demand in the fact that it is obedience to the commandment of God.[78]

Even a theologian who was far from being associated with the so-called "German Christians," the former editor of the *Theological Dictionary of the New Testament*, Gerhard Kittel, confessed that he had prayed for years that his people might be saved from their distress and disgrace.[79] Should then the emergence of Adolf Hitler not be regarded as God's answer to prayers of that kind? Had not Adolf Hitler himself invoked the power of "Providence" when he was amazingly spared from assassination attempts? [80]

But not only Christians in Nazi Germany ventured such "providential" interpretations of history. When in 1941 the invasion of the German Army in Russia was most threatening, Patriarch Sergius of the Russian Orthodox Church in Moscow confidently wrote in a circular addressed to the laity and clergy of his district that, like on previous occasions, "with the help of God, we will once again chase away the enemy." [81] Of course, we could argue with Luther that God simply raises an even more violent ruler to dispose of a violent one.[82] This would mean that God does not condone either of them but simply uses them in his providential activity to restore order and justice. The factor of historical survival or eminence therewith does not legitimate a certain power or authority as providential.[83]

There are still amazing historical events, however, that invite true theological evaluation. For instance, when the Gothic hordes of Alaric ransacked Rome in 410 many people interpreted this as signaling the wrath of the ancient gods.[84] These gods were angry, because the people had forsaken the ancient cults and adopted Christianity. However, the church father Augustine endeavored to show in his book, *The City of God,* that this was not the case. He claimed that the decline and fall of Rome was due to the moral depravity of paganism. A generation later the presbyter Salvianus of Marseilles explained the decline of Rome not as a judgment on the heathen but on the Christians.[85] The unrighteousness of the Christians in church and society had led to the fall of Rome as the punishment of God. Whom should we then trust, the interpretation of the pagans, or that of Augustine, or of Salvianus? Perhaps we should first realize "that the interpretation of an historical event as a special revelation of Providence too easily becomes a piously disguised form of self-justification." [86] It is one thing to believe that through God's providential action, even in the historical process, his kingdom will finally triumph and another to conceive divine providence atomistically as a fragmentary demonstration of his power.

We are unable to claim with Friedrich Schiller that world history is world judgment.[87] It is also difficult to agree with the attempt of G. F. W. Hegel to conceive of world history as a theodicy of God in which the thinking spirit is reconciled with evil.[88] Yet should we follow Dorothee Sölle when she claims that the pain, injustice, and suffering of the innocent lead to the dethronement of God almighty, the king, father, and ruler of the whole world? [89] Has not Dietrich Bonhoeffer claimed that God has allowed himself to be edged out of the world so that God has become weak and powerless? [90] Was William Hamilton right when he claimed to carry out the legacy of Bonhoeffer and asserted that the traditional sovereign and omnipotent God is difficult to perceive or meet? He surmised that "in place of this God, the impotent God, suffering with men, seems to be emerging." [91] Thomas J. J. Altizer then finally speaks of the death of God as an event in history. "We must realize," he states, "that the death of God is an historical event, that God has died in our cosmos, in our history, in our *Existenz*." [92]

It would indeed be futile to attempt a justification of the historical process as a result of God's providential activity. Luther's emphasis on the theology of the cross should serve as a warning against such endeavors. In the *Heidelberg Disputation* (1518) he asserts: "True theology and recognition of God are in the crucified Christ." [93] In the example of Christ Luther realized that God completes when he destroys, "that he makes alive when he puts one on the cross, that he saves when he judges," yet that he discloses himself when he disguises himself.[94] Luther consequently concluded that God works under the appearance of the opposite. Bonhoeffer emphasized this "weakness" of God too. But unlike some of his followers, he also confessed in his *Letters and Papers from Prison* very much like Luther: "I believe that God is no timeless fate, but that he waits for and answers sincere prayers and responsible actions." [95]

It would be too sweeping a statement, however, to confess that discerning God's providential involvement in the historical process is simply a matter of faith. Such sentiment could easily lead to credulity and to the attitude of regarding any historical oddity as the result of God's will. This could even be more the case, since in several respects the causal explanations of historical events contain a significantly higher degree of subjectivity than those in the natural sciences: [96]

(1) In the natural sciences an established causal connection between two stages of experience can be repeated by anyone at any time. Historical events, however, are singular, and their presumed sequence cannot be subjected to experimental scrutiny (e.g.: Does World War I always lead to World War II?).

(2) In the natural sciences paradoxical phenomena (e.g., duality of wave and corpuscle) can be explained as complementary. Differing historical perspectives, however, usually exclude each other (e.g., the attempts to explain the reason for the devastation of Rome in 410).

(3) In the natural sciences the causal sequence between two stages of experience can always be established. If hypothetical forces have to be assumed to establish such a sequence, such procedure usually leads to new advancements in science. With historical events

the causal sequence is often not evident and history appears as a sequence of accidents (e.g., the legal phrase "an act of God").

Since we do not want to justify God's providence by pointing to historical accidents nor by simply equating in deterministic fashion the whole historical process with God's providence, a criterion to assess the trustworthiness of God's providential activity in the historical process must be gained from other sources.

It is important here to remember that God is introduced in the Scriptures as the one for whom nothing is impossible and who determines the course of history. Yet it is even more important to recall that this is done to express the conviction that God will bring his plan of salvation to completion (Gen. 18:14 and Luke 1:37), but not to impress on us the notion that the whole history runs according to God's preconceived plan. When Jesus was asked for a theological interpretation of the death of the Galileans that Pilate had slain, or the eighteen men who were killed by the tower that collapsed at Siloam (Luke 13:1-5), he deliberately refused to equate history with God's judgment. The same was true when his disciples asked him for the reason why a man was born blind (John 9:3). Yet Jesus did not simply shrug his shoulders and declare that history is without meaning. In the first two instances he answered in existential fashion that events like these remind us of our own morality and sinfulness. In the last case he commented according to the Evangelist that it served to manifest the works of God.[97]

In other words, historical events are not an end in themselves. They are also not just part of the larger context of world history. Ultimately historical events have eschatological significance. They are "a living reminder of the End, speaking sometimes with certainty and more often in utter ambiguity." [98] Though the New Testament even alerts us to watch for the signs of the end, it is obvious for the New Testament writers that history does not provide us with a timetable for the things to happen before the eschatological fulfillment (Matt. 24:32f. and 36f.).

While we must agree with the biblical testimony that the historical process will find its fulfillment and completion in the eschaton, we must refrain from the temptation to identify God with one of the causes of the historical process or with the cause. We should rather side with Friedrich Gogarten when he reminds us that, by accepting us in his sonship, God has granted us the freedom to lead our lives responsibly without again interfering through divine providence.[99] God wants us to be his governors in the world. A governor without freedom and responsibility would be a mere puppet and not a responsive and responsible being. Yet responsibility does not exclude divine providence. It rather necessitates providence. We should be God's governors and because of this responsible God-relationship we need God's guidance. This can be illustrated with the Old Testament understanding of *berith* (covenant) which also plays an essential role in the Christian faith. We see how important the notion of covenant is when we remember that "testament" as used in Old or New Testament really means covenant. According to Old Testament thinking a covenant is always offered by a mightier power to an inferior one; it is never a contract between equals.[100] Finite humanity fulfilling its task as God's governor is this inferior agent who needs God's assistance and guiding providence.

We have seen that God grants his assistance and guiding providence in providing the trustworthiness of both the natural and the moral process. He also grants the trustworthiness of the historical process. However, human life and history in any form is unwarranted. Therefore the believer does not perceive it as an accident but as the result of God's undeserved creational and sustaining activity. Yet the trustworthiness of the historical process is not so much understood to result from the God who provides order. Certainly, through the impact of the natural and moral processes on history order is provided and chaos averted. But the primary thrust of the historical process is directed towards grace and fulfillment, and not towards order and sustenance. Especially through the unresolved tensions of history God reminds us that we "groan inwardly as we wait for adoption as sons" and that even the whole creation still waits "with eager longing for the revealing of the sons of God" (Rom. 8:19-23). We recognize that our world is in transition from "in the beginning God created heaven and earth" to "and God will be all in all." Consequently our position as God's administrators of this world and as the executors of the historical process is not a permanent one.

That special piece of history, called salvation history, continually reminds us that we are not just created by God but towards God. Thus the unresolved riddles of our historical existence will find their resolution in the larger context of salvation. While God in his general providence "provides both order and grace as the matrix of existence," [101] (human) existence is not a self-contained phenomenon. It is open towards its future which is foreshadowed in the Christ event as the promise and the proleptic anticipation of a new creation.

We must now talk about the special providence of God.

3. Special Providence of God (Miracles)

In our brief survey of God's general providence we have seen how God provides a trustworthy basis for human activity. In granting order for our existence God primarily sanctions natural constellations already prevailing in our world. Only in the eschatological provision of grace did we notice that God's providential activity will extend beyond the presently available. Does this mean that within the historical context we cannot expect anything new and that the phenomenon of novelty will only emerge when the eschaton commences?

Especially in the evolutionary processes of life we have seen that the elimination of novelty from the historical context would hardly fit. The evolution of life in its present form was not something simply to be expected, but it included both novelty and predictability. Turning to God's self-disclosure as it culminated in Jesus Christ, we notice too that there is constancy and surprise. God's involvement with humanity developed along certain lines (e.g., covenant, promise and fulfillment, law and gospel, etc.), but at the same time there are events that were totally unexpected, such as the crossing of the Red Sea, the election of David, and the coming of the Messiah. Even the Christian existence itself stands under the same dialectic. On the one hand it is an existence as predictable as any other human existence. But at the same time the Christian is allowed to anticipate proleptically something of the eschatologically envisioned goal; as a Christian he is a new creation already now. This means that the eschaton as novelty is not just a future phenomenon, it is to some extent a present experience. Realistically to affirm this eschatological novelty we must understand that God's providence extends beyond the provision of order in his general providence. In analogy to the unexpectedness of God's self-disclosure we must also talk about God's special providence as his provision of novelty in his miraculous activity. We must deal here primarily with the problem and significance of novelty, and with the issue of prayer as a response to and a request for God's providential care. Yet to do justice to God's ultimate provision of salvation we must also talk about the prospect of a new humanity as foreshadowed in God's special providence.

a. The problem of novelty

In talking about novelty in terms of God's special providence we should first clarify what we mean with this term. Just to replace the more traditional term miracle with the term novelty would not solve anything, since much of the problem involved in talking about miracles stems from the confusion about what a miracle is. Novelty or miracle is here theologically understood as an act of God which runs counter to our usual sense of experience and which becomes visible in the objective world. A miracle is an exception. Something that occurs every day we usually do not call miracle or novelty. Augustine, for instance, said very appropriately about Jesus' feeding the five thousand: "For certainly the government of the whole world is a greater miracle than the satisfying of five thousand men with five loaves; and yet no man wonders at the former; but the latter men wonder at, not because it is greater, but because it is rare." [102] The problem posed by a novelty, however, is not its exceptional character, but that it becomes visible in the objective world. Miracles thus are erratic blocks and are in danger of becoming stumbling blocks. The reason for this is that as an act of God they pertain to the metaphysical dimension, while as something that has become visible they belong to the dimension of nature.

Through the emergence of the natural sciences a more and more stringent distinction was made between the natural, the object matter of the natural sciences, and the supernatural, the realm of God. If God is to be understood as the agent of a miracle, one commonly assumed that he could not proceed in a natural manner but in a supernatural one. Thus the potential conflict was laid between those who felt that the natural context of events does not allow for divine disruptions, and those who asserted that God can at any time interfere with the natural constellations. It is interesting here to remember that at the time of Augustine, the distinction between the natural and the supernatural had not yet been made. He was still free to explain: "A portent, therefore, happens not contrary to nature, but contrary to what we know as nature." [103]

It was not until the ninth century, through translations of the works of Pseudo-Dionysius, that the term "supernatural" finally made its appearance in Western theology.[104] Yet only from the 13th century onward, primarily with the help of Thomas Aquinas, did "supernatural" become a commonly accepted theological term. Thomas Aquinas, for instance, clearly distinguished between the natural and the supernatural when he defined: "Firstly, there is natural change, which is done in the natural way by the appropriate agent. Secondly, there is miraculous change, which is done by a supernatural agent, above the normal order and course of nature—as for instance the raising of the dead to life." [105] Yet Thomas did not want to see the natural in opposition to the supernatural. Like most people in the Middle Ages,

Thomas perceived God as the one who connects the natural with the supernatural so that the natural order is enveloped in the supernatural and provides origin, sustenance, and goal for the natural.[106]

Aquinas agreed with Augustine that a miracle is "something difficult and unusual." But then he added that it is also something "surpassing the capabilities of nature [*supra facultatem naturae*] and the expectations of those who wonder at it." [107] A miracle therefore is not simply something unusual and unexpected. It is something altogether wondrous, having its cause, namely God, hidden absolutely and from everyone. Since Thomas defined a miracle as an act of God which is outside the normal pattern of nature and surpasses its capabilities, he even ventured to say: "Creation and the justifying of the sinner, while they are acts of God alone, are strictly speaking not miracles, because they are acts not meant to be accomplished by other causes." Thus a miracle, as an act of God, does not take place outside the natural realm but within it, replacing the natural course of things.

Such a definition rightly emphasizes that at certain points God's creative activity is present in nature in an unusual way. Yet it makes one wonder too whether God is not significantly less present in the usual proceedings of nature. Putting nature in antithesis to the supernatural, as had become more and more the custom in medieval scholastic theology, was intended to emphasize the supremacy of God. God is above and beyond nature. By reserving, however, for God the supernatural as a unique and separate realm or mode of action, he was inadvertently placed into a rather aloof position. The general acceptance of the distinction between natural and supernatural coincided with the growing significance and independence attributed to the natural sciences. Thus unintentionally the course was set for relegating God more and more to the supernatural and eventually for divorcing him completely from the natural realm. Thus nature was gradually perceived as running independently according to its own laws. In the 15th century such an eminent scholar as Nicholas of Cusa still attempted to bridge the widening chasm between theology and science by assuming a coincidence of opposites in which all finite contradictions would merge into an infinite unity.[108] But his influence was not lasting; natural science dominated more and more, eventually excluding supernatural possibilities.

Until fairly recently Roman Catholic thinking followed the line of argument advanced by Thomas Aquinas. This means that a miracle would be asserted if a certain phenomenon, e.g., the healing of a sick person, could not be sufficiently explained by assuming only natural causes.[109] God's involvement in the context of a miracle was thus conceived of as an action separate from the workings of other (natural) forces. However, two dangers could arise from this kind of thinking: (1) It could easily lead to the conclusion that God is not the sole agent of all processes. God interferes only at specific, unusual points through miraculous actions. (2) It might also make the occasions for divine interventions fewer and fewer, as our natural knowledge of the world increases. This latter point is demonstrated by the decreasing number of actual miracles officially admitted by the Roman Catholic Church. Gradually God becomes so transcendent that in more and more cases the natural events make good sense without reference to him. God is then relegated to a supernatural sphere that has no bearing on our everyday life.

Protestant theology, however, did not fare much better than the Roman Catholic Church. Some theologians attempted a similar distinction between the natural and the supernatural as Thomas Aquinas and arrived at analogous results. Most other theologians, however, attempted to "reconcile" the biblical miracles with the increasing command that science was gaining over the natural world. For instance, since 17th century German Protestantism no longer found the world view of Jesus tenable, the theory of accommodation was developed. It proposed to distinguish between the conceptuality with which Jesus proclaimed his message and the actual intention of his proclamation. Johann Salomo Semler further refined this theory in the 18th century, saying for example with regard to demons that the Jews of Jesus' time believed that certain dangerous diseases were caused by demons.[110] Though Jesus did not share this belief with his contemporaries, he accommodated himself to their thinking and performed what in the eyes of the Jews of his time were miraculous exorcisms. The intention of Jesus' "miraculous" actions, however, was to free these people from their fear of demons.

A generation earlier the English deist Thomas Woolston had claimed that the New Testament miracles could not have occurred in the way they were depicted by the evangelists, since, if visualized, these events lead to numerous contradictions.[111] Yet similar to Semler, Woolston did not want to suggest that the New Testament miracles were merely fictitious. According to Woolston some miracles, such as the story of the empty tomb, were most likely bare of historical content, but others certainly did contain a historical kernel. Woolston, however, left it open what this historical kernel was. He suggested that in the form in which they were told by the evangelists the New Testament miracles were at best only allegorical or mystical.

In the 18th century many natural explanations of the New Testament miracles were advanced. For instance, Jesus' walking on the water was explained as wading in shallow water while his disciples believed he was actually walking on the water. The feeding of the five thousand was interpreted as the result of Jesus' attractive preaching. His audience was so fascinated by him that they regarded eating for the time being as secondary. Of course, not everyone was satisfied with such evidently compromising explanations. To the dismay of Semler, Hermann Samuel Reimarus, for example, denounced the New Testament miracles completely as deliberate inventions and fraud by the disciples.[112] The norm for the supernatural activity of God was now set by our scientific knowledge of the world. What was naturally possible according to the then available scientific knowledge was also regarded as supernaturally conceivable. Still recently Rudolf Bultmann followed this line of thinking when he claimed: "It is impossible to use electric light and radio and to avail ourselves of modern medical and surgical discoveries and at the same time to believe in the New Testament world of daemons and spirits." [113]

In recent years, however, we have realized more and more that the order and structure we discover in nature is not something that is there as a given, but it is partly something we introduce into nature. The English astronomer Sir Arthur S. Eddington expressed this best when he said:

> We have found that where science has progressed the farthest, the mind has but regained from nature that which the mind has put into nature. We have found a strange footprint on the shores of the unknown. We have devised profound theories, one after another, to account for its origin. At last, we have succeeded in reconstructing the creature that made the foot-print. And Lo! It is our own.[114]

We also remember that the so-called laws of nature are not laws according to which events must occur, though we usually expect this, but they are laws patterned according to our experience of the way events generally happen. We have further noticed that the substructure of reality is undetermined, allowing for the kind of novelty that, for instance, characterizes the evolutionary process.

It would be wrong, however, to assume that our present understanding of nature again allows for God's miraculous interference.

The idea of God interfering with nature is also foreign to the biblical understanding of God's working. When we check the biblical witnesses we notice that God's miraculous activity is not viewed as something contrary to or superimposed on nature. "There is no talk of a sealed-in world or of iron-clad laws which must be broken through." [115] Since the biblical witnesses are convinced that God is involved in the totality of the world, miracles are viewed then as a new and surprising mode of God's ongoing activity. In other words, God's special providence is only a peculiar but important case of his general providential activity. Paul Tillich stated this very precisely: "Providence is not interference; it is creation. It uses all factors, both those given by freedom and those given by destiny, in creatively directing everything toward its fulfillment. . . . It is not an additional factor, a miraculous physical or mental interference in terms of supernaturalism." [116]

God's miraculous activity occurs within and through the present structure of nature. This does not imply, however, that a miracle as miracle becomes evident in the natural context. What becomes visible are rather two significant consequences of a miracle:

(1) We observe that something ran counter to our usual sense experience.[117] It may just be a striking constellation of causes, conforming with the laws of nature, and occurring at the appropriate moment. For instance, such a constellation would be the strong east wind that according to Exodus 14:21 commenced to blow at the right moment and enabled the Israelites to escape through the Red Sea, while it did not allow the pursuing Egyptians to take the same route. However, our observation that something ran counter to our usual sense experience could also be due to a special (causal) act that overrides the normal sequence of cause and effect in human affairs. An example for this kind of event would be the healing of the paralytic (Mark 2:11). Though medical science knows of exceptional instances in which paralyzed persons can regain the function of their limbs, there is no law that says that it will indeed be so. One can at most hope for such an event, but one cannot expect it as one does with events occurring with regularity.

(2) The other consequence of a miracle that becomes visible is the miraculous event as an item of the past. Once the miracle had occurred, we could have seen that the Israelites had arrived at the other side of the Sea and we could have watched how the formerly paralyzed person was walking again. Once these results are visible, we will

have to employ the help of all available expertise to bring the states prior and after the miracle into a causal relationship. Being in charge of the natural context in which we live we will want to find the natural causes that made the miraculous event possible.

When confronted with a miracle our Christian faith will inform us that it was not just nature that made this "miraculous" change possible, but at the same time was the result of God's mighty hand through his special providential activity. Yet is such a twofold view of reality possible or does it simply give the same constellation a different name? It would be helpful here to remember the dilemma that scientists initially faced when they wanted to determine the nature of the elementary particles. They were confronted with the seemingly exclusive duality between wave and corpuscle until the Danish physicist Niels Bohr introduced the principle of complementarity, suggesting that wave and particle properties are complementary aspects of a single reality. This principle allows for a twofold view of reality, a view which is not based on a temporary deadlock in scientific research, but reflects "an essential characteristic of reality." [118] Let us now apply this insight to the binary components of a miracle, namely the natural cause and effect sequence and God's miraculous activity of using these causes in an unusual or unprecedented way. We would then have to conclude that though the visible presence of the one (nature) seems to exclude the presence of the other (God), only both complementary aspects together point to the whole of reality.

A miracle therefore does not replace faith by demonstrating the presence of God through sign language. It rather necessitates faith so that we allow for and affirm the total twofold reality that encounters us. William Pollard has captured this situation very aptly when he said: "What to the faithful is an act of divine mercy showing forth our Lord's restorative power is for the pagan merely a piece of extraordinarily good luck. What to the faithful is a manifestation of divine judgment is to the pagan only a misfortune." [119] But with these remarks we are already touching upon the significance of miracles as it discloses itself especially in the salvational process.

b. The significance of novelty and the salvational process

According to the biblical witnesses, miracles are intrinsically related to the salvational process. Today even the most critical analysts of the New Testament sources admit that Jesus did indeed perform acts that his contemporaries regarded as miraculous and that we still consider highly unusual.[120] Jesus accompanied his teaching ministry by healing sick persons, such as the paralytic (Mark 2:11), Peter's mother-in-law (Mark 1:31), and people obsessed with unclean spirits (Mark 1:26).

Yet Jesus' miraculous activity is not without analogies. We know that miracles are reported about some of his contemporaries which show an astounding similarity to Jesus' miracles. Apollonius of Tyana, for instance, an itinerant neo-Pythagorean teacher and contemporary of Jesus, is supposed to have raised people from the dead and healed many who were sick.[121] Though some of the miracles may simply have been attributed to persons in antiquity to emphasize their importance, it would be overreacting to conclude that none of these miracles allegedly performed did actually take place. Even the similar structure of miracle stories of the gospels and of miracle stories in other literary sources of antiquity would not disprove their factuality.[122] There are not too many variations possible in the way in which a miracle can be effectively told. Since the power to perform miracles, however, was at that point also considered a status symbol, symbolizing a special relationship to the gods, each claim to truth must be carefully analyzed. The possibility cannot be excluded that even some of the miracles attributed to Jesus are without historical basis, merely serving to underscore his exceptional status.

The New Testament witnesses did not seem to be threatened by the existence of other miracle stories. They were even convinced that the performance of miracles was not the exclusive prerogative of Jesus. For instance, they tell us that Jesus himself warned of false Christs and prophets of the end-times who would perform great signs and wonders (Mark 13:22). The apostles also knew of people who used sorcery to perform miraculous deeds (cf. Acts 8:9). If we want to obtain a complete picture of the significance of the miracles of Jesus it is insufficient to interpret them exclusively in the light of Near Eastern or Greco-Roman religious thought.

Since Jesus' miracles were concomitant with his mission we must understand them primarily from the goal of his life and destiny. If we can agree with the New Testament witnesses that Jesus announced the kingdom of God and brought it about through his life and destiny (Mark 1:14f.), then the miracles are signs and proleptic anticipation of the kingdom of God.[123] Miracles are therefore never used by Jesus to demonstrate his power and to legitimate himself (cf. Matt. 12:38f.). They are rather signs that illustrate his message. They show that God is not a distant God far away, but a God actively involved in the creational process. But God does not simply confirm present tendencies, he is willing to give them a new and unprecedented turn. This creative activity of God results in a decisive confrontation with the anti-Godly powers. According to the New Testament witnesses Jesus did not perform his miracles in aloof detachment from the affairs of the day. Authorized by God, he fought and overcame the destructive anti-Godly powers and each of his victories then became visible in a miracle. In a picturesque and dramatic way the evangelists tell us that these powers recognized Jesus and exclaimed in anguish: "What have you to do with me, Jesus, Son of the Most High God? I adjure you by God, do not torment me" (Mark 5:7).

We have seen that God fends off the destructive anti-Godly powers through his orders of preservation in the natural, moral, and historical processes. Through his miracles, however, he does not just maintain order, but, in a creative act, initiates a completely new order. The anti-Godly powers are not merely kept in check, but at one specific point they are overcome, they have to retreat. Therefore miracles are signs of the commencing kingdom and reign of God.[124] When sick people are restored to health, dead are brought back to life, biologically impairing phenomena (such as hunger) are overcome, and physically limiting phenomena (such as space and gravity) eliminated, we obtain glimpses of an entirely new creation. The seer in the Book of Revelation, envisioning the eschatological perfection, conveys a similar picture when he says: "Death shall be no more, neither shall there be mourning nor crying nor pain any more, for the former things have passed away" (Rev. 21:4).

Of course, Jesus' miracles are only temporary points of victory over the anti-Godly powers. The people healed may become sick again, the people brought back to life will die again, and the people fed will once again be hungry. Does this mean that the present structure of reality is so overpowering that even miracles would at best provide a temporary escape and not an indication that the present structure of reality will be taken up into a new structure, the new world to come? We could only answer this question in the affirmative if we were to neglect the resurrection of Jesus Christ as the miracle through which all other miracles of Jesus are endowed with ultimate validity. Jesus' resurrection was not a resuscitation or a return to life after which another and final death followed. As Paul victoriously exclaimed: In Jesus' resurrection death was overcome through a new form of life (1 Cor. 15:55ff.). Here the promised transformation of the whole cosmos had commenced.

The reality shown to us in the resurrection of Jesus Christ was no restoration of our present cosmos, it was an indication and anticipation of a new cosmos.[125] Because this miracle, the inauguration of a new reality, happened with and because of Jesus, we are allowed to accept all the miracles that he himself performed and all miracles that are still performed in his authority as signposts foreshadowing and pointing to a new world to come. Miracles therefore have eschatological significance. They point to the promised eschaton and they anticipate it proleptically, indicating that our present world is not endowed with permanence but on its course to a new world. Through his special providence God reminds us that the orders of preservation are just that, orders that preserve the world for its fulfillment and perfection in the new world to come. In his special providence God also shows us that these orders are only of penultimate quality. Though they are usually reliable, they are not so restrictive as to exclude novelty, even in the sense of the ultimate and universal novelty of the new creation.[126]

We must refrain, however, from the utopian assumption that there is a developmental continuity between our present structure of reality and salvation in and through Christ. As we have learned from Teilhard de Chardin, the evolutionary pressure provides at best the elements for the christogenesis, but this pressure will not bring it about. To achieve salvation neither evolution nor revolution suffices. Salvation can only be brought about through something unprecedented and new, through the creational activity of God as foreshadowed in the Christ event.

It should be noted at least parenthetically that a miracle taken by itself does not necessarily have convincing power. It does not necessitate the conclusion that we are confronted here with God's salvational activity. For instance, many of those who saw that the sick were restored to health were amazed and glorified God (Mark 2:12). Jesus' "friends" and the scribes did not deny either that Jesus had performed unusual deeds. But they concluded that he either was "beside himself" or he was connected with "Beelzebul, and by the prince of demons he casts out the demons" (Mark 3:21f.). A miraculous act by itself is silent, it does not disclose whether it is endowed by God with eschatological significance, whether it is simply the sign that we are confronted with an especially gifted person, such as a true miracle worker, or whether it is a seductive act of the anti-Godly powers. For Jesus, however, sign and proclamation go together. As we can see with his "friends" and the scribes, those who rejected his message did not change their minds once they were confronted with his miracles. They had heard the miraculous message of the commencement of the salvational process and rejected it together with its signs. Here the conclusion of the parable of the rich man and Lazarus conveys a most telling insight: "If they do not hear Moses and the prophets, neither will they be convinced if someone should rise from the dead" (Luke 16:31).

c. The impact of prayer

In our consideration of God's care for humanity we did not want to leave the impression that God's preserving and promising activity relegates us to inactivity. If such were the case it would violate our position of being God's governors in the world. Once we turn to the impact of prayer on God's providential care, we will soon notice that we are encouraged to be actively involved in this providential work. We could even say that the experience of God who hears and answers our prayers is the heart of the question of providence.[127] If God does not interact with us in a dialogical way, similar to the sentiment expressed in Stoic thought, we would be confronted with an impersonal "it," with the laws of nature or with a merciless fate. Then prayer would be nothing but an attempt to calm our nerves. Prayer would have to be understood as an attempt to obtain self-control, analogous in its intention to Far Eastern meditation exercises.

But the New Testament is full of exhortations to pray, which leave no doubt that an actual I-Thou relationship between God and humanity is envisioned in prayer (cf. Matt. 7:7; 21:22; John 15:7). Consequently we are told that one does not address God in a carefree, casual attitude. A prayer should not be done in a boasting attitude, convinced that God has no choice but to agree with the contents of our prayers (Matt. 6:5-7). Instead a prayer should be precise and made in humility. It is not without significance that in the prayer which Jesus taught his disciples the assertion of the holiness of God's name comes first (Matt. 6:9).[128]

This emphasis on God's holiness does not just inform the attitude of our prayers but also their content. For instance, the promise of Christ according to the Gospel of John: "Whatever you ask the Father in my name, he may give it to you" (John 15:16), does not imply that God will grant us anything for which we ask him. Dietrich Bonhoeffer captured the meaning of prayer well when he said: "God does not give us everything we want, but he does fulfill all his promises." [129] Prayer is not a frivolous attempt to discover how far-reaching God's power is, for example, whether he can reverse the sequence of winter and spring, but it is rather the reliance for Christ's sake on the promise expressed in the Psalms: "Call upon me in the day of trouble; I will deliver you, and you shall glorify me" (Ps. 50:15). Since Christ has overcome the destructive anti-Godly powers, we, as his followers, are encouraged to step on his side and call upon God to deliver us or others from the impact of these powers too.

Martin Luther was right when he said that God's order or command and the prayers of Christians are the two pillars that support the entire world and without which the world would disintegrate.[130] God promised to consider the content of our prayers in his preserving, sustaining, and creative activity. Through our prayers we are on God's side, cooperating with him and dialoging with him concerning the future of the world. Prayer therefore can have many contents. First of all we must mention here adoration and praise of God. Again Luther reminds us that we should not only call upon God in our plight. We should also thank him for his help and rescue, remember his acts of kindness, and praise him for them, because "he is the Creator, the Benefactor, the Promiser, and the Savior."[131] Luther can rightly say that it is sinful if we cease to pray to God. A life without prayer is no longer in tune with God as the creative source of all life; it mistakenly presumes that our world is self-sufficient. Prayer serves here as a reminder for us to recall the one from whom we have everything that is. Therefore we should ask God even for things that we seemingly take for granted, such as good weather or a good harvest.[132] With this last sentence we have already touched upon the large category of petitions which seem to form the main content of most prayers.

Luther also encourages us to bring before God all our anxieties, such as personal afflictions like poverty and sickness, or even sinfulness. He asserts that we should not exclude any petitions whether they envision temporal or eternal goals.[133] Georgia Harkness rightly prioritizes this all-inclusive scope of petitions when she says that "to seek God's forgiveness for past and present sin, and thus to find hope for the future, is an essential part of Christian prayer."[134] If we do not include in our prayers the plea for forgiveness of sin, our dialog with God will always be disturbed. Both in prayers and in our expectations will we act out of our own sinful and selfish interests, but not out of conformity with God. Petitions are therefore first concerned with inner strength and renewal. Of course, this will include more than just forgiveness, it will also be a prayer for inner peace in times of conflict, for clarity of outlook, new strength at moments of fatigue, and for power to cope with the daily demands of life. The following stanza from the gospel hymn "What a Friend We Have in Jesus" seems to express this kind of prayerful attitude very appropriately:

> Have we trials and temptations?
> Is there trouble anywhere?
> We should never be discouraged;
> Take it to the Lord in prayer.
> Can we find a friend so faithful,
> Who will all our sorrows share?
> Jesus knows our every weakness;
> Take it to the Lord in prayer.[135]

From the acknowledgement of God's benevolent activity in Jesus Christ new strength and peace of mind can be gained. God as the ruler of the universe cares about us little unimportant beings so much that he comes to us in the human form of Jesus Christ. This God who cares is also the one who gives strength to the weary and lifts up those who are in low esteem (Luke 1:52).

In our considerations of petitional prayers, we dare not forget the frequent petitions for physical health and healing. Since prayers are not intended to be a substitute for work, petitions for recovery from physical illness should never replace appropriate medical care. However, the two are not mutually exclusive. The same insight must guide our attitude toward so-called faith healing. Though each case of a miraculous healing must be subjected to careful scrutiny, we know that unusual and unforeseen recoveries from grave illness do occur. There is also no doubt that some people have the gift to heal.[136] We have seen, however, that this power need not stem from God. It can also have been obtained from the anti-Godly seductive powers.

Again we are confronted with the fact that a miraculous event is silent, it does not disclose its originator. However, in prayer we have a means with which to "discern the spirits." [137] If we are existentially involved in an event of so-called faith healing or in any other miraculous event, we are able to discern the source of this healing power. The existential involvement will usually assume one of three forms: We are the one who has the gift to heal, we are the one who has been healed, or we are an immediately involved bystander (relative). If our relationship with God in prayer is strengthened, we may safely assume that the healing power was a gift of God. It will then not become commercialized or used for self-advertising and self-exaltation. Following the example of Jesus it will rather be used to illustrate the Christian gospel and humbly and gratefully to further the human good. If the relationship with God in prayer is weakened, however, we can hardly attribute this power to God. Its source must be the anti-Godly powers who enable seemingly divine miracles, often even accompanied externally with Christian symbols, to seduce people. If the relationship in prayer, however, remains unaffected, we may simply regard this healing power as an unusual, "natural" gift of God, similar to the superior healing gifts of medical doctors.

Since we discover more and more that a human being is a psycho-somatic unity, we realize that psychic disturbances, such as depressions and neuroses, can bring about physical ailments, such as disturbances of the digestive system, malfunctioning of the glands, and heart and kidney diseases.[138] Psychic disturbances are frequently intertwined with spiritual crises. Regaining psychic and spiritual strength and balance is then often accompanied by a physical healing process. The strengthening, alleviating, and comforting impact of prayer cannot be underestimated. Prayer can indeed be effectively "used" to calm our nerves. Such use, however, does not result in a dialog with God but moves on the meditative level of our own psyche. We should refrain from calling it prayer, but term it more appropriately meditation. Though it dare not become a substitute for prayers, it serves a rather useful function in our turbulent times to attain a state of tranquility and peacefulness of mind. Of course, we should not expect that the dialog with God in true prayers is followed by an automatic physical improvement. Restoration of psychic and spiritual health is usually a very slow process and occasionally it will not be attained at all. If we take seriously the dialog character of prayer, we must also be ready for God's non-compliance with our petitions.

When we finally come to petitions concerning natural events, we must bear in mind that this is primarily the realm where we will affirm the natural protective orders of God. Yet it is part of our task as God's administrators to remind him of those who are especially exposed to the dangerous possibilities of the natural forces, such as miners, travelers, pilots, and sailors. Again prayers are not intended to replace protective measures, but to accompany and perhaps enhance them. Similarly, it is our prerogative and duty to pray in adverse conditions, such as storms, floods, and other disasters that their impact will be softened or averted. Since a prayer is never uttered in selfish interest, we will keep in mind not only the well-being of ourselves but of others. This means the same adoration, praise, and petitions that we extend on our behalf we extend also on behalf of others.

In all our prayers we always conclude with the expressed or tacit admission with which the Evangelist tells us that Jesus concluded in Gethsemane the most fervent prayer ever uttered: "Nevertheless, not as I will, but as thou wilt" (Matt. 26:39). A Christian prayer is not a demand for God's surrender, but rather the prerogative and duty of a dialog with the one who has formed the earth and the whole universe, and who has been our dwelling place in all generations (Ps. 90:1f.).

d. Towards a new humanity

Since we started our investigation of the human nature with the observation that humanity is in turmoil, it could be misleading to conclude it with the affirmation of the impact of prayer. The Christian understanding of humanity might then easily be misunderstood as a flight from earthly reality, an escape route into the transcendental. If these fears proved true, we would have to agree with the classical Marxist assessment that the Christian faith serves as a spiritual tranquilizer that clouds our vision of reality and that hinders us from tackling the problems of the day. Yet in attempting to understand human nature we related the human phenomenon to the categories of inanimate and animate nature, to other human beings, and to God. This already implied that humanity, though intimately related to its creator, cannot be understood apart from the created. Moreover, its position as God's governor endows it with a special obligation for all the created including its own kind.

If stewardship characterizes our attitude toward nature, we dare not expect less in the inter-human realm. Our relationship with God does not hinder our involvement in the affairs of the day. It rather enables and urges us to treat the world not as something to be taken for granted but as a unique creation on its way to its God-provided destiny. Having realized this we can never treat any person's life we touch as a means only but must always regard it as an end. This categorical imperative that Immanuel Kant emphasized nearly two hundred years ago, has not lost its urgency.[139] It is still binding for us, lest we deny our calling to become God's governors in this world and manage the world on our own. To give our activities the semblance of significance and ultimate value we would then have to absolutize our standpoints and become solipsistic, communal, or ethnic dictators.

Closely connected to the realization that we are God's governors in this world, and in part even underlying it, is the awareness that we are created in God's image. Yet we have noticed that from the very beginning of humanity the human family has always fallen short of being God's image. We may wonder therefore whether this goal can ever be realized. But there is Jesus of Nazareth, the human face of God, of whom the Scriptures say that he was obedient to God until death (Phil. 2:8). The hope-provoking fact about Jesus, however, is not that he lived up to the ideal of being God's image, but that in doing so he did this in our interest. Consequently, whatever happened to him is also a God-promised possibility for us. In other words, through and in Christ the realization of being God's image has become a human possibility.

In the Judeo-Christian community the hope emerged for a new world, a new world society under God's immediate reign. This hope found its culmination in the life and destiny of Jesus. Jesus as the Christ, as the hoped for Messiah, portrayed in his life-style the absolute obedience to God's will, he proclaimed the immediacy, even the arrival of the kingdom of God, and through his resurrection he showed the way to a new world to come. Each of these facets of Jesus' life and destiny complement and interpret each other. They stand for both the arrival and the promise of a new humanity and a new world order.

In contrast to the people around them the first Christians followed the example of their Lord and loved each other.[140] While this expression of love and concern for each other has been compromised a thousand times, Friedrich Engels, the collaborator with Karl Marx, makes a very significant observation when he says: "In the popular risings of the Christian West . . . the religious disguise is only a flag and a mask for attacks on an economic order which is becoming antiquated. This is finally overthrown, a new one arises and the world progresses." [141] Engels recognized that in the name of the Judeo-Christian tradition actual societal changes take place, whereas in other societies reform movements "are clothed in religion but they have their source in economic causes; and yet, even when they are victorious, they allow the old economic conditions to persist untouched."

We must now ask what allows for and engenders this transformation of society in the "Christian West." What was it that drew millions of people to emigrate to the "New World" and what stimulated them to turn it into a beacon of hope for many others living under oppression and poverty? What was it that lured at least one third of the world population to embrace Marxist doctrines, a teaching that still serves as a sign of freedom from domination and slavery in many younger nations? Though economic reasons are a powerful stimulus, they fail to explain the whole picture, because often the already affluent intellectuals are especially attracted to Marxist doctrines.

Of course, we could say that the endeavor to transform society results from the peculiarly human phenomenon of pressing on to ever new horizons, of being open for the world and for constantly new experiences. Again this answer fails to account for the fact that primarily the "Christian West" served as the starting point for societal transformations. Perhaps the religious component cannot just be understood with Engels as a disguise, but as the propelling and driving force for the creation of a new society. The Judeo-Christian hope for a new world order and for a new humanity served as the stimulus for the Marxist vision of a "socialized humanity." [142] The Judeo-Christian faith also stood behind the assertion in *The Declaration of Independence* "that men are created equal, that they are endowed by their Creator with certain inalienable rights, that among these are life, liberty, and the pursuit of happiness."

But we would contradict what we have observed earlier about human sinfulness if we would not recognize at the same time that the Marxist vision is tarnished by countless acts of new oppression. *The Declaration of Independence* too significantly qualified the insight of equality within the human family when it called the American Indians "merciless savages" who attack the white immigrants. Regardless of these frequent lapses the search for a responsible world society continues. It involves not just rudiments of the Judeo-Christian tradition as in the Marxist vision or in the American *Declaration of Independence* but Christians themselves of many nationalities and confessions are active in it. Inspired by the hope that is within them they are willing to give account for it (1 Pet. 3:15) and contribute through a common effort to a deeper unity and deeper insight. For Christians humanity is not a fact that can be taken for granted, but it is understood as a process, constantly being created and re-creating itself.[143]

The Christian vision of a new world order gains constantly new hope and refinement through its connection with Jesus Christ as the originator and source of the hope for a new humanity.[144] Consequently it is distinguished from all ideologies and movements it engendered, through its intensity and clarity. The living dialog of call and response between Christ and his followers ensures that the hope for a new humanity, though not without a material basis, is different from what can be expected through genetic input and environmental conditioning alone. Therefore it will result in a truly new creation of a loving process.[145] This dialog will also ensure that we are not taking the future in our own hands and replace the old tyrannies of oppression with new tyrannies of liberation.

We do not affirm a powerless God, whose intentions we have to correct, but the creator of the world and the author of history whose goal we are allowed and encouraged to anticipate proleptically. He "has chosen to create human beings as makers of their own history with full freedom inherent in their individual and collective destinies." [146] Since prayer is not just a mental or oral activity, but involves the enfleshment of our dialog with God, the pressing toward alleviation of hunger, inequality, and prejudice and the striving for a new humanity is a direct outgrowth of the impact of prayer. We must understand ourselves as the hands and arms of God, moulding ourselves and others and being moulded into a foretaste of the eschatological kingdom.

The representatives of liberation theology rightly remind us that we are accountable to the global human family and that we must become living witnesses to the coming of the kingdom. But is it not just a futurist eschatological vision when the seer of the Book of Revelation says:

> Behold, the dwelling of God is with men. He will dwell with them, and they shall be his people, and God himself will be with them; he will wipe away every tear from their eyes, and death shall be no more, neither shall there be mourning nor crying nor pain any more, for the former things have passed away? Rev. 21:3f.

Admittedly, such eschatological fulfillment is truly God's own work and seems to have no place in our present world. Yet if we take seriously God's covenant extended to us in Christ, this eschatological vision is not just otherworldly. Paul rightly reminds us: "And we all, with unveiled face, reflecting the glory of the Lord, are being changed into his likeness from one degree of glory to another" (2 Cor. 3:18).

We can object that this prospect of sanctification, this progressive transformation into God's true representatives, is too costly. If this were our response we would not exert any inspiring and corrective influence on the global human family. We would rather tacitly condone present turmoil, violence, and oppression. Any vision of a new humanity, whether utopian or ideological, would be superior to such a stand and offer at least a semblance of hope. On the other hand, we can participate in God's covenant community and become beacons of hope for a new humanity. Such a venture, however, will not be convenient. As the frequent imperatives in the Pauline letters indicate, it will mean a continuous battle against our sinful desires to join the mainstream of society. We will also become offensive to those who want to perpetuate traditional patterns of oppression, injustice, and exploitation, and who mistakenly look for Christians to uphold the status quo.

Where Christians are living out their allegiance to the Lord, the cross of Christ takes on new meaning. Since both cross and tomb could not hold on to our Lord, the symbols of apparent defeat were turned into signs of triumph over the powers of destruction. The cross then becomes a rallying point for the oppressed and the powerless and a sign of inspiration that in this sign we will win and erect bastions of a new humanity of solidarity and ultimate dependence upon the Lord of history. Through Christ's life and destiny we know that all the processes in the universe will ultimately serve to make God's kingdom triumph. Therefore we are confident that he "will vindicate his people and have compassion on his servants" (Ps. 135:14) so that the hopes he inspired will not be in vain.

Summary and Final Observations

In this chapter we attempted to discover how God's protective and guiding care can instill hope into our alienated existence. Again we want to note some important points:

(1) God's care for his creation is not adequately expressed by assuming his deterministic, mechanistic, persuasive, or immanent presence. It is neither predictable nor can it be tapped to attain control over oneself or one's environment.

(2) God's sustaining, protective, and guiding presence through his general providence is not experienced uniformly. It is differentiated according to the various areas and modes of his presence, in nature, morals, and history. In none of these areas his presence excludes freedom within the processes. Humanity can alter and predict the course of these processes to various degrees, the least in the natural process, the most in the historical process. Consequently their guiding character is least perspicuous in the historical realm and most in the natural realm.

(3) The general providence of God emphasizes primarily his pro-

tective and sustaining care. A teleological direction of this care cannot be perceived phenomenologically. Salvation history, however, provides us with a tool to interpret the historical process, and following from there of all processes, reminding us of their transitory and unfulfilled character.

(4) The special providence of God adds to our cosmic journey the character of novelty. While God's general providence emphasized the reliability of the process and its continuity with the past, his special providence points to the future fulfillment and establishes a connection with the promised goal of the process. God's special providence does not occur in contradiction to nature, but in contrast to the way we usually experience nature.

(5) Miracles are temporary anticipations for the hoped-for completion of the world. They point toward the eschatological fulfillment and announce its coming. They receive their validation from the resurrection of Jesus Christ through whom the new world order was anticipated. Since it was the Christ who was resurrected, such permanent fulfillment is promised for his followers and for all creation.

(6) The dialog character of prayer is a living reminder that our world is still incomplete, we do not yet live by vision but by audition. Prayer allows us to participate in the preserving and creative process through dialog with the power that decides upon our present existence, our past, and our future.

(7) Our cosmic journey will find its destiny in a new humanity, a new heaven and a new earth. The eschatological promise of this new creation serves as a continuous stimulus for partial anticipation of this new creation. Since it is still promise, it announces the eschatological proviso to all overzealous enthusiasts. And since it is God's promise, it assures us that the trustworthiness of our natural, moral, and historical process, though not foolproof, can and will be sustained toward its eschatological resolution.

We have reached the end our investigation. Of course, many more facets of humanity's interaction with its environment could have been pointed out. Since a human being is basically a forward-reaching being, anthropology or the science about humanity is a never-finished topic. It is always expanding, adducing new facts and insights. Yet we wanted to elaborate only the most basic structures of human existence to rediscover the origin, direction, and goal of our journey through space and time.

First we looked at the structure and possible development of our universe in order to assess humanity's place and destiny. We soon realized that the universe is less fixed in its structure than one might initially assume when one considers exclusively macrocosmic constellations. Space, time, matter, and even the cause and effect sequence can become rather elusive under the scrutinizing eyes of contemporary investigation. The eternal duration of the universe is not a promising factor either from which we can gain strength for our own plans. At the conclusion of long aeons we either face a run-down universe with no rejuvenation in sight or a cataclysmic collapse of the world, after which there might be a new beginning, totally disjunctive, however, from everything previous.

Looking secondly at the phenomenon of life, we soon realized that the transition between living and non-living forms of being are elusive. This shows the intimate dependence between living beings and their natural environment. In its amazing variety the growing stream of life demonstrates a surprising unity, both in its structures and in its transitions from one species to another. When we finally reach humans as the youngest members of the living family, we are not astonished that in many ways they resemble their fellow creatures. However, if we regard humans simply as higher animals, we miss the essence and place of humanity. Humans are not just part of the living species, but due to their many peculiarly human features they have achieved an unprecedented dominion over all other living creatures and over the inanimate world.

When we consider thirdly the astounding historical success of humanity, we might at first be inclined to see immense potential for further and higher development. But humanity's cultural development in creating a world of its own depends on the resources of the finite natural world in which it finds itself, and therefore its progress will necessarily be limited. In terms of moral improvement there a wider and wider gap seems to open between humanity's technical potential and the insight to use this potential responsibly.

Yet there is still a fourth referent for humanity—God as the creator of the world and the author of history. Since God is experienced and understood as creatively involved with human and world history as its initiator, granter, and redeemer, he can endow human destiny with eternal significance. In the light of God, humanity is not just a link in the natural context, but with its peculiarly human features it gains significance as God's administrator in this world. However, humanity is continuously prone to neglect its relationship with God and therefore its status as a God-responsible being. Though we might conclude that this is an innate shortcoming of humanity, it cannot be classified as a genetic defect. Knowingly and willingly humans desert their special relationship with God. While the incentive for this anti-Godly behavior does not come from humans themselves, their willing consent reinforces their personal responsibility.

But the amazing fact is that God does not cease to care for humanity. In the preservational orders of nature, of moral behavior, and of history he allows the human family to live a life either in alienation from God or in harmony with him. Since God extends his caring hand indiscriminately over good and evil people, his preservational orders are often misunderstood as autonomous structures. A Christian, however, sees in them God's caring hand. This experience is reinforced for Christians through God's miraculous special providence in which God allows for novelty within these orders to preserve and protect life. This creative process of God will culminate in God's final novelty, the creation of a new world. Glimpses of a new creation have been foreshadowed in the life and destiny of Jesus Christ and continue to be seen in God's present involvement in the world. God's caring attitude toward humanity, however, does not dismiss humans from their position as God's administrators. Through the example and sign of hope, God has established in Jesus Christ, he invites them to participate in his own care, both for their fellow human beings and for the rest of creation. Only by experiencing that someone cares with infinite compassion for us finite beings, do we become truly human beings. We are free to care for others with the same intensity as we would care for ourselves.

The structures of human existence that we discovered in inanimate and animate nature do not suffice to illuminate the origin, direction, and goal of our cosmic journey. Only from the one who provides our existence with origin as well as with structure do we obtain an understanding of our journey. We realize that we are not helplessly and hopelessly adrift in space and time. Elevated to become God's administrators and in part anticipating the eschatological goal before us, we regain a sense of direction and dignity, and a point of reference. This does not mean that the inanimate and animate structures become irrelevant. On the contrary, in the light of God's ultimacy and universality, their particularity and specificity can no longer be assumed to be of accidental occurrence. There is purpose and direction in the universe. It loses its cold and impersonal character and assumes life and warmth. The experience of a God who cares endows our existence with meaning, and, at the same time, permits us to understand the whole world as God's creation. The world was not created for our exploitation or self-glorification. Our uniquely human position notwithstanding, the cosmos was created together with us to enjoy God and to be enjoyed by him forever.

Notes

INTRODUCTION

1. Konrad Lorenz, *On Aggression*, trans. by M. K. Wilson (New York: Harcourt, Brace & World, 1966), p. 41, rightly comments: "The rushed existence into which industrialized, commercialized man has precipitated himself is actually a good example of an inexpedient development caused entirely by competition between members of the same species. Human beings of today are attacked by so-called manager diseases, high blood pressure, renal atrophy, gastric ulcers, and torturing neuroses; they succumb to barbarism because they have no more time for cultural interests."

2. Theodore Roszak, *The Making of a Counter Culture. Reflections on the Technocratic Society and Its Youthful Opposition* (Garden City, N.Y.: Doubleday, 1968). See also his compilation of *Sources. An Anthology of Contemporary Materials Useful for Preserving Personal Sanity While Braving the Great Technological Wilderness* (New York: Harper, Colophon Books, 1972), which again provides an excellent introduction to alternative life-styles. Charles A. Reich, *The Greening of America* (New York: Random House, 1970), p. 351, perceptively claims "that the great and urgent need of these times is transcendence." Yet we wonder whether his advocacy of "Consciousness III" which "posits an extended family in the spirit of the Woodstock Festival without individual 'ego trips' or 'power trips,'" (p. 384), can really satisfy this need. While his diagnosis is accurate, his proposed remedy does not provide the regrounding and redirection our industrial civilization needs. Student unrest and countercultural movements of the industrialized countries presuppose a society of affluence and of plenty. Since then, however, we have discovered that we actually are entering a stage of scarcity. Industrial civilization has not only deceived its advocates, it has also led astray the countercultural forces.

3. Cf. Wolfhart Pannenberg, *What Is Man? Contemporary Anthropology*

in Theological Perspective, trans. by Duane A. Priebe (Philadelphia: Fortress, 1970), pp. 2ff., in his very enlightening comments on humanity's contemporary situation.

4. Søren Kierkegaard, *Stages on Life's Way,* trans. by W. Lowrie (Princeton: Princeton University, 1940), p. 402.

5. Jürgen Moltmann, in his provocative book, *Man. Christian Anthropology in the Conflicts of the Present,* trans. by J. Sturdy (Philadelphia: Fortress, 1974), pp. 1-15, addresses himself very appropriately to a relational definition of humanity when he attempts to "define" humanity by comparing it with animals, with other members of the human family, and with the divine. Yet instead of attempting to answer the question of humanity in the context in which it emerged, he relies in his constructive part very heavily on the socio-political context at the expense of the scientific context.

6. Ludwig Feuerbach in his preface to Jacob Moleschott, *Lehre der Nahrungsmittel. Für das Volk,* 2nd ed. (Erlangen: F. Enke, 1853).

7. Cf. Marcus Tullius Cicero, *On the Commonwealth,* trans. with notes and intr. by G. H. Sabine and S. B. Smith (Columbus: Ohio State University, 1929), p. 143 (1. 37), where in reference to Greek custom Cicero suggests that all people are either Roman or barbarian (non-Roman).

8. Juvenal, *Satires,* trans. by J. Mazzaro, with intro. and notes by R. E. Braun (Ann Arbor: University of Michigan, 1965), p. 222, n. 4 (Sat. 11.27).

9. Augustine, *Confessions and Enchiridion,* trans. and ed. by A. C. Outler, Vol. 7 of *The Library of Christian Classics* (Philadelphia: Westminster, 1955), p. 31.

1. THE UNIVERSE

1. Friedrich Engels, *Dialectics of Nature,* trans. and ed. by Clemens Dutt, pref. and notes by J. B. S. Haldane (New York: International Publishers, 1940), pp. 24f. A still reliable and informative introduction to the issues touched on in this chapter and the next, especially in their historical context, is provided by Sir William Cecil Dampier, *A History of Science and Its Relations with Philosophy & Religion,* postscript by I. Bernard Cohen, 4th ed. (Cambridge: University Press, 1966).

2. Immanuel Kant, *Critique of Pure Reason,* trans. by N. K. Smith (London: Macmillan, 1929), pp. 402ff. (A435ff., B463ff.).

3. Cf. for the following Werner Heisenberg, *Physics and Philosophy. The Revolution in Modern Science,* intr. by F. S. C. Northrop (New York: Harper, 1958), esp. pp. 5-26, in Northrop's excellent introduction to Heisenberg; or Heisenberg's more technical book, *The Physical Principles of the Quantum Theory,* trans. by C. Eckart and F. C. Hoyt (Chicago: University, 1930).

4. For the following cf. George A. Williams, *Elementary Physics: Atoms, Waves, Particles* (New York: McGraw-Hill, 1969), pp. 334-347, or any other good book in elementary physics.

5. Cf. Louis de Broglie, *Matter and Light. The New Phyics,* trans. by

W. H. Johnston (New York: W. W. Norton, 1939), pp. 111-119, and pp. 154ff., where he acknowledges the duality of light (and matter) while calling for further research to attain a comprehensive understanding of light.

6. Kant, pp. 80f. (A39, B56).

7. Augustine, *The City of God,* trans. by M. Dods, intr. by Thomas Merton (New York: Random House, Modern Library, 1950), p. 350 (11.6).

8. Cf. the very lucid discussion of this problem in Max Born, *Einstein's Theory of Relativity,* rev. ed. in collab. with Günther Leibfried and Walter Biem (New York: Dover, 1962), pp. 226ff., which also serves as an excellent introduction to many other issues connected with Einstein's theory. For a popularly written introduction to Einstein cf. George Gamow, *Matter, Earth, and Sky,* 2nd ed. (Englewood Cliffs, NJ: Prentice-Hall, 1965), pp. 190-201.

9. Pierre Simon Marquis de Laplace, *A Philosophical Essay on Probabilities,* trans. by F. W. Truscott and F. L. Emory, intr. by E. T. Bell (New York: Dover, 1951), p. 4. For a good critique of Laplace's claim cf. Georg Hendrik von Wright, *Causality and Determinism* (New York: Columbia University, 1974), pp. 116-119.

10. Cf. Werner Heisenberg, *Philosophic Problems of Nuclear Science,* trans. by F. C. Hayes (New York: Pantheon, 1952), pp. 16ff., where he shows the decisive character of the observer in determining the location and the velocity of the electron.

11. For details concerning the determination of the mean life and its relationship to the half-life, or the time needed for half the amount of the radioactive atoms of a substance to disintegrate, cf. Irving Kaplan, *Nuclear Physics,* 2nd ed. (Reading, MA: Addison-Wesley, 1963), pp. 231 and 237.

12. Cf. Heisenberg, *Physics and Philosophy,* pp. 30ff.

13. *Philosophic Problems of Nuclear Science,* p. 51.

14. For the considerable discussion among scientists and philosophers of sciences concerning the nature and role of indeterminacy see the excellent remarks of William A. Wallace, *Causality and Scientific Explanation.* Vol. 2: *Classical and Contemporary Science* (Ann Arbor: University of Michigan, 1974), esp. pp. 163-308. The basic issue at stake is here whether indeterminacy is objective in the sense that it characterizes matter or reality, or whether it is merely a characteristic of human knowledge of such reality (cf. Wallace, p. 307). Yet even if we concede that indeterminacy is only a characteristic of our knowledge of reality and could some day be replaced by a newly gained deterministic view of reality, what would hinder us to assure that at a still more distant point in history another indeterministic view of reality might emerge? In other words, the transition from the once assumed all-embracing deterministic view of reality to an indeterministic one has irrevocably shaken our confidence in stringent determinism.

15. This impressive example is provided by Pascual Jordan, *Der Naturwissenschaftler vor der religiösen Frage. Abbruch einer Mauer,* 2nd ed. (Oldenburg: Gerhard Stalling, 1964), pp. 154f.

16. Karl Heim, *Das Weltbild der Zukunft. Eine Auseinandersetzung zwischen Philosophie, Naturwissenschaft und Theologie* (Berlin: C. A. Schwetschke, 1904), p. 260.

17. Cf. Rudolf Carnap, *Philosophical Foundations of Physics. An Introduction to the Philosophy of Science,* ed. by Martin Gardner (New York: Basic Books, 1966), p. 207, who states in his accurate description of the prevailing notion of causality in nature: "Perhaps it would be less confusing if the word 'law' were not used at all in physics. It continues to be used, because there is no generally accepted word for the kind of universal statement that a scientist uses as the basis for prediction and explanation. In any case, it should be kept clearly in mind that, when a scientist speaks of a law, he is simply referring to a description of an observed regularity. It may be accurate, it may be faulty. If it is not accurate, the scientist, not nature, is to blame."

18. *Der Naturwissenschaftler vor der religiösen Frage,* p. 157.

19. For a very popular introduction to the general theory of relativity and the cosmological impulses it exerted cf. Gamow, *Matter, Earth, and Sky,* esp. pp. 572-597. A more conventional, but very readable introduction to the general theory of relativity and its implications is given in the comprehensive book of Donald H. Menzel, Fred L. Whipple, and Gerard de Vaucouleurs, *Survey of the Universe* (Englewood Cliffs, NJ: Prentice-Hall, 1970), pp. 747-766.

20. Cf. Hermann Bondi, *Cosmology,* 2nd ed. (Cambridge: University Press, 1960), pp. 98ff., and William R. Corliss, *Mysteries of the Universe* (New York: Thomas Y. Crowell, 1967), pp. 67ff.

21. Cf. Martin Rees, Remo Ruffini, and John A. Wheeler, *Black Holes, Gravitational Waves and Cosmology: An Introduction to Current Research* (New York: Gordon and Breach, 1974), p. 153.

22. Cf. Georges Lemaitre, "Note on de Sitter's Universe," *Publications of the Massachusetts Institute of Technology,* Series II, No. 29 (May, 1925), pp. 188-192.

23. *Matter, Earth, and Sky,* pp. 592ff.; cf. also his *The Creation of the Universe* (New York: Viking, 1952), pp. 55ff.

24. Fred Hoyle, *The Nature of the Universe* (New York: Harper, 1950), p. 85.

25. Rees, Ruffini, Wheeler, p. 215; and W. D. Arnett and Donald D. Clayton, "Explosive Nucleosynthesis in Stars," *Nature,* Vol. 227 (August 22, 1970), pp. 780-784.

26. Cf. *Survey of the Universe,* pp. 781ff.

27. Cf. for a brief introduction to Dirac's hypothesis Emilio Segrè and Clyde E. Wiegand, "The Antiproton," *Scientific American,* Vol. 194 (June, 1956), p. 37; and Maurice Duquesne, *Matter and Antimatter,* trans. by A. J. Pomerans (New York: Harper, 1960), pp. 67ff. It is interesting for the rapid advancement of scientific insight that in this book Duquesne still had to concede in 1960 "that antimatter cannot be produced experimentally at present" (p. 122).

28. Carl D. Anderson, "Facts About the Nucleus of the Atom," *Annual Report of the Board of Regents of the Smithsonian Institute* (1935) (Washington: U.S. Government Printing Office, 1936), pp. 235-247.

29. D. E. Dorfan, *et al.,* "Observations on Antideuterons," *Physical Review*

Letters, Vol. 14, No. 14 (June 14, 1965), pp. 1003-1006; and Segrè and Wiegand, "The Antiproton," pp. 37-41. It is interesting that Segrè and Wiegand already wonder whether there would also exist an anti-universe consisting of anti-matter. Evidently, the principle of symmetry provides a strong impulse for scientific hypotheses.

30. Maurice Goldhaber, "Speculations on Cosmogony," *Science*, Vol. 124 (August 3, 1956), pp. 218f., where he advances this theory in distinction to the theories of a big bang and of continuous creation.

31. Cf. Hannes Alfvén, *Worlds—Antiworlds. Antimatter in Cosmology* (San Francisco: W. H. Freeman, 1966), who in following his teacher, Oskar Klein, advocates the theory of a matter-antimatter universe without denying that the issue whether such a universe actually exists is not yet decided.

32. Isaac Asimov, *The Universe. From Flat Earth to Quasar* (New York: Walker, 1966), p. 257.

33. Geoffrey and Margaret Burbidge, *Quasi-Stellar Objects* (San Francisco: W. H. Freeman, 1967), pp. 210ff.

34. Cf. Hannes Alfvén, "Antimatter and Cosmology," *Scientific American*, Vol. 216 (April, 1967), pp. 106-112, who cautiously advocates the existence of matter and antimatter galaxies.

35. Fred Hoyle, *From Stonehenge to Modern Cosmology* (San Francisco: W. H. Freeman, 1972), p. 56.

36. Cf. Hermann Bondi, *Cosmology*, pp. 140-156.

37. Fred Hoyle, *The Nature of the Universe*, rev. ed. (New York: Harper, 1960), p. 126; and Raymond A. Lyttleton, "An Electric Universe?" in *Rival Theories of Cosmology. A Symposium and Discussion of Modern Theories of the Structure of the Universe*, ed. by H. Bondi, W. B. Bonner, R. A. Lyttleton, and G. J. Whitrow (London: Oxford University, 1960), pp. 25ff.

38. Hoyle, *The Nature of the Universe*, p. 132.

39. *Ibid.*, pp. 139f.

40. So rightly George McVittie, *Fact and Theory in Cosmology* (New York: Macmillan, 1961), p. 171, in his reservations against the steady state theory.

41. According to Asimov, p. 292.

42. Maarten Schmidt and Francis Bello, "The Evolution of Quasars," *Scientific American*, Vol. 224 (May 1971), pp. 55-69, assert that though not all the problems connected with quasars are solved, it may be fairly well assumed that their redshift is to be interpreted cosmologically. Since up to a certain point the number of quasars rises steeply with increasing redshift, one might then assume that at a relatively early age of the universe these quasars populated the universe fairly densely, while today they are heading toward the outer "edges" of the universe: Needless to say that Fred Hoyle, "The Crisis in Astronomy," in *Physics 50 Years Later*, ed. by Sanborn C. Brown (Washington, D.C.: National Academy of Sciences, 1973), pp. 63-78, is dissatisfied with interpreting the increased redshift for quasars as meaning cosmologically more distant. He in turn wonders whether a larger redshift always means a more distant object (p. 77).

43. Menzel, Whipple, de Vaucouleurs, *Survey of the Universe*, pp. 783ff., give more extensive pertinent information on the various types of background radiation, all pointing into a similar direction. Cf. also the more popular but helpful account of cosmic background radiation in Lloyd Motz, *The Universe. Its Beginning and End* (New York: Charles Scribner, 1975), pp. 70ff.

44. Cf. the translated excerpt from Clausius' paper on entropy, *"Über die bewegende Kraft der Wärme,"* in *A Source Book in Physics*, ed. by William F. Magie (Cambridge, MA: Harvard University, 1935), pp. 228-236.

45. To my knowledge Arthur S. Eddington, *The Nature of the Physical World. The Gifford Lectures 1927* (New York: Macmillan, 1929), pp. 68ff., was the first to introduce the term "time arrow." For a popular introduction to the problems of time cf. G. J. Whitrow, *The Nature of Time* (New York: Holt, Rinehart and Winston, 1972), esp. pp. 146-162.

46. Cf. for the following Motz, *The Universe*, pp. 307-317. Richard Schlegel, in his stimulating article, "Time and Entropy," in the significant collection *Time in Science and Philosophy. An International Study of Some Current Problems*, ed. by Jiri Zeman (Amsterdam: Elsevier, 1971), p. 34, assumes that an expansion of the universe, continuing forever with a fixed amount of matter "would hardly be compatible with the finite average density of matter that we find today in the universe." He therefore considers "two alternatives to an infinite time based on an infinitely extending cosmic progressive change: (1) a creation-of-the-universe event in the finite past; (2) a temporally cyclic universe." In the second case Schlegel finds that while the progressive change within any one cycle would clearly define an increasing time, such progressive change extending through one cycle to the next would be lacking. Thus, properly speaking, "the universe would not have a time measure beyond a single cosmic cycle," time would necessarily be finite.

47. When Motz, p. 317, claims that "men have (in their own existence) not only the promise of life renewed but also the promise of almost infinite variety in such life," he seems to grossly overestimate the unknown and unpredictable character of such a "reprocessed universe." Life eternal that he projects is based on speculation bordering on wishful thinking, but not on sound scientific insights. For the problems connected with a cyclic universe cf. also William Bonner, *The Mystery of the Expanding Universe* (New York: Macmillan, 1964), pp. 96-103 and 204ff. For a very stimulating discussion of "the black box model of collapse and the reprocessing of the universe," cf. the enlightening remarks by Rees, Ruffini, and Wheeler, pp. 302-307, who call the possible results of the paradox of collapse "the greatest crisis of physics of all time" (p. 307).

48. Cf. Motz, pp. 283ff.; and George Gamow, *A Star Called the Sun* (New York: Viking, 1964), pp. 160f.

49. Pierre Teilhard de Chardin, *The Vision of the Past*, trans. by J. M. Cohen (New York: Harper & Row, 1966), pp. 168ff.

2. THE PHENOMENON OF LIFE

1. Archimedes of Syracuse according to *The Oxford Dictionary of Quotations*, 2nd ed. (Oxford: University Press, 1953), p. 14.
2. Cf. Ernst Benz in his stimulating book, *Evolution and Christian Hope: Man's Concept of the Future from the Early Fathers to Teilhard de Chardin*, trans. by H. G. Frank (Garden City, NY: Doubleday, 1966), pp. 76ff.
3. Cf. the instructive book by William P. D. Wightman, *The Growth of Scientific Ideas* (New Haven: Yale University, 1964), pp. 325 and 355, where he points out that the idea of spontaneous generation was first eloquently put forth by Aristotle in his book *The Generation of Animals*. Yet Aristotle's idea of spontaneous generation does not contradict the previously quoted Latin proverb *ex ovo ovum*, since spontaneously generated animals were never "perfect" at the point of generation, but were at the stage of larvae. In the Middle Ages, however, sometimes the idea of spontaneous generation actually meant the spontaneous generation of "perfect" animals, such as mice or fish. Cf. also for the following historical part the excellent presentation by George Schwartz and Philip W. Bishop, eds., foreword by Linus Pauling, *Moments of Discovery*, 2 vols. (New York: Basic Books, 1958), who provide both excerpts of historical writings and comments on such issues as the origin of life (for our particular issue cf. Vol. 1, pp. 401f.).
4. William Shakespeare, *Anthony and Cleopatra* in *Shakespeare: The Complete Works*, ed. by G. B. Harrison (New York: Harcourt, Brace and Co., 1952), p. 1238 (Act II/7).
5. Isaac Asimov, in his informative book, *The Wellsprings of Life* (New York: Abelard-Schuman, 1960), p. 155.
6. Cf. the comprehensive treatment of the relationship between theology and science by Ian G. Barbour, *Issues in Science and Religion* (Englewood Cliffs, NJ: Prentice-Hall, 1966), p. 318, who comes to the same conclusion.
7. For a popular but reliable introduction to these issues cf. Wolfhard Weidel, *Virus*, trans. by L. Streisinger (Ann Arbor: University of Michigan, 1959).
8. Cf. the numerous examples of adaptation through mutation cited by Theodosius Dobzhansky, *Evolution, Genetics, and Man*, 6th rep. (New York: John Wiley, 1966), esp. pp. 96-106.
9. Stanley L. Miller, "Production of Some Organic Compounds under Possible Primitive Earth Conditions" (1955) in *Synthesis of Life*, ed. by Charles C. Price (Stroudsburg, PA: Dowden, Hutchinson & Ross, 1974), pp. 7-17.
10. Cf. for the following Sidney W. Fox, "How Did Life Begin?" *Science*, Vol. 132 (July 22, 1960), pp. 200-208, here p. 202.
11. Fox, p. 207. Cf. also Cyril Ponnamperuma, "Primordial Organic Chemistry and the Origin of Life" (1970), reprinted in *Synthesis of Life*, ed. by Charles C. Price, pp. 33-61, who even goes so far as to claim that "in the long run the search for extraterrestrial life can hardly meet with failure" (pp. 57f.).

12. Carl Sagan, "The Origin of Life in a Cosmic Context," in *Cosmochemical Evolution and the Origins of Life. Proceedings of the Fourth International Conference on the Origin of Life and the First Meeting of the International Society for the Study of the Origin of Life. Barcelona, June 25-28, 1973.* Vol. 1: *Invited Papers,* ed. by J. Oró, S. L. Miller, C. Ponnamperuma, and R. S. Young (Boston: D. Reidel, 1974), p. 498.

13. Cf. John Keosian, "Life's Beginnings—Origin or Evolution?" in *Cosmochemical Evolution and the Origins of Life,* Vol. 1, p. 292, who rightly cautions against the idea that one can easily re-enact experimentally the origin of life. "There is only one evolution—the evolution of matter from elementary particles through atoms and molecules to systems of higher and higher levels of organization. Each new level ushers in new properties which could not be predicted from properties of the lower level."

14. James D. Watson and Francis H. C. Crick, "Molecular Structure of Nucleic Acids," *Nature,* Vol. 171 (April 25, 1953), pp. 737f. For a reliable and popular introduction to the genetic code cf. George and Muriel Beadle, *The Language of Life. An Introduction to the Science of Genetics* (Garden City, NY: Doubleday, 1966); cf. also for the following Louis Levine, *Biology of the Gene,* 2nd ed. (St. Louis: C. V. Mosby, 1973), pp. 1-33.

15. Cf. Leslie C. Dunn, *A Short History of Genetics. The Development of Some of the Main Lines of Thought: 1864-1939* (New York: McGraw-Hill, 1965), pp. 227ff.

16. Jacques Monod, *Chance and Necessity. An Essay on the Natural Philosophy of Modern Biology,* trans. by A. Wainhouse (New York: Alfred A. Knopf, 1971), p. 143.

17. Francis H. C. Crick, "Origin of the Genetic Code," *Nature,* Vol. 213 (Jan. 14, 1967), p. 119.

18. Francis H. C. Crick, "The Origin of the Genetic Code," *Journal of Molecular Biology,* Vol. 38 (Dec. 28, 1968), p. 377, where he gives an excellent description of his proposal concerning the origin of the genetic code.

19. *Ibid.,* 373ff., quotation p. 375.

20. Cf. Leslie E. Orgel, "Evolution of the Genetic Apparatus," *Journal of Molecular Biology,* Vol. 38 (Dec. 28, 1968), p. 381f.

21. For the following cf. Laura L. Hsu and Sidney W. Fox, "Interactions between Diverse Proteinoids and Microspheres in Simulations of Primordial Evolution," *BioSystems,* Vol. 8 (1976), esp. pp. 89f. Cf. also Sidney W. Fox, "The Matrix for Protobiological Quantum: Cosmic Casino or Shapes of Molecules?" *International Journal of Quantum Chemistry: Quantum Biology Symposium* (1975), pp. 307-320.

22. Robert F. Goldberger, "Autogenous Regulation of Gene Expression," *Science,* Vol. 183 (March 1, 1974), p. 810.

23. Sidney W. Fox and Klaus Dose, *Molecular Evolution and the Origin of Life.* Foreword by A. Oparin (San Francisco: W. H. Freeman, 1972), p. 253.

24. Cf. W. Thieman and W. Darge, "Experimental Attempts for the Study of the Origin of Optical Activity on the Earth," in *Cosmo-*

chemical Evolution and the Origins of Life, Vol. 1, pp. 263-283, esp. p. 282, who give a good overview of the various attempts to solve the problem of stereochemical preference and then claim that there is a physical force that induces this preference, though they admit that at present this force cannot be fully verified through experiments. Cf. also Henry R. Mahler and Eugene H. Cordes, *Biological Chemistry,* 2nd ed. (New York: Harper & Row, 1966), p. 51, who say: "Just why all the amino acids that occur in proteins are exclusively L is not clear. . . . It may well be that the choice of the L forms was dictated by chance rather than by a distinct preference based on one or more physical forces."

25. Edward Anders, Royoichi Hayatsu, and Martin H. Studier, "Organic Compounds in Meteorites," *Science,* Vol. 182 (Nov. 23, 1973), p. 783. Cf. for the following also the excellent article by N. H. Horowitz and Jerry S. Hubbard, "The Origin of Life," in *Annual Review of Genetics,* Vol. 8, ed. by Herschel L. Roman et al. (1974). esp. pp. 400ff.

26. Keith Kvenvolden, James Lawless, Katherine Pering, et al., "Evidence for Extraterrestrial Amino-Acids and Hydrocarbons in the Murchison Meteorite," *Nature,* Vol. 228 (Dec. 5, 1970), p. 924.

27. Cf. Anders, Hayatsu, Studier, "Organic Compounds in Meteorites," p. 789.

28. Aleksandr Oparin in his foreword to Fox and Dose, *Molecular Evolution and the Origin of Life,* p. vii. ·

29. Kvenvolden, Lawless, Pering, "Evidence for Extraterrestrial Amino-Acids and Hydrocarbons in the Murchison Meteorite," p. 924.

30. *Ibid.,* p. 926.

31. For this and the following quotations see Monod, *Chance and Necessity,* p. 144f.

32. Cf. for the following Pascual Jordan, *Der Naturwissenschaftler vor der religiösen Frage,* pp. 337ff. Of course, this theory seems very unlikely, since it would exclude the existence of bacteria with dextro-rotatory proteins. It is more likely that very early in the evolutionary process there were organisms containing D-rotatory substances and others containing L-rotatory substances. Some may even have contained both. Yet gradually organisms containing L-substances survived "somehow" and outpaced all other organisms. Cf. George Wald, "The Origin of Optical Activity" (1957), in Charles C. Price, ed., *Synthesis of Life,* p. 242, who advances this theory which actually leaves unanswered the essential question: "Why are L-configurations predominant?"

33. Walter Sullivan, *We Are Not Alone. The Search for Intelligent Life on Other Worlds,* rev. ed. (New York: McGraw-Hill, 1970), esp. pp. 245ff., serves as a good introduction to the various enterprises in the search for life on other stellar objects. Cf. also I. S. Shklovskii and Carl Sagan, *Intelligent Life in the Universe* (New York: Dell Publishing, 1966), and the very informative collection by Cyril Ponnamperuma, ed., *Exobiology* (Amsterdam: North Holland Publishing, 1972), which includes articles about "Organic Molecules in Space" and "Distribution and Significance of Carbon Compounds on the

Moon." For a very sobering report see Sidney W. Fox, "The Apollo Program and Amino Acids," *Science and Public Affairs. Bulletin of The Atomic Scientists*, Vol. 29 (December, 1973), pp. 46-51.

34. Giordano Bruno, *On the Infinite Universe and Worlds*, in Dorothea Waley Singer, *Giordano Bruno. His Life and Thought*, with an annotated trans. of his work *On the Infinite Universe and Worlds* (New York: Greenwood, 1968), pp. 257f. (1st dialog); Immanuel Kant, *Allgemeine Naturgeschichte und Theorie des Himmels*, in *Werke in zehn Bänden*, ed. by Wilhelm Weischedel, Vol. 1 (Darmstadt: Wissenschaftliche Buchgesellschaft, 1968), p. 381 (A180).

35. Loren Eiseley, *The Immense Journey* (New York: Random House, 1957), p. 162.

36. Cf. as an example for the Middle Ages Nicholas of Cusa, *Of Learned Ignorance*, trans. by G. Heron, intr. by D. J. B. Hawkins (New Haven: Yale University, 1954), pp. 118f. (3.13), where he emphasizes the "balanced design" of the universe and the "admirable order" through which each new element depends upon its agreement with the remaining elements.

37. Plato, *Timaeus*, in *The Complete Collected Dialogues of Plato Including the Letters*, ed. by Edith Hamilton and Huntington Cairns with intr. and prefatory notes (New York: Bollingen Foundation, 1961), pp. 1162f. (esp. 29e-31b).

38. Aristotle, *Historia Animalium*, trans. by D'Arcy W. Thompson, Vol. 4 of *The Works of Aristotle*, ed. by J. A. Smith and W. D. Ross (Oxford: Clarendon, 1910), n.p. (8.1, 588b).

39. For this and the following quotation see the exhaustive study by Arthur O. Lovejoy, *The Great Chain of Being. A Study of the History of an Idea. William James Lecture: 1933* (Cambridge, MA: Harvard University, 1936), p. 183.

40. John Milton, *Paradise Lost*, in *The Complete English Poetry of John Milton*, ed. by John T. Shawcross (New York: New York University, 1963), p. 325 (book 5, 509-512).

41. Alexander Pope, *An Essay on Man*, ed. by Maynard Mack, in *The Poems of Alexander Pope*, Vol. 3.1 (London: Methuen, 1970), p. 44f. (esp. 1. 237-246).

42. James Thomson, *The Seasons*, in *The Complete Poetical Works of James Thomson*, ed. by J. Logie Robertson (London: Oxford University, 1951), p. 65 (Summer, 333-337).

43. Immanuel Kant, *Allgemeine Naturgeschichte und Theorie des Himmels*, p. 386 (A187). Cf. also part 1 of this treatise which Kant prefaces with a quotation from Pope.

44. Cf. Edward Young in *Young's Night Thoughts* (New York: Worthington, 1889), p. 7 (Night 1), where he says: "Distinguish'd link in being's endless chain! Midway from nothing to the Deity!"

45. John Locke, *An Essay Concerning Human Understanding*, ed. by Alexander C. Fraser, Vol. 2 (New York: Dover, 1959), p. 68 (book 3.6.12).

46. Cf. Gottfried Wilhelm Leibniz, *The Monadology*, in *Philosophical Papers and Letters*, trans. and ed. with an intr. by Leroy E. Loemker, Vol. 2 (Chicago, IL: University of Chicago, 1956), pp. 1044,

1052, and 1055 (par. 1, 47f., 62ff.); cf. also for a brief introduction to Leibniz' monadology Hans Schwarz, *The Search for God. Christianity—Atheism—Secularism—World Religions* (Minneapolis: Augsburg, 1975), p. 55.

47. Leibniz, *A New System of the Nature and the Communication of Substances, As Well as the Union between the Soul and the Body* (1965) in *Philosophical Papers and Letters*, Vol. 2, p. 749 (16).

48. Leibniz, *The Principles of Nature and of Grace, Based on Reason* (1714), in *Philosophical Papers and Letters*, Vol. 2, p. 1043 (18).

49. Cf. Samuel Johnson, "Nature and Origin of Evil. Review of a Free Inquiry" (1757), in Vol. 13 of *The Works of Samuel Johnson in 16 Volumes* (New York: Lamb, 1903), pp. 223ff., where he rejects the idea of a Great Chain of Being on grounds that such chain could not have being and that there are too many vacuities in this chain. Cf. also Voltaire, *"Chaine des Êtres Créés,"* in *Philosophical Dictionary*, trans. with intr. and glossary by Peter Gay, pref. by André Mauroin Vol. 1 (New York: Basic Books, 1962), pp. 161ff.

50. Paul Heinrich Dietrich Holbach, *Systeme de la Nature*, Vol. 1 (A Londres, 1780), pp. 85ff. (1.6).

51. Jean Baptiste Robinet, *De la Nature*, 3rd ed., Vol. 1 (Amsterdam: E. van Harrevelt, 1766), pp. 20ff.

52. *Ibid.*, Vol. 5 (1768), p. 148, as quoted by Arthur O. Lovejoy, *The Great Chain of Being*, pp. 274f.

53. Erasmus Darwin, *Zoonomia or The Laws of Organic Life*, Vol. 1 (Dublin: P. Byrne and W. Jones, 1794), p. 551 (39.4), *Overtures to Biology. The Speculations of Eighteenth Century Naturalists* (New Haven: Yale University, 1964), esp. pp. 159-175, in his treatment of Erasmus Darwin. Cf. also Desmond King-Hele, *Erasmus Darwin* (New York: Charles Scribner's, 1963), esp. pp. 63-96. It is strange that in *The Origin of Species* Charles Darwin does not even mention once his grandfather who expressed many of Charles Darwin's theses more correctly than his famous descendant (cf. King-Hele, p. 81).

54. Jean Baptiste de Lamarck, *Zoological Philosophy*, trans. with an intr. by Hugh Elliot (New York: Hafner, 1963), p. 122.

55. Cf. Friedrich Engels, *Dialectics of Nature*, p. 236, where he claims that Darwin lumped together two absolutely separate things, selection by the pressure of overpopulation and selection by greater capacity of adaptation of altered circumstances. A bizarre and unfortunate example of exclusive emphasis on environmental influence was the rule of Lysenkoism in Russia. For details cf. Zhores A. Medvedev, *The Rise and Fall of T.D. Lysenko*, trans. by I. M. Lerner (New York: Columbia, 1969), esp. pp. 35ff.

56. Cf. Thomas Robert Malthus, *Population: The First Essay*. Foreword by Kenneth E. Boulding (Ann Arbor: University of Michigan, 1959), pp. 21ff.

57. *Charles Darwin's Autobiography with His Notes and Letters Depicting the Growth of the 'Origin of Species,'* ed. by Sir Francis Darwin, intr. by George G. Simpson (New York: Henry Schuman, 1950), p. 54.

58. For this quotation and the following paragraph cf. Sir William C.

Dampier, *A History of Science and Its Relations with Philosophy & Religion*, p. 277.

59. Cf. for the following Darwin, *The Origin of Species*, in *The Origin of Species and The Descent of Man* (New York: Random House, Modern Library, n.d.), p. 98 (chapter 4).

60. *Ibid.*, p. 373.

61. *Ibid.*, p. 367.

62. *Ibid.*, p. 370.

63. *Charles Darwin's Autobiography*, p. 55.

64. According to William Irvine, *Apes, Angels, and Victorians. The Story of Darwin, Huxley, and Evolution* (New Yor'.: McGraw-Hill, 1955), p. 107.

65. *Ibid.*, p. 108.

66. Darwin, *The Origin of Species*, p. 374.

67. Irvine, p. 108.

68. *Charles Darwin's Autobiography*, p. 61.

69. Darwin, *The Descent of Man*, in *The Origin of Species and The Descent of Man* (New York: Random House, Modern Library, n.d.), p. 390; cf. also Ernst Haeckel, *The History of Creation or The Development of the Earth and Its Inhabitants by the Action of Natural Causes*, trans. from the 8th German ed. by Sir E. Ray Lankester, 2 Vols. (New York: D. Appleton, 1925).

70. *The Descent of Man*, pp. 430f.

71. *Ibid.*, pp. 512f.

72. For the following quotations see *ibid.*, pp. 468, 914, and 494.

73. *Ibid.*, pp. 915ff.

74. Irvine, p. 197.

75. Herbert Spencer, *First Principles*, 6th ed. (Akron, OH: Werner, 1900), p. 367 (par. 145).

76. Cf. Hugh Elliot, *Herbert Spencer* (Westport, Conn.: Greenwood, 1970 [1917]), p. 3; cf. also the interesting volume by Edward Youmans, *Herbert Spencer on the Americans and the Americans on Herbert Spencer* (New York: D. Appleton, 1882; reprint: New York: Arno, 1973).

77. Karl Marx, "Letter to Friedrich Engels" (Dec. 19, 1860), excerpt in Karl Marx and Frederick Engels, *Selected Correspondence, 1846-1895*, trans. with expl. notes by Donna Torr (New York: International Publishers, 1962), p. 126. Cf. also p. 125, for Marx' comments on Darwin in a letter to Ferdinand Lassalle. Cf. also the interesting book by Conway Zirkle, *Evolution, Marxian Biology, and the Social Scene* (Philadelphia: University of Pennsylvania, 1959), esp. pp. 85ff., where she deals with the discovery of Darwin by Marx and Engels.

78. *The Origin of Species*, p. 122 (chap. 5: summary).

79. Irvine, p. 92.

80. Trans. by Eva R. Sherwood and Bateson in *The Origin of Genetics. A Mendel Source Book*, ed. by Curt Stern and Eva R. Sherwood (San Francisco: W. H. Freeman, 1966), pp. 1-55.

81. Cf. for the following the excellent book by Monroe W. Strickberger, *Genetics* (New York: Macmillan, 1968), pp. 97ff.

82. Cf. the instructive paper by Clarence P. Oliver, "Dogma and the

Early Development of Genetics," in *Heritage from Mendel,* ed. by R. Alexander Brink (Madison: University of Wisconsin, 1967), p. 3f.

83. Cf. for the following Hermann J. Muller, "The Problem of Genic Modification" (1927), in *Studies in Genetics. The Selected Papers of H. J. Muller* (Bloomington: Indiana University, 1962), p. 275.

84. So also George G. Simpson, "The Meaning of Darwin," in *Charles Darwin's Autobiography,* p. 9.

85. Hermann J. Muller and Lewis M. Mott-Smith, "Evidence that Natural Radioactivity Is Inadequate to Explain the Frequency of 'Natural' Mutations" (1930), in *Studies in Genetics. The Selected Papers of H. J. Muller,* p. 278.

86. *Ibid.,* p. 284.

87. "The Role Played by Radiation Mutations in Mankind" (1941), in *Studies in Genetics. The Selected Papers of H. J. Muller,* pp. 549f.

88. Cf. Strickberger, *Genetics,* p. 526, who claims that with the size of our present human population "the number of new spontaneous mutations easily extends into millions."

89. Arne Müntzing, *Genetics: Basic and Applied. A Survey of Methods and Main Results* (Stockholm, Sweden: LTs Förlag, 1961), pp. 418f.

90. Cf. George G. Simpson, "The History of Life," in *Evolution after Darwin. The University of Chicago Centennial,* ed. by Sol Tax, Vol. 1: *The Evolution of Life. Its Origin, History and Future* (Chicago: University of Chicago, 1960), pp. 160f; and Julian Huxley, *Evolution in Action* (New York: Harper & Row, 1953), pp. 41f. and 52f.

91. So Theodosius Dobzhansky, *Evolution, Genetics, and Man* (New York: John Wiley, 1966), p. 82; and Ronald A. Fisher, *Creative Aspects of Natural Law* (Cambridge: University Press, 1950), esp. pp. 13ff.

92. Richard Goldschmidt, *The Material Basis of Evolution* (New Haven: Yale University, 1940), esp. pp. 396f.; and Otto Schindewolf, *Grundfragen der Paläontologie. Geologische Zeitmessung—Organische Stammesentwicklung — Biologische Systematik* (Stuttgart: E. Schweizerbart'sche Verlagsbuchhandlung, 1950), pp. 406ff.

93. Cf. J. S. Weiner, *The Piltdown Forgery* (London: Oxford University, 1955).

94. Haeckel, *The History of Creation,* Vol. 1, pp. 355ff.

95. Cf. Otto Schindewolf, "Phylogenie und Anthropologie aus paläontologischer Sicht," in *Neue Anthropologie,* ed. by Hans-Georg Gadamer and Paul Vogler, Vol. 1 (Stuttgart: Georg Thieme, 1972), pp. 251f. and 270. Theodosius Dobzhansky, *Mankind Evolving. The Evolution of the Human Species* (New Haven: Yale University, 1962), p. 165, though critical of Haeckel's formulation of the fundamental biogenetic law admits "that many features of human ontogeny make no sense at all except on the assumption that they are retentions of the developmental patterns of remote ancestors. The celebrated gill arches, which are formed in human embryos and in those of other land-dwelling vertebrates, are also present in embryos of fishes, but in the latter they eventually become the supports of functioning gills. Can one avoid the inference that our ancestors had gills that were used as such?"

96. Cf. for the following Dobzhansky, *Mankind Evolving*, pp. 167f., and the extensive treatment of this issue by Philip L. Carpenter, *Immunology and Serology*, 2nd ed. (Philadelphia: W. B. Saunders, 1965), pp. 202ff., who provides extensive statistical material.

97. Cf. for a good introduction to these phenomena, Marcel Florkin, *A Molecular Approach to Phylogeny* (New York: Elsevier, 1966), esp. p. 31, where he adduces interesting statistics for the number of differences in cytochrome c of different species, and pp. 158f., where he does the same for insulin. Monroe W. Strickberger, *Genetics*, p. 806, however, rightly warns that we should not determine the relationship between species exclusively by comparisons of the amino acid sequence in a polypeptide, such as cytochrome c. For instance, according to an analysis of cytochrome c protein man would be more closely related to kangaroos than to horses, which, as we know from other evidence, cannot be true. Yet Strickberger, p. 807, admits that "as an aid in understanding evolutionary relationships rather than as the sole criterion for such relationships, comparisons between amino acid sequences will undoubtedly offer valuable contributions."

98. For the following cf. the amazingly comprehensive book by John Z. Young, *An Introduction to the Study of Man* (Oxford: Clarendon, 1971), pp. 406ff.; cf. also the popular and informative book by Carroll L. and Mildred A. Fenton, *The Fossil Book. A Record of Prehistoric Life* (Garden City, NY: Doubleday, 1958), pp. 53f.; for an extensive discussion of the oldest fossils cf. M. G. Rutten, *The Origin of Life by Natural Causes* (Amsterdam: Elsevier, 1971), esp. pp. 219ff.

99. Philip H. Gosse, *Omphalos: An Attempt to Untie the Geological Knot* (London: John van Voorst, 1857), pp. 347f.

100. For the following cf. Georges Cuvier, *Essay on the Theory of the Earth*, mineralogical notes and account of Cuvier's geological discoveries by Jameson, observations on the geology of North America by Samuel L. Mitchill (New York: Kirk & Mercein, 1818), pp. 166f. Cf. also Francis C. Haber, "Fossils and the Idea of a Process of Time in Natural History," in *Forerunners of Darwin: 1745-1859*, ed. by H. Bentley Glass, Owsei Temkin, and William L. Straus, Jr. (Baltimore: Johns Hopkins, 1959), esp. pp. 254f. Cf. also Frank D. Adams, *The Birth and Development of the Geological Studies* (New York: Dover, 1954), pp. 265ff.

101. Cf. Young, pp. 437ff.

102. Cf. Gerhard Heberer, "Die Herkunft der Menschheit," in *Propyläen Weltgeschichte*, ed. by Golo Mann and Alfred Hess, Vol. 1 (Berlin: Propyläen, 1961), pp. 127ff.; and Otto Schindewolf, "Phylogenie und Anthropologie aus paläontologischer Sicht," p. 283. Heberer talks here of an "animal-man transition field" in which the tool-user became a tool-maker.

103. Cf. Dobzhansky, *Mankind Evolving*, p. 173.

104. L. S. B. Leakey, *Adam's Ancestors. The Evolution of Man and His Culture*, 4th ed. (New York: Harper & Row, Torchbook, 1960), p. 3.

105. *Mankind Evolving*, p. 175.

106. Cf. for the following the instructive information in Paul Overhage,

Menschenformen im Eiszeitalter. Umwelten—Gestalten—Entwicklungen (Frankfurt am Main: Josef Knecht, 1969), p. 191. For the *homo erectus* cf. also Dobzhansky, *Mankind Evolving*, pp. 176ff.

107. Cf. for the following Overhage, pp. 409ff.
108. Cf. for the following two paragraphs, *Mankind Evolving*, pp. 179-191.
109. *Ibid.*, p. 191.

3. HUMANITY—A UNIQUE SPECIES

1. Cf. Otto H. Schindewolf, "Phylogenie und Anthropologie aus palä-ontologischer Sicht," in *Neue Anthropologie,* ed. by Hans-Georg Gadamer and Paul Vogler, Vol. 1, pp. 276ff., where he advances the possibility that hominoid apes lost some of the faculties which our common ancestors once possessed. Thus one can speak of a progressive simiation [becoming ape-like] on the part of the hominoid apes, and a progressive hominization on our part.
2. For the following cf. *ibid.,* pp. 279ff.
3. Bernhard Rensch, *Biophilosophy,* trans. by C. A. M. Sym (New York: Columbia University, 1971), p. 70.
4. For the following cf. Adolf Remane, "Die Bedeutung der Evolutionslehre für die allgemeine Anthropologie," in *Neue Anthropologie,* Vol. 1, pp. 320ff. For other examples of the presence of tradition in anthropoid apes cf. Sherwood L. Washburn and David A. Hamburg, "The Implications of Primate Research," in *Primate Behavior. Field Studies of Monkeys and Apes,* ed. by Irven DeVore (New York: Holt, Rinehart and Winston, 1965), p. 619f.; cf. also Irenäus Eibl-Eibesfeldt in his thorough and stimulating book, *Ethology. The Biology of Behavior,* trans. by E. Klinghammer (New York: Holt, Rinehart and Winston, 1970), pp. 221ff., who furnishes many examples of the development of tradition among animals.
5. Homer, *Odyssey,* trans. by S. H. Butcher and A. Lang, in *The Complete Works of Homer. The Iliad and the Odyssey* (New York: Modern Library, n.d.), pp. 268f. (book 17).
6. Cf. Adolf Remane, "Die Bedeutung der Evolutionslehre für die allgemeine Anthropologie," p. 322; and R. Allen and Beatrice T. Gardner, "Teaching Sign Language to a Chimpanzee," *Science,* Vol. 165 (Aug. 15, 1969), pp. 664-672. For a popular and informative report on experiments with chimpanzees and the scientific conclusions reached cf. also Eugene Linden, *Apes, Men, and Language* (New York: Saturday Review Press, 1974).
7. Konrad Lorenz, *On Aggression,* pp. 151ff.
8. Cf. for the following Detlev Ploog, "Kommunikation in Affengesellschaften und deren Bedeutung für die Verständigungsweisen des Menschen," in *Neue Anthropologie,* Vol. 2, p. 170.
9. Otto H. Schindewolf, "Phylogenie und Anthropologie aus paläontologischer Sicht," in *Neue Anthropologie,* Vol. 1, p. 282.
10. So Remane, p. 324. Additionally Irenäus Eibl-Eibesfeldt, *Der vorprogrammierte Mensch. Das Ererbte als bestimmender Faktor im menschlichen Verhalten* (Munich: Deutscher Taschenbuch Verlag, 1976), p. 100, points out that the findings of the first weapons by

paleoanthropologists go hand in hand with the findings of violently damaged human skulls. Thus increasing individualization may not be the sole factor that contributed to this destructive human behavior, but also the invention of weapons which humanity still today has not learned to handle peacefully.

11. For the first part of this section cf. Kurt Wezler, "Menschliches Leben in der Sicht des Physiologen," in *Neue Anthropologie*, Vol. 2, pp. 336-382; cf. also John Z. Young, *An Introduction to the Study of Man*, pp. 222-250, for many valuable statistics. John Z. Young, however, does not seem to differentiate clearly enough between growth of anthropoid apes and of humans. Though both show a characteristic retardation in growth, this is much more extended for humans than for anthropoid apes. Therefore it is also somewhat confusing to say with J. M. Tanner: "The characteristic form of the human growth curve is shared by apes and monkeys," especially since he has to admit immediately in parenthesis: "(or at least by chimpanzees and rhesus, the only species on which we have data)." "Human Growth and Constitution," in *Human Biology. An Introduction to Human Evolution, Variation and Growth*, ed. by G. A. Harrison *et al.* (New York: Oxford University, 1964), p. 317. For the recent acceleration in the development of human beings cf. the significant essay by Adolf Portmann, "Die Entwicklungsbeschleunigung der Jugend als biologisches und soziales Problem," in *Entlässt die Natur den Menschen? Gesammelte Aufsätze zur Biologie und Anthropologie*, 2nd ed. (Munich: A. Piper, 1971), pp. 253-281.

12. Cf. for this and the following paragraph, Wezler, pp. 344-352, for pertinent statistical evidence. For the evolution and peculiarity of the human brain cf. Theodosius Dobzhansky, *Mankind Evolving*, pp. 199-202.

13. Cf. for the following Wezler, pp. 340ff.; and William C. Osman Hill, *Evolutionary Biology of the Primates* (London: Academic Press, 1972), pp. 66ff.

14. Cf. for the following Wezler, pp. 371f.

15. Cf. for the following *ibid.*, pp. 377f.; and John Z. Young, *An Introduction to the Study of Man*, pp. 516f.

16. Cf. for this paragraph Eibl-Eibesfeldt, "Stammesgeschichtliche Anpassungen im Verhalten des Menschen," in *Neue Anthropologie*, Vol. 2, pp. 13-18; and his *Ethology*, pp. 403-408, where he reports on pertinent studies conducted by other scientists.

17. Cf. for the following Eibl-Eibesfeldt, "Stammesgeschichtliche," pp. 13 and 50f.; cf. also *Ethology*, p. 442.

18. For the quotations in this paragraph see Margaret Mead, *From the South Seas. Studies of Adolescence and Sex in Primitive Societies*, Part 3: *Sex and Temperament in Three Primitive Societies* (New York: William Morrow, 1939), pp. 279f., and Ashley Montagu, ed., in his intr. to *Man and Aggression*, 2nd ed. (New York: Oxford, 1973), p. xvii.

19. For the next two paragraphs cf. the excellent book by John Money and Anke A. Ehrhardt, *Man & Woman, Boy & Girl. The Differentiation and Dimorphism of Gender Identity from Conception to Maturity*

(Baltimore: Johns Hopkins University, 1972), esp. p. 117; Patricia Draper, "Cultural Pressure on Sex Differences," *American Ethnologist*, Vol. 2 (November, 1975), esp. pp. 602ff. (quotation on p. 603); and Eibl-Eibesfeldt, *Menschenforschung auf neuen Wegen. Die naturwissenschaftliche Betrachtung kultureller Verhaltensweisen* (Vienna: Fritz Molden), pp. 40f.

20. Eibl-Eibesfeldt. *Ethology*, p. 453.

21. Sigmund Freud, *"Warum Krieg?"* Letter to Albert Einstein (Sept., 1932), in *Gesammelte Werke. Chronologisch geordnet*, Vol. 16: *Werke aus den Jahren 1932-1939* (London: Imago, 1950), p. 24, where he says: "It is part of the inborn inequality of mankind which cannot be eliminated that distinguishes mankind in leaders and dependents." For the following Eibl-Eibesfeldt, *Ethology*, pp. 446ff.

22. Wolfgang Wickler, in his interesting book, *The Sexual Code. The Social Behavior of Animals and Men*, intr. by Konrad Lorenz, illustr. by Hermann Kacher (Garden City, NY: Doubleday, 1972), p. 281, rightly says: "Man is different from animals. His behavior is that of a thinking being, so it cannot be assessed in terms of biology alone; but neither can it be assessed without biology." Cf. also Konrad Lorenz, "Psychology and Phylogeny" (1954), in *Studies in Animal and Human Behavior*, Vol. 2, trans. by R. Martin (Cambridge, MA: Harvard University, 1971), p. 194, who points out the difficulty of adapting innate norms to today's problems and emphasizes "the gradually developing inadequacy of species-specific *killing inhibitions*." For this particular problem cf. his book *On Aggression*.

23. Cf. the examples cited by Lorenz, *On Aggression*, pp. 282f.

24. Cf. for the following paragraph Bernhard Hassenstein, "Das spezifisch Menschliche nach den Resultaten der Verhaltensforschung," in *Neue Anthropologie*, Vol. 2, esp. pp. 64ff.; and Eibl-Eibesfeldt, *Ethology*, pp. 232-237.

25. So Hassenstein, p. 77.

26. For the following cf. Hassenstein, pp. 81f. Cf. also Byron A. Campbell and James R. Misanin, "Basic Drives," in *Annual Review of Psychology*, Vol. 20 (Palo Alto, CA: Annual Reviews, 1969), p. 77, who rightly claim that the so-called "basic drives," such as hunger, thirst, sex, and maternal behavior are themselves controlled by "a complex of interactions among environmental stimuli, hormonal states, physiological imbalance, previous experience, etc."

27. Cf. Harry J. Jerison, *Evolution of the Brain and Intelligence* (New York: Academic Press, 1973), esp. pp. 401 and 424, who also provides extensive statistical material.

28. Cf. for the following Hugo Spatz, "Gedanken über die Zukunft des Menschenhirns und die Idee vom Übermenschen," in *Der Übermensch. Eine Diskussion*, ed. by Ernst Benz (Stuttgart: Rhein-Verlag, 1961), pp. 342f. Cf. also Alan Bilsborough, "Some Aspects of the Evolution of the Human Brain" in *The Biology of Brains. Proceedings of a Symposium Held at the Royal Geographical Society London on September 28 and 29, 1972*, ed. by W. B. Broughton (New York: John Wiley, 1974), p. 211, who suggests that "structural and organizational

changes have perhaps been of greater importance in the evolution of the human brain than mere increase in size."

29. Cf. for the following Spatz, p. 344.
30. Cf. Spatz, pp. 371f. Spatz, however, refers here to Julian Huxley, *Evolution in Action* (New York: Harper & Row, Perennial Library, 1966), pp. 124-129, who is convinced of the progress of human "psycho-social evolution," as it expresses itself, for instance, in the discovery of the primacy of the human personality in which society is seen as existing for the individual and not vice versa.
31. Charles Darwin, *The Descent of Man,* 471 (chap. 4). Cf. also James Henry Breasted, *The Dawn of Conscience* (New York: Charles Scribner's, 1936), pp. 11ff., who describes the *"first rise of a civilization of profound moral vision"* in Egypt and compares it with Stone Age barbarism in Europe and the total lack of equal justice in ancient Babylonia.
32. Cf. Spatz, pp. 370f., and 365f. Cf. also C. W. M. Whitty, "Changes in Conduct and Personality Following Localized Brain Lesions," in *Biology and Personality: Frontier Problems in Science, Philosophy and Religion,* ed. by Ian T. Ramsey (New York: Barnes & Noble, 1965), pp. 139-149, who also cites some typical consequences of certain kinds of brain damage.
33. Pierre Teilhard de Chardin, *The Phenomenon of Man,* trans. by B. Wall, intr. by Sir Julian Huxley (New York: Harper, 1959), pp. 249f.
34. For an instructive introduction to some of the detectable genetically caused diseases cf. Alun Jones and Walter F. Bodmer, *Our Future Inheritance: Choice or Chance? A Study by a British Association Working Party* (London: Oxford University, 1974), pp. 106 and esp. pp. 45-82, where they also provide lists of some of the detectable diseases.
35. Leroy Augenstein, "Shall We Play God?" in *Changing Man: The Threat and the Promise,* ed. by Kyle Haselden and Philip Hefner (Garden City, NY: Doubleday, 1968), p. 97, is toying with this idea. For the difficulties involved in "genetic surgery" cf. Jones and Bodmer, p. 110. Cf. also the caution of Hermann J. Muller, "Means and Aims in Human Genetic Betterment," in *The Control of Human Heredity and Evolution,* ed. by Tracy M. Sonneborn, 5th ed. (New York: Macmillan, 1967), p. 113.
36. G. Pontecorvo, "Prospects for Genetic Analysis in Man," in *The Control of Human Heredity and Evolution,* ed. by Tracy M. Sonneborn, p. 83; cf. also Joshua Lederberg, "Biological Future of Man," in *Man and His Future.* A Ciba Foundation Volume, ed. by Gordon Wolstenholme (London: J. & A. Churchill, 1967), pp. 269f.
37. Augenstein, pp. 91f.
38. Cf. Jones and Bodmer, p. 113.
39. So Lederberg, "Genetic Engineering and the Amelioration of Genetic Defect" (1970), in *Human Genetics, Readings on the Implications of Genetic Engineering,* ed. by Thomas R. Mertens (New York: John Wiley, 1975), p. 94, with regards to the so-called "clone-a-man" process.

40. Cf. G. H. Beale, "Das Verändern der Erbeigenschaften der Zelle," in *Unsere Welt 1985*, ed. by Robert Jungk and H. J. Mundt (Munich: Kurt Desch, 1967), pp. 65f.
41. Hermann J. Muller, "Genetic Progress by Voluntarily Conducted Germinal Choice," in *Man and His Future*, ed. by Gordon Wolstenholme, p. 255.
42. Cf. n. 41 and Muller, "Human Evolution by Voluntary Choice of Germ Plasm" (1961), in *Human Genetics*, esp. pp. 130-138, as samples of the numerous articles Muller devoted to this topic.
43. Jean Rostand, *Can Man Be Modified?* (New York: Basic Books, 1959), p. 80.
44. For the following cf. Maya Pines, *The Brain Changers. Scientists and the New Mind Control* (New York: Harcourt Brace Javanovich, 1973), pp. 86-115; and Hudson Hoaglund, "Potentialities in the Control of Behavior," in *Man and His Future*, pp. 306f.
45. Cf. Weston La Barre, *The Peyote Cult*, enl. ed. (New York: Schocken, 1969).
46. B. F. Skinner, *About Behaviorism* (New York: Alfred A. Knopf, 1974), p. 219.
47. *Ibid.*, p. 171.
48. B. F. Skinner, "Freedom and the Control of Men" (1955/56), in *Cumulative Record. A Selection of Papers*, 3rd ed. (New York: Appleton-Century-Crofts, 1972), p. 4.
49. B. F. Skinner, *Beyond Freedom and Dignity* (New York: Alfred A. Knopf, 1971), p. 200.
50. *Ibid.*, p. 206.
51. Cf. for the following Skinner, "Freedom and the Control of Men," pp. 7ff.
52. For the following cf. *ibid.*, pp. 10f.
53. B. F. Skinner, *Walden Two* (New York: Macmillan, 1948).
54. Skinner, "Freedom and the Control of Men," p. 14.
55. *Ibid.*, p. 16.
56. Cf. Skinner, *Beyond Freedom and Dignity*, pp. 125f., for further discussion on what constitutes "the good." For some of the discussion on Skinner, especially with regard to his "abolition of freedom" cf. *Beyond the Punitive Society. Operant Conditioning: Social and Political Aspects*, ed. by Harvey Wheeler (San Francisco: W. H. Freeman, 1973), which also contains a very helpful reply by Skinner to his critics.
57. For the following cf. Konrad Lorenz, "Ganzheit und Teil in der tierischen und menschlichen Gemeinschaft" (1950), in *Mensch und Tier. Streifzüge durch die Verhaltensforschung* (Munich: Piper, 1973), pp. 242f.
58. So among others Otto H. Schindewolf, "Phylogenie und Anthropologie aus paläontologischer Sicht," in *Neue Anthropologie*, Vol. 1, pp. 276f.; and Lorenz, "Ganzheit und Teil," pp. 248f.
59. Cf. for the following Lorenz, "Ganzheit und Teil," pp. 251f.
60. So Lorenz, *Das sogenannte Böse. Zur Naturgeschichte der Aggression*, 33rd ed. (Vienna: G. Borotha Schoeler, 1973), p. 333. The earlier English translation, *On Aggression*, p. 251, has this quote somewhat

misleadingly modified to: "The imagination of man's heart is not really evil from his youth up, as we read in Genesis." Niko Tinbergen, a long-time friend of Lorenz, arrives at similar conclusions. Cf. Tinbergen's essay "The Search for Animal Roots of Human Behavior" (1964), in *The Animal in Its World. Explorations of an Ethologist, 1932-1972*, Foreword by Peter Medawar, Vol. 2 (Cambridge, MA: Harvard University, 1973), pp. 171ff.

61. Cf. for the following Lorenz, *On Aggression*, pp. 241f. Edward O. Wilson, *Sociobiology. The New Synthesis* (Cambridge, MA: Harvard University, 1975), pp. 246f., however, objects here saying: "The evidence of murder and cannibalism in mammals and other vertebrates has now accumulated to the point that we must completely reverse the conclusion advanced by Konrad Lorenz in his book *On Aggression*. Murder is far more common and hence 'normal' in many vertebrate species than in man." Of course, the question must be asked here what Wilson understands by murder. If he does not mean reflective killing, but an intentional and wilful act, then humanity may indeed be the more dangerous species. No other living beings have ever staged systematic genocides, such as the Nazis against the Jews, or as did other "cultured" nations by "relocating" native populations.

62. For the following cf. Lorenz, "Ganzheit und Teil," pp. 254f.; and *On Aggression*, pp. 251ff. Cf. also Tinbergen, "Functional Ethology and the Human Sciences" (1972), in *The Animal in Its World*, Vol. 2, pp. 220f., where he mentions the problems of human disadaptation and readaptation in our urbanized, crowded, and anonymous living conditions.

63. Cf. Lorenz in his provocative book *Civilized Man's Eight Deadly Sins*, trans. by M. K. Wilson (New York: Harcourt Brace Javanovich, 1974), pp. 12ff.

64. For the following two paragraphs cf. Lorenz in his concluding chapter *On Aggression*, pp. 275-299, which has the characteristic title "Avowal of Optimism."

65. *On Aggression*, p. 299; our quotation is from the German original, *Das sogenannte Böse*, p. 368.

66. Cf. for the following Bernhard Hassenstein, "Das spezifisch Menschliche nach den Resultaten der Verhaltensforschung," in *Neue Anthropologie*, Vol. 2, p. 83; quotation p. 96. For the interactive model of human aggression cf. also the helpful summary in Irenäus Eibl-Eibesfeldt, *Der vorprogrammierte Mensch*, pp. 115ff. Cf. also the caution rightly expressed by Muzafer and Carolyn W. Sherif, "Motivation and Intergroup Aggression: A Persistent Problem in Levels of Analysis," in the significant volume, *Development and Evolution of Behavior. Essays in Memory of T. C. Schneirla*, ed. by Lester R. Aronson et al. (San Francisco: W. H. Freeman, 1970), pp. 576f., when they say: "Attempts to deal with human aggression exclusively through motivational concepts amount to ignoring the stimulational background and context." Similarly, Edward O. Wilson, *Sociobiology*, p. 551, objects to Lorenz saying: "While Skinner and others reduced man to an equipotent response machine, Konrad Lorenz, Desmond Morris and others saw man as a biological species adapted to

particular environments." Wilson in turn suggests that a species does neither just respond to stimuli nor is it only environmentally fixed. It rather uses whatever is advantageous to evolution. While Lorenz might agree with Wilson on this issue, the point that Lorenz makes is not that humanity is solely adapted to particular environments, but that the rate at which humanity introduced environmental changes overextended its possibilities for fast enough responses. Theodosius Dobzhansky, "On Some Fundamental Concepts of Darwinian Biology," in *Evolutionary Biology*, Vol. 2, ed. by Th. Dobzhansky, Max K. Hecht, and William C. Steere (New York: Appleton-Century-Crofts, 1968), p. 28, perhaps summed up best the relationship between environmental stimulus and adaptive response when he said: "The fundamental thesis of the biological theory of evolution is that evolution is, at least in the main, an adaptive response of life to the challenges of the environment, mediated through natural selection. It does not follow, however, that the adaptedness always increases as the evolution progresses. Man is not necessarily better adapted to his environment than flies, or corals, or bacteria are to theirs." This assessment would still leave room for the concern of Lorenz that in human history environmental changes and human response to these changes are getting more and more out of tune.

When Ashley Montagu in his introduction to *Man and Aggression,* p. xix, passionately declared: "Certainly the views of Ardrey and Lorenz and others like them concerning man's nature have no scientific validity whatever," he overstated his case. The crucial question is not whether there is a basic aggressive drive in humanity, but whether today's technological and socio-economic conditions engender and reinforce aggressive destructiveness, instead of channeling human energies into a constructive direction.

67. Hassenstein, pp. 83f.
68. Lorenz, *Civilized Man's Eight Deadly Sins,* pp. 42 and 59.
69. Cf. the concluding statement by Toffler, *Future Shock* (New York: Random House, 1970), p. 430, where he says: "For, by making imaginative use of change to channel change, we can not only spare ourselves the trauma of future shock, we can reach out and humanize distant tomorrows."
70. Alvin Toffler, *The Eco-Spasm Report* (New York: Bantam Book, 1975), where he says on the cover: "What is happening is the breakdown of industrial civilization on the planet and the first fragmentary appearance of a wholly new civilization."
71. Hans Schwarz, "The Eschatological Dimension of Ecology," *Zygon,* Vol. 9 (Dec., 1974), esp. pp. 325-329.
72. This idea was first vigorously advanced by William and Paul Paddock, *Famine—1975! America's Decision: Who Will Survive* (Boston: Little, Brown and Co., 1967), esp. pp. 205ff. When we read this proposal we are struck by the cold-blooded rationality of the argument.
73. Garrett Hardin, "Lifeboat Ethics. The Case Against Helping the Poor," *Psychology Today,* Vol. 8 (Sept., 1974), pp. 38-43 and 123-126. Cf. also Garrett Hardin, *Exploring New Ethics for Survival* (New

York: Viking, 1972). For the discussion of the various aspects of a lifeboat ethics cf. the valuable contributions in the special issue of *Soundings. An Interdisciplinary Journal*, Vol. 59 (Spring, 1976): "World Famine and Lifeboat Ethics: Moral Dilemmas in the Formation of Public Policy," ed. by George R. Lucas, Jr.

74. Robert L. Heilbroner, *An Inquiry into the Human Prospect* (New York: W. W. Norton, 1974), p. 17.

75. *Ibid.*, p. 22.

76. *Ibid.*, p. 137.

77. *Ibid.*, p. 138.

78. *Ibid.*, p. 144. As a good response to Heilbroner's book cf. the papers in *Zygon*, Vol. 10 (Sept., 1975), resulting from a symposium on "The Human Prospect: Heilbroner's Challenge to Religion and Science (Washington, D.C., Oct. 23-24, 1974)."

79. Ernst Bloch, *Das Prinzip Hoffnung*, Vol. 3 (Frankfurt/Main: Suhrkamp, 1969), p. 1628 (chap. 55).

80. Bloch, *On Karl Marx*, being an abridged trans. by J. Maxwell of *Das Prinzip Hoffnung* (New York: Herder & Herder, 1971), p. 172. Similar thoughts are also expressed in Bloch, *Tübinger Einleitung in die Philosophie* (Frankfurt/Main: Suhrkamp, 1970), p. 234.

81. Cf. Bloch, *Tübinger Einleitung*, p. 242.

82. For this quotation and the next see Bloch, *Naturrecht und menschliche Würde* (Frankfurt/Main: Suhrkamp, 1961), p. 219.

83. *Ibid.*, p. 258.

84. *Ibid.*, p. 210.

85. Jürgen Moltmann, "Messianismus und Marxismus," in *Über Bloch*, ed. by Martin Walser, Ivo Frenzel, Jürgen Moltmann, et al., 2nd ed. (Frankfurt/Main: Suhrkamp, 1968), p. 59, rightly observes that since Bloch did not answer the quest for God with his paneschatological idea of the (material) kingdom, he could also not come to terms with the quest for humanity. Cf. also Moltmann, "Hope and Confidence: A Conversation with Ernst Bloch," *Dialog*, Vol. 7 (Winter, 1968), pp. 42-55.

86. For the following cf. Mao Tse-tung, "On Practice. On the Relation Between Knowledge and Practice, Between Knowing and Doing" (1937), in *Selected Works of Mao Tse-tung*, Vol. 1 (Peking: Foreign Languages Press, 1967), p. 308.

87. *Mao Tse-tung's Quotations. The Red Guard's Handbook*, intr. by Steward Fraser (Nashville, TN: International Center. George Peabody College for Teachers, 1967), p. 203.

88. Mao Tse-tung, "Dialectical Materialism" (March, 1940), trans. by Dennis J. Doolin and Peter J. Golas in their article "On Contradiction in the Light of Mao Tse-tung's Essay on 'Dialectical Materialism,'" *The China Quarterly* (July-September, 1964), p. 42.

89. Frederic Wakeman, *History and Will, Philosophical Perspectives of Mao Tse-tung's Thought* (Berkeley: University of California, 1973), p. 166. It is significant in this context that according to a newspaper report during the 1975 visit to China Helmut Schmidt, the Chancellor of the Federal Republic of Germany, had a 100-minute visit with Mao Tse-tung, on which occasion Mao talked with Schmidt among other

items extensively about Immanuel Kant, Ernst Haeckel, the most fervent German disciple of Darwin, and Karl von Clausewitz. Cf. *Detroiter Abend-Post* (November 8, 1975) in a front page article.

90. *Mao Tse-tung's Quotations,* p. 222.
91. Mao Tse-tung, "On Practice," in *Selected Works,* Vol. 1, p. 304.
92. For this and the following quotations see *Mao Tse-tung's Quotations,* pp. 5; 3; 9; 11; 24.
93. For this paragraph cf. *Mao Tse-tung's Quotations,* pp. 29f. and 187; for quotations see *ibid.,* pp. 26, 269, and 275. Very interestingly Jerome Ch'en, *Mao and the Chinese Revolution with Thirty-seven Poems by Mao Tse tung,* trans. by M. Bullock and Jerome Ch'en (London: Oxford University, 1965), p. 6, points out the intense hatred "which is so essential a part of Mao's personality." Though it has been used toward liberating and educating China, it has also been directed against anybody who would disagree with Mao's way of bringing about his envisioned goal.
94. Cf. *Christian Faith and the Chinese Experience.* Workshop Reports from an Ecumenical Colloquium in Louvain, Belgium, September 9-14, 1974 (Lutheran World Federation/Pro Mundi Vita, 1974), p. 21. See also the very instructive papers of this Colloquium published in the same volume. Another important publication of the Lutheran World Federation/Pro Mundi Vita on China contains the papers of an ecumenical seminar held at Båstad, Sweden, January 29 to February 2, 1974, on *Theological Implications of the New China.* For information on the astounding accomplishments of the "New China" cf. *China. The Peasant Revolution,* ed. by Ray Wylie (London: World Student Christian Federation, 1972); and Maxwell S. Stewart, *China Revisited.* Public Affairs Pamphlet No. 505 (New York: Public Affairs Committee, 1974).
95. Wakeman, *History and Will,* p. 20.
96. So rightly Leo Goodstadt, *China's Search for Plenty. The Economics of Mao Tse-tung* (New York: Weatherhill, 1973), p. 203. Jack Chen in his highly informative book, *Inside the Cultural Revolution* (New York: Macmillan, 1975), p. 439, even claims that now "China has resolutely rejected the way of superindustrialism, the 'affluent society.' China has wisely understood that conditions of life on our planet today call for a life-style of homely frugality and that to adopt such a life-style is not a denial of happiness but a wise caution in facing the future." If this statement is true, and many signs indicate it is, then not only young nations could learn from China, but highly developed ones too, in order to rethink their priorities and aspirations.
97. Cf. for the following *ibid.,* pp. 235ff. While he mentions that in private discussions Chinese Communists are insistent that the Cultural Revolution has corrected these phenomena, he claims that the many reports from all areas of the country indicate that heretical ideas continue. According to Goodstadt these conflicting stories imply that Mao's endeavors fall short of a total triumph. Chen, p. 436, admits that the main danger for China today comes from the emergence of a new class of bourgeois, from the revisionists in leading positions in the state and inside the Party apparatus. One might wonder here

whether a truly egalitarian society is not too much an eschatological goal to be *fully* realized in the present. Even a permanent revolution, of which the Cultural Revolution seemed to be part, can lead to the formation of an elitist group of revolutionaries.

98. Quoted in Leo Goodstadt, *op. cit.*, p. 235, from a regional broadcast in mainland China (October 10, 1970).

99. *Mao Tse-tung's Quotations*, p. 203.

100. Cf. the perceptive reservations that Holmes Welch, *Buddhism under Mao* (Cambridge, MA: Harvard University, 1972), pp. 383ff., expressed against Mao's totally this-worldly and rationalistic approach to life. For the total grip of the party's system on the people cf. the penetrating and very critical analysis in *Escape from Red China*, by Robert Loh as told to Humphrey Evans (New York: Coward-McCann, 1962), which, however, was written before the Cultural Revolution.

101. Cf. the excellent essay by Roger Garaudy, "The Meaning of Life and History in Marx and Teilhard de Chardin: Teilhard's Contribution to the Dialogue Between Christian and Marxists," trans. by N. Lindsay, in *Evolution, Marxism & Christianity. Studies in the Teilhardian Synthesis*, ed. by the Pierre Teilhard de Chardin Association of Great Britain and Ireland (London: Garnstone, 1967), esp. pp. 61f.

102. Cf. Pierre Teilhard de Chardin, *The Future of Man*, trans. by N. Denny (New York: Harper & Row, 1964), pp. 253f.

103. For this and the following quotations see, *ibid.*, pp. 228; 229; and 230. Cf. also Pierre Teilhard de Chardin, *Activation of Energy*, trans. by R. Hague (New York: Harcourt Brace Jovanovich, 1971), pp. 212ff., where he mentions that human interdependence will bring with it a heightened vision of responsibility.

104. For the following cf. *The Future of Man*, pp. 232f., for quotations see *ibid.*, p. 233. Cf. also Pierre Teilhard de Chardin, *Human Energy*, trans. by J. M. Cohen (London: Collins, 1969), pp. 133f., where he is more hesitant, though still hoping that science will find the right substitutes at the appropriate time.

105. *The Future of Man*, p. 240.

106. For this and the following quotations see *ibid.*, p. 265.

107. For the following remarks and quotations see *ibid.*, p. 286.

108. *Human Energy*, p. 153.

109. For the following cf. *The Future of Man*, p. 34.

110. For the following cf. *ibid.*, pp. 214f.

111. For the following cf. *ibid.*, pp. 34 and 235f.

112. *Human Energy*, p. 160.

113. *The Future of Man*, p. 223.

114. *Human Energy*, p. 143.

115. Pierre Teilhard de Chardin, *Christianity and Evolution*, trans. by R. Hague (New York: Harcourt Brace Javanovich, 1969), p. 175.

116. Pierre Teilhard de Chardin, *The Divine Milieu. An Essay on the Interior Life*, trans. by B. Wall (New York: Harper & Row, 1960), pp. 133f.

117. Cf. the comprehensive and critical analysis of Teilhard's system in Henri de Lubac, *The Religion of Teilhard de Chardin*, trans. by R. Hague (New York: Desclee, 1967), pp. 108f. For other shorter, but

helpful introductions to Teilhard cf. Philip Hefner, *The Promise of Teilhard. The Meaning of the Twentieth Century in Christian Perspective* (Philadelphia: J. B. Lippincott, 1970); and Robert Hale, *Christ and the Universe. Teilhard de Chardin and the Cosmos* (Chicago: Franciscan Herald, 1972).

118. Cf. Lubac, p. 198, who points to the difference between Bergson and Teilhard. For Henri Bergson cf. his book *Creative Evolution,* trans. by A. Mitchell (New York: Henry Holt, 1911), esp. pp. 89 and 96f.

119. *Christianity and Evolution,* p. 80.

120. Cf. the questions posed by Lubac, pp. 200f.; and Teilhard, *Christianity and Evolution,* p. 148, where he comes close to making this assertion.

4. God's Own Creation

1. Cf. Xenophanes of Colophon (24ff.) who says: "He sees as a whole, thinks as a whole, and hears as a whole. But without toil he sets everything in motion, by the thought of his mind. And he always remains in the same place, not moving at all, nor is it fitting for him to change his position at different times" (trans. in Kathleen Freeman, *Ancilla to the Pre-Socratic Philosophers. A Complete Translation of the Fragments in Diels, 'Fragmente der Vorsokratiker'* [Oxford: Basil Blackwell, 1952], p. 23). Cf. also Kathleen Freeman, *The Pre-Socratic Philosophers. A Companion to Diels, 'Fragmente der Vorsokratiker'* (Oxford: Basil Blackwell, 1953), p. 93, who points out the influence Xenophanes had on Parmenides and Plato with this concept of God as the One.

2. Cf. "Taittiriya Upanishad" (III), in *The Principal Upanishads,* ed. with intr., text and notes by S. Radhakrishnan (London: Allen & Unwin, 1953), p. 553, where it says: "That, verily, from which these beings are born, that, by which, when born they live, that into which, when departing, they enter. That, seek to know. That is *Brahman.*"

3. Hans Schwarz, *The Search for God,* pp. 21f.

4. Cf. for the following Frederick Copleston, *A History of Philosophy,* Vol. 3 (Westminster, MD: Newman, 1959), p. 261; and Dorothea W. Singer, *Giordano Bruno,* p. 50.

5. Giordano Bruno, *On the Infinite Universe and Worlds,* in Singer, p. 363 (5th dialog).

6. *Ibid.,* p. 365 (5th dialog).

7. *Ibid.,* p. 257 (1st dialog).

8. *Ibid.,* pp. 261f. (1st dialog).

9. We wonder whether one can say with Paul H. Michel, *The Cosmology of Giordano Bruno,* trans. by R. E. W. Maddison (Ithaca, NY: Cornell University, 1973), p. 122, that according to Bruno the soul of the universe cannot be equated with God, but is located between God and the universe. For Bruno there only seems to be a distinction, and not a very strong one, between God and the universe, but not between the soul of the universe and God.

10. For details of the trial cf. Singer, pp. 158-180.
11. Cf. Copleston, Vol. 4, p. 209.
12. Benedict de Spinoza, *Short Treatise on God, Man, & His Well-Being,* trans. and ed. with an intr., commentary, and a Life of Spinoza by A. Wolf (New York: Russell & Russell, 1963), p. 21 (chap. 2).
13. *Ibid.,* p. 25.
14. Cf. Spinoza, *Ethics,* preceded by *On the Improvement of the Understanding,* ed. with an intr. by James Gutmann (New York: Hafner, 1960), p. 188 in Spinoza's preface to part 4 of his *Ethics.*
15. *Short Treatise,* p. 27 (chap. 2).
16. *Ibid.,* p. 41 (chap. 3).
17. *Ibid.,* p. 47 (chap. 5).
18. *Ibid.,* p. 56 (chap. 8).
19. *Ibid.,* p. 40 (chap. 2).
20. *Ibid.,* p. 57 (chap. 9).
21. *Ibid.,* pp. 30f. (chap. 2).
22. Benedict de Spinoza, *Ethics,* p. 41 (part 1: def.).
23. Cf. *ibid.,* p. 48 (part 1: prop. 11).
24. Cf. Thomas Carson Mark, *Spinoza's Theory of Truth* (New York: Columbia University, 1972), p. 10 n.3, who convincingly points out that God and nature do not have the same meaning for Spinoza, though for him they refer to the same thing and have the same extension.
25. Hubertus Genzinus Hubbeling, *Spinoza's Methodology* (Assen: Van Gorcum, 1964), p. 19.
26. Cf. Martin Luther, *Confession Concerning Christ's Supper* (1528), in *Luther's Works,* ed. by Jaroslav Pelikan and Helmut T. Lehmann, Vol. 37 (Philadelphia: Muhlenberg, 1961), p. 228. Cf. also Spinoza, *Ethics,* p. 52 (part 1: prop. 15), where he says: "that by 'body' we understand a certain quantity possessing length, breadth, and depth, limited by some fixed form; and that to attribute these to God, a being absolutely infinite, is the greatest absurdity."
27. *Ethics,* p. 55 (part 1: prop. 15).
28. A good introduction to Hegel's thoughts is provided by Walter Kaufmann, *Hegel, Reinterpretation, Texts, and Commentary* (New York: Doubleday, 1965). Especially helpful for our problem is Erik Schmidt, *Hegel's System der Theologie* (Berlin: Walter de Gruyter, 1974); and Erik Schmidt, *Hegels Lehre von Gott. Eine kritische Darstellung* (Gütersloh: C. Bertelsmann, 1952). For the following cf. Loyd D. Easton, *Hegel's First American Followers. The Ohio Hegelians: John B. Stallo, Peter Kaufmann, Moncure Conway, and August Willich, with Key Writings* (Athens, OH: Ohio University, 1966); and *The American Hegelians. An Intellectual Episode in the History of Western America,* ed. by William H. Goetzmann (New York: Alfred A. Knopf, 1973); and William J. Brazill, *The Young Hegelians* (New Haven: Yale University, 1970). For the quotation see Karl Barth, *Protestant Theology in the Nineteenth Century. Its Background & History,* trans. by B. Cozens and J. Bowden (London: SCM, 1972), p. 384.

29. Georg Wilhelm Friedrich Hegel, *Das Leben Jesu* (1795), in *Hegels theologische Jugendschriften*, ed. by Herman Nohl (Tübingen, 1907), p. 75, where Hegel then continues: "The plan of the world is ordered according to reason. Reason teaches man to learn his destiny, an unconditional purpose of his life. Though it has often been darkened, it has never been totally extinguished, even in darkness there has always been retained a faint flickering *[Schimmer]* of reason."

30. Hegel, *Wissenschaft der Logik*, in *Sämtliche Werke*, ed. by Hermann Glockner, Vol. 4 (Stuttgart: Fr. Frommann, 1928), pp. 45f.

31. Hegel, *Vorlesungen über die Philosophie der Religion*, Vol. 1: *Begriff der Religion*, ed. by Georg Lasson (Hamburg: Felix Meiner, 1966), p. 295.

32. Cf. Hegel, *System der Philosophie, Dritter Teil: Die Philosophie des Geistes*, in *Sämtliche Werke* (Glockner), Vol. 10, p. 35, where Hegel says: "*The Absolute is the Spirit;* this is the highest definition of the Absolute."

33. *Ibid.*, pp. 451ff. (par. 562ff.) and pp. 458f. (par. 572f.).

34. *Ibid.*, p. 39 (par. 385), pp. 46f. (par. 387), and pp. 382ff. (par. 483-486).

35. Hegel, *Vorlesungen*, Vol. 3, *Sämtliche Werke* (Glockner), Vol. 19, p. 8.

36. Hegel, *Die Philosophie des Geistes*, in *Sämtliche Werke* (Glockner), Vol. 10, pp. 37f. (par. 384).

37. Hegel, *The Phenomenology of Mind*, trans. by J. B. Baillie (London: George Allen & Unwin, 1961), p. 769.

38. Cf. Erik Schmidt, *Hegels System der Theologie*, p. 135.

39. Hegel, *Vorlesungen*, Vol. 2, in *Sämtliche Werke* (Glockner), Vol. 16, pp. 197f.

40. Cf. Hegel, *Philosophy of Nature*, trans. by A. V. Miller. Foreword by J. N. Findlay (Oxford: Clarendon, 1970), pp. 12ff. (par. 246f.).

41. Hegel, *System der Philosophie*, Part 1: *Die Logik*, in *Sämtliche Werke* (Glockner), Vol. 8, p. 296 (par. 127).

42. Cf. for the following Hegel, *Vorlesungen*, Vol. 2, in *Sämtliche Werke* (Glockner), Vol. 16, pp. 51f. and 253f.

43. Cf. Arthur Schopenhauer, *Panerga und Paralipomena. Kleinere philosophische Schriften*, in *Sämtliche Werke*, ed. by Paul Deussen, Vol. 4 (Munich: R. Piper, 1913), esp. pp. 159-165. Schopenhauer's criticism of Hegel is one of the fiercest in the history of philosophy and never abated throughout Schopenhauer's life. It contributed much to Schopenhauer's own difficulties in his academic and philosophic career.

44. So Johannes Hirschberger, *Geschichte der Philosophie*, Vol. 2: *Neuzeit und Gegenwart* (Freiburg: Herder, 1960), p. 370.

45. George L. Kline, "Hegel and the Marxist-Leninist Critique of Religion," in *Hegel and the Philosophy of Religion. The Wofford Symposium*, ed. with an intr. by Darrel E. Christensen (The Hague: Martinus Nijhoff, 1970), p. 194, rightly emphasized that from the very beginning Karl Marx was "not the least bit interested in a faithful interpretation of Hegel (or anyone else), but passionately interested in adapting and applying Hegel's (and everybody else's) ideas—using them as weapons in the historical struggle of socio-economic classes."

46. Schopenhauer, *Panerga,* in *Sämtliche Werke,* ed. by W. Freiherr von Löhneysen, Vol. 4 (Wiesbaden: Insel-Verlag, 1960), p. 143.

47. Cf. for the following Hegel, *Lectures on the Philosophy of Religion,* trans. by E. B. Speirs and J. B. Sanderson (New York: Humanities, 1962). Vol. I, pp. 96f., where he observes especially with reference to Spinozism that a strictly pantheistic understanding of God has never been advanced. Cf. for the following paragraphs also the excellent book by Iwan Iljin, *Die Philosophie Hegels als kontemplative Gotteslehre* (Berne: A. Francke, 1946), esp. pp. 341, 350, and 368, quote p. 352, who points out very convincingly both limitations and promise of Hegel's system.

48. Cf. the excellent essay by Wolfhart Pannenberg, "Die Bedeutung des Christentums in der Philosophie Hegels," in *Hegel Studien,* Beiheft 11: *Stuttgarter Hegel-Tage 1970,* ed. by Hans-Georg Gadamer (Bonn: Bouvier, 1974), esp. pp. 188ff. Pannenberg rightly emphasizes that, though some statements in Hegel can be interpreted pantheistically, neither pantheism nor panentheism are actually appropriate terms to characterize Hegel's thought.

49. For the following cf. Hans Schwarz, "Theistic or Non-theistic Talk about God?," *Theologische Zeitschrift (Basel),* Vol. 26 (May-June, 1970), pp. 199-214, esp. pp. 199ff.

50. Ralph Cudworth, *The True Intellectual System of the Universe,* trans. by J. Harrison (London: Thomas Tegg, 1845), Vol. 1, p. xl, in his preface.

51. *Ibid.,* Vol. 2, p. 515; for the following see *ibid.,* Vol. 1, p. 217; Vol. 2, pp. 616f. n. 3; and Vol. 3, p. 441.

52. *Ibid.,* Vol. 3, p. 440.

53. *Ibid.,* Vol. 4, p. 338.

54. Cf. Emanuel Hirsch, *Geschichte der neueren evangelischen Theologie,* Vol. 1 (Gütersloh: C. Bertelsmann, 1949), p. 192, who comments that this faith was common to all Cambridge Platonists. The idea of a harmonious relationship between God and the world is in part engendered by the belief in the Great Chain of Being which forms a ladder of perfections and links together the whole universe with God. Again the Great Chain of Being was a concept affirmed by all the Cambridge Platonists. Cf. C. A. Patrides, ed., *The Cambridge Platonists* (London: Edward Arnold, 1969), p. 35, in his introductory remarks.

55. Anthony Earl of Shaftesbury, *Characteristics of Men, Manners, Opinions, Times,* etc., ed. with intr. and notes by John M. Robertson, Vol. 2 (Gloucester, MA: Peter Smith, 1963), p. 19. Ernst Cassirer, *The Platonic Renaissance in England,* trans. by J. P. Pettegrove (New York: Gordian, 1970), pp. 159f., who is very critical of the Cambridge Platonists because of their reactionary spirit, states that "it is principally Shaftesbury who saves the Cambridge School from the fate of a learned curiosity and makes it a philosophic force in the centuries to come." Cassirer shows, too, the profound influence the Cambridge Platonists had on Shaftesbury when he developed his own system of philosophy.

56. Cf. Hirsch, Vol. 1, pp. 370f.

57. For the following cf. *ibid.,* Vol. 1, p. 366.

58. Shaftesbury, Vol. 2, pp. 98 and 69.
59. *Ibid.*, p. 54.
60. *Ibid.*, p. 16.
61. *Ibid.*, Vol. 1, p. 240, where Shaftesbury also distinguishes between a "perfect Theist," believing in a designing and ordering principle or mind, necessarily good and permanent, a "perfect Atheist" rejecting such principle or mind, and a "Polytheist" believing in several such principles, and a "Daemonist," for whom these governing mind or minds are not absolutely and necessarily good. Shaftesbury himself, of course, sides with the "perfect Theist."
62. So Stanley Grean, in his instructive book, *Shaftesbury's Philosophy of Religion and Ethics. A Study in Enthusiasm* (Athens, OH: Ohio University, 1967), p. 51.
63. As a good introduction to Voltaire and of how he relates God and nature cf. Émile Bréhier, *The History of Philosophy*, Vol. 5: *The Eighteenth Century*, trans. by W. Baskin (Chicago: University of Chicago, 1967), pp. 143-154, which also lists some additional literature. Cf. also Rosemary Z. Lauer, *The Mind of Voltaire. A Study in His "Constructive Deism"* (Westminster, MD: Newman, 1961).
64. Voltaire, *The Elements of Sir Isaac Newton's Philosophy*, trans. by J. Hanna (London: Frank Cass, 1967), p. 184.
65. Voltaire, *"âme* (soul)," in *Philosophical Dictionary*, Vol. 1, p. 63.
66. Voltaire, *Traité de Métaphysique* (1734) reproduced from the Kehl text, pref., notes and variants by H. Temple Patterson (Manchester: Manchester University, 1957), p. 58. Cf. also Copleston, *A History of Philosophy*, Vol. 6, p. 23, who refers to the same passage.
67. Cf. Voltaire, *"matiere* (matter)," in *Philosophical Dictionary*, Vol. 2, pp. 374ff., where he also claims that in line with the thinking of antiquity, God the creator should be conceived of as the one who brought order into chaos rather than the one who created out of nothingness.
68. Voltaire, *The Elements of Sir Isaac Newton's Philosophy*, p. 258.
69. Voltaire, "God—Gods," in *A Philosophical Dictionary*, Vol. 5, in *The Works of Voltaire. A Contemporary Version. Edition de la Pacification* (Paris: E. R. DuMont, 1901), Vol. 9, p. 242. Originally this article was not part of Voltaire's *Dictionary*, but it was an article he contributed to the *Encyclopedia*.
70. *Critique of Pure Reason*, p. 526 (A631ff.; B659ff.).
71. For the following survey of process thought cf. Hans Schwarz, *The Search for God*, pp. 59-69.
72. Alfred North Whitehead, *Process and Reality. An Essay in Cosmology* (New York: Macmillan, 1960), p. 519. For a good introduction to the thought of Whitehead cf. Edward Pols, *Whitehead's Metaphysics. A Critical Examination of 'Process and Reality'* (Carbondale: Southern Illinois University, 1967). Another excellent introduction to Whitehead is provided by Victor Lowe, Charles Hartshorne, and A. H. Johnson, *Whitehead and the Modern World. Science, Metaphysics, and Civilization. Three Essays on the Thought of Alfred North Whitehead*, pref. by A. Cornelius Benjamin (Freeport, NY: Books for Libraries Press, 1972).

73. Whitehead, *The Interpretation of Science. Selected Essays,* ed. with intr. by A. H. Johnson (Indianapolis: Bobbs-Merrill, 1961), p. 181.

74. Whitehead, *Religion in the Making. Lowell Lectures 1926* (New York: Macmillan, 1926), p. 76.

75. *Process and Reality,* p. 521.

76. Cf. *Religion in the Making,* p. 157.

77. *Process and Reality,* p. 523.

78. *Religion in the Making,* p. 158.

79. *Process and Reality,* p. 532. This statement does not imply that Whitehead understands God as a projection of a father image. God is rather for him the ground of all reality including that of our finite being. This is substantiated when he says at another occasion: God can be conceived "as the supreme ground for limitation, it stands in His very nature to divide the Good from the Evil, and to establish Reason 'within her dominion supreme.'" So Whitehead, *Science and the Modern World. Lowell Lectures 1925* (New York: Macmillan, 1960), p. 258.

80. Charles Hartshorne, *Man's Vision of God and the Logic of Theism* (Chicago: Willett, Clark & Co., 1941), p. 12. For a good introduction to both Hartshorne and Whitehead which also shows their similarities and differences cf. *Two Process Philosophers, Hartshorne's Encounter with Whitehead,* ed. by Lewis S. Ford (Tallahassee, Florida: American Academy of Religion, 1973) *AAR Studies in Religion,* No. 5.

81. Hartshorne, *The Logic of Perfection and Other Essays in Neoclassical Metaphysics* (La Salle, IL: Open Court, 1962), p. 4.

82. Hartshorne, *Beyond Humanism. Essays in the New Philosophy of Nature* (Lincoln: University of Nebraska, Bison Book, 1968), p. 7.

83. *Ibid.,* pp. 315f.

84. Hartshorne, *A Natural Theology for Our Time* (La Salle, IL: Open Court, 1967), p. 128.

85. *Critique of Pure Reason,* pp. 396-421 (A426-460; B454-488).

86. Cf. for the following Dietrich Bonhoeffer, *Letters and Papers from Prison,* ed. by Eberhard Bethge, rev. ed. (New York: Macmillan, 1967), p. 178.

87. Cf. for the following the excellent comments by Walter Kaufmann, "The Young Hegel and Religion," in *Hegel. A Collection of Critical Essays,* ed. by Alasdair MacIntyre (Garden City, NY: Doubleday Anchor Book, 1972), pp. 95f. and G. W. F. Hegel in his revised introduction to *The Positivity of the Christian Religion* (1800), in Hegel, *On Christianity. Early Theological Writings,* trans. by T. M. Knox, intr. by Richard Kroner (New York: Harper Torchbooks, 1961), pp. 171f. (quote p. 171). Cf. also Hans Schwarz, *The Search for God,* especially chapter 3 on the "Questionableness of the Human Situation."

88. Cf. for the following David Löfgren in his excellent study, *Die Theologie der Schöpfung bei Luther* (Göttingen: Vandenhoeck & Ruprecht, 1960), p. 166, and Martin Luther, *Lectures on Galatians* (1535), chapters 1-4, in *Luther's Works,* Vol. 26, p. 95, in his exegesis of Gal. 2:6, where he says: "Now the whole creation is a face or mask

of God. But here we need the wisdom that distinguishes God from His mask. The world does not have this wisdom."

89. For this and the following quotation see Luther, *In Genesin Declamationes* (1527), in *D. Martin Luthers Werke. Kritische Gesamtausgabe* (Weimar: Hermann Böhlhaus, 1883-), Vol. 24, p. 55, 1. 7 and p. 56, 1. 1, in his comments on Gen. 1:27. This edition is hereafter referred to as WA, followed by volume number in Arabic numerals, the subvolume, if any, in Roman numerals, the parts thereof, if any, in Arabic numerals, and the page(s) and line(s) in Arabic numerals; cf. WA (volume) 24, (page) 55f., (lines) 7-7 and 1-1; and Luther, *Lectures on Genesis* (1535-45), Chapters 21-25 in *Luther's Works*, Vol. 4, p. 249, in his exegesis of Gen. 24:1-4.

90. Cf. Arthur Weiser, *Das Buch der zwölf Kleinen Propheten*, Vol. 1 (Göttingen: Vandenhoeck & Ruprecht, 1959), pp. 96f., in his exegesis of Hosea 13:4 where he states that, in analogy to the cultic revelatory formula of the Decalog, God is pronounced as the only One in contrast to the then prevalent syncretism.

91. Cf. Walther Zimmerli, *Grundriss der alttestamentlichen Theologie* (Stuttgart: W. Kohlhammer, 1972), p. 17.

92. Cf. Gerhard von Rad, *Old Testament Theology*, Vol. 1: *The Theology of Israel's Historical Traditions*, trans. by D. M. G. Stalker (Edinburgh: Oliver & Boyd, 1962), pp. 121ff., who points out the significance of this creed.

93. G. Ernest Wright, in his very instructive essay, "Reflections Concerning Old Testament Theology," in *Studia Biblica et Semitica Theodoro Christiano Vriezen Dedicata* (Wageningen: H. Veenman & Zonen, 1966), p. 382, states the matter very clearly: "The biblical event was a happening in time which was deemed of special importance because God's word was present within it, interpreting its meaning. The historical happening and its interpretation, the deed and the word of God as its commentary, these constitute the biblical event."

94. Cf. Jürgen Moltmann, *Theology of Hope. On the Ground and the Implications of a Christian Eschatology*, trans. by J. W. Leitch (New York: Harper, 1967), p. 109.

95. Moltmann, pp. 137ff., has pointed out especially well the significance of this change for the understanding of eschatology. Yet the emergence of a viewpoint comprising the whole universe is equally important for the relationship between salvation history and history.

96. This is especially noticeable in the Gospel of Luke in which God's self-disclosure in Christ is depicted as the center of history. Cf. Hans Conzelmann, in his illustrative study, *The Theology of St. Luke*, trans. by G. Buswell (New York: Harper, 1960), esp. pp. 150f.

97. Rudolf Bultmann, *Theology of the New Testament*, Vol. 1, trans. by K. Grobel (New York: Charles Scribner's, 1951), pp. 43f.

98. Bultmann, *The Presence of Eternity. History and Eschatology* (New York: Harper, 1957), p. 37.

99. Bultmann, "New Testament and Mythology," in *Kerygma and Myth. A Theological Debate*, ed. by Hans Werner Bartsch, trans. by R. H. Fuller, Vol. 1 (London: SPCK, 1953), p. 5.

100. *The Presence of Eternity*, p. 151.

101. A good example is Ernst Fuch's essay, "Christus das Ende der Geschichte," *Evangelische Theologie*, Vol. 8 (1948/49), pp. 447-461, written in reply to Oscar Cullmann's book *Christ and Time*.

102. Karl Barth, *Church Dogmatics*, Vol. 3.1: *The Doctrine of Creation*, trans. by J. W. Edwards *et al.* (Edinburgh: T. & T. Clark, 1958), p. 60.

103. *Church Dogmatics*, Vol. 4.2: *The Doctrine of Reconciliation*, ed. by G. W. Bromiley and T. F. Torrance (Edinburgh: T. & T. Clark, 1958), p. 806.

104. Oscar Cullmann, *Christ and Time. The Primitive Christian Conception of Time and History*, trans. by F. V. Filson (London: SCM, 1962), p. 83.

105. *Ibid.*, p. 137, where Cullmann also observes that the Christ event as the midpoint of time is in its part illuminated by the Old Testament preparation for this midpoint. Thus the Old Testament does not become superfluous once we have reached the New.

106. Cullmann, *Salvation in History*, trans. by S. G. Sowers (London: SCM, 1967), p. 294.

107. Cf. for the following *ibid.*, pp. 154ff., esp. p. 156.

108. *Ibid.*, p. 166.

109. *Ibid.*, p. 163.

110. *Ibid.*, pp. 151f.

111. Wolfhart Pannenberg, "Redemptive Event and History," in *Basic Questions in Theology. Collected Essays*, Vol. 1, trans. by G. H. Kehm (Philadelphia: Fortress, 1970), p. 41.

112. Wolfhart Pannenberg, thesis 3 of his "Dogmatic Theses on the Doctrine of Revelation," in *Revelation as History*, ed. by Wolfhart Pannenberg, trans. by D. Granskou (New York: Macmillan, 1968), p. 135.

113. *Ibid.*, pp. 136ff.

114. For this paragraph cf. Pannenberg, "Insight and Faith," in *Basic Questions in Theology*, Vol. 2, pp. 28-45, esp. pp. 28, 33, 36, 40, and 44; quotation taken from p. 36.

115. James Plastaras, *Creation and Covenant* (Milwaukee: Bruce, 1968), p. 5.

116. von Rad, "The Theological Problem of the Old Testament Doctrine of Creation" (1936), in *The Problem of the Hexateuch and Other Essays*, trans. by E. W. T. Dicken, intr. by Norman W. Porteous (Edinburgh: Oliver & Boyd, 1965), p. 138. Cf. also his *Old Testament Theology*, Vol. 1, p. 139.

117. Von Rad, *loc. cit.*, p. 134.

118. Especially Regin Prenter, *Creation and Redemption*, trans. by Th. I. Jensen (Philadelphia: Fortress, 1967), p. 200, emphasized that creation and redemption belong together. He says: "Creation is the beginning of redemption, and redemption is the consummation of creation."

119. von Rad, "Theological Problem," p. 140.

120. Cf. von Rad, *Wisdom in Israel*, trans. by James D. Martin (Nashville: Abingdon, 1972), pp. 162 and 225f.; cf. also Ps. 97:6, where the psalmist says: "The heavens proclaim his righteousness; and all the peoples behold his glory."

121. Cf. for the following Th. C. Vriezen, *An Outline of Old Testament Theology* (Newton, MA: Charles T. Branford, 1970), p. 332.
122. Cf. for the following the enlightening comments of Gustav Mensching, *Die Religion. Erscheinungsformen, Strukturtypen und Lebensgesetze* (Stuttgart: Curt E. Schwab, 1959), pp. 300ff., and Karl Jaspers, *Origin and Goal of History*, trans. by M. Bullock (New Haven: Yale University, 1953), p. 24.
123. For a good introduction to these and related issues cf. Henricus Renckens, *Israel's Concept of the Beginning. The Theology of Genesis 1-3*, trans. by Ch. Napier (New York: Herder and Herder, 1964), esp. pp. 36ff.
124. So Bernhard W. Anderson, *The Beginning of History. Genesis* (London: Lutterworth, 1963), p. 30.
125. Karl Barth, *Church Dogmatics*, Vol. 3.1: *The Doctrine of Creation*, p. 81, wants to dismiss and resist "to the very last any idea of the inferiority or untrustworthiness or even worthlessness of a 'non-historical' depiction and narration of history." Yet in using the terms "prehistory" and "saga" for the creation accounts, he degrades the historical character of these accounts. When he defines saga as "an intuitive and poetic picture of a pre-historical reality of history which is enacted once and for all within the confines of time and space," he clouds even more the issue of the historicity of these accounts. There is only one "pre-historical reality of history," namely God himself. Everything else is history or it is non-existent.
126. So Gerhard von Rad, *Genesis. A Commentary*, trans. by J. H. Marks (Philadelphia: Westminster, 1961), p. 47.
127. Cf. Alexander Heidel, *The Babylonian Genesis. The Story of the Creation* (Chicago: University of Chicago, Phoenix Books, 1963), p. 9, and 42-45, for a summary and the text of *Enuma elish.*
128. Cf. the fine survey by Hans-Joachim Kraus, *Geschichte der historisch-kritischen Erforschung des Alten Testaments von der Reformation bis zur Gegenwart* (Neukirchen/Moers: Erziehungsverein, 1956), pp. 274-283. Among the representatives of Pan-Babylonism must be counted Hugo Winckler, Alfred Jeremias, and Peter Jensen. Friedrich Delitzsch, though pursuing his own ideas, is closely affiliated with them. Cf. Delitzsch, *Babel and Bibel. A Lecture of the Significance of Assyrological Research for Religion. Delivered before the German Emperor*, trans. by Th. J. McCormack (Chicago: Open Court, 1902), p. 3. In a later publication, *Die grosse Täuschung* (Stuttgart: Deutsche Verlagsanstalt, 1920), Friedrich Delitzsch rejected the Old Testament completely as sub-Christian and showed an amazingly militant anti-Semitic attitude.
129. So Werner Foerster, *"ktizo,"* in *Theological Dictionary of the New Testament*, ed. by Gerhard Kittel, trans. by G. W. Bromiley, Vol. 3 (Grand Rapids, MI: William B. Eerdmans, 1965), p. 1008, with reference to these passages. While Foerster mentions that Deutero-Isaiah used *bara* twenty times, Karl Heinz Bernhardt, *"bara* (Etymology, Occurrences)," in *Theological Dictionary of the Old Testament*, ed. by G. Johannes Botterweck and Helmer Ringgren, trans. by J. T. Willis, Vol. 2 (Grand Rapids, MI: William B. Eerdmans, 1975), p. 245, is

more accurate by distinguishing Trito-Isaiah from Deutero-Isaiah and therefore mentions that Deutero-Isaiah used *bara* seventeen times. For the meaning and theological use of *bara* in the Old Testament, cf. Helmer Ringgren, "*bara* (III: Meaning, IV: Theological Usage)," in *TDOT*, Vol. 2, pp. 246ff.

130. Cf. von Rad, *Genesis*, pp. 47f., in his exegesis of Gen. 1:1-2, in which he emphasizes the effortlessness of God's creative activity. Regin Prenter's comments, *Creation and Redemption*, p. 194, are certainly exaggerated when he says that creation "is God's struggle against death in order that life may be preserved. Creation takes place as God overcomes the powers of chaos, death, and destruction."

131. Cf. Foerster, p. 1008.

132. Cf. for the following paragraph Gerhard von Rad, *Old Testament Theology*, Vol. 1, p. 143, who points out that the understanding of God creating the world through his word has analogies in the Egyptian and Babylonian creation myths.

133. Bernhard W. Anderson, *Understanding the Old Testament* (Englewood Cliffs: Prentice-Hall, 1966), p. 174, rightly says that "the Yahwist was not concerned primarily with the creation of heaven and earth, or with man's relation to the cosmic scene, but rather with man's *earthly* environment."

134. Cf. Emil Brunner, *Dogmatics*, Vol. 2: *The Christian Doctrine of Creation and Redemption*, trans. by O. Wyon (Philadelphia: Westminster, 1952), pp. 9ff., for an excellent treatment of the issue of creation out of nothingness.

135. For the following cf. von Rad, *Old Testament Theology*, Vol. 1, p. 148, in his instructive remarks on the interrelatedness of cosmological knowledge and theological penetration of this knowledge. It is doubtful whether one can distinguish as clearly "between the Christian doctrine of creation and every existent or conceivable world-view" as Karl Barth, *Church Dogmatics*, Vol. 3.1, p. 343, assumed. Theology and world view necessarily influence each other, because theological assertions are always dependent on the conceptual tools with which they are expressed.

136. Cf. for the following the very lucid explanations by Henricus Renckens, *Israel's Concept of the Beginning*, pp. 51ff.

137. Paul Tillich, *Systematic Theology*, Vol. 1 (Chicago: University of Chicago, 1951), p. 254.

138. So Gordon D. Kaufman, *Systematic Theology. A Historicist Perspective* (New York: Charles Scribner's, 1968), p. 276. Then he supplements this statement immediately saying: "the second [event in history] involved ontological development within the world itself, being the appearance of a qualitatively different level of being within the world."

139. Foerster, "*ktizo*," *TDNT*, p. 1028.

140. Rudolf Bultmann, *Theology of the New Testament*, Vol. 1, p. 228, who states this with reference to Paul. Cf. also Ethelbert Stauffer, *New Testament Theology*, trans. by J. Marsh (New York: Macmillan, 1955), p. 59.

141. Cf. Stauffer, p. 57f., who points out the significance of God creating through his word.

142. Cf. Gerhard Kittel, *"lego,"* in *TDNT,* Vol. 4, pp. 131f. Cf. also Rudolf Schnackenburg, *The Gospel according to St. John,* Vol. 1: *Introduction and Commentary on Chapters 1-4,* trans. by K. Smyth (New York: Herder and Herder, 1968), p. 232, in his exegesis of John 1:1, where he says: The phrase " 'in the beginning' . . . is chosen deliberately with reference to Gen. 1:1, since the Logos proclaimed by the hymn is the 'Word' by which God created all things."

143. Cf. Kittel, p. 131, who discusses these issues.

144. For the following cf. Siegfried Schulz, *Das Evangelium nach Johannes* (Göttingen: Vandenhoeck & Ruprecht, 1972), pp. 18f., in his exegesis of John 1:1.

145. For the following cf. Hans Walter Wolff, *Anthropology of the Old Testament,* trans. by M. Kohl (Philadelphia: Fortress, 1974), p. 95.

146. Cf. Ludwig Köhler, *Old Testament Theology,* trans. by A. S. Todd (Philadelphia: Westminster, 1957), p. 129, who rightly states that the Hebrew word *adam* "means rather men taken as a whole, and it is only late and slowly that the individual idea replaces the collective." Cf. also Fritz Maas, *"adham,"* in *TDOT,* Vol. 1, pp. 79 and 83f.

147. Cf. von Rad, *Genesis,* p. 58.

148. von Rad, *ibid.,* p. 75, in his exegesis of Gen. 2:7. Cf. also Josef Plöger, *"adhamah,"* in *TDOT,* Vol. 1, pp. 95f.

149. For the following cf. Wolff, p. 96ff.

150. To divide in this respect between the natural processes and God's immediate activity is advocated, however, in the Papal encyclical *Humani Generis* (Aug. 12, 1950), when it affirms: "The *magisterium* of the Church does not forbid 'evolutionary' doctrine, insofar as it truly inquires about the origin of the human body arising from already existing and living matter—however, Catholic faith commands us to hold that the souls are immediately created by God" (text: Henricus Denzinger, *Enchiridion Symbolorum* [Barcinone: Herder, 1965], p. 779 [3896]). It is noteworthy that the parenthetical clause, "however, Catholic faith commands us to hold that the souls are immediately created by God," is missing in the English translation. Cf. Denzinger, *The Sources of Catholic Dogma,* trans. by R. J. Deferrari (St. Louis: B. Herder, 1957), pp. 645f. (2327). John A. Hardon, *The Catholic Catechism. A Contemporary Catechism of the Teachings of the Catholic Church* (Garden City, NY: Doubleday, 1975), pp. 92ff., reaffirms this dual origin of humanity. Karl Rahner, *Hominisation. The Evolutionary Origin of Man as a Theological Problem,* trans. by W. T. O'Hara (New York: Herder and Herder, 1965), provides a very interesting and significant interpretation of the encyclical. First he affirms the intention of the encyclical that man is not merely an extension of matter (pp. 20f.). Yet he does not want to leave the impression that "God's operation becomes an activity in the world side by side with the activity of creatures, instead of being the transcendent ground of all activity of all creatures," (p. 96). Therefore he argues that "the statement that God directly creates the soul of a human being does not imply any denial of the statement that the parents procreate the human being in his unity. It makes the statement more precise by indicating that this procreation belongs to that kind of

created efficient causality in which the agent by virtue of divine causality essentially exceeds the limits set by his own essence" (p. 99). We totally agree with Rahner's insistence that especially the creation of human life, but, we might add, the peculiar creation of any form of life, is not something to be expected. Because of the manifold possibilities of the hereditary process, (pro)creation always includes novelty and surprise. The encyclical statement, however, makes it rather difficult to arrive at this notion. We also wonder whether it really supports Rahner's complementary view of the creative process, with which we identify, that it is a strictly natural phenomenon and, at the same time, a totally God-wrought activity. We suspect that the encyclical rather advocates a twofold view of the creative process, that God and nature do their respective part to bring about a new human being.

151. *Psalm 147* (1532), in *Luther's Works*, Vol. 14, p. 114, in his exegesis of Ps. 147:13 (own trans.).

152. Cf. Gerhard von Rad, *Genesis,* pp. 81f., in his exegesis of Gen. 2:21ff.

153. Especially Claus Westermann, *Genesis,* Vol. 1 (Neukirchen-Vluyn: Neukirchener Verlag, 1974), pp. 316f., emphasizes that according to Gen. 2:23 the creation attains its goal in the mutuality of man and woman.

154. For the following cf. von Rad, *Genesis,* pp. 57f., in his exegesis of Gen. 1:26ff. For a more extensive treatment of the *imago Dei* cf. our chapter 6 (Humanity's Shattered Image).

155. For this paragraph cf. the enlightening comments of Gerhard von Rad, *Old Testament Theology,* Vol. 1, pp. 144-147. Westermann, *Genesis,* Vol. 1, p. 218, in his exegesis of Gen. 1:26a rightly comments that here the proprium of humanity is understood in its being over against God. This relationship with God is nothing added to being human, but is constitutive of the human condition. Cf. also Friedrich Horst, "Face to Face. The Biblical Doctrine of the Image of God," *Interpretation,* Vol. 4 (July, 1950), pp. 259-270, who provides a good biblical survey of the concept and concludes that for the Christian "the sum total of all gifts described in his possession of the divine image, await their fulfillment in the future of the Kingdom of God" (p. 270).

156. Cf. Wolff, *Anthropology,* pp. 160ff., who also adduces evidence of Egyptian analogies to the understanding of humanity being created in the image of God.

157. *Ibid.,* p. 161.

158. von Rad, *Genesis,* p. 58, in his exegesis of Gen. 1:26-28.

159. Emil Brunner, *Man in Revolt. A Christian Anthropology,* trans. by O. Wyon (Philadelphia: Westminster, 1967), p. 346.

160. For a good introduction to the so-called women's liberation movement cf. the carefully researched and informative book by Maren Lockwood Carden, *The New Feminist Movement* (New York: Russell Sage Foundation, 1974). Very rightly she sees as one of the causes of the new feminist movement in the United States the highly mechanized household which made homemaking unsatisfactory and the high emphasis in society on personal development through remunerative work (p. 158). It is significant, however, that according to her the new

feminists usually do not want to be men-like, but want to make the work world of men more human (pp. 166f.).

161. So Martin Hengel, "Was ist der Mensch? Erwägungen zur biblischen Anthropologie heute," in *Probleme biblischer Theologie. Gerhard von Rad zum 70. Geburtstag*, ed. by Hans Walter Wolff (Munich: Chr. Kaiser, 1971), p. 118.

162. Lynn White Jr., "The Historical Roots of Our Ecological Crisis" (1967), in *Ecology and Religion in History*, ed. by David and Eileen Spring (New York: Harper Torchbook, 1974), p. 24.

163. *Ibid.*, p. 23.

164. Arnold Toynbee, "The Religious Background of the Present Environmental Crisis" (1972), in *Ecology and Religion in History*, pp. 148f.

165. For the understanding of the Spirit, especially in its life-giving and sustaining functions, cf. the thought-provoking article by Wolfhart Pannenberg, "The Doctrine of the Spirit and the Task of a Theology of Nature," *Theology*, LXXV (January, 1972), pp. 8ff.

166. So Hengel, p. 117, and von Rad, *Old Testament Theology*, Vol. 1, p. 145.

167. For the understanding of personhood cf. the excellent remarks by Helmut Thielicke, *Der Evangelische Glaube. Grundzüge der Dogmatik*, Vol. 2: *Gotteslehre und Christologie* (Tübingen: J. C. B. Mohr/ Paul Siebeck, 1973), pp. 123-139, esp. pp. 138ff.; cf. also the penetrating analysis by Wolfhart Pannenberg, in "Der Mensch—Ebenbild Gottes?" in *Glaube und Wirklichkeit. Kleinere Beiträge zum christlichen Denken* (Munich: Chr. Kaiser, 1975), pp. 66ff. Already in an earlier essay "The Question of God," in *Basic Questions in Theology*, Vol. 2, pp. 227ff., Pannenberg pointed out that the idea of a person originates in the phenomenology of religious experience. Therefore one can talk only about a human being as a person in the full sense, if one recognizes a personal God. So again later in Pannenberg, *The Idea of God and Human Freedom*, trans. by R. A. Wilson (Philadelphia: Westminster, 1973), esp. pp. 92f.

168. Hans-Joachim Schoeps, *Was ist der Mensch? Philosophische Anthropologie als Geistesgeschichte der neuesten Zeit* (Göttingen: Musterschmidt, 1960), p. 16.

169. Cf. the accurate analysis by Schoeps, pp. 23f.

5. THE HUMAN PREDICAMENT AND THE CAUSE OF EVIL

1. So Karl Menninger, in his perceptive book *Whatever Became of Sin?"* (New York: Hawthorn, 1973), pp. 13ff.

2. Cf. *ibid.*, pp. 44ff.

3. Jean-Paul Sartre, *No Exit*, in *No Exit and Three Other Plays*, trans. by L. Abel (New York: Random House, Vintage Books, 1949), p. 47.

4. Hans Schwarz, *The Search for God*, p. 96.

5. Sigmund Freud, "Moral Responsibility for the Content of Dreams" (1925), in *Collected Papers*, ed. by James Strachey, Vol. 5 (London: Hogarth, 1950), p. 157. For a good introduction to Freud's understanding of the human predicament and the Christian notion of origi-

nal sin cf. Sharon MacIsaac, *Freud and Original Sin* (New York: Paulist, 1974).

6. Cf. for the following the comprehensive work of Helmut Harsch, *Das Schuldproblem in Theologie und Tiefenpsychologie* (Heidelberg: Quelle & Meyer, 1965), p. 69.

7. Erich Fromm, *The Heart of Man. Its Genius for Good and Evil* (New York: Harper & Row, 1964), pp. 48f.

8. Sigmund Freud, "Three Contributions to the Theory of Sex," in *The Basic Writings of Sigmund Freud,* trans. and ed. with an intr. by A. A. Brill (New York: Random House, Modern Library, 1938), pp. 617f., and 621f.

9. Sigmund Freud, *New Introductory Lectures on Psychoanalysis* (1933), in *The Complete Introductory Lectures on Psychoanalysis,* trans. and ed. by James Strachey (New York: W. W. Norton, 1966), p. 569.

10. Sigmund Freud, *Civilization and Its Discontents,* trans. and ed. by James Strachey (New York: W. W. Norton, 1962), p. 59.

11. *Ibid.,* p. 67.

12. *Ibid.,* p. 68.

13. *Ibid.,* p. 68.

14. *Ibid.,* p. 89.

15. *New Introductory Lectures,* p. 531.

16. "Beyond the Pleasure Principle" (1920), in *The Standard Edition of the Complete Psychological Works of Sigmund Freud,* ed. by James Strachey, Vol. 18 (London: Hogarth, 1955), p. 53.

17. Cf. Paul Ricoeur, in his penetrating analysis of Freud in *Freud and Philosophy. An Essay on Interpretation* (New Haven: Yale University, 1970), pp. 302ff.

18. *Civilization and Its Discontents,* p. 69. Perhaps this would mean that Freud does not advocate a (destructive) death instinct in humanity, but he rather describes the intrinsically human awareness of finitude and the resulting endeavor to overcome finitude. Muzafer and Carolyn W. Sherif, "Motivation and Intergroup Aggression: A Persistent Problem in Levels of Analysis," in *Development and Evolution of Behavior,* p. 566, are only partially correct when they assert that Freud's conception of a death instinct is scientifically unwarranted. While we must agree with their rejection of a simple idea of a death instinct, Freud's conception is more complex and also more accurate than they assume.

19. So Ernest Becker, *The Denial of Death* (New York: Free Press, 1973), p. 277. In this persuasive book Ernest Becker largely follows the thinking of Freud by relying heavily on Otto Rank, a student of Freud, and shows that humanity's haunting experience of death provides the main stimulus for its activities. In a posthumously published book, *Escape from Evil* (New York: Free Press, 1975), a sequel to *The Denial of Death,* Becker now attempts to show that "man's natural and inevitable urge to deny mortality and achieve a heroic self-image are the root causes of human evil" (p. xvii). In other words, humanity's attempt to become like God, to deny its finitude, are both the stimulus to heroic deeds and the cause of all evil. Of course, the question must be asked here whether humanity's activities are just a reflection of its basic denial of what it is not, namely God, or whether

they can and should also be understood as an attempt to live up to what humans ought to be, God's administrators. The Pauline self-assessment, for instance, that humanity knows the good, but does the evil, indicates that human activities cannot just be attributed unilaterally to one stimulus. When Becker in the end hopes for "that minute measure of reason to balance destruction" *(Escape from Evil,* p. 170), he seems to implicitly admit this, since "reason" in this context ought to serve as a means of self-preservation or as something that allows humanity to live as it ought to live.

20. Carl Gustav Jung, *Psychological Types,* trans. by H. G. Baynes, rev. by R. F. C. Hull, being Vol. 6 of *The Collected Works of C. G. Jung,* ed. by William McGuire, 2nd ed. (Princeton: Princeton University, 1971), pp. 163 (268) and 377 (625). Cf. also Helmut Harsch, *Das Schuldproblem in Theologie und Tiefenpsychologie,* p. 115.

21. Cf. Jolande Jacobi, *The Psychology of C. G. Jung,* trans. by R. Manheim (New Haven: Yale University, 1962), pp. 34f.

22. Cf. for the following Harsch, p. 116.

23. *Psychology and Alchemy* (1935/36), in *The Collected Works of C. G. Jung,* Vol. 12, trans. by R. F. C. Hull (New York: Bollingen, Pantheon Books, 1953), p. 211 (329); cf. also *ibid.,* pp. 11f. (12ff.) where Jung points out the importance, especially for the Christian believer to bring into harmony the archetype with the conscious mind, lest the archetype simply becomes a religious veneer without participation in and influence on the conscious mind.

24. Cf. Jung's criticism of Freud when he says that Freud overemphasizes "the pathological aspect of life" and interprets "man too exclusively in the light of his defects." So Jung, "Freud and Jung: Contrasts" (1929), in *Collected Works,* Vol. 4, p. 335 (773).

25. "The Phenomenology of the Spirit in Fairytales" (1948), in *Collected Works,* Vol. 9.1, 2nd ed., p. 230 (420). Jung continues his comments on the fall saying perceptively: "Man's whole history consists from the very beginning in a conflict between his feeling of inferiority and his arrogance."

26. *The Relations Between the Ego and the Unconscious* (1916), in *Collected Works,* Vol. 7, p. 171 (266).

27. *Ibid.,* p. 238 (405).

28. Cf. *ibid.,* pp. 138f. (225) and 156 (246).

29. *Psychology and Religion* (1937), in *Collected Works,* Vol. 11, 2nd ed., p. 77.

30. Cf. "Psychotherapists or the Clergy?" (1932), in *Collected Works,* Vol. 11, 2nd ed., pp. 340f. (522f.).

31. "A Psychological Approach to the Dogma of the Trinity" (1948), in *Collected Works,* Vol. 11, 2nd ed., pp. 196ff. (290ff.). Since Jung wants to maintain humanity's responsibility for evil, he is careful not "to impute all evil to God." Yet on the other hand he is convinced that "through the intervention of the Holy Ghost, however, man is included in the divine process, and this means that the principle of separateness and autonomy over against God—which is personified in Lucifer as the God-opposing will—is included in it too." We wonder, however, whether the biblical promise that God will be all in all is to

be interpreted to signify the hope for an eventual unification of good and evil. The eschatological thrust of the New Testament indicates that evil is beyond integration, it can only be overcome through elimination.

32. Jung, "Gut und Böse in der analytischen Psychologie—Beitrag zur Aussprache," in *Gut und Böse in der Psychotherapie. Ein Tagungsbericht,* ed. by Wilhem Bitter (Stuttgart: Ernst Klett, 1959), p. 41. Cf. also p. 39, where Jung says with reference to the principle of evil or the devil: "I personally find it difficult to still find validity in the idea of the *privatio boni";* i.e., evil being only a lack of the good as Augustine assumed.

33. Cf. Edward S. Tauber and Bernard Landis, "On Erich Fromm," in *In the Name of Life. Essays in Honor of Erich Fromm,* ed. by Bernard Landis and Edward S. Tauber, with assistance of Erica Landis (New York: Holt, Rinehart and Winston, 1971), p. 1. In this collection we find excellent essays on various aspects of Fromm's work plus a selective bibliography of his own writings.

34. Erich Fromm, *Escape from Freedom* (New York: Holt, Rinehart and Winston, 1960 [1941]), p. 24.

35. For this statement and the following cf. Fromm, "Psychoanalysis and Zen Buddhism," in D. T. Suzuki, Erich Fromm, and Richard De Martino, *Zen Buddhism &Psychoanalysis* (New York: Harper, 1960), pp. 86f.

36. These and the following quotes are from *Escape from Freedom,* pp. 29, 32, and 36.

37. Fromm, *Man for Himself. An Inquiry Into the Psychology of Ethics* (New York: Rinehart, 1959 [1947]), p. 40.

38. *Ibid.,* p. 40.

39. *Ibid.,* p. 42. Don S. Browning, in his book, *Generative Man: Psychoanalytic Perspectives* (Philadelphia: Westminster, 1973), pp. 115f., which serves as a helpful guide to the anthropology of major contemporary psychoanalysts, rightly cautions that in the light of such statements it is hardly fair to charge Fromm with "glib utopianism and perfectionism."

40. *Escape from Freedom,* pp. 173 and 179.

41. For this quotation and the following paragraph cf. *The Heart of Man,* pp. 22 and 23.

42. For this quotation and this paragraph cf. *ibid.,* pp. 150, 138, 120f., 48, 45, and 50.

43. Fromm, *The Anatomy of Human Destructiveness* (New York: Holt, Rinehart and Winston, 1973), p. 438.

44. Cf. Ramon Xirau, "Erich Fromm: What Is Man's Struggle?" in *In the Name of Life,* p. 151, who points out that Fromm believes "that the history of human religiousness . . . is the history of a progressive dealineation, and a progressive affirmation of free will, reason, and love between men."

45. It is not quite correct to say with Ludwig Köhler, *Old Testament Theology,* p. 178, that "the priestly writer knows nothing of Paradise, Fall, or cursed ground." While it is true that the priestly writer does not narrate a story of the fall as such, his narrative of the flood de-

picts the emergence of sin on a global, not an individual scale. For the discussion with Köhler cf. the perceptive comments by Walther Zimmerli, *Grundriss der alttestamentlichen Theologie,* p. 153.

46. So von Rad, *Genesis,* p. 98.
47. Cf. for this and the following Zimmerli, *Grundriss,* p. 148.
48. Vriezen, *An Outline of Old Testament Theology,* p. 414.
49. *Vorlesungen über die Philosophie der Religion,* Vol. 1, in *Sämtliche Werke* (Glockner), Vol. 15, p. 285; and *Vorlesungen über die Geschichte,* in *Sämtliche Werke* (Glockner), Vol. 11, p. 413.
50. Friedrich Schiller, *Etwas über die erste Menschengesellschaft. Übergang des Menschen zur Freiheit und Humanität* (1789), in *Gesammelte Werke in fünf Bänden,* ed. by Reinhold Netolitzky (Gütersloh: C. Bertelsmann, 1959), p. 103.
51. *The Heart of Man,* p. 20.
52. "The Phenomenology of the Spirit in Fairytales," in *The Collected Works of C. G. Jung,* Vol. 9.1, 2nd ed., p. 230 (420).
53. Cf. *The Phenomenon of Man,* pp. 301f., where he says: "The involuting universe . . . proceeds step by step by dint of billion-fold trial and error. It is this process of groping, combined with the two-fold mechanism of reproduction and heredity . . . , which gives rise to the . . . tree of life." Cf. also p. 310, where he picks up the same terminology in talking about the "evil of disorder and failure" as a necessity in the evolutionary process.
54. For the following cf. the very instructive comments by Zimmerli, *Grundriss,* pp. 148f.
55. Cf. von Rad, *Genesis,* pp. 87f., in his exegesis of Gen. 3:6, who presents this interpretation.
56. Cf. Johannes Fichtner, *"ophis* (Gen. 3)," in *TDNT,* Vol. 5, p. 573, who emphasizes the creational aspect of the serpent.
57. This assumption is advanced by Erich Fromm, *You Shall Be As Gods. A Radical Interpretation of the Old Testament and Its Tradition* (New York: Holt, Rinehart and Winston, 1966), p. 24.
58. Similarly, von Rad, *Genesis,* p. 86, in his exegesis of Gen. 3:4f.
59. Cf. *ibid.,* pp. 86f.; and Renckens, *Israel's Concept of the Beginning,* pp. 274f.
60. Cf. Zimmerli, *Grundriss,* p. 152.
61. So rightly Vriezen, *An Outline of Old Testament Theology,* p. 415.
62. Cf. for the interpretation of Gen. 3:15 Fichtner, *"ophis* (Gen. 3)," *TDNT,* Vol. 5, pp. 574f. At this point no indication is made yet that the animosity between snake and humanity will be overcome. But such animosity will no longer exist in the messianic time. Then the original harmony will be re-established; cf. Isa. 11:1-8.
63. Cf. for the following Vriezen, *An Outline of Old Testament Theology,* pp. 304f., who also comments on the difficulty of a monotheistic religion to allow for evil without directly attributing it to God.
64. Cf. Werner Foerster, *"daimon,"* in *TDNT,* Vol. 2, p. 11, who says with reference to our passage: "OT monotheism is thus maintained, since no power to which man might turn in any matter is outside the one God of Israel."
65. Cf. for the following the good treatment of the concept of Satan by

Rivkah Schärf Kluger, *Satan in the Old Testament,* trans. by H. Nagel (Evanston: Northwestern University, 1967), esp. pp. 34ff.

66. Cf. von Rad, "*diabolos* (The OT View of Satan)," in *TDNT*, Vol. 2, p. 73.

67. Cf. for further details Kluger, pp. 72ff.

68. Cf. for the following von Rad, "*diabolos*," pp. 73f. Cf. also the exhaustive treatment of the understanding of Satan by Herbert Haag, *Teufelsglaube,* with contributions by Katharine Elliger, Bernhard Lang, and Meinrad Limbeck (Tübingen: Katzmann, 1974), here pp. 204f., who emphasizes the pernicious aspect of Satan in the Book of Job.

69. Cf. for the following Kluger, p. 132.

70. Cf. Haag, p. 200; cf. also Lars Gösta Rignell, *Die Nachtgesichte des Sacharja. Eine exegetische Studie* (Lund: Håkan Ohlsson, 1950), p. 101. Kluger, p. 142, comments here in Jungian fashion: "In Zech. 3:1ff. the differentiation process has advanced further. *The separation of Satan, the dark side of God, is followed by the corresponding release of God's light side.*"

71. For the whole paragraph cf. von Rad, "*diabolos*," pp. 74f.; cf. also Kluger, p. 161. Haag, pp. 213f. rightly cautions us here that in 1 Chron. 21:1 Satan does not replace Yahweh, but the wrath of Yahweh that was kindled against Israel.

72. Kluger, p. 79. It is also doubtful whether Haag, p. 217, is correct when he perceives the emergence of Satan in the Old Testament as a result of the ever stronger tendency to prevent the transcendence and holiness of God from being tarnished by impurities. While we agree that there is undoubtedly a discernible progressive understanding of God in the Old Testament, it is much more the nature of (political) reality that seems to become more and more incongruous with the salvific expectations, once the exile was past history and nothing decisive occurred to re-establish the Jewish empire. If one wanted to remain a faithful believer in the realization of God's promissory history, one had to look for impeding forces outside God (and humanity). For the problems of a gradual clarification of the understanding of God cf. Hans Schwarz, *The Search for God,* chap. 6: "From a Tribal God to the Savior of Mankind," pp. 158-178.

73. So Zimmerli, *Grundriss,* p. 150.

74. So Georg Fohrer, *History of Israelite Religion,* trans. by D. E. Green (Nashville: Abingdon, 1972), p. 375.

75. For the following cf. Kluger, pp. 87ff., and 133. Cf. also Georg Fohrer, *Das Buch Hiob,* in *Kommentar zum Alten Testament,* Vol. 16 (Gütersloh: Gerd Mohn, 1963), p. 44, for a brief description of the text. Fohrer, however, makes no mention of Satan in this context. For a translation of the Babylonian Job cf. "I will praise the Lord of Wisdom" ("Poem of the Righteous Sufferer") trans. by Robert H. Pfeiffer, in *Ancient Near Eastern Texts Relating to the Old Testament,* ed. by James B. Pritchard (Princeton: Princeton University, 1950), pp. 434-437.

76. Kluger, p. 135.

77. For this paragraph cf. the excellent book by Geo Widengren, *Die*

Religionen Irans (Stuttgart: W. Kohlhammer, 1965), here esp. pp. 74-78, where he provides us with a concise description of Zarathustra's teachings. For a brief summary of Zoroastrianism cf. also Hans Schwarz, *The Search for God,* pp. 124-127.

78. In *The Songs of Zarathushtra. The Gatas,* trans. from the Avesta by D. F. A. Bode and P. Nanavutty, Foreword by Radhakrishnan (London: George Allen & Unwin, 1952), p. 49, Yasna 30:3f., reads: "(3) Now in the beginning, these two Mainyu, the twins, revealed themselves in thought, word, and deed as the Better and the Bad; and, from these two, the wise chose aright, but not so the unwise. (4) And thus, when these two Mainyu first came together, they generated life and the absence of life, and so shall human existence continue till the end of time: the worst life for the Followers of the Lie, but the supreme beatific vision for the Followers of Truth."

79. So Geo Widengren in his instructive essay, "The Principle of Evil in the Eastern Religions," in *Evil.* Essays by Carl Kerenyi, et al. Edited by the Curatorium of the C. G. Jung Institute, Zürich. Translated by R. Manheim and H. Nagel (Evanston: Northwestern University, 1967), pp. 35f.

80. Kluger's remark, *Satan in the Old Testament,* p. 157, that "for the Persian religion, dualism is the *point of departure"* may be slightly exaggerated, since the point of departure is the one God Ahura Mazda.

81. So Foerster, *"diabolos* (The Later Jewish View of Satan)," in *TDNT,* Vol. 2, p. 76.

82. So D. S. Russell, *The Method & Message of Jewish Apocalyptic* (Philadelphia: Westminster, 1964), p. 252, in his instructive treatment of the understanding of Satan in the intertestamental period.

83. Of course, we must keep in mind the relatively late date of this book, perhaps even being later than some of the New Testament books. Cf. *The Apocalypse of Abraham,* ed. with a trans. by G. H. Box, assist. by J. I. Landsman (London: SPCK, 1919), pp. xvf.

84. It is interesting that in 2 Enoch 31:6 and in the Apocalypse of Moses the fall is attributed to Satan. Especially in the latter book the significant observation is made that, after being expelled from heaven because of disobeying God's orders, Satan speaks through the mouth of the serpent and entices Eve and causes her to sin (Apoc. Mos. 17:4). This identification of Satan with the serpent is then picked up in the New Testament Book of Revelation (cf. Rev. 12:9).

85. Russell, p. 253, n. 4, reiterates the comment made by G. H. Box in his translation of 4 Ezra in *The Apocrypha and Pseudepigrapha of the Old Testament in English,* ed. by R. H. Charles, Vol. 2 (Oxford: Clarendon, 1963), p. 563, when he says: The statement that the Law which is implanted in human nature is unable to gain mastery over the evil inclination "contradicts the teaching of rabbinic theology."

86. Cf. for the following Foerster, *"satanas,"* in *TDNT,* Vol. 7, p. 156.

87. Cf. H. H. Rowley, *The Relevance of Apocalyptic. A Study of Jewish and Christian Apocalypse from Daniel to the Revelation* (New York: Association, 1963), p. 172.

88. William Foxwell Albright, *From the Stone Age to Christianity.*

Monotheism and the Historical Process (Baltimore: Johns Hopkins, 1957), p. 362.

89. So Foerster, in his concise but comprehensive article *"diabolos* (The NT View of Satan," in *TDNT,* Vol. 2, p. 79.

90. Cf. for the following the instructive analysis in Joachim Jeremias, *New Testament Theology. The Proclamation of Jesus,* trans. by J. Bowden (New York: Charles Scribner's, 1971), pp. 93-96. When Haag, *Teufelsglaube,* pp. 317f., sees in Luke 10:18 the only authentic word of Jesus in which he refers to Satan, he is too critical of the biblical tradition. By interpreting this word of Jesus to announce the fall of Satan as the accuser, Haag perceives on the one hand that Jesus had gained the victory over the anti-Godly powers, while he rejects on the other hand the idea that Satan still has any threatening function. Yet such an understanding of salvation as totally realized is unwarranted. While Jesus undoubtedly announced the rule of God and actualized it, there is still an outstanding eschatological component to this rule. The victory is only gained in a proleptic way. As the apocalyptic passages in the synoptics indicate, Satan is not a reality to be neglected. Jesus has broken the power of the evil one, but he has not completely destroyed it or made it irrelevant as Haag seems to indicate. (Cf. Foerster, *"satanas* [Satan in the New Testament], in *TDNT,* Vol. 7, p. 160). In distinguishing Jesus' understanding of Satan and of the demons from that of his contemporaries and even from that of the evangelists, Haag seems to advocate a theory of accommodation.

91. Cf. the excellent book of Trevor Ling, *The Significance of Satan. New Testament Demonology and Its Contemporary Relevance* (London: SPCK, 1961), p. 18. This implies that an exorcism per se is not necessarily a beneficial act. It depends in whose authority the exorcism has been performed.

92. So Foerster, *"satanas,"* p. 160.

93. Cf. Rudolf Bultmann, *The Gospel of John. A Commentary,* trans. by G. R. Beasley-Murray *et al.* (Philadelphia: Westminster, 1971), p. 331, in his exegesis of John 9:3; cf. also Siegfried Schulz, *Das Evangelium nach Johannes,* p. 141, to this passage.

94. Cf. Foerster, pp. 156f., who emphasizes the expulsion of the accuser.

95. Cf. Joachim Jeremias, *The Lord's Prayer,* trans. by J. Reumann (Philadelphia: Fortress, Facet Books, 1969), p. 29; and Ernst Lohmeyer, *Das Vater-unser* (Göttingen: Vandenhoeck & Ruprecht, 1962), pp. 144f.

96. Cf. the excellent description in Bultmann, *Theology of the New Testament,* Vol. 2, pp. 15-32.

97. Cf. Foerster, p. 163, for the exegesis of this passage. Foerster rightly comments that since this verse asserts "that the devil is determined by the fact that he is the devil . . . it forbids us to ask what the devil was before he became the devil." This means it rejects any speculations concerning the origin of the devil which were so popular in later Judaism.

98. Bultmann, *Theology of the New Testament,* Vol. 2, p. 17.

99. *Ibid.,* Vol. 2, p. 21. Raymond E. Brown, *The Gospel According to John (I-XII)* Garden City, NY: Doubleday, 1966), p. lvi, offers an

interesting suggestion. While admitting that Bultmann's thesis that John is dependent on an early oriental Gnosticism cannot be disproved, he suggests that in many ways such a hypothesis is unnecessary. Brown in turn proposes that "OT speculation about personified Wisdom and the vocabulary and thought patterns of sectarian Judaism, like the Qumran community, go a long way toward filling in the background of Johannine theological vocabulary and expression." Such Jewish influence would then indicate that the Johannine understanding of the function and position of Satan is largely a consequent development of Old Testament and later Jewish thought.

100. Friedrich Schleiermacher, *The Christian Faith,* trans. by H. R. Mackintosh and J. S. Stewart (Edinburgh: T. & T. Clark, 1960), p. 161 (par. 44). When Schleiermacher, however, still permits the use of the concept of a devil in religious teaching, occasionally in liturgy, in poetry, and, of course, in song (pp. 169f.), we wonder whether this would not confuse the issue more than it clarifies it, provided we accept Schleiermacher's premise of the irrelevancy of the devil.

101. Cf. Bultmann, "New Testament and Mythology," in *Kerygma and Myth. A Theological Debate,* esp. p. 5.

102. So rightly Stauffer, *New Testament Theology,* p. 67.

103. Cf. Wolfgang Trillhaas, *Dogmatik* (Berlin: Alfred Töpelmann, 1962), p. 148, who rightly says that "neither the doctrine of angels nor of the devil has salvational significance." Yet we wonder whether one can neglect Satan or the devil completely and just talk about the demonic as does Paul Tillich. Then the anti-Godly function and quality of the powers of darkness would be understated in favor of an exclusively monotheistic understanding of God.

104. Cf. Otto Böcher, *Das Neue Testament und die dämonischen Mächte* (Stuttgart: Katholisches Bibelwerk, 1972), p. 74, who points out the influence that pagan piety had on the development of the fear of demons and witches in medieval Christianity.

105. Immanuel Kant, *Religion within the Limits of Reason Alone,* trans., intr. and notes by Theodore M. Greene and Hoyt H. Hudson, with a new essay "The Ethical Significance of Kant's Religion," by John R. Silber, 2nd ed. (Lasalle, IL: Open Court, 1960), p. 27.

106. Cf. for the following *ibid.,* p. 30.

107. Emil Brunner, *Man in Revolt,* pp. 126f., rightly observed: "Kant's idea of radical evil remains the most serious attempt ever made by any philosopher—who does not bring his system into conformity with the Christian revelation—about evil."

108. Reinhold Niebuhr, *The Nature and Destiny of Man. A Christian Interpretation. Gifford Lectures,* Vol. 1: *Human Nature* (New York: Charles Scribner's, 1949), p. 180.

109. *Heidelberg Disputation* (1518), in *Luther's Works,* Vol. 31, p. 39 (thesis 4).

110. Kaufman, *Systematic Theology,* p. 310.

111. *Heidelberg Disputation,* p. 45 (expl. of thesis 6).

112. *The Bondage of Will* (1525), in *Luther's Works,* Vol. 33, p. 180.

113. *Ibid.,* pp. 65f.

114. Cf. Paul Althaus, in his excellent treatment of Luther's theology, *The Theology of Martin Luther*, trans. by R. C. Schultz (Philadelphia: Fortress, 1966), p. 168, who concludes: "Thus Luther can regard Satan both as the instrument and as the enemy of God."

115. *Church Dogmatics*, Vol. 3.3: *The Doctrine of Creation*, p. 351. It is unfortunate that the German *"das Nichtige"* (the nothing) is simply rendered in English with "nothingness."

116. *Ibid.*, p. 360; and Otto Weber, *Karl Barth's Church Dogmatics. An Introductory Report on Volumes I:1 to III:4*, trans. by A. C. Cochrane (Philadelphia: Westminster, 1953), p. 194, who translates *"das Nichtige"* more appropriately with "the Nihil."

117. This aspect is especially emphasized by Scandinavian Lutheranism. Cf. as a good example the excellent remarks by Regin Prenter, *Schöpung und Erlösung* (Göttingen: Vandenhoeck & Ruprecht, 1960), pp. 228ff. Unfortunately the later English translation omitted the whole excursus "On Angels and Demons." Cf. also Gustaf Aulén, *Christus Victor. An Historical Study of the Three Main Types of the Idea of Atonement*, trans. by A. G. Hebert (New York: Macmillan, 1956), esp. pp. 153-159.

118. This has been elaborated especially well by Karl Heim, *Jesus the Lord*, trans. by D. H. van Daalen (Edinburgh: Oliver and Boyd, 1959), p. 102.

119. *Church Dogmatics*, Vol. 3:3, p. 354.

6. HUMAN SINFULNESS

1. Cf. Wolfgang Trillhaas, *Dogmatik*, p. 199, who affirms that seen from the inside, original sin and actual sin come indistinguishably together.

2. Cf. for the Old Testament usage Gottfried Quell, *"hamartano* (Sin in the OT)" in *TDNT*, Vol. 1, pp. 268f.

3. For the exegesis of this verse cf. *ibid.*, p. 277; and Hans-Joachim Kraus, *Psalmen*, Vol. 1 (Neukirchen Kreis Moers: Neukirchener Verlag, 1960), pp. 386f.

4. Cf. for the following Gustav Stählin and Walter Grundmann, *"hamartano* (The Concept of Sin in Judaism)," in *TDNT*, Vol. 1, p. 290.

5. Cf. Mark 1:24, and Joachim Jeremias, *New Testament Theology*, p. 94, in his interpretation of this verse.

6. Ernst Fuchs, *Studies of the Historical Jesus*, trans. by A. Scobie (Naperville, IL: Alec R. Allenson, 1964), p. 21, rightly states that Jesus "dares to affirm the will of God as though he himself stood in God's place." Then he continues saying: But the people "could not tolerate his claim to assert through his own conduct that God's will was a gracious will." Cf. also Norman Perrin, *Rediscovering the Teaching of Jesus* (New York: Harper & Row, 1967), pp. 102-108, who elucidated the eschatological significance of Jesus' table fellowship with sinners and the connection of this fellowship with the Lord's Supper.

7. Cf. Walter Grundmann, *"hamartano* (Sin in the NT)," in *TDNT*, Vol. 1, p. 304.

8. For the understanding of *krisis* cf. also the excellent analysis in Bultmann, *Theology of the New Testament,* Vol. 2, pp. 37ff.

9. Cf. Grundmann, "*hamartano,*" *TDNT,* p. 308.

10. Cf. also Gerhard von Rad, *Genesis,* p. 119, in his exegesis of Gen. 8:21f.

11. Cf. Charles A. and Emilie G. Briggs, *A Critical and Exegetical Commentary on The Book of Psalms,* Vol. 2 *(The International Critical Commentary)* (New York: Charles Scribner's, 1907), pp. 6f., in his exegesis of Ps. 51:5. Cf. also Kraus, *Psalmen,* Vol. 1, p. 387.

12. Cf. for the following Karl Heim, *The World: Its Creation and Consummation. The End of the Present Age and the Future of the World in the Light of the Resurrection,* trans. by R. Smith (Philadelphia: Muhlenberg, 1962), pp. 123f., who very perceptively points out that Paul does not make Adam responsible for the origin of sin and of death, but sin and death penetrated into the world of humanity through the first man as through a door. Sin and death bear here almost anthropomorphic features. Cf. also 1 Cor. 15:54ff.

13. Cf. Anders Nygren, *Commentary on Romans,* trans. by C. C. Rasmussen, (Philadelphia: Fortress, 1949), pp. 210f., in his exegesis of Rom. 5:12.

14. Augustine, *Treatise on Rebuke and Grace,* in *A Select Library of the Nicene and Post-Nicene Fathers of the Christian Church,* ed. by Philip Schaff, Vol. 5 (Grand Rapids, MI: Wm. B. Eerdmans, 1956), p. 485 (33).

15. Cf. W. Rohnert, *Die Dogmatik der evangelisch-lutherischen Kirche* (Braunschweig: Hellmuth Wollermann, 1902), p. 198, who recites a whole catalog of qualities that humanity enjoyed prior to the fall. Francis Pieper, *Christian Dogmatics,* Vol. 1 (St. Louis, MO: Concordia, 1950), pp. 551ff., even ponders whether original sin caused immediate death or only started the process of dying which results in complete separation of body and soul. For the discussion of the "original state" in the history of the church cf. *Chr. Ernst Luthardt's Kompendium der Dogmatik,* ed. by Robert Jelke, 14th ed. (Leipzig: Dörffling & Franke, 1937), pp. 200-203.

16. So Pelagius according to Mari Mercator, "Commonitorium de Coelestio," in *Patrologiae Cursus Completus,* ed. by J.-P. Migne, *Series Latina Prior,* Vol. 48 (Paris: J.-P. Migne, 1862), col. 85 (2.2ff.). This series will be abbreviated as Migne, PSL, plus volume and column numbers.

17. *The Biology of Ultimate Concern* (New York: New American Library, 1967), pp. 68f.

18. *Ibid.,* p. 72.

19. Cf. Bultmann, *Theology of the New Testament,* Vol. 1, p. 253, in his exegesis of Rom. 5:13f.

20. So Paul Althaus, *The Ethics of Martin Luther,* trans. with a foreword by R. C. Schultz (Philadelphia: Fortress, 1972), p. 30.

21. Reinhold Niebuhr, *The Nature and Destiny of Man,* vol. 1, p. 186, rightly states that pride is one of the basic sins if not the basic sin. It is even more basic than sensuality, since the latter is, in some way, derived from the former.

22. Wolfhart Pannenberg, *What Is Man?*, p. 36, rightly speaks here of a "perversion of the relation between control and trust that expresses the perverseness of man himself."

23. Cf. for the following Grundmann, *"hamartano," TDNT*, p. 311. For the historical and theological problems of Romans 7 cf. Otto Michel, *Der Brief an die Römer*, 11th ed. (Göttingen: Vandenhoeck & Ruprecht, 1957), pp. 156ff.; cf. also for the different options Paul Althaus, *Paulus und Luther über den Menschen. Ein Vergleich*, 3rd. ed. (Gütersloh: Carl Bertelsmann, 1958), esp. p. 33.

24. Augustine, *City of God*, p. 707 (19.25). The more popular wording: "The virtues of the pagans are splendid vices," however, is apocryphal and wrongly attributed to Augustine. Cf. Friedrich Loofs, *Leitfaden zur Dogmengeschichte*, ed. by Kurt Aland, 6th ed. (Tübingen: Max Niemeyer, 1959), p. 333, n. 4.

25. When Handley C. G. Moule, *The Epistle to the Romans* (London: Pickering & Inglis, n.d.), p. 202, says with reference to Romans 7 that "there is a conflict in the Christian man, regenerate, yet taken, in a practical sense, apart from his Regenerator," Moule seems to be too pessimistic. The victory is gained, yet the full disclosure of the victory is not yet attained. Cf. Bultmann, *Theology of the New Testament*, Vol. 1, pp. 330ff., in his excellent treatment of the relationship between the Pauline imperative and indicative. Bultmann here recognizes that "the *imperative*, 'walk according to the Spirit,' not only does not contradict the *indicative* of justification (the believer is rightwised) but results from it." In other words, salvation though still outstanding is not just in the future.

26. Pelagius, *Epistola ad Demetriadem*, in Migne, PSL, Vol. 30, col. 17f. (2).

27. Pelagius, *Expositio in Epist. ad Rom.*, in Migne, PSL, Vol. 30, col. 723, in his exposition of Rom. 12.

28. Pelagius, *Epistola ad Demetriadem*, in Migne, PSL, Vol. 30, col. 18f. (3).

29. Pelagius according to Augustine, *On the Grace of Christ*, in *A Select Library of the Nicene and Post-Nicene Fathers of the Christian Church*, ed. by Philip Schaff, Vol. 5, p. 219 (5.4).

30. Coelestius according to Augustine, *On Man's Perfection in Righteousness*, in *A Select Library*, Vol. 5, pp. 160 and 163 (2.1 and 6.15).

31. Pelagius according to Augustine, *On Nature and Grace*, in *A Select Library*, Vol. 5, p. 123 (7.8).

32. So Reinhold Seeberg, *Text-Book of the History of Doctrines*, trans. by Ch. E. Hay, Vol. 1: *History of Doctrines in the Ancient Church* (Grand Rapids, MI: Baker, 1952), p. 334, in his extensive treatment of Pelagianism.

33. Julian in Augustine, *Operis Imperfecti Contra Julianum*, in Migne, PSL, Vol. 45, col. 1254 (3.19).

34. Coelestius according to Augustine, *On Original Sin*, in *A Select Library*, Vol. 5, p. 239 (6.6), where Coelestius is quoted saying: "Sin is not born with a man—it is subsequently committed by the man: for it is shown to be a fault, not of nature, but of the will."

35. Pelagius, *Expositio in Epist. ad Rom.*, in Migne, PSL, Vol. 30, col. 694, in his exposition of Rom. 5.

36. Cf. for the following the excellent description of Greco-Roman antiquity in Jaroslav Pelikan, *The Christian Tradition. A History of the Development of Doctrine*. Vol. 1: *The Emergence of the Catholic Tradition (100-600)* (Chicago: University of Chicago, 1971), pp. 280f. Gerald Bonner, *Augustine and Modern Research on Pelagianism. The Saint Augustine Lecture 1970* (Wetteren, Belgium: Cultura, 1972), p. 34, mentions another possible root of Pelagianism when he suggests: "The contribution of Pelagius to Pelagianism was to provide a theological basis to defend Christian asceticism against any charge of Manichaeism and to justify the assurance that a virtuous life is possible for the Christian if he will only try." Pelagius would then be understood as fighting off a negative attitude towards the created while at the same time insisting on the potential goodness of the created. Of course, such dualistic attitude towards the world is already prevalent in Plato and in most philosophical and religious systems of the Mediterranean.

37. Cf. for this and the following Plato, *Laws*, in *The Collected Dialogues of Plato Including the Letters*, pp. 1325 and 1300 (741 and 709 b-c).

38. Ovid, *Metamorphoses*, with an Engl. trans. by Frank Justus Miller, Vol. 2 (Cambridge, MA: Harvard University, 1964), p. 33 (9.429f.).

39. Marcus Tullius Cicero, *De Divinatione*, Book 1.2, ed. by Arthur Stanley Pease (Urbana: University of Illinois, 1920), p. 322 (1.56.127).

40. According to Gaius Suetonius Tranquillus, *The Twelve Caesars*, trans. by R. Graves (Baltimore, MD: Penguin Books, 1957), p. 144 (Tiberius, 69).

41. So R. A. Norris, *Manhood and Christ. A Study in the Christology of Theodore of Mopsuestia* (Oxford: Clarendon, 1963), p. 179. Cf. also H. B. Swete, *Theodori Episcopi Mopsuesteni*, in *Epistolas B. Pauli Commentarii. The Latin Version with Greek Fragments*, with intr., notes, and indices, Vol. 2: *1 Thessalonians-Philemon* (Cambridge: University Press, 1882), pp. 332-337, where Theodore emphasizes emphatically that Adam was created in a state of mortality, and that therefore mortality was not our punishment for Adam's sin.

42. Augustine, *On Grace and Free Will, in A Select Library*, Vol. 5, p. 444 (2.2).

43. Augustine, *City of God*, p. 457 (14.11).

44. Augustine, *On Rebuke and Grace*, in *A Select Library*, Vol. 5, p. 485 (33.12).

45. Augustine, *On Forgiveness of Sins, and Baptism*, in *ibid.*, Vol. 5, p. 74 (3.14).

46. Augustine, *Against Julian*, trans. by M. A. Schumacher, in *The Fathers of the Church. A New Translation*, ed. by Roy J. Deferrari, Vol. 35 (New York: Fathers of the Church, 1957), p. 386 (6.24.75).

47. Augustine, *On Marriage and Concupiscence*, in *A Select Library*, Vol. 5, pp. 276 and 278 (1.32.37).

48. So rightly Friedrich Loofs, *Leitfaden zur Dogmengeschichte*, p. 307, n. 9.

49. Augustine, *On the Grace of Christ,* in *A Select Library,* Vol. 5, p. 224 (18.17).
50. Augustine, *Against Julian* in *The Fathers of the Church,* Vol. 35, p. 356 (6.15.47).
51. Augustine, *Against Two Letters of the Pelagians,* in *A Select Library,* Vol. 5, p. 379 (1.7.13); and Augustine, *Operis Imperfecti contra Julianum,* in Migne, PSL, Vol. 45, col. 1294 (3.109), where he says: *"Ecce quare dixi, Neminem liberum ad agendum bonum sine adiutorio Dei."*
52. Cf. Reinhold Seeberg, *Lehrbuch der Dogmengeschichte,* Vol. 2: *Die Dogmenbildung in der Alten Kirche,* 3rd ed. (Darmstadt: Wissenschaftliche Buchgesellschaft, 1965), p. 518.
53. So *ibid.,* p. 542. Seeberg also observes that Augustine always insisted that God chose certain ones to salvation while he left others to their just destiny. Yet Augustine never wanted to admit that God also determines them to sin.
54. Cf. Augustine, *Letters,* Vol. 5 (204-270), trans. by W. Parsons, in *The Fathers of the Church,* Vol. 32, p. 84 (217).
55. Augustine, *On the Gift of Perseverance,* in *A Select Library,* Vol. 5, p. 531 (17).
56. Desiderius Erasmus, *On the Freedom of the Will,* in *Luther and Erasmus: Free Will and Salvation,* trans. and ed. by E. Gordon Rupp and Philip S. Watson, Vol. 17 of *The Library of Christian Classics* (Philadelphia: Westminster, 1969), p. 90. Cf. also the interesting study of Harry J. McSorley, *Luther: Right or Wrong? An Ecumenical-Theological Study of Luther's Major Work, The Bondage of Will* (Minneapolis: Augsburg, 1969), who shows that Erasmus did not do justice to traditional Catholic doctrine, while Luther, apart from a necessitarian argument, shows in his biblical exegesis a truly Catholic stance (p. 369).
57. *On the Freedom of the Will,* p. 87.
58. *Ibid.,* p. 90.
59. Cf. Luther, *On the Bondage of Will,* in *Luther and Erasmus: Free Will and Salvation,* pp. 191f.
60. *The Judgment of Martin Luther on Monastic Vows* (1525), in *Luther's Works,* Vol. 44, p. 277.
61. *Against Latomus* (1521), in *Luther's Works,* Vol. 32, p. 160.
62. "The Gospel for New Year's Day" (1522), in *Luther's Works,* Vol. 52, p. 151. In his exposition of Luke 2:21, Luther says: "Our person, nature, and entire existence are corrupted through Adam's fall. Therefore not a single work can be good in us, until our nature and personal being are changed and renewed."
63. Luther, *Assertio Omnium Articulorum M. Lutheri per Bullam Leonis X* (1520), in WA 7, 105, 30ff.
64. *Lectures on Genesis,* chapters 21-25 (1535-45), in *Luther's Works,* Vol. 4, p. 355. In his exegesis of Gen. 25:22a, Luther says: "Procreation is a work of God, and of God alone. And it is surely true that if it were not tainted with such loathsome lust and depravity, we could not help being amazed at the value and the miraculous quality of such a great work."
65. Luther, *Enarratio Psalmi LI* (1532), WA 40 II, 381, 6ff., in his

exegesis of Psalm 51:5. The English (American) edition of *Luther's Works*, Vol. 12, pp. 348f., relies on the published text instead of the manuscript and therefore does not contain this reference to "being conceived in sin."

66. *An Open Letter on the Harsh Book against the Peasants* (1525), in *Luther's Works*, Vol. 46, p. 76.
67. *On the Bondage of Will*, p. 232.
68. *Ibid.*, p. 201.
69. *Lectures on Genesis*, chapters 26-30 (1535-45), in *Luther's Works*, Vol. 5, p. 47, in his exegesis of Gen. 26:9. Luther also mentions there that he learnt this from his teacher Staupitz.
70. *Predigten des Jahres 1532*, in WA 36, 61, 8f. Here Luther says that speculators will break their neck if they want to know about how God reigns the world.
71. *Assertio Omnium Articulorum M. Lutheri per Bullam Leonis X* (1520), in WA 7, 143f.
72. *Decem Praecepta Wittenbergensi Praedicata Populo* (1518), in WA 1, 427, 15f., where he quotes Augustine's insight that humanity is a "corrupt entity."
73. *Large Catechism* (1529), in *The Book of Concord. The Confessions of the Evangelical Lutheran Church*, trans. and ed. by Theodore G. Tappert (Philadelphia: Fortress, 1959), p. 419.
74. *Lectures on Genesis*, chapters 21-25 (1535-45), in *Luther's Works*, Vol. 4, p. 180, in his exegesis of Gen. 22:19; and cf. *Predigten über das 2. Buch Mose. 1524-1527*, in WA 16, 42, 5f., where Luther admits that God always does good in those who are his.
75. *In Epistolam S. Pauli ad Galatas Commentarius* (1531), in WA 40 I, 293, 8ff., in his exegesis of Gal. 2:20. Cf. also the English translation of the commentary, *Lectures on Galatians* (1535), chapters 1-4, in *Luther's Works*, Vol. 26, p. 174.
76. Cf. for the following Irenaeus, *Against Heresies*, in *The Ante-Nicene Fathers. Translations of the Writings of the Fathers down to A.D. 325*, ed. by Alexander Roberts and James Donaldson, Vol. 1: *The Apostolic Fathers—Justin Martyr—Irenaeus* (Grand Rapids, MI: Wm. B. Eerdmans, n.d.), p. 544 (5.16.2); and cf. Gerhard von Rad, *"ikon* (The Divine Likeness in the OT)," in *TDNT*, Vol. 2, pp. 390f., who also remarks very interestingly: "In Gen. 5:1ff. reference is made to the physical progeny of the first man, and it is said of Seth, Adam's son, that he was begotten in the image and likeness of Adam. This statement is most important. It ensures the theological actuality for all generations of the witness to the divine likeness." Cf. further Paul Althaus, *Die christliche Wahrheit. Lehrbuch der Dogmatik* (Gütersloh: Gerd Mohn, 1959), pp. 336ff., for his very perceptive treatment of the issue of humanity being created in the image of God.
77. *City of God*, pp. 365 (11.22) and 387 (12.7).
78. *Summa Theologiae*, Latin text and Engl. trans., intr. notes, appendices and glossaries, Blackfriar Edition (New York: McGraw-Hill, n.d.), Vol. 26, p. 38 (la 2ae.82.3).
79. *Ibid.*, Vol. 26, p. 35 (la 2ae.82.2).
80. Cf. *The Summa Theologica*, literally trans. by Fathers of the English

Dominican Province, Vol. 8 (London: Burns Oates & Washbourne, 1942), p. 352 (la 2ae.110.3), where Thomas says that human virtues dispose man fittingly "to the nature whereby he is a man; whereas infused virtues dispose man in a higher manner and towards a higher end, and consequently in relation to some higher nature, i.e., in relation to a participation of the Divine Nature."

81. *Ibid.*, Vol. 8, p. 350 (la 2ae.110.2).

82. Cf. for the following the perceptive analysis by Helmut Thielicke, *Theological Ethics*, Vol. 1: *Foundations*, ed. by William H. Lazareth (Philadelphia: Fortress, 1966), pp. 197-211, to the issue of the Roman Catholic ontological perception of humanity being created in the image of God. When he states that "Roman Catholic thinking is profoundly ontological, Reformation thinking profoundly personalistic," then this is true for the time of the Reformation, but, as we will see, it is no longer true in this exclusive sense for our present time.

83. "Decree on Justification" (5), in Henricus Denzinger, *The Sources of Catholic Dogma*, p. 250 (797).

84. So rightly Thielicke, *Theological Ethics*, Vol. 1, p. 207. Since he does not distinguish between image and similitude, he rightly says that the *"imago* qualities of man" are not affected through the fall.

85. Martin Luther, *Über das 1. Buch Mose. Predigten* (1527), in WA 24, 51, 12f., in his exegesis of Gen. 1:27.

86. *On the Bondage of Will*, in *Luther and Erasmus: Free Will and Salvation*, p. 140.

87. John Calvin, *Institutes of the Christian Religion*, ed. by John T. McNeill, trans. by F. L. Battles, Vol. 20 of *The Library of Christian Classics* (Philadelphia: Westminster, 1960), pp. 255 (2.2.1) and 277 (2.2.17). Cf. also T. F. Torrance, *Calvin's Doctrine of Man* (Grand Rapids, MI: Wm. B. Eerdmans, 1957), pp. 88ff., in his excellent analysis of this evident dichotomy. Torrance rightly claims that it is important to be aware of Calvin's distinction between the natural and the spiritual. While humanity is deprived of its spiritual gifts, it is only corrupted in its natural gifts. He also admits that though "it is difficult to see how there can be any ultimate reconciliation between Calvin's doctrine of total perversity and his doctrine of a remnant of the *imago dei*, though the very fact that he can give them both in the same breath seems to indicate that he had no difficulty in reconciling them."

88. Johann Gerhard, *The Image of God*, in *The Doctrine of Man in Classical Lutheran Theology*, ed. by Herman A. Preus and Edmund Smits (Minneapolis: Augsburg, 1962), p. 62.

89. Cf. Althaus, *Die christliche Wahrheit*, p. 340.

90. Barth, *Church Dogmatics*, Vol. 3.2, p. 324, opts for an analogy of relationship instead of an analogy of being between God and humanity.

91. Barth, *Church Dogmatics*, Vol. 3.1, p. 200, arrives at the same conclusions in his excellent comments on the *imago dei* issue. Cf. also Zimmerli, *Grundriss der alttestamentlichen Theologie*, pp. 27f.

92. *Man in Revolt*, p. 136; cf. also Thielicke, *Theological Ethics*, Vol. 1, p. 167, esp. n.18.

93. G. C. Berkouwer, *Man: The Image of God*, trans. by D. W. Jellema (Grand Rapids, MI: Wm. B. Eerdmans, 1962), esp. pp. 145ff.
94. Cf. for the following Michael Schmaus, *Der Glaube der Kirche. Handbuch katholischer Dogmatik*, Vol. 1 (Munich: Max Hueber, 1969), p. 336.
95. *Ibid.*, p. 650.
96. Cf. for the following excellent remarks by Trillhaas, *Dogmatik*, pp. 203f., concerning the relationship between humanity being created in the image of God and human sinfulness.
97. *City of God*, p. 441 (14.1).
98. *Ibid.*, p. 609 (18.1).
99. *Ibid.*, p. 477 (14.28).
100. *Ibid.*, p. 445 (14.4).
101. *Ibid.*, pp. 695 (19.17) and 692 (19.14).
102. *Ibid.*, p. 763 (21.1).
103. Cf. *ibid.*, p. 458 (14.11), and the introduction by Thomas Merton, pp. ixf.
104. Albrecht Ritschl, *The Christian Doctrine of Justification and Reconciliation. A Positive Development of the Doctrine*, trans. and ed. by H. R. Mackintosh and A. B. Macaulay, 2nd. ed. (Edinburgh: T. & T. Clark, 1902), pp. 383f.
105. *Ibid.*, p. 335.
106. *Ibid.*, p. 338.
107. Rolf Schäfer, *Ritschl. Grundlinien eines fast verschollenen dogmatischen Systems* (Tübingen: J. C. B. Mohr/Paul Siebeck, 1968), p. 98, n. 3, rightly talks here about the force of Ritschl's system which would disallow for any notion that God could even remotely be responsible for sin. Therefore Ritschl is forced to assume that the cause of sin lies alone in human freedom. Schäfer also points out the great influence of Schleiermacher on Ritschl's notion of the communal understanding of (original) sin. Cf. Schleiermacher, *The Christian Faith*, pp. 288ff. (par. 71).
108. Ritschl, *The Christian Doctrine of Justification and Reconciliation*, p. 349.
109. *Ibid.*, p. 337.
110. *Ibid.*, p. 335.
111. *Man in Revolt*, p. 125. Ritschl then did not accomplish the task he set himself, "to transcend the dilemma which hovers between Pelagius and Augustine" (Ritschl, *The Christian Doctrine of Justification and Reconciliation*, p. 335).
112. David L. Mueller, in his excellent book, *An Introduction to the Theology of Albrecht Ritschl* (Philadelphia: Westminster, 1969), p. 73, mentions Walter Rauschenbusch, Reinhold Niebuhr, and also the Swiss Socialists Leonhard Ragaz and Hermann Kutter, who picked up this emphasis on the corporate dimension of sin from Ritschl. For Reinhold Niebuhr cf. esp. *Nature and Destiny of Man*, Vol. 1, esp. pp. 208-219; also *The Children of Light and the Children of Darkness. A Vindication of Democracy and a Critique of Its Traditional Defence* (New York: Charles Scribner's, 1960), esp. pp. 1-41; and

Moral Man and Immoral Society. A Study in Ethics and Politics (New York: Charles Scribner's, 1936).

113. *A Theology for the Social Gospel* (New York: Macmillan, 1917), pp. 77f. Cf. also *The Righteousness of the Kingdom,* ed. and intr. by Max L. Stackhouse (Nashville: Abingdon, 1968), which contains an extensive and helpful introduction, plus a bibliography of Rauschenbusch's own writings and selected secondary literature.

114. *A Theology for the Social Gospel,* p. 90.

115. *Ibid.,* p. 87.

116. *Ibid.,* p. 79.

117. *Ibid.,* p. 81.

118. *Ibid.,* p. 80.

119. *Ibid.,* p. 99.

7. UNDER GOD'S CARE

1. William Pollard, *Chance and Providence. God's Action in a World Governed by Scientific Law* (New York: Charles Scribner's, 1958), p. 7.

2. Cf. Richard Rubenstein, *After Auschwitz. Radical Theology and Contemporary Judaism* (Indianapolis: Bobbs-Merrill, 1966), pp. 87 and 153f.

3. Arthur Schopenhauer, *The World as Will and Idea,* trans. by R. B. Haldane and J. Kemp, Vol. 3 (London: Routledge & Kegan Paul, 1957), p. 395.

4. For the following cf. Gottfried Wilhelm Leibniz, *The Monadology* 60ff.), in *The Monadology and Other Philosophical Writings,* pp. 250-253.

5. It is important to learn from the success and failure of the physico-theology of the 17th and 18th century in its dialog with science during the first phase of the Enlightenment, since we must engage in a similar dialog to face the challenges of the present second phase of the Enlightenment. For a comprehensive introduction to physico-theology cf. Wolfgang Philip, *Das Werden der Aufklärung in theologiegeschichtlicher Sicht* (Göttingen: Vandenhoeck & Ruprecht, 1957), esp. pp. 21ff.

6. Friedrich Schleiermacher, *The Christian Faith,* pp. 725f. (par. 164.3).

6a. David R. Griffin, *God, Power, and Evil: A Process Theodicy* (Philadelphia: Westminster, 1976), pp. 310 and 309. The redemptive deficiency becomes especially noticeable in his appendix "Theodicy and Hope for a Future Life" (pp. 311-313).

7. B. Carra de Vaux, *"kismet,"* in *Encyclopedia of Religion and Ethics,* ed. by James Hastings, Vol. 7, p. 738.

8. de Vaux, *"fate* (Muslim)," in *ibid.,* Vol. 5, p. 794; cf. also the very informative and balanced article by M. Mujeeb, "Man and God in Islam: Freedom and Obligation as Found in the Qur'an," in *Islam. Guru Nanak Quincentenary Celebration Series* (Patiala: Punjabi University, 1969), pp. 34ff.

9. Xenophanes of Colophon (21:13), in Kathleen Freeman, *Ancilla to*

the Pre-Socratic Philosophers. A Complete Translation of the Fragments in Diels, "Fragmente der Vorsokratiker," p. 22.

10. Cf. Arrian in his *Discourses of Epictetus* (1.16), in *The Stoic and Epi-
curean Philosophers. The Complete Extant Writings of Epicurus, Epictetus, Lucretius, Marcus Aurelius*, ed. with an intr. by Whitney J.
Oates (New York: Random House, 1940), pp. 252f.

11. Chrysippus according to Joannis Stobaeus, *Ecologarum Physicarum et
Ethicarum*, ed. by August Meineke, Vol. 1 (Leipzig: B. G. Teubner,
1860), p. 46 (1.5.180), says: "*Haimarmene* is the law *(logos)* of the
cosmos . . . the law according to which the things that were made,
occurred, the things that are taking place, do take place, the things
that will occur, come into being." For the translation of *logos* cf. *A
Greek-English Lexicon*, comp. by Henry G. Liddell and Robert Scott,
A New Edition rev. by Henry S. Jones (Oxford: Clarendon, 1958),
p. 1058 (III/7).

12. For the skeptical mood in Greek philosophy cf. Edwyn Bevan, *Stoics
and Sceptics*, Four Lectures Delivered in Oxford During Hilary Term
1913 for the Common University Fund (reprint: New York: Barnes &
Noble, 1959), pp. 121f.

13. Cleanthes of Assos as quoted by Seneca, *Ad Lucilium Epistulae
Morales* (107.11), with an Eng. trans. by Richard M. Gummere, Vol.
3 (Cambridge, MA: Harvard University, 1962), p. 228.

14. *The Consolation of Philosophy*, intr. by Irwin Edman (New York:
Random House, Modern Library, 1943), p. 120 (end of book 5).

15. Cf. Victor Wolfgang von Hagen, *The Ancient Sun Kingdoms of the
Americas*, illus. by Alberto Beltrán (Cleveland: World, 1961), pp.
159-162.

16. Cf. the instructive book by Franz Cummont, *Astrology and Religion
Among the Greeks and Romans* (New York: Dover, 1960 [1912]).

17. For Luther's position cf. Heinrich Bornkamm, *Luther's World of
Thought*, trans. by M. H. Bertram (St. Louis, MO: Concordia, 1958),
pp. 185ff.

18. Cf. WATR (TR standing for table talks), 3, 114, 23-26 (2952b).

19. WATR, 4, 543, 7-16 (4846).

20. *Table Talk*, in *Luther's Works*, Vol. 54, pp. 458f. (5573). Here Luther
lists a whole series of arguments against astrology.

21. For the following cf. Luther, "*Randbemerkungen Luthers zu den Sen-
tenzen des Petrus Lombardus*" (1510/11), in WA 9, 66, 29-34.

22. For the following cf. Friedrich Baumgärtel, "*pneuma* (B. Spirit in
the OT)," in *TDNT*, Vol. 6, p. 366, where he calls the *ruah* Yahweh
"a dynamic creative principle" and "the personal creative power of
God" with which "God is also at work as Sustainer of His creation."
Philip Hefner in his thought-provoking essay, "The Self-Definition of
Life and Human Purpose: Reflections Upon the Divine Spirit and the
Human Spirit," *Zygon*, Vol. 8 (Sept.-Dec., 1973), p. 399, rightly
claims that "the Spirit of God resides in the foundational matrix out
of which all reality, including man, lives." This Spirit, according to
Hefner, also "symbolizes the ongoing presence or dynamic actualiza-
tion of this power of God," (p. 398).

23. *Letters and Papers from Prison,* ed. by Eberhard Bethge, rev. ed. (New York: Macmillan, 1967), pp. 174f.

24. For the following cf. the illuminating remarks by William Pollard, *Chance and Providence,* pp. 74-78.

25. *Ibid.,* p. 68.

26. George G. Simpson, *The Meaning of Evolution. A Study of the History of Life and of Its Significance for Man* (New Haven: Yale University, 1950), p. 310. Of course, we do not want to leave the impression, and Simpson does not intend to do so either, that everything within the evolutionary process is totally unpredictable. There are always covariances within the evolutionary process and certain limits which are not exceeded or below which a certain species will not drop (cf. for instance, the minimum weight of mammals). Thus there evolves an internal balance within the evolutionary system tending toward optimal conditions of existence and survival. Cf. the excellent article by Paul Overhage, "Gebundene Mannigfaltigkeit," in *Gott in Welt. Festgabe für Karl Rahner,* Vol. 2, ed. by Herbert Vorgrimmler (Herder: Freiburg, 1964), esp. pp. 842ff.

27. Simpson, pp. 310f., even ventures to claim that this "new evolution involves knowledge, including the knowledge of good and evil." In other words humanity is again confronted with the primordial choice between good and evil as it was once in paradise. Cf. also Hermann J. Muller, "The Guidance of Human Evolution," in *Evolution After Darwin,* ed. by Sol Tax, Vol. 2, p. 460, where he asserts: "From now on, evolution is whatever we make it, provided that we choose the true and the good."

28. So rightly Pollard, *Chance and Providence,* p. 178.

29. *"Kaspar Crucigers Sommerpostille"* (1544), in WA 21, 521, 20-25, in a sermon on Rom. 11:33-36.

30. Cf. the important collection ed. by Charles E. Curran, *Absolutes in Moral Theology?* (Cleveland: Corpus Books, 1968), which contains an interesting essay by Robert H. Springer, "Conscience, Behavioral Science and Absolutes," pp. 19-56, in which he concludes that "greater relativity in the abstract will yield sounder moral conclusions in the concrete." Cf. also the informative sourcebook compiled by C. Ellis Nelson, *Conscience. Theological and Psychological Perspectives* (New York: Newman, 1973).

31. So Emil Brunner, *Justice and the Social Order,* trans. by M. Hottinger (New York: Harper, 1945), p. 6.

32. Origen, *Contra Celsum,* trans. with intr. & notes by Henry Chadwick (Cambridge: University Press, 1953), p. 293 (5.37).

33. Cf. Lactantius, *The Divine Institutes,* trans. by Sr. M. F. McDonald, in *The Fathers of the Church,* Vol. 49, pp. 356ff. (5.12).

34. Cf. Thomas Hobbes, *Leviathan,* ed. with an intr. by C. B. Macpherson (Baltimore, MD: Penguin, 1968), p. 189 (chap. 14), who perceives natural law primarily under the aspect of a contract.

35. Augustine, *Reply to Faustus the Manichaean,* in *A Select Library,* Vol. 4, p. 283 (22.27).

36. *The City of God,* p. 690 (19.13).

37. Augustine, *On the Psalms,* in *A Select Library,* Vol. 8, p. 580 (119.117).
38. Augustine, *Reply to Faustus the Manichaean,* p. 284 (22.28).
39. Augustine, *Letters,* Vol. 3 (131-164), trans. by Sr. Wilfrid Parsons, in *The Fathers of the Church,* Vol. 20, p. 331 (157).
40. Thomas Aquinas, *Summa Theologiae* (Blackfriar Ed.), Vol. 28, p. 52.
41. *Ibid.,* p. 7 (1a 2ae.90.1).
42. *Ibid.,* p. 16 (1a 2ae.90.4).
43. *Ibid.,* p. 22 (1a 2ae.91.2).
44. *Ibid.,* pp. 65ff. (1a 2ae.93.5).
45. *Ibid.,* p. 95 (1a 2ae.94.6).
46. *Ibid.,* p. 87 (1a 2ae.94.4).
47. *Lectures on Romans. Glosses and Scholia* (1515/16), in *Luther's Works,* Vol. 25, p. 345, for the exegesis of Rom. 8:3 (cf. WA 56, 355, 14).
48. Cf. *Predigten des Jahres 1546,* in WA 51, 126, 9f., where Luther says reason is "the biggest whore that the devil has."
49. *Lectures on Galatians* (1535), in *Luther's Works,* Vol. 26, p. 307, in his exegesis of Gal. 3:19.
50. *Ibid.,* p. 308.
51. *A Simple Way to Pray* (1535), in *Luther's Works,* Vol. 43, p. 203, explaining the fourth commandment.
52. *Predigten über das 2. Buch Mose, 1524-1527,* in WA 16, 512, 3-6, in his exegesis of the third commandment.
53. Cf. for the following, *Against the Heavenly Prophets in the Matter of Images and Sacraments* (1525), in *Luther's Works,* Vol. 40, pp. 97f.
54. WATR 2, 374, 17ff.
55. *Psalm 101,* in *Luther's Works,* Vol. 13, p. 161, in his exegesis of Ps. 101:1.
56. *Lectures on Deuteronomy* (1525), in *Luther's Works,* Vol. 9, p. 108, in his exegesis of Dtn. 10.
57. *On Temporal Authority: To What Extent It Should Be Obeyed* (1523), in *Luther's Works,* Vol. 45, p. 119.
58. *Ibid.,* p. 129.
59. Cf. Luther's argument in *The Judgement of Martin Luther on Monastic Vows* (1521), *in Luther's Works,* Vol. 44, p. 336.
60. Jean Jacques Rousseau, *Emile or Education,* trans. by B. Foxley (New York: E. P. Dutton, 1928), pp. 5ff. Cf. also William Boyd, *The Educational Theory of Jean Jacques Rousseau* (New York: Russell & Russell, 1963), p. 190, who rightly claims that in *Émile* Rousseau does not want to turn his back on civilization. "He is merely seeking for a method of keeping men as near nature as possible under existing social conditions."
61. *The Social Contract,* in *Political Writings,* trans. and ed. by Frederick Watkins (New York: Thomas Nelson, 1953), pp. 38f.
62. Cf. John Locke, *An Essay Concerning Human Understanding,* ed. by Alexander C. Fraser, Vol. 1 (New York: Dover, 1959), p. 118, after he discarded the concept of innate ideas.
63. For Hume cf. Hans Schwarz, *The Search for God,* pp. 76ff.; and for the empirical foundation of laws, cf. David Hume, *A Treatise of Hu-*

man *Nature,* in *Hume on Human Nature and the Understanding,* ed. by Antony Flew (New York: Collier, 1962), p. 279.

64. Cf. the eloquent argument in Brunner, *Justice and Social Order,* p. 8.
65. *The Biology of the Ten Commandments,* trans. by D. Smith (New York: McGraw-Hill, 1972), pp. 76, 123, and 160f.
66. Cf. Siegfried Morenz, *Egyptian Religion,* trans. by A. E. Keep (London: Methuen, 1973), esp. p. 112, where he refers to the so-called "Book of the Dead," and pp. 121ff. where he classifies the commandments in ancient Egypt as wisdom literature. This latter reference is particularly illuminating, since it attests to the acquisition of right conduct through insight and not just through divine revelation. Cf. H. Saddhatissa, *Buddhist Ethics—Essence of Buddhism* (London: George Allen & Unwin, 1970), pp. 111f., and Kashi Nath Upadhyaya, *Early Buddhism and the Bhagavadgita* (Delhi: Motilal Banarsidass, 1971), pp. 413f. Cf. also Moritz Merker, *Die Massai* (New York: Johnson Reprint, 1968 [1910]), pp. 335. Of course, one should notice here that the Masai are a Semitic tribe, a fact which Merker emphasizes by showing their common heritage with the ancestors of the Old Testament Israelites.
67. Wickler, *The Biology of the Ten Commandments,* pp. 44f., who refers to Merker's study on the Masai.
68. *Predigten über das 2. Buch Mose. 1524-1527,* in WA 16, 380, 19f., in a sermon on Ex. 19.
69. Cf. the excellent article by Arnold W. Ravin, "Science, Values, and Human Evolution," *Zygon,* Vol. 11 (June, 1976), pp. 138-154, here p. 151.
70. Wickler, *The Biology of the Ten Commandments,* pp. 171ff.
71. *Ibid.,* p. 179.
72. For the following cf. Werner Elert, *The Christian Ethos,* trans. by C. J. Schindler (Philadelphia: Muhlenberg, 1957), pp. 77f.
73. For the following cf. Walter Künneth, *Politik zwischen Dämon und Gott. Eine christliche Ethik des Politischen* (Berlin: Lutherisches Verlagshaus, 1954), pp. 139f.
74. *Church Dogmatics,* Vol. 3.4: *The Doctrine of Creation,* p. 45.
75. Cf. for the following Bonhoeffer, *Ethics,* ed. by Eberhard Bethge, trans. by N. H. Smith (New York: Macmillan, 1955), p. 207.
76. Immanuel Kant in his *Foundations of the Metaphysics of Morals,* in *Foundations of the Metaphysics of Morals and What Is Enlightenment?* trans. with intr. by Lewis White Beck (Indianapolis: Bobbs-Merrill, 1959), esp. pp. 38ff., argues on the basis of "pure reason" that there are certain moral norms that, when universalized, will support human existence while others, when universalized, will impede it.
77. *Predigten des Jahres 1531,* in WA 34 II, 237, 3f., in a sermon on the festival of St. Michael's.
78. *"Zwölf Thesen der Kirchlichen Einheitsfront in Württemberg"* (May 11, 1934), in *Die Bekenntnisse und grundsätzlichen Äusserungen zur Kirchenfrage,* Vol. 2: *Das Jahr 1934,* ed. by Kurt Dietrich Schmidt (Göttingen: Vandenhoeck & Ruprecht, 1935), p. 73.
79. Cf. Gerhard Kittel, in Karl Barth and Gerhard Kittel, *Ein theologischer Briefwechsel* (Stuttgart: W. Kohlhammer, 1934), p. 12.

80. Cf. Alan Bullock, *Hitler. A Study in Tyranny*, rev. ed. (New York: Harper, 1962), p. 744. Bullock even comments (p. 723): "Anything, however trivial, which went right in the last two years of the war served Hitler as further evidence that he had only to trust Providence and all would be well."

81. Sergius, *Die Wahrheit über die Religion in Russland*, trans. by L. Wyss (Zollikon-Zürich: Evangelischer Verlag, 1944), p. 16.

82. Cf. *Admonition to Peace. A Reply to the Twelve Articles of the Peasants in Swabia* (1525), in *Luther's Works*, Vol. 46, p. 32.

83. So rightly G. C. Berkouwer in his excellent book *The Providence of God*, trans. by L. Smedes (Grand Rapids, MI: Wm. B. Eerdmanns, 1952), p. 179.

84. Cf. Thomas Merton in his intr. to Augustine, *The City of God*, p. ixf.

85. Cf. Salvianus, *On the Government of God*, trans. by Eva M. Sanford (New York: Octagon Books, 1966), p. 223 (7.23), and Eva Sanford in her intr. pp. 3f.

86. Berkouwer, *The Providence of God*, p. 180.

87. Cf. Schiller's poem *"Resignation"* (1786), *Gesammelte Werke in fünf Bänden*, Vol. 3, p. 394.

88. *The Philosophy of History*, pref. by Charles Hegel, trans. by J. Sibree, intr. by C. J. Friedrich (New York: Dover, 1956), p. 15. Similarly it is difficult for us to agree with him (p. 36) when he says: "God governs the world; the actual working of his government—the carrying out of his plan—is the History of the World."

89. *Christ the Representative. An Essay in Theology After the "Death of God,"* trans. by D. Lewis (Philadelphia: Fortress, 1967), pp. 150f., where she quotes Bonhoeffer's assertion referred to in n.90.

90. *Letters and Papers from Prison*, p. 196.

91. *The New Essence of Christianity* (New York: Association, 1966), p. 54, where he says this with reference to Bonhoeffer's previously mentioned statement.

92. "America and the Future of Theology," in Thomas J. J. Altizer and William Hamilton, *Radical Theology and the Death of God* (Indianapolis: Bobbs-Merrill, 1966), p. 11.

93. Cf. the explanation of thesis 20 of the *Heidelberg Disputation*, in *Luther's Works*, Vol. 31, p. 53.

94. So rightly Erich Seeberg, *Luthers Theologie in ihren Grundzügen*, 2nd ed. (Stuttgart: W. Kohlhammer, 1950), pp. 54f.

95. *Letters and Papers from Prison*, p. 34.

96. For the following cf. Albert C. Outler, *Who Trusts in God. Musings on the Meaning of Providence* (New York: Oxford University, 1968), pp. 45f.

97. Cf. Bultmann, *The Gospel of John*, p. 331, esp. n. 3, in his exegesis of John 9:1-7.

98. Evgenii Lampert, *The Apocalypse of History. Problems of Providence and Human Destiny* (London: Faber and Faber, 1948), p. 176, who very convincingly asserts an apocalyptic and eschatological interpretation of history.

99. Friedrich Gogarten, *The Reality of Faith. The Problem of Subjectivism in Theology* (Philadelphia: Westminster, 1959), pp. 55ff.

100. Cf. the excellent remarks by Ludwig Köhler, *Old Testament Theology*, p. 62; cf. also Johannes Behm, *"diatheke,"* in *TDNT*, Vol. 2, p. 134, where he says: "Diatheke is from first to last the 'disposition' of God, the mighty declaration of the sovereign will of God in history, by which He orders the relation between Himself and men according to His own saving purpose, and which carries with it the authoritative divine ordering, the one order of things which is in accordance with it."

101. Outler, *Who Trusts in God*, p. 52.

102. *Lectures or Tractates on the Gospel according to St. John*, in Vol. 7 of *A Select Library*, p. 158.

103. *The City of God*, p. 776 (21.8).

104. For the following cf. the enlightening book by John P. Kenny, *The Supernatural. Medieval Theological Concepts to Modern* (Staten Island, NY: Alba House, 1972), pp. 94f.

105. *Summa Theologiae* (Blackfriar Ed.), Vol. 49, p. 159 (3a 13 2r).

106. Cf. *ibid.*, Vol. 14, p. 79 (1a 105 5r).

107. For this and the following quote see *Summa Theologiae*, Vol. 14, pp. 83ff. (1a 105 7).

108. Cf. Nicholas of Cusa, *The Vision of God*, intr. by Evelyn Underhill (New York: Frederick Ungar, 1960 [1928]), pp. 46f.

109. Cf. the comprehensive study of Louis Monden, *Signs and Wonders. A Study of the Miraculous Element in Religion* (New York: Desclee, 1966). Cf. also the definitions of a miraculous healing in Lourdes according to the informative book by Ruth Cranston, *The Miracle of Lourdes* (New York: McGraw-Hill, 1955), pp. 103f.

110. For the following cf. Johann Salomo Semler, *Versuch einer biblischen Dämonologie oder Untersuchung der Lehre der heil. Schrift vom Teufel und seiner Macht* (Halle: Carl Hermann Hemmerde, 1776), esp. pp. 283ff. and 344f.

111. For the following cf. Emanuel Hirsch, *Geschichte der neueren evangelischen Theologie*, Vol. 1, pp. 316ff.

112. Hermann Samuel Reimarus, *The Goal of Jesus and His Disciples*, intr. and trans. by George W. Buchanan (Leiden: E. J. Brill, 1970), pp. 118f.

113. So Bultmann in his famous essay on "New Testament and Mythology," in *Kerygma and Myth*, Vol. 1, p. 5.

114. *Space, Time, and Gravitation: An Outline of the General Relativity Theory* (Cambridge: University, 1921), pp. 200f.

115. Berkouwer, *The Providence of God*, p. 222.

116. *Systematic Theology*, Vol. 1, p. 267.

117. Cf. for the following the excellent remarks of Mark Pontifex, *Freedom and Providence* (New York: Hawthorn, 1960), p. 114.

118. Cf. the significant remarks of William Pollard, *Chance and Providence*, pp. 141ff.; cf. also Günter Howe, "Zu den Äusserungen von Niels Bohr über religiöse Fragen," *Kerygma und Dogma*, Vol. 4 (January, 1958), pp. 26f., where Howe points out the implications of Bohr's principle of complementarity for our understanding of reality.

119. Pollard, *Chance and Providence*, p. 66.

120. Cf. Herbert Braun, *Jesus. Der Mann aus Nazareth und seine Zeit* (Berlin: Kreuz, 1969), pp. 43f.; and Ernst Käsemann, "Zum Thema

der Nichtobjektivierbarkeit," *Evangelische Theologie*, Vol. 12 (1952/53), p. 457.

121. Cf. the very instructive investigation by Gerd Petzke, *Die Traditionen über Apollonius von Tyana und das Neue Testament* (Leiden: E. J. Brill, 1970), pp. 157 and 179; cf. also Philostratus, *The Life of Apollonius of Tyana*, trans. by F. C. Conybeare, Vol. 1 (Cambridge, MA: Harvard University, 1969), p. 367 (4.6).

122. Cf. Rudolf Bultmann, *The History of the Synoptic Tradition*, trans. by J. Marsh (Oxford: Basil Blackwell, 1963), pp. 210 and 231ff., who tries to explain their similar structure from the assumption of a common origin.

123. Cf. for the following Bultmann, *Theology of the New Testament*, Vol. 1, esp. pp. 7f. and 23, who shows that Jesus sees the fulfillment of the prophetic predictions of salvation already beginning in his own miracles. Cf. also Anton Fridrichsen, *The Problem of Miracle in Primitive Christianity*, trans. by R. A. Harrisville and J. S. Hanson (Minneapolis: Augsburg, 1972), pp. 72f.

124. Joachim Jeremias, *New Testament Theology*, p. 95, rightly claims that the victories over the instruments of Satan "are a foretaste of the eschaton."

125. William Manson, "Eschatology in the New Testament," in *Eschatology. Four Papers Read to the Society for the Study of Theology*, by William Manson et al. (Edinburgh: Oliver and Boyd, 1952), p. 6, rightly says: "The Resurrection of Jesus is not simply a sign which God granted in favor of His Son, but is the inauguration, the entrance into history, of *the times of the End*." Karl Heim, *The World: Its Creation and Consummation*, also shows very convincingly the eschatological significance of Christ's resurrection. Yet he seems to envision not an eschatological perfection but a return of the created world "to its original state" (p. 134). Such a view, however, would have to assume that there was already perfection in the beginning. At most the biblical creation stories seem to indicate a state of original goodness, but not one of perfection. God's creation is on its way from its inception to its completion, but is not returning to its beginning.

126. Robert M. Grant in his excellent book *Miracle and Natural Law in Graeco-Roman and Early Christian Thought* (Amsterdam: North-Holland, 1952), p. 269, says concerning the New Testament miracle stories: They "were actually symbols, stories conveying pictures of the freedom and the power of God, who was at work in human history and would ultimately vindicate those who trusted and obeyed him." Grant sees the dividing line between Graeco-Roman thought and Christian faith in the trust of the laws of nature, however conceived, and the faith in the freedom and power of God, as "demonstrated" in his miracles. This freedom in God in turn endows humanity with freedom. Though we are part of nature, we cannot be reduced to nature since we are God's governors. This special position is a source of hope in the fulfillment of our and the world's future.

127. Cf. Georgia Harkness, *The Providence of God* (New York: Abingdon, 1960), p. 121, who also reminds us that this is the place at which many people's faith in providence is shipwrecked.

128. Jeremias, *The Lord's Prayer,* esp. p. 22.
129. *Letters and Papers from Prison,* p. 213.
130. *Sermons on the Gospel of St. John* (1537), in *Luther's Works,* Vol. 24, p. 81, in his exposition of John 14:12.
131. *Lectures on Genesis* (1535-1545), in *Luther's Works,* Vol. 3, p. 117, in his exegesis of Gen. 17:7.
132. WA 37, 425, 2-8, in a sermon on Ps. 65 (1534).
133. *Instructions for the Visitors of Parish Pastors in Electoral Saxony* (1528), in *Luther's Works,* Vol. 40, p. 279.
134. *The Providence of God,* p. 128.
135. Hymn 459 of the *Service Book and Hymnal,* authorized by the Lutheran churches cooperating in the Commission on the Liturgy and Hymnal (Minneapolis: Augsburg, 1958).
136. For a curious mixture of Christian and non-Christian approaches to healing cf. the interesting book by Sybil Leek, *The Story of Faith Healing* (New York: Macmillan, 1973), who according to the cover of the book is "a practicing witch and psychic."
137. This has been pointed out very convincingly by Karl Heim, *The Transformation of the Scientific World View,* trans. by W. A. Whitehouse (London: SCM, 1953), pp. 192f., in his excellent remarks concerning the structure and significance of miracles.
138. Harkness, *The Providence of God,* pp. 135ff.; cf. also Paul Tournier, *The Healing of Persons,* trans. by E. Hudson (New York: Harper, 1965); and the popular report by Howard R. and Martin E. Lewis, *Psychosomatics. How Your Emotions Can Damage Your Health* (New York: Viking, 1972).
139. *Foundations of the Metaphysics of Morals,* p. 47.
140. Cf. Friedrich Engels, "On the History of Early Christianity" (1894/95), in Karl Marx and Friedrich Engels, *On Religion,* intr. by Reinhold Niebuhr (New York: Schocken, 1964), p. 320.
141. For this quotation and the following see *ibid.,* p. 317f., in a footnote by Engels.
142. Cf. Karl Marx, "Theses on Feuerbach" (1845), in *On Religion,* p. 72, where he talks about the new society as a *"human* society, or socialized humanity."
143. Philip Hefner, in his thoughtful essay, "Toward a New Doctrine of Man: The Relationship of Man and Nature," in *Zygon,* Vol. 2 (June, 1967), pp. 144f., appropriately reminds us that humanity is not a solid, given entity, but "a bundle of energy, organized in a certain manner, proceeding in a certain direction."
144. Cf. the instructive book by Paul Bock, *In Search of a Responsible World Society. The Social Teachings of the World Council of Churches* (Philadelphia: Westminster, 1974), esp. p. 226. Wolfhart Pannenberg, "Der Mensch—Ebenbild Gottes?" in *Glaube und Wirklichkeit,* p. 65, rightly says that humanity is destined to realize its true humanity in communion with God. Since this goal of history of humanity's humanization has already become visible in Jesus, the process of becoming fully human has become the theme for all subsequent history: All people shall participate in the true humanity as it appeared in Jesus Christ.

145. Cf. the very interesting remarks by Hugo Assmann, *Theology for a Nomad Church,* trans. by Paul Burns, intr. by Frederick Herzog (Maryknoll, NY: Orbis, 1976), p. 141, where he says: "If the formative context of material structures is not joined by the loving process of call and response, the result is a simple product of the environment and not the new man."

146. Denis Goulet, *A New Moral Order. Studies in Development Ethics and Liberation Theology,* Foreword by Paulo Feire (Maryknoll, NY: Orbis, 1974), p. 130. It is significant for the interdependence between the evolutionary advancement and the striving for a new humanity that Goulet finds in Teilhard the main advocate for this eschatological vision of a new humanity.

Selected Bibliography

(For further bibliographic information, particularly of more specialized nature, please consult the footnotes.)

1. ISSUES IN SCIENCE AND RELIGION:

Austin, William H. *The Relevance of Natural Science to Theology.* New York: Macmillan, 1976.

Barbour, Ian G. *Christianity and the Scientist.* New York: Association, 1960.

———. *Issues in Science and Religion.* Englewood Cliffs, NJ: Prentice-Hall, 1966.

———. *Myths, Models, and Paradigms. A Comparative Study in Science and Religion.* New York: Harper, 1974.

———, ed. *Science and Religion. New Perspectives on a Dialogue.* New York: Harper Forum Book, 1968.

———. *Science & Secularity. The Ethics of Technology.* New York: Harper, 1970.

Bayne, Stephen F. *Space Age Christianity.* Foreword by William F. Lewis. New York: Morehouse-Barlow, 1963.

Booth, Edwin P., ed. *Religion Ponders Science.* New York: Appleton-Century, 1964.

Broad, Charlie D. *Religion, Philosophy, and Psychical Research. Selected Essays.* New York: Harcourt & Brace, 1953.

Bube, Richard H., ed. *The Encounter Between Christianity and Science.* Grand Rapids, MI: Wm. B. Eerdmans, 1968.

———. *The Human Quest. A New Look at Science and the Christian Faith.* Waco, TX: Word Books, 1971.

Burhoe, Ralph Wendell, ed. *Science and Human Values in the 21st Century.* Philadelphia: Westminster, 1971.

Cauthen, Kenneth. *Science, Secularization & God. Towards a Theology of the Future.* New York: Abingdon, 1969.

Clark, Cecil H. D. *The Scientist and the Supernatural.* London: Epworth, 1966.

Clark, Robert E. D. *Christian Belief and Science. A Reconciliation and a Partnership.* Philadelphia: Muhlenberg, 1961.

——. *The Universe: Plan or Accident? The Religious Implications of Modern Science.* Philadelphia: Muhlenberg, 1961.

Coulson, Charles A. *Christianity in an Age of Science.* New York: Oxford University, 1953.

——. *Science and Christian Belief.* Chapel Hill, NC: University of North Carolina, 1955.

——. *Science, Technology and the Christian.* New York: Abingdon, 1960.

Dampier, Sir William C. *A History of Science and Its Relations with Philosophy and Religion.* 4th ed. Postscript by I. Bernhard Cohen. London: Cambridge University, 1966.

Dillenberger, John. *Protestant Thought and Natural Science. A Historical Interpretation.* Garden City, NY: Doubleday, 1960.

Esterer, Arnulf K. *Towards a Unified Faith.* New York: Philosophical Library, 1963.

Gilkey, Langdon. *Religion and the Scientific Future. Reflections on Myth, Science, and Theology.* New York: Harper, 1970.

Habgood, John. *Truths in Tension. New Perspectives on Religion and Science.* Foreword by Sir Bryan Matthews. New York: Holt, Rinehart and Winston, 1964.

Hartshorne, M. Holmes. *The Promise of Science and the Power of Faith.* Philadelphia: Westminster, 1958.

Heim, Karl. *Christian Faith and Natural Science.* Translated by N. H. Smith. London: SCM, 1953.

——. *The Transformation of the Scientific World View.* Translated by W. A. Whitehouse. London: SCM Press, 1953.

Heinecken, Martin J. *God in the Space Age.* Philadelphia: John C. Winston, 1959.

Journal of the American Scientific Affiliation. Edited by Richard H. Bube. Stanford University, CA: 1949- (quarterly).

Kennedy, Gail, ed. *Evolution and Religion. The Conflict Between Science and Theology in Modern America.* Boston: D. C. Heath, 1957.

Klotz, John W. *Modern Science in the Christian Life.* St. Louis: Concordia, 1961.

Koestler, Arthur. *The Sleepwalkers. A History of Man's Changing Vision of the Universe.* New York: Macmillan, 1959.

Long, Edward LeRoy Jr. *Religious Beliefs of American Scientists.* Philadelphia: Westminster, 1952.

——. *Science & Christian Faith. A Study in Partnership.* New York: Association, 1950.

MacCormac, Earl R. *Metaphor and Myth in Science and Religion.* Durham, NC: Duke University, 1976.

McNeur, Ronald W. *Space-Time-God.* Philadelphia: Westminster, 1961.

Mascall, Eric L. *Christian Theology and Natural Science. Some Questions on Their Relations.* New York: Ronald, 1956.

——. *The Openness of Being. Natural Theology Today. The Gifford Lectures, 1970-1971.* Philadelphia: Westminster, 1972.

Miles, Thomas R. *Religion and the Scientific Outlook.* London: George Allen & Unwin, 1959.

Milne, Edward A. *Modern Cosmology and the Christian Idea of God.* Oxford: Clarendon Press, 1952.

Mixter, Russell L., ed. *Evolution and Christian Thought Today.* Grand Rapids, MI: Wm. B. Eerdmans, 1959.

Morton, John. *Man, Science and God.* London: Collins, 1972.

Peacocke, A. R. *Science and the Christian Experiment.* London: Oxford University, 1971.

Polanyi, Michael. *Science, Faith and Society.* Chicago: University of Chicago, 1966.

Pollard, William G. *Physicist and Christian. A Dialogue Between the Communities.* Greenwich, CT: Seabury, 1961.

———. *Science and Faith: Twin Mysteries* (A Youth Forum Book). New York: Thomas Nelson, 1970.

Rabut, Oliver A. *God in an Evolving Universe.* Translated by W. Springer. New York: Herder and Herder, 1966.

Ramm, Bernard. *The Christian View of Science and Scripture.* Grand Rapids, MI: Wm. B. Eerdmans, 1954.

Ramsey, Ian T., ed. *Biology and Personality: Frontier Problems in Science, Philosophy and Religion.* New York: Barnes & Noble, 1966.

———. *Religion and Science: Conflict and Synthesis. Some Philosophical Reflections.* London: SPCK, 1964.

Raven, Charles E. *Christianity and Science.* New York: Association, 1955.

———. *Natural Religion and Christian Theology. The Gifford Lectures, 1951.* 2 vols. Cambridge: University Press, 1953.

Richardson, Alan. *The Bible in the Age of Science.* London: SCM, 1961.

Russell, Bertrand. *Religion and Science.* New York: Oxford University, Galaxy Book [1935], 1961.

Rust, Eric C. *Nature and Man in Biblical Thought.* London: Lutterworth, 1953.

———. *Science and Faith. Towards a Theological Understanding of Nature.* New York: Oxford University, 1967.

Schaaffs, Werner. *Theology, Physics, and Miracles.* Translated by R. L. Renfield, Washington, D.C.: Canon Press, 1974.

Schilling, Harold K. *The New Consciousness in Science and Religion.* Philadelphia: United Church Press, 1973.

———. *Science and Religion. An Interpretation of Two Communities.* New York: Scribner, 1962.

Shapley, Harlow, ed. *Science Ponders Religion.* New York: Appleton-Century-Crofts, 1960.

Sinnott, Edmund W. *Two Roads to Truth. A Basis for Faith Under the Great Tradition.* New York: Viking, 1953.

Smethurst, Arthur F. *Modern Science and Christian Beliefs.* New York: Abingdon, 1955.

Snow, Charles P. *The Two Cultures: and A Second Look. An Expanded Version of The Two Cultures and the Scientific Revolution.* New York: Cambridge University, 1964.

Stagg, Frank. *Polarities of Man's Existence in Biblical Perspective.* Philadelphia: Westminster, 1973.

Teilhard de Chardin, Pierre. *Science and Christ*. Translated by R. Hague. London: Collins, 1965.

Torrance, Thomas F. *God and Rationality*. London: Oxford University, 1971.

———. *Theological Science. Based on the Hewett Lectures for 1959*. London: Oxford University, 1969.

Towers, Bernard. *Concerning Teilhard, and Other Writings on Science and Religion*. London: Collins, 1969.

Van der Ziel, Aldert. *The Natural Sciences and the Christian Message*. Minneapolis: T. S. Denison, 1960.

White, Edward A. *Science and Religion in American Thought. The Impact of Naturalism*. New York: AMS, 1968.

Whitehead, Alfred North. *The Interpretation of Science. Selected Essays*. Edited by A. H. Johnson. Indianapolis: Bobbs-Merrill, 1961.

———. *Science and the Modern World. Lowell Lectures, 1925*. New York: Macmillan, 1960.

Wier, Frank E. *The Christian Views Science*. New York: Abingdon, 1969.

Yarnold, Greville D. *The Spiritual Crisis of the Scientific Age*. New York: Macmillan, 1959.

Yinger, J. Milton. *The Scientific Study of Religion*. New York: Macmillan, 1970.

Zygon. Journal of Religion & Science. Edited by Ralph Wendell Burhoe. University of Chicago, 1966- (quarterly).

2. ORIGIN AND STRUCTURE OF THE UNIVERSE:

Alfvén, Hannes. *Worlds-Antiworlds. Antimatter in Cosmology*. San Francisco: W. H. Freeman, 1966.

Asimov, Isaac. *The Universe: From Flat Earth to Quasar*. New York: Walker, 1966.

Bergmann, Peter G. *The Riddle of Gravitation*. New York: Scribner, 1968.

Bondi, Hermann. *Cosmology*. 2nd ed. Cambridge: University Press, 1960.

———. *Relativity and Common Sense: A New Approach to Einstein*. Garden City, NY: Doubleday, Anchor Book, 1964.

Bonnor, William B. *The Mystery of the Expanding Universe*. New York: Macmillan, 1964.

Born, Max. *Einstein's Theory of Relativity*. Rev. ed. In collaboration with Günther Leibfried and Walter Biem. New York: Dover, 1962.

Burbidge, Geoffrey, and Burbidge, Margaret. *Quasi-Stellar Objects*. San Francisco: W. H. Freeman, 1967.

Butterfield, Herbert. *The Origins of Modern Science, 1300-1800*. Rev. ed. New York: Macmillan, 1957.

Carnap, Rudolf. *Philosophical Foundations of Science. An Introduction to the Philosophy of Science*. Edited by Martin Gardner. New York: Basic Books, 1966.

Corliss, William R. *Mysteries of the Universe*. New York: Thomas Y. Crowell, 1967.

Eddington, Sir Arthur S. *The Nature of the Physical World. The Gifford Lectures, 1927*. Ann Arbor, MI: University of Michigan [1928], 1958.

———. *The Philosophy of Physical Science.* Cambridge: Cambridge University, 1939.

Eiseley, Loren. *The Firmament of Time.* New York: Atheneum, 1960.

Feuer, Lewis S. *Einstein and the Generations of Science.* New York: Basic Books, 1974.

Gamow, George. *The Creation of the Universe.* New York: Viking, 1952.

———. *Matter, Earth, and Sky.* 2nd ed. Englewood Cliffs, NJ: Prentice-Hall, 1965.

———. *A Star Called the Sun.* New York: Viking, 1964.

———. *Thirty Years That Shook Physics: The Story of Quantum Theory.* Garden City, NY: Doubleday, 1966.

Heisenberg, Werner. *Across the Frontiers.* Translated by P. Heath. New York: Harper, 1974.

———. *Philosophic Problems of Nuclear Science.* Translated by F. C. Hayes. New York: Pantheon, 1952.

———. *The Physical Principles of the Quantum Theory.* Translated by C. Eckart and F. C. Hoyt. New York: Dover, 1930.

———. *Physics and Beyond: Encounters and Conversations.* Translated by A. J. Pomerans. New York: Harper Torchbook, 1971.

———. *Physics and Philosophy. The Revolution in Modern Science.* New York: Harper Torchbook, 1958.

Hoyle, Fred. *Encounter with the Future,* New York: Simon and Schuster, Credo Perspectives, 1965.

———. *The Nature of the Universe.* Rev. ed. New York: Harper & Row, 1960.

———. *From Stonehenge to Modern Cosmology.* San Francisco: W. H. Freeman, 1972.

Jastrow, Robert. *Red Giants and White Dwarfs. The Evolution of Stars, Planets and Life.* New York: Harper, 1967.

Kaplan, Irvin. *Nuclear Physics.* 2nd ed. Reading, MA: Addison-Wesley, 1963.

McVittie, George. *Fact and Theory in Cosmology.* New York: Macmillan, 1961.

Margenau, Henry. *The Nature of Physical Reality. A Philosophy of Modern Physics.* New York: McGraw-Hill, 1950.

Menzel, Donald H.; Whipple, Fred L.; and de Vaucouleurs, Gerard. *Survey of the Universe.* Englewood Cliffs, NJ: Prentice-Hall, 1970.

Motz, Lloyd. *The Universe—Its Beginning and End.* New York: Scribner, 1975.

Munitz, Milton K. *Space, Time and Creation. Philosophical Aspects of Scientific Cosmology.* New York: Collier, 1961.

———. ed. *Theories of the Universe. From Babylonian Myth to Modern Science.* Glencoe, IL: Free Press, 1957.

Nagel, Ernest. *The Structure of Science. Problems in the Logic of Scientific Explanation.* New York: Harcourt, Brace & World, 1961.

Rees, Martin; Ruffini, Remo; and Wheeler, John A. *Black Holes, Gravitational Waves and Cosmology: An Introduction to Current Research.* New York: Gordon and Breach, 1974.

Russell, Bertrand. *The Analysis of Matter.* With a new introduction by Lester E. Denonn. New York: Dover [1927], 1954.

Wallace, William A. *Causality and Scientific Explanation.* Vol. II: *Classical and Contemporary Science.* Ann Arbor: University of Michigan, 1974.

Whitehead, Alfred North. *Process and Reality: An Essay in Cosmology.* New York: Macmillan, 1929.

———. *Science and Philosophy.* Patterson, NJ: Littlefield, Adams [1948], 1964.

Whitrow, G. J. *The Nature of Time.* New York: Holt, Rinehart and Winston, 1972.

Williams, George A. *Elementary Physics: Atoms, Waves, Particles.* New York: McGraw-Hill, 1969.

von Wright, Georg Hendrik. *Causality and Determinism.* New York: Columbia University, 1974.

Zeman, Jirí, ed. *Time in Science and Philosophy. An International Study of Some Current Problems.* Amsterdam: Elsevier, 1971.

3. THE PHENOMENON OF LIFE:

Appleman, Philip, ed. *Darwin.* New York: W. W. Norton, 1970.

Asimov, Isaac. *The Wellsprings of Life.* New York: Abelard-Schuman, 1960.

Beadle, George, and Beadle, Muriel. *The Language of Life. An Introduction to the Science of Genetics.* Garden City, NY: Doubleday, 1966.

Bertalanffy, Ludwig von. *Problems of Life. An Evaluation of Modern Biological Thought.* London: Wattc, 1952.

Blum, Harold F. *Time's Arrow and Evolution.* 3rd ed. Princeton, NJ: Princeton University, 1968.

Borek, Ernest. *The Code of Life.* Rev. ed. New York: Columbia University, 1969.

———. *The Sculpture of Life.* New York: Columbia University, 1973.

Boschke, F. L. *Creation Still Goes On.* Translated by L. Parks. New York: McGraw-Hill, 1964.

Darwin, Charles. *Charles Darwin's Autobiography with His Notes and Letters Depicting the Growth of the "Origin of Species."* Edited by Sir Francis Darwin. Introduction by George G. Simpson. New York: Henry Schuman, 1950.

———. *The Origin of Species by Means of Natural Selection, or The Preservation of Favored Races in the Struggle for Life and the Descent of Man and Selection in Relation to Sex.* New York: Random House, Modern Library, n.d.

Dobzhansky, Theòdosius. *The Biology of Ultimate Concern.* New York: New American Library, 1967.

———. *Evolution, Genetics, and Man.* 6th rep. New York: John Wiley, 1966.

———. *Genetics and the Origin of Species.* 3rd ed., rev. New York: Columbia University, 1951.

———. *Mankind Evolving. The Evolution of the Human Species.* New Haven: Yale University, 1962.

Eiseley, Loren. *Darwin's Century: Evolution and the Men Who Discovered It.* Garden City, NY: Doubleday, Anchor Book, 1961.

———. *The Immense Journey.* New York: Vintage, 1958.

Elliot, Hugh. *Herbert Spencer.* Westport, CT: Greenwood, 1970.

Florkin, Marcel. *A Molecular Approach to Phylogeny*. New York: Elsevier, 1966.

Fox, Sidney W., and Dose, Klaus. *Molecular Evolution and the Origin of Life*. Foreword by A. Oparin. San Francisco: W. H. Freeman, 1972.

Fraenkel-Conrat, Heinz. *Design and Function at the Threshold of Life: The Viruses*. New York: Academic Press, 1962.

Francoeur, Robert T. *Perspectives in Evolution*. Baltimore, MD: Helicon, 1965.

Glass, H. Bentley, ed. *Forerunners of Darwin: 1745-1859*. Baltimore: Johns Hopkins, 1959.

Greene, John C. *Darwin and the Modern World View*. Baton Rouge: Louisiana State University, 1961.

———. *The Death of Adam: Evolution and Its Impact on Western Thought*. Ames: Iowa State University, 1959.

Grene, Marjorie. *The Understanding of Nature Essays in the Philosophy of Biology*. Boston, MA: D. Reidel, 1974.

Himmelfarb, Gertrude. *Darwin and the Darwinian Revolution*. Garden City, NY: Doubleday, Anchor Book, 1959.

Huxley, Julian. *Evolution in Action*. New York: Harper, 1953.

Irvine, William. *Apes, Angels and Victorians. The Story of Darwin, Huxley, and Evolution*. New York: McGraw-Hall, 1955.

Keosian, John. *The Origin of Life*. 2nd ed. New York: Reinhold, 1968.

King-Hele, Desmond. *Erasmus Darwin*. New York: Scribner, 1963.

Kornberg, Arthur. *DNA Synthesis*. San Francisco: W. H. Freeman, 1974.

Lasker, Gabriel, W., ed. *The Process of Ongoing Human Evolution*. Detroit: Wayne State University, 1960.

Lewis, John. *Man and Evolution*. New York: International Publishers, 1962.

Lovejoy, Arthur O. *The Great Chain of Being. The Study of the History of an Idea. William James Lecture, 1933*. New York: Harper Torchbook, 1965.

Lyttleton, Raymond A. *Mysteries of the Solar System*. Oxford: Clarendon Press, 1963.

Macvey, John W. *Alone in the Universe?* New York: Macmillan, 1963.

Mahler, Henry R., and Cordes, Eugene H. *Biological Chemistry*. 2nd ed. New York: Harper, 1971.

Malthus, Thomas Robert, *Population*. Edited and introduced by Gertrude Himmelfarb. New York: Modern Library, 1970.

Monod, Jacques. *Chance and Necessity. An Essay on the Natural Philosophy of Modern Biology*. Translated by A. Wainhouse. New York: Alfred A. Knopf, 1971.

Montagu, Ashley. *Darwin, Competition and Cooperation*. New York: Henry Schuman, 1952.

Muller, Hermann J. *Studies in Genetics. The Selected Papers of H. J. Muller*. Bloomington: Indiana University, 1962.

Orgel, Leslie E. *The Origin of Life: Molecules and Natural Selection*. New York: Wiley, 1973.

Ponnamperuma, Cyril, ed. *Exobiology*. New York: North Holland, 1972.

Price, Charles C., ed. *Synthesis of Life*. Stroudsburg, PA: Dowden, Hutchinson & Ross, 1974.

Rensch, Bernhard. *Biophilosophy.* Translated by C. A. M. Sym. New York: Columbia University, 1971.

Ritterbush, Philip C. *Overtures to Biology. The Speculations of Eighteenth-Century Naturalists.* New Haven: Yale University, 1964.

Rutten, Martin G. *The Origin of Life by Natural Causes.* Amsterdam: Elsevier, 1971.

Schwartz, George, and Bishop, Philip W., eds. *Moments of Discovery,* 2 vols. Foreword by Linus Pauling. New York: Basic Books, 1958.

Senet, André. *Man in Search of His Ancestors. The Romance of Paleontology.* Translated by M. Barnes. New York: McGraw-Hill, 1955.

Shklovskii, I. S., and Sagan, Carl. *Intelligent Life in the Universe.* New York: Dell, 1966.

Simpson, George G. *The Major Features of Evolution.* New York: Columbia University, 1953.

Sinnott, Edmund W. *The Biology of the Spirit.* New York: Viking, 1955.

Strickberger, Monroe W. *Genetics.* New York: Macmillan, 1968.

Sullivan, Walter. *We Are Not Alone. The Search for Intelligent Life on Other Worlds.* Rev. ed. New York: McGraw-Hill, 1966.

Tax, Sol, ed. *Evolution After Darwin. The University of Chicago Centennial.* 3 vols. Chicago: University of Chicago, 1960.

Teilhard de Chardin, Pierre. *The Appearance of Man.* Translated by J. M. Cohen. Preface by Robert T. Francoeur. New York: Harper, 1965.

———. *The Vision of the Past.* Translated by J. M. Cohen. New York: Harper, 1966.

Waddington, Conrad H. *The Nature of Life.* New York: Atheneum, 1962.

Wetter, Gustav A. *Dialectical Materialism. A Historical and Systematic Survey of Philosophy in the Soviet Union.* Translated by P. Heath. Rev. ed. Westport, CT: Greenwood, 1973.

4. God's Own Creation:

Anderson, Bernard W. *The Beginning of History: Genesis.* London: Lutterworth, 1963.

Balthasar, Hans Urs von. *The God Question and Modern Man.* Foreword by John Macquarrie. Translated by H. Graef. New York: Seabury, 1967.

———. *A Theology of History.* New York: Sheed and Ward, 1963.

Barth, Karl. *Church Dogmatics.* Vol. 3.1: *The Doctrine of Creation.* Translated by J. W. Edwards *et al.* Edinburgh: T. & T. Clark, 1958.

Brunner, Emil. *Dogmatics.* Vol. 2: *The Christian Doctrine of Creation and Redemption.* Translated by O. Wyon. Philadelphia: Westminster, 1952.

Bultmann, Rudolf. *The Presence of Eternity: History and Eschatology.* New York: Harper, 1957.

Cullmann, Oscar. *Christ and Time. The Primitive Christian Conception of Time and History.* Translated by F. V. Filson. London: SCM, 1962.

———. *Salvation in History.* Translated by S. G. Sowers. London: SCM, 1967.

Eliade, Mircea. *Cosmos and History. The Myth of the Eternal Return.* Translated by W. R. Trash. New York: Harper Torchbook, 1959.

Gay, Peter. *Deism: An Anthology.* Princeton, NJ: Van Nostrand, 1968.

Geertz, Clifford. *The Interpretation of Cultures. Selected Essays.* New York: Basic Books, 1973.

Gilkey, Langdon. *Maker of Heaven and Earth. A Study of the Christian Doctrine of Creation.* Garden City, NY: Doubleday, Anchor Book, 1959.

Grean, Stanley. *Shaftesbury's Philosophy of Religion and Ethics. A Study in Enthusiasm.* Athens, OH: Ohio University, 1967.

Harris, Marvin. *The Rise of Anthropological Theory. A History of Theories of Culture.* New York: Thomas Y. Crowell, 1971.

Hartshorne, Charles. *Beyond Humanism. Essays in the New Philosophy of Nature.* Lincoln, NE: University of Nebraska, Bison Book, 1968.

————. *Creative Synthesis and Philosophic Method.* LaSalle, IL: Open Court, 1970.

————. *The Logic of Perfection and Other Essays in Neoclassical Metaphysics.* LaSalle, IL: Open Court, 1962.

————. *Man's Vision of God and the Logic of Theism.* Chicago: Willett, Clark, 1941.

————. *A Natural Theology for Our Time.* LaSalle, IL: Open Court, 1967.

Hegel, Georg Wilhelm Friedrich. *The Phenomenology of Mind.* Translated by J. B. Baillie. London: George Allen & Unwin, 1961.

————. *Philosophy of Nature.* Translated by A. V. Miller. Foreword by J. N. Findlay. Oxford: Clarendon, 1970.

Heidel, Alexander. *The Babylonian Genesis. The Story of Creation.* 2nd ed. Chicago: University of Chicago, Phoenix Book, 1951.

Heim, Karl. *The World: Its Creation and Consummation. The End of the Present Age and the Future of the World in the Light of the Resurrection.* Translated by R. Smith. Philadelphia: Muhlenberg, 1962.

Hume, David. *Hume on Religion.* Edited with an Introduction by Richard Wollheim. Cleveland: World, 1963.

Kaufman, Gordon D. *Systematic Theology. A Historicist Perspective.* New York: Scribner, 1968.

Lowe, Victor; Hartshorne, Charles; and Johnson, A. H. *Whitehead and the Modern World. Science, Metaphysics, and Civilization. Three Essays on the Thought of Alfred North Whitehead.* Preface by A. Cornelius Benjamin. Freeport, NY: Books for Libraries Press, 1972.

Malinowski, Bronislaw. *A Scientific Theory of Culture and Other Essays.* Preface by Huntington Cairns. Chapel Hill: University of North Carolina, 1944.

Metz, Johannes, ed. *The Evolving World and Theology.* Vol. 26 of *Concilium. Theology in an Age of Renewal.* New York: Paulist, 1967.

Michel, Paul Henri. *The Cosmology of Giordano Bruno.* Translated by R. E. W. Maddison. Ithaca, NY: Cornell University, 1973.

Niebuhr, Reinhold. *Beyond Tragedy. Essays on the Christian Interpretation of History.* New York: Scribner, [1937] 1951.

Overman, Richard H. *Evolution and the Christian Doctrine of Creation. A Whiteheadian Interpretation.* Philadelphia: Westminster, 1967.

Pannenberg, Wolfhart. *The Idea of God and Human Freedom.* Translated by R. A. Wilson. Philadelphia: Westminster, 1973.

————, ed. *Revelation as History.* Translated by D. Granskou. New York: Macmillan, 1968.

Paterson, Antoinette Mann. *The Infinite Worlds of Giordano Bruno.* Springfield, IL: Charles C. Thomas, 1970.

Patrides, C. A. *The Cambridge Platonists.* London: Edward Arnold, 1969.

Pittenger, W. Norman. *The Historic Faith and a Changing World.* New York: Oxford University, 1950.

von Rad, Gerhard. *Genesis. A Commentary.* Translated by J. H. Marks. Philadelphia: Westminster, 1961.

Renckens, Henricus. *Israel's Concept of the Beginning. The Theology of Genesis 1-3.* New York: Herder and Herder, 1964.

Reumann, John. *Creation & New Creation. The Past, Present, and Future of God's Creative Activity.* Minneapolis: Augsburg, 1973.

Rust, Eric C. *Evolutionary Philosophies and Contemporary Theology.* Philadelphia: Westminster, 1969.

Singer, Dorothea Waley. *Giordano Bruno. His Life and Thought.* With an annotated translation of his work, *On the Infinite Universe and Worlds.* New York: Greenwood, 1968.

de Spinoza, Benedictus. *Short Treatise on God, Man & His Well-Being.* Translated and edited with an introduction, commentary, and a Life of Spinoza by A. Wolf. New York: Russell & Russell, 1963.

Van der Ziel, Aldert. *Genesis and Scientific Inquiry.* Minneapolis: T. S. Denison, 1965.

Voltaire. *Voltaire on Religion : Selected Writings.* Translated and Introduced by Kenneth W. Appelgate. New York: Frederick Ungar, 1974.

Vriezen, Th. C. *An Outline of Old Testament Theology.* 2nd rev. and enl. ed. Newton, MA: Charles T. Branford, 1970.

Westermann, Claus. *Creation.* Translated by J. J. Scullion. Philadelphia: Fortress, 1974.

Zimmerli, Walther. *The Old Testament and the World.* Translated by J. J. Scullion. London: SPCK, 1976.

5. THE NATURE OF HUMANITY:

Anthropology Today. Del Car, CA: CRM Books, 1971.

Ardrey, Robert. *African Genesis. A Personal Investigation into the Animal Origins and Nature of Man.* New York: Athaneum, 1963.

Balthasar, Hans Urs von. *A Theological Anthropology.* New York: Sheed and Ward, 1967.

Berkouwer, G. C. *Man: The Image of God.* Translated by D. W. Jellema. Grand Rapids, MI: Wm. B. Eerdmans, 1962.

Brunner, Emil. *Man in Revolt. A Christian Anthropology.* Translated by O. Wyon. Philadelphia: Westminster, 1947.

Buber, Martin. *Between Man and Man.* Translated by R. G. Smith. New York: Macmillan, 1948.

———. *I and Thou.* With a Postscript by the author added. Translated by R. G. Smith, 2nd ed. New York: Scribner, 1958.

———. *The Knowledge of Man. Selected Essays.* Edited with an introductory essay by Maurice Friedman. Translated by M. Friedman and R. G. Smith. New York: Harper, 1965.

Cairns, David. *The Image of God in Man.* London: SCM, 1953.

Collingwood, Francis J. *Man's Physical and Spiritual Nature.* New York: Holt, Rinehart and Winston, 1963.

Dobzhansky, Theodosius. *Genetic Diversity and Human Equality.* Foreword by Ward Madden. New York: Basic Books, 1973.

Gadamer, Hans-Georg, and Vogler, Paul, eds. *Neue Anthropologie.* 7 vols. Stuttgart: Georg Thieme, 1972-1974.

Jantsch, Erich. *Design for Evolution. Self-Organization and Planning in the Life of Human Systems.* New York: George Braziller, 1975.

LeFevre, Perry. *Understandings of Man.* Philadelphia: Westminster, 1966.

Lecomte du Noüy, Pierre. *Human Destiny.* New York: Longmans, Green & Co., 1947.

Marty, Martin E. and Peerman, Dean G., eds. *New Theology No. 10* (Bios and Theology). New York: Macmillan, 1973.

Mascall, Eric L. *The Importance of Being Human. Some Aspects of the Christian Doctrine of Man.* New York: Columbia University, 1958.

Matson, Floyd W. *The Idea of Man.* New York: Dell, 1976.

Mead, Margaret, *et al.,* eds. *Science and the Concept of Race.* New York: Columbia University, 1968.

Moltmann, Jürgen. *Man. Christian Anthropology in the Conflicts of the Present.* Translated by J. Sturdy. Philadelphia: Fortress, 1974.

Montagu, Ashley. *Anthropology and Human Nature.* Boston: P. Sargent, 1957.

———, ed. *Frontiers of Anthropology.* With introduction and notes. New York: Putnam, 1974.

Morris, Desmond. *Naked Ape: Zoologist's Study of the Human Animal.* New York: McGraw-Hill, 1967.

Nelson, J. Robert, ed. *No Man Is Alien. Essays on the Unity of Mankind.* Leiden: E. J. Brill, 1971.

Niebuhr, Reinhold. *The Nature and Destiny of Man. A Christian Interpretation.* 2 vols. New York: Scribner, 1949.

Pannenberg, Wolfhart. *What Is Man? Contemporary Anthropology in Theological Perspective.* Translated by D. A. Priebe. Philadelphia: Fortress, 1970.

Pittenger, Norman W. *The Christian Understanding of Human Nature.* Philadelphia: Westminster, 1964.

Platt, John R., ed. *New Views of the Nature of Man. The Monday Lectures. The University of Chicago. Spring, 1965.* Chicago: University of Chicago, 1965.

Polanyi, Michael. *The Study of Man. The Lindsay Memorial Lectures, 1958.* Chicago: University of Chicago, 1962.

Rahner, Karl. *Hominisation. The Evolutionary Origin of Man as a Theological Problem.* Translation by W. T. O'Hara. New York: Herder and Herder, 1965.

Sinnott, Edmund W. *Life and Mind.* Yellow Springs, OH: Antioch, 1956.

———. *Matter, Mind and Man. The Biology of Human Nature.* New York: Harper, 1957.

Smith, Ronald Gregor. *The Whole Man. Studies in Christian Anthropology.* Philadelphia: Westminster, 1969.

Stevenson, Leslie. *Seven Theories of Human Nature.* New York: Oxford University, 1975.

Tax, Sol, ed. *Horizons of Anthropology.* Chicago: Aldine, 1964.
———, ed. *International Symposium on Anthropology. New York, 1952. Anthropology Today: Selections.* Chicago: University of Chicago, 1952.
Teilhard de Chardin, Pierre. *Man's Place in Nature. The Human Zoological Group.* Translated by R. Hague. New York: Harper, 1966.
———. *The Phenomenon of Man.* Introduction by Julian Huxley. Translated by B. Wall. New York: Harper, 1959.
Thorpe, William H. *Animal Nature and Human Nature.* Garden City, NY: Doubleday, Anchor Book, 1974.
———. *Biology and the Nature of Man.* London: Oxford University, 1963.
Wolff, Hans Walter. *Anthropology of the Old Testament.* Translated by M. Kohl. Philadelphia: Fortress, 1974.
Young, John Z. *An Introduction to the Study of Man.* Oxford: Clarendon, 1971.

6. THE HUMAN POTENTIAL:

Baillie, John. *The Belief in Progress.* New York: Scribner, 1951.
Benthall, Jonathan, ed. *The Limits of Human Nature. Essays Based on a Course of Lectures Given at the Institute of Contemporary Arts, London.* With an introduction. London: Butler & Tanner, 1973.
Benz, Ernst. *Evolution and Christian Hope: Man's Concept of the Future from the Early Fathers to Teilhard de Chardin.* Translated by Heinz G. Frank. Garden City, NY: Doubleday, Anchor Book, 1968.
Bloch, Ernst. *On Karl Marx.* An abridged translation by J. Maxwell from *Das Prinzip Hoffnung.* New York: Herder & Herder, 1971.
———. *A Philosophy of the Future.* Translated by J. Cumming. New York: Herder & Herder, Azimuth Book, 1970.
Breasted, James Henry. *The Dawn of Conscience.* New York: Scribner, 1934.
Browning, Geraldine O.; Alioto, Joseph L. Farber, Seymour M., eds. *Teilhard de Chardin: In Quest of the Perfection of Man. An International Symposium.* Cranbury, NJ: Associated University Presses, 1973.
Calder, Nigel. *The Mind of Man. An Investigation into Current Research on the Brain and Human Nature.* New York: Viking, 1970.
Callahan, Daniel. *The Tyranny of Survival.* New York: Macmillan, 1973.
Chen, Jack. *Inside the Cultural Revolution.* New York: Macmillan, 1975.
Ch'en Jerome. *Mao and the Chinese Revolution.* With Thirty-seven Poems by Mao Tse-Tung. Translated by M. Bullock and Jerome Ch'en. London: Oxford University, 1965.
Delgado, José M. R. *Physical Control of the Mind. Toward a Psychocivilized Society.* New York: Harper, 1969.
DeVore, Irven, ed. *Primate Behavior: Field Studies of Monkeys and Apes.* New York: Holt, Rinehart & Winston, 1965.
Dubos, René. *Beast or Angel? Choices that Make Us Human.* New York: Scribner, 1974.
———. *A God Within.* New York: Scribner, 1972.
Ehrl·ch. Paul R.; Ehrlich, Anne H.; and Holdren, John P. *Human Ecology Problems and Solutions.* San Francisco: W. H. Freeman, 1973.

Ehrlich, Paul R. *The Population Bomb.* New York: Ballantine, 1968.

Eibl-Eibesfeldt, Irenäus. *Ethology. The Biology of Behavior.* Translated by E. Klinghammer. New York: Holt, Rinehart & Winston, 1970.

Ghiselin, Michael T. *The Economy of Nature and the Evolution of Sex.* Berkeley: University of California, 1974.

Gonzalez-Ruiz, Jose-Maria. *The New Creation: Marxist and Christian?* Translated by M. J. O'Connell. Maryknoll, NY: Orbis, 1976.

Goodstadt, Leo. *China's Search for Plenty. The Economics of Mao Tse-tung.* New York: Weatherhill, 1973.

Handler, Philip, ed. *Biology and the Future of Man.* New York: Oxford University, 1970.

Hardin, Garrett. *Exploring New Ethics for Survival. The Voyage of the Spaceship Beagle.* New York: Viking, 1972.

Harrison, Geoffrey A., *et al. Human Biology. An Introduction to Human Evolution, Variation and Growth.* New York: Oxford University, 1964.

Haselden, Kyle, and Hefner, Philip, eds. *Changing Man: The Threat and the Promise.* Garden City, NY: Doubleday, 1968.

Hefner, Philip. *The Promise of Teilhard. The Meaning of the Twentieth Century in Christian Perspective.* Philadelphia: J. B. Lippincott, 1970.

Heilbroner, Robert L. *An Inquiry into the Human Prospect.* New York: W. W. Norton, 1974.

Huxley, Julian. *The Human Crisis.* Seattle: University of Washington, 1963.

Jerison, Harry J. *Evolution of the Brain and Intelligence.* New York: Academic Press, 1973.

Jones, Alun, and Bodmer, Walter F. *Our Future Inheritance: Choice or Chance?* London: Oxford University, 1974.

Laszlo, Ervin. *The World System: Models, Norms, Applications.* New York: George Braziller, 1973.

Linden, Eugene. *Apes, Men, and Language.* New York: Saturday Review Press, 1974.

Lorenz, Konrad. *Civilized Man's Eight Deadly Sins.* Translated by M. K. Wilson. New York: Harcourt Brace Jovanovich, 1974.

———. *On Aggression.* Translated by M. K. Wilson. New York: Harcourt, Brace & World, 1966.

———. *Studies in Animal and Human Behavior.* 2 vols. Translated by R. Martin. Cambridge: Harvard University, 1971.

Mao Tse-tung's Quotations. The Red Guard's Handbook. Introduction by Steward Fraser. Nashville: International Center, George Peabody College for Teachers, 1967.

Mao, Tse-tung. *Selected Works.* 4 vols. Peking: Foreign Languages Press, 1967-69.

Meadows, Donella H., *et al. The Limits to Growth. A Report for the Club of Rome's Project on the Predicament of Mankind.* New York: Universe Books, 1972.

Mertens, Thomas R., ed. *Human Genetics. Readings on the Implications of Genetic Engineering.* New York: John Wiley, 1975.

Mesarovic, Mihajlo, and Pestel, Eduard. *Mankind at the Turning Point. The Second Report to the Club of Rome.* New York: E. P. Dutton, 1974.

Montagu, Ashley, ed. *Culture and Human Development. Insights into Growing Human.* Englewood Cliffs, NJ: Prentice-Hall, 1974.

————. *The Direction of Human Development.* New and rev. ed. New York: Hawthorn, 1970.

————. *Man and Aggression.* New York: Oxford University, 1973.

Passmore, John. *The Perfectibility of Man.* London: Duckworth, 1970.

Piaget, Jean. *Biology and Knowledge. An Essay on the Relations between Organic Regulations and Cognitive Processes.* Translated by B. Walsh. Chicago: University of Chicago, 1971.

The Pierre Teilhard de Chardin Association of Great Britain and Ireland, ed. *Evolution, Marxism and Christianity: Studies in the Teilhardian Synthesis.* London: Garnstone, 1967.

Pines, Maya. *The Brain Changers. Scientists and the New Mind Control.* New York: Harcourt, Brace, Javanovich, 1974.

Polanyi, Michael. *Knowing and Being.* Edited by Marjorie Grene. Chicago: University of Chicago, 1969.

Skinner, B. F. *About Behaviorism.* New York: Alfred A. Knopf, 1974.

————. *Beyond Freedom and Dignity.* New York: Bantam, 1972.

————. *Cumulative Record. A Selection of Papers.* 3rd ed. New York: Appleton-Century-Crofts, 1972.

————. *Walden Two.* New York: Macmillan, 1948.

Sonneborn, Tracy M., ed. *The Control of Human Heredity and Evolution.* 5th ed. New York: Macmillan, 1967.

Spring, David, and Spring, Eileen, eds. *Ecology and Religion in History.* New York: Harper Torchbook, 1974.

Teilhard de Chardin, Pierre. *Activation of Energy.* Translated by R. Hague. New York: Harcourt Brace Javanovich, 1971.

————. *Christianity and Evolution.* Translated by R. Hague. New York: Harcourt Brace Javanovich, 1971.

————. *The Divine Milieu. An Essay on the Interior Life.* Translated by B. Wall. New York: Harper Torchbook, 1965.

————. *The Future of Man.* Translated by N. Denny. New York: Harper Torchbook, 1969.

————. *Toward the Future.* Translated by R. Hague. New York: Harcourt Brace Javanovich, 1975.

————. *Human Energy.* Translated by J. M. Cohen. London: Collins, 1969.

Tinbergen, Niko. *The Animal in Its World: Explorations of an Ethologist, 1932-1972.* Vol. 2: *Laboratory Experiments and General Papers.* Cambridge: Harvard University, 1973.

Toffler, Alvin. *The Eco-Spasm Report.* New York: Bantam Books, 1975.

————. *Future Shock.* New York: Bantam, 1971.

Wakeman, Frederic. *History and Will. Philosophical Perspectives of Mao Tse-tung's Thought.* Berkeley: University of California, 1973.

Wheeler, John Harvey, ed. *Beyond the Punitive Society. Operant Conditioning: Social and Political Aspects.* San Francisco: W. H. Freeman, 1973.

Wickler, Wolfgang. *The Sexual Code. The Social Behavior of Animals and Men.* Introduction by Konrad Lorenz. Garden City, NY: Doubleday, 1972.

Wilson, Edward Osborne. *Sociobiology: The New Synthesis.* Cambridge, MA: Harvard University, 1975.

Zimmerli, Walther. *Man and His Hope in the Old Testament.* Naperville, IL: Alec R. Allenson, 1971.

7. THE HUMAN PREDICAMENT, SIN, AND THE CAUSE OF EVIL:

Anshen, Ruth Nanda. *The Reality of the Devil: Evil in Man.* New York: Harper, 1972.

Becker, Ernest. *The Denial of Death.* New York: Free Press, 1973.

———. *Escape from Evil.* New York: Free Press, 1975.

Berkouwer, G. C. *Sin.* Translated by Ph.C. Holtrop. Grand Rapids: Wm. B. Eerdmans, 1971.

Bonhoeffer, Dietrich. *Creation and Fall. A Theological Interpretation of Genesis 1-3.* Translated by J. C. Fletcher. New York: Macmillan, 1959.

Bowker, John. *Problems of Suffering in Religions of the World.* Cambridge: Cambridge University, 1970.

Browning, Don S. *Generative Man: Psychoanalytic Perspectives.* Philadelphia: Westminster, 1973.

Buber, Martin. *Good and Evil.* Translated by R. G. Smith. New York: Scribner, 1953.

Camus, Albert. *Resistance, Rebellion, and Death.* Translated with and introduction by Justin O'Brien. New York: Alfred A. Knopf, 1966.

Cherbonnier, Edmond La B. *Hardness of Heart. A Contemporary Interpretation of the Doctrine of Sin.* Garden City, NY: Doubleday, 1955.

Doniger, Simon, ed. *The Nature of Man in Theological and Psychological Perspective.* New York: Harper, 1962.

Evil; Essays by Carl Kerenyi (and others). Translated by Ralph Manheim and Hildegard Nagel. Edited by the Curatorium of the C. G. Jung Institute, Zürich. Evanston: Northwestern University, 1967.

Ferguson, John. *Pelagius. A Historical and Theological Study.* Cambridge. W. Heffer, 1956.

Freud, Sigmund. *The Basic Writings of Sigmund Freud.* Translated and edited with an introduction by A. A. Brill. New York: Random House, Modern Library, 1938.

Fromm, Erich. *The Anatomy of Human Destructiveness.* New York: Holt, Rinehart and Winston, 1973.

———. *Escape from Freedom.* New York: Holt, Rinehart and Winston, 1960.

———. *The Heart of Man. Its Genius for Good and Evil.* New York: Harper, 1964.

———. *Man for Himself. An Inquiry into the Psychology of Ethics.* New York: Rinehart, 1959.

Fromm, Erich, and Xirau, Ramon, eds. *The Nature of Man.* Readings selected, edited and furnished with an introductory essay. New York: Macmillan, 1968.

Gerhard, Johann. *The Image of God,* in *The Doctrine of Man in Classical Lutheran Theology.* Edited by Herman A. Preus and Edmund Smits. Minneapolis: Augsburg, 1962.

Hefner, Philip. *Faith and the Vitalities of History. A Theological Study Based on the Work of Albrecht Ritschl.* New York: Harper, 1966.

Hick, John. *Evil and the God of Love.* New York: Harper, 1966.

Jacobi, Jolande. *The Psychology of C. G. Jung. An Introduction with Illustrations.* Translated by R. Manheim. New Haven: Yale University, 1962.

Jung, Carl Gustav. *The Collected Works.* 18 vols. 2nd ed. Princeton, NJ: Princeton University, 1968- .

Kallas, James. *Jesus and the Power of Satan*. Philadelphia: Westminster, 1968.
———. *The Real Satan. From Biblical Times to the Present*. Minneapolis: Augsburg, 1975.
Kelly, Henry Ansgar. *The Devil, Demonology and Witchcraft. The Development of Christian Beliefs in Evil Spirits*. Garden City, NY: Doubleday, 1974.
———. *Towards the Death of Satan. The Growth and Decline of Christian Demonology*. London: Geoffrey Chapman, 1968.
Kemp, Eric W., ed. *Man: Fallen and Free. Oxford Essays on the Condition of Man*. London: Hodder and Stoughton, 1969.
Kluger, Rivkah Schärf. *Satan in the Old Testament*. Translated by H. Nagel. Evanston: Northwestern University, 1967.
Lewis, C. S. *The Great Divorce*. New York: Macmillan, 1945.
———. *The Problem of Pain*. New York: Macmillan, 1959.
Ling, Trevor. *The Significance of Satan. New Testament Demonology and Its Contemporary Relevance*. London: SPCK, 1961.
Lotz, David W. *Ritschl & Luther. A Fresh Perspective on Albrecht Ritschl's Theology in the Light of His Luther Study*. New York: Abingdon, 1974.
Luther and Erasmus: Free Will and Salvation. Translated and edited by E. Gordon Rupp and Philip S. Watson. Vol. 17 of *The Library of Christian Classics*. Philadelphia: Westminster, 1969.
MacIsaac, Sharon. *Freud and Original Sin*. New York: Paulist, 1974.
McSorley, Harry J. *Luther: Right or Wrong? An Ecumenical-Theological Study of Luther's Major Work, The Bondage of Will*. Minneapolis: Augsburg, 1969.
Menninger, Karl. *Whatever Became of Sin?* New York: Hawthorn, 1973.
———. *Love against Hate*. With the collaboration of Jeanetta Lyle Menninger. New York: Harcourt, Brace, 1942.
———. *Man against Himself*. New York: Harcourt, Brace, 1938.
Metz, Johannes B. *Moral Evil under Challenge*. Vol. 56 of *Concilium. Theology in the Age of Renewal*. New York: Herder and Herder, 1970.
Mueller, David L. *An Introduction to the Theology of Albrecht Ritschl*. Philadelphia: Westminster, 1969.
Niebuhr, Reinhold. *Man's Nature and His Communities. Essays on the Dynamics and Enigmas of Man's Personal and Social Existence*. New York: Scribner, 1965.
———. *Moral Man and Immoral Society. A Study in Ethics and Politics*. New York: Scribner, [1936] 1960.
Olson, Alan M., ed. *Disguises of the Demonic. Contemporary Perspectives on the Power of Evil*. New York: Association, 1975.
Pike, Nelson, ed. *God and Evil. Readings on the Theological Problem of Evil*. Englewood Cliffs, NJ: Prentice-Hall, 1964.
Rank, Otto. *Psychology and the Soul*. Translated by W. D. Turner. New York: A. S. Barnes, Perpetua Book, 1961.
Rauschenbusch, Walter. *Christianizing the Social Order*. New York: Macmillan, 1913.
———. *The Righteousness of the Kingdom*. Edited and introduced by Max L. Stackhouse. New York: Abingdon, 1968.

———. *A Theology for the Social Gospel.* New York: Macmillan, [1917] 1960.

Reik, Theodor. *Myth and Guilt. The Crime and Punishment of Mankind.* New York: George Braziller, 1957.

Ricoeur, Paul. *Freud and Philosophy. An Essay on Interpretation.* Translated by D. Savage. New Haven: Yale University, 1970.

———. *The Symbolism of Evil.* Translated by E. Buchanan. New York: Harper, 1967.

Ritschl, Albrecht. *The Christian Doctrine of Justification and Reconciliation. The Positive Development of the Doctrine.* 2nd ed. Translated and edited by H. R. Mackintosh and A. B. Macaulay. Edinburgh: T. & T. Clark, 1902.

Rondet, Henri. *Original Sin. The Patristic and Theological Background.* Translated by C. Finegan. Staten Island, NY: Alba House, 1972.

Soelle, Dorothee. *Suffering.* Translated by E. R. Kalin. Philadelphia: Fortress, 1975.

Tennant, F. R. *The Sources of the Doctrines of the Fall and Original Sin.* Introductory by Mary Frances Thelen. New York: Schocken [1903], 1968.

Thielicke, Helmut. *Death and Life.* Translated by E. H. Schroeder. Philadelphia: Fortress, 1970.

Torrance, T. F. *Calvin's Doctrine of Man.* New ed. Grand Rapids: Wm. B. Eerdmans, 1957.

Trooster, Stephanus. *Evolution and the Doctrine or Original Sin.* Translated by J. A. Ter Haar. New York: Newman, 1968.

8. Providence, Miracles, and the Prospect of a New Humanity:

Alves, Rubem A. *A Theology of Human Hope.* Foreword by Harvey Cox. Washington: Corpus Books, 1969.

Balthasar, Hans Urs von. *Prayer.* Translated by A. V. Littledale. New York: Sheed and Ward, 1961.

Benoit, Pierre; Murphy, Roland; and Van Iersel, Bastiaan, eds. *The Presence of God.* Vol. 50 *of Concilium. Theology in the Age of Renewal.* New York: Paulist, 1969.

Berdyaev, Nikolai. *The Destiny of Man.* Translated by N. Duddington. London: Geoffrey Bles, [1937] 1948.

———. *The Fate of Man in the Modern World.* Translated by D. A. Lowrie. Ann Arbor: University of Michigan, [1935] 1961.

Berkouwer, G. C. *The Providence of God.* Translated by L. Smedes. Grand Rapids, MI: Wm. E. Eerdmans, 1952.

Bockle, Franz, ed. *Man in a New Society.* Vol. 75 of *Concilium. Religion in the Seventies.* New York: Herder and Herder, 1972.

Brunner, Emil. *The Divine Imperative. A Study in Christian Ethics.* Translated by O. Wyon. Philadelphia: Westminster, [1937] 1947.

Cailliet, Émile. *The Recovery of Purpose.* New York: Harper, 1959.

de Dietrich, Suzanne. *The Witnessing Community. The Biblical Record of God's Purpose.* Philadelphia: Westminster, 1958.

Elert, Werner. *The Christian Ethos.* Translated by C. J. Schindler. Philadelphia: Muhlenberg, 1957.

Farrar, Austin. *Love Almighty and Ills Unlimited. An Essay on Providence and Evil Containing the Nathaniel Taylor Lectures for 1961.* Garden City, NY: Doubleday, 1961.

Fuller, Reginald H. *Interpreting the Miracles.* Philadelphia: Westminster, 1963.

Geffré, Claude, and Guttiérez, Gustavo, eds. *The Mystical and Political Dimension of the Christian Faith.* Vol. 6 of *Concilium. New Series.* No. 10: *Theology of Liberation.* New York: Herder and Herder, 1974.

Grant, Robert M. *Miracle and Natural Law in Graeco-Roman and Early Christian Thought.* Amsterdam: North-Holland, 1952.

Harkness, Georgia. *The Providence of God.* New York: Abingdon, 1960.

Hazelton, Roger. *God's Way with Man. Variations on the Theme of Providence.* New York: Abingdon, 1956.

Hull, John M. *Hellenistic Magic and the Synoptic Tradition.* Naperville, IL: Alec R. Allenson, 1974.

Keller, Ernst, and Keller, Marie-Luise. *Miracles in Dispute. A Continuing Debate.* Translated by M. Kohl. Philadelphia: Fortress, 1969.

Leibnitz, *Selections.* Edited by Philip P. Wiener. New York: Scribner, 1961.

Lewis, C. S. *Letters to Malcolm: Chiefly on Prayer.* New York: Harcourt, Brace, & World, 1964.

————. *Miracles. A Preliminary Study.* New York: Macmillan, 1947.

Malinowski, Bronislaw. *Magic, Science and Religion and other Essays.* With an introduction by Robert Redfield. Garden City, NY: Doubleday, Anchor Book, 1954.

Margenau, Henry. *Scientific Indeterminism and Human Freedom. Wimmer Lecture XX.* Latrobe, PA: Archabbey Press, 1968.

Metz, Johannes B. *Theology of the World.* Translated by W. Glen-Doepel. New York: Herder and Herder, 1969.

Meyer, Carl S., and Mayer, Herbert T., eds. *The Caring God. Perspectives on Providence.* St. Louis: Concordia, 1973.

Miguez Bonino, Jose. *Doing Theology in a Revolutionary Situation.* Philadelphia: Fortress, Confrontation Book, 1975.

Moltmann, Jürgen. *Hope and Planning.* Translated by M. Clarkson. New York: Harper, 1971.

————. *Theology of Hope. On the Grounds and the Implications of a Christian Eschatology.* Translated by J. W. Leitch. New York: Harper, 1967.

Monden, Louis. *Signs and Wonders. A Study of the Miraculous Element in Religion.* Foreword by Avery Dulles. New York: Desclee, 1966.

Moule, C. F. D., ed. *Miracles. Cambridge Studies in Their Philosophy and History.* London: A. R. Mowbray, 1965.

Munk, Arthur W. *History and God. Clues to His Purpose.* New York: Ronald, 1952.

Outler, Albert C. *Who Trusts in God. Musings on the Meaning of Providence.* New York: Oxford University, 1968.

Pittenger, W. Norman. *God's Way with Men. A Study of the Relationship between God and Man in Providence, "Miracle," and Prayer.* London: Hodder and Stoughton, 1969.

————. *Theology and Reality. Essays in Restatement.* Greenwich, CT: Seabury, 1955.

Pollard, William G. *Chance and Providence. God's Action in a World Governed by Scientific Law.* New York: Scribner, 1958.

Pontifex, Mark. *Freedom and Providence,* Vol. 22 of *The Twentieth Century Encyclopedia of Catholicism.* Edited by Henri Daniel-Rops. New York: Hawthorn, 1960.

Schwarz, Hans. *On the Way to the Future. A Christian View of Eschatology in the Light of Current Trends in Religion, Philosophy, and Science.* Minneapolis: Augsburg, 1972.

Schrey, Heinz-Horst, ed. *Faith & Action: Basic Problems in Christian Ethics. A Selection of Contemporary Discussions.* Introduction by Helmut Thielicke. Edinburgh: Oliver & Boyd, 1970.

Segundo, Juan Luis. *A Theology for Artisans of a New Humanity.* Translated by J. Drury. Vol. 5: *Evolution and Guilt.* New York: Maryknoll, 1974.

———. *A Theology for Artisans of a New Humanity.* Translated by J. Drury. Vol. 2: *Grace and the Human Condition.* New York: Maryknoll, 1973.

Thomas, M. M., and Converse, Paul E. *Revolution and Redemption.* New York: Friendship, 1955.

Thomas, M. M. *Salvation and Humanisation.* Madras: Christian Literature Society, 1971.

Van Nuys, Kelvin. *Science and Cosmic Purpose.* New York: Harper, 1949.

Wickler, Wolfgang. *The Biology of the Ten Commandments.* Translated by D. Smith. New York: McGraw-Hill, 1972.

Index of Names

Index of Subjects

Index of Biblical References

EXTRA-BIBLICAL

DATE DUE

GAYLORD			PRINTED IN U.S.A.